D1562623

The Call of the GAME

STEVE McKEE

The Call of the GAME

McGRAW-HILL BOOK COMPANY

New York St. Louis San Francisco
Hamburg Mexico Toronto

1 2 3 4 5 6 7 8 9 DOCDOC 8 7 6

ISBN 0-07-045354-3

LIBRARY OF CONGRESS CATALOGING-IN-PUBLICATION DATA

McKee, Steve.
The call of the game.
1. Sports—United States. 2. Tournaments—United States. I. Title.
GV583.M345 1987 796′.0973 86-10535
ISBN 0-07-045354-3

BOOK DESIGN BY PATRICE FODERO

To Noreen

CONTENTS

The Year

January 22–23, 1983	Two-Man Bobsled Championships, Lake Placid, N.Y.
January 29–30	Women's National Powerlifting Championships, Chicago
February 2–5	National Figure Skating Championships, Pittsburgh
February 14–15	Westminster Kennel Club Dog Show, Madison Square Garden
February 19–20	Continental Team Tiddlywinks Championships, MIT, Boston
February 22	N.Y. Knicks vs. Dallas Mavericks, Madison Square Garden
February 26	Birkebeiner Cross Country Ski Race, Cable, Wisc.
March 2	Chicago Sting vs. Memphis Americans, Chicago Stadium
March 7	USFL Birmingham Stallions vs. Michigan Panthers, Birmingham, Ala.
March 9–12	National Amateur Quail Field Dog Trials, north of Pensacola, Fla.
March 18–20	North American Sled Dog Championships, Fairbanks, Alaska

April 2–4	NCAA Basketball Championships, Albuquerque, N.M.
April 7–11	Masters Golf Tournament, Augusta National Golf Course, Ga.
April 19	Boston Marathon
April 23	New York Yankees vs. Minnesota Twins, Yankee Stadium
April 29	Friday Night Fights at Felt Forum, Madison Square Garden
May 7	Kentucky Derby, Churchill Downs, Louisville, Ky.
May 12	Chicago Cubs vs. Philadelphia Phillies, Wrigley Field, Chicago
May 14–15	National Rugby Championships, Winnemac Stadium, Chicago
May 17–21	National Volleyball Championships, Memphis, Tenn.
May 27	Indianapolis 500
June 6–11	National Fencing Tournament, University of San Francisco
June 14	San Francisco Giants vs. Houston Astros, Candlestick Park
June 18–19	National Track and Field Championships, Indianapolis
June 25–26	Synchronized Swimming Championships, Yale, New Haven, Conn.
July 4–7	All-Star Baseball Game, Comiskey Park, Chicago
July 19	New York Yankees vs. Minnesota Twins, Yankee Stadium
July 20–21	National Juggling Championships, SUNY-Purchase, N.Y.
July 28	New York Mets vs. Cincinnati Reds, Shea Stadium
August 7	Team America vs. Tampa Bay Rowdies, RFK Stadium, Washington, D.C.
August 9	Atlanta Braves vs. SF Giants, Fulton County Stadium, Atlanta
August 12–13	Outdoor Speed Roller Skating Championships, Ft. Worth, Tex.

August 14	Texas Rangers vs. Cleveland Indians, Arlington Stadium, Tex.
August 18	Cardinals vs. Houston Astros, Busch Stadium, St. Louis
August 19–21	National Waterskiing Championships, Du Quoin, Ill.
August 23	Pirates vs. Astros, Three Rivers Stadium, Pittsburgh
August 29	Kickoff Classic, Nebraska vs. Penn State, The Meadowlands, N.J.
August 30–September 11	U.S. Open Tennis, National Tennis Center, Flushing, N.Y.
September 18–26	America's Cup, Newport, R.I.
September 21	Boston Red Sox vs. New York Yankees, Fenway Park
October 11–16	World Series, Baltimore Orioles vs. Philadelphia Phillies
October 16	National Jousting Tournament, The Mall, Washington, D.C.
October 23	New York City Marathon
November 11	Chicago Bulls vs. Boston Celtics, Chicago Stadium
November 13	Chicago Bears vs. Philadelphia Eagles, Soldier Field, Chicago
November 13	Chicago Blackhawks vs. Edmonton Oilers, Chicago Stadium
November 18	Denver Nuggets vs. Houston Rockets, Denver
November 20	Denver Broncos vs. Seattle Seahawks, Mile High Stadium, Denver
November 25	Larry Holmes vs. Marvis Frazier, Caesar's Palace, Las Vegas
November 27	Los Angeles Lakers vs. Chicago Bulls, The Forum, Los Angeles

December 1–3	National Finals Rodeo, The Myriad, Oklahoma City, Okla.
December 10	Allentown College vs. Muhlenberg College, Center Valley, Pa.
January 2, 1984	Orange Bowl, Nebraska vs. University of Miami, Miami, Fla.
January 4	World Jai Alai Miami
January 22	Super Bowl, Washington Redskins vs. L.A. Raiders, Tampa Stadium, Fla.

Acknowledgments

I would like to thank Jim Lampley of ABC Sports; Art Kaminsky and Janet Pawson, my agents; and Tom Quinn, my editor at McGraw-Hill. They believed in me and my year on the road.

I would also like to thank:
Alaska: Roger Brigham, Sports Editor, *Anchorage Daily News,* without his commitment the trip would not have happened. Janis Helton, my original—and still best—critic. Dean Gottehrer, because it all started when I enrolled in his class in 1978. Bob and Claire Murphy; Pat Kling; the Villanoes; the Caldarolas; James Laudwein, S.J. And John McDermott, because he always understood
California: Michael and Lisa Kirk; Mrs. Robert Murphy, Billy and Mary Murphy, Anne Murphy
Colorado: Tom and Robin Downey
Connecticut: Dennis Philbin; Chinatip Loungsri
Delaware: Frank and Anita Sciacca
Florida: My sister, Kathy, and Jon Martin; Dan Kubala.
Illinois: Irene Sullivan—for the key to her heart as well as her apartment—and Will Reller; John Husar, the Chicago *Tribune*
Maryland: Frank and Anita Sciacca
Massachusetts: The McDermott clan
Nebraska: Jim and Annemarie Gross, for their heartland hospitality

New York: Peter Callaghan and West; John and Vi Farley; Cynthia Merman, who first gave shape to the manuscript; Susan Mayer, Tom Quinn's assistant at McGraw-Hill; the Gampps and the Murphys; Ira Berkow, the *New York Times;* Dozier Hasty and the staff of the *Brooklyn Heights Press;* Dave Pieratt

North Carolina: Sr. Francis Sheridan

Ohio: Tom and Judy Green; Pete Carey, Mr. and Mrs. Charles Carey

Oregon: Dolores Kueffler and Pat Hunter; Jane Salisbury

Pennsylvania: My mother, who never asked her son to get a real job; Joanne and Max Kirk; Mr. and Mrs. McEntee and the rest of the York Crowd; Jim Masterson, Peggy Masterson; Bruce and Chris Arians; the D'Ottavios; Chris and Marianne Cashman; Neil Kilty, OSFS

Rhode Island: Cindy Kirk; Debbie Vierra

Texas: Walter Damtoft, *American Way* magazine; Les Wollam

Washington: Ed Reading

Washington, D.C.: Frank and Anita Sciacca; John Ogulnik, National Public Radio; Curtis Riddle, *USA Today*

I would like to acknowledge: Leslie Anderson and Jack Fiveash; Jana Angelakis; Dave Baldridge; Mary Lou Bartram and Alice Blum; Rick Blane; Brenda Lee Bonogofsky; Debbie and Dennis Brown; Jimmy Bryan; Mr. and Mrs. Roger Castino; John Castino; Duke Cullimore; Mr. and Mrs. Harris Dunlap; Bill Gudiz; Lois Hollan; Caldwell Jones; Josh at the Open; Linda Long; Peter Moreau; Dave Neubert; Tom Osenton; Lyle Schwartz; Chris Snyder; Cary Taylor; John Vanak; Dr. Myron Wheat, Jr.; Tony Wise.

Author's Note

This is the story of what I did in 1983. Or as much of the story as would fit comfortably between the covers of one book. So, first, I'd like to apologize to all the people I met along the way who didn't make the final cut. Their stories may be absent, but I remember well and am deeply grateful for their generosity of spirit.

Regarding those who do appear within these pages: In most instances, I've used real names of real people and the real stories they told me. Only occasionally have names been changed or identities altered. There is only one composite character. Nicky from Newark is the result of conversations with four professional scalpers I first met in Albuquerque.

INTRODUCTION

Super Bowl Sunday, 1984. A quarter mile from Tampa Stadium. The game was three hours away. Scalpers and scalpees were everywhere (shouts of "Who needs tickets?" and signs like "Wanted: Three girls with six tickets!"). Parents clutching children clutching penants. Teenagers smoking dope. The 2001 Lounge ("21 naked ladies, including exotic dancers in the flying saucer!"). Used car lots. Shopping plazas. Packs of people all dressed in the same color. A man clutching a sign the size of a small sail: "Jesus Saves Sinners from Hell—John 3:16–21." Stretch limousines cruising toward the VIP entrance. Motor home encampments sprung to life. Fans mugging for television cameras. Coolers of beer perched on trunks.

A sudden realization: I've seen all this before. Many times before. At fifty-five events in thirty-one different sports in the past 369 days.

Once again I was caught up in a crowd being pulled to the center of the universe. Seventy-two thousand people pouring into Tampa Stadium from all directions like sand through a funnel. Expectations boiled, the excitement so thick it could have held a football three feet off the ground.

We were on our way to the game. We wouldn't be watching this one on television. We were here. Now and forever. Whenever Super Bowl XVIII popped into a conversation, we could sit back real casual-like and say, "Yeah, we was there. We saw it. Down in Tampa. Raiders-Redskins. What a game. Shoulda been there."

It was this frantic sense of urgency that I recognized more than anything or anyone I could see or hear around me. After 54,000 miles through twenty-four states and the District of Columbia, I understood clearly and suddenly that I could have finished my year on the road no place else but here. The Super Bowl was my entire trip neatly wrapped into one quick Sunday afternoon.

I laughed at myself. Had I known the final event would embody everything I'd already seen, I might have skipped the first fifty-four. I'd have saved myself heaps of aggravation.

Minor irritations had plagued me all year. Would I have enough money to finish the trip? Would the van ever stop leaking oil? Would the van ever get more than ten miles to the gallon? I almost froze to death while trying to sleep in the back of the van in Lake Placid last January. Sharp contrast to an ill-advised swing through Texas in mid-August. In Pittsburgh I got hit over the head with a broomstick. In Philadelphia the van was trashed and all my clothes were stolen. In Louisville, I thought I was dying, although I wasn't and I didn't.

Doing this trip also meant leaving Alaska, where I'd been living since 1975. Alaska is a state of mind as well as a state of the union, and forsaking "The Great Land" wasn't easy. Once my year began, I searched for sporting events alone while my wife, Noreen, studied for her Master's in New York City.

All in all, I had to admit, there was much about the 54,000 miles I'd covered in the past year that I could've done well enough without.

But this was no time to cop an attitude. I had wanted to spend a year on the road traveling to America's sports events, and now I'd done it.

Now was the time to remember.

Figure skating (television misses that sport completely). Lorenzo Charles's last-second dunk to beat Houston in the NCAAs. Following Arnie at the Masters. Joan Benoit's stunning Boston Marathon record. The Indy 500 (*everything* about the Indy 500). Fred Lynn's grand slam to win the fiftieth anniversary All-Star Game for the American League. The historic upset at the America's Cup in Newport, Rhode Island. The National Jousting

Tournament on a classic fall day on the Mall in Washington, D.C. Miami's impossible victory over Nebraska in the Orange Bowl three weeks ago.

And the people. Anthony Gatto, the ten-year-old phenom at the National Juggling Festival. Ivan Lendl at the U.S. Open Tennis Championships. Katie McDonald attempting to qualify for the first women's Olympic Marathon Trials by running the New York City Marathon. Reggie McKenzie of the Seattle Seahawks. The aging rodeo cowboy, Skipper Voss. Jim Lampley of ABC Sports, who surprised me by consenting to a lengthy interview.

The unexpected joys. A visit to Fenway Park. An afternoon at Wrigley Field. Finding the best hot dog. Continental Team Tiddlywinks at MIT. An early season hockey game between Chicago and Edmonton becoming one of the most gripping contests of the year. Winning a "Croix de Candlestick" in San Francisco. The National Waterskiing Championships in Du Quoin, Illinois. And every stop I made in Chicago.

But surely the most surprising of the unplanned pleasures of a year on the road had been the road itself. All those miles of getting there became as important as being there. The moving toward, the going to, was integral to the rhythms and shape of the year. The road exacts its price in loneliness, but pays its dividend in familiarity. The van's wooden steering wheel, its torn seat, a clear view through the windshield became my companions on the road. Getting there involved anticipation and expectation, plus a certain tension because I never knew if I'd get in the gate once I got there. Being there answered all my questions, and even while attending events I often found myself looking forward to the road, and the next event, and to getting there.

I moved to Alaska in 1975, about the same time live satellite television made it to the forty-ninth state. Until recently, Fairbanks was five hours behind the East Coast (it's now only four), and it's always been right below the North Pole and as far west as Hawaii. Watching television in Alaska changed the way I watched television. Sunday afternoon football began at 7 A.M.; a World Series night game at three o'clock in the afternoon. Sitting in my observation tower 3,000 miles above, the better part of a country removed from and five hours behind the Lower 48, I discovered I was watching not only the game but all those people watching the game as well. I was a spectator twice removed, and, dependent as I was on the tube, I began to question its veracity.

I can't remember exactly when I decided to travel the country in search of sports events. The closest I can come to the germ of the idea is a conversation with friends in June of 1979. We talked about doing a book, a big coffee-table-sized book, filled with pictures of sports fans. All kinds of sports fans from hundreds of events from all around the country. I suggested that along with the pictures there should be some sort of narrative to tie it all together. Couple that idea to my growing distrust of television, and by February 1981 I'd decided to travel the country attending as many sports events as possible in one year and then write about it. I remember it was February because it's a difficult month to forget in Alaska. That's also when I presented the idea to my wife, Noreen. She said okay, just like that, then said make sure you do it right.

But what was "right"? The trip hadn't happened quite the way I thought it would back in January. I'd assumed the year would unfold seamlessly, with a recognizable beginning, middle, and end, and all I'd have to do was get it down on paper. But that hadn't happened. The trip started, it stopped, it started all over again.

There'd also been no one way to collect the entire year. Traveling in the van I kept my notes on tape, but when I went to an event without the van I used a diary. Occasionally I didn't take any notes at all, but then spent my down time in New York City after the event writing to friends and telling them everything I'd seen and done.

I chose 1983 because the Olympics figured to dominate the entire 1984 year in sports, and I wanted my year to belong to me. There were, of course, events I had to attend: World Series, NCAAs, Indy 500, Kentucky Derby, et al. But between those events, I was free to do what I wanted, provided I could get there and back again. I included two marathons and a cross-country ski race. I went to the Westminster Kennel Club Dog Show at Madison Square Garden, plus the Amateur Field Dog Trials in Pensacola, Florida. The North American Sled Dog Championships in March was more an excuse to visit Alaska.

But all the games—major and minor, big and little—really just served as my excuse to travel the country. Only on rare occasion did I concentrate on the event itself. That was the one thing television could do well: tell who had won and who had lost and why. I wanted to get there and to be there, but then see who else was there and hear what they had to say.

In the early weeks of the trip I had considered myself The Everyfan, traveling on behalf of all sports fans in America, off to tell them what it was like to be there, everywhere, at all the events they only watched on television. That conceit faded rather quickly, although it never died completely. At times I fancied myself a painter assigned to capture the definitive portrait of Sports in America. But that was impossible, too. Attending one event meant not attending at least one other. Talking to one person meant not talking to everyone else. Pursuing one story meant ignoring the rest. The best I could do was examine some individual brush strokes along the way. If the big picture was to be brought together at all, that would be up to me and an ugly brown van criss-crossing the country looking for the next game down the road.

CHAPTER 1

* * *

This wasn't what I had in mind at all. Lake Placid, New York, 1 A.M., 20 degrees below zero. Outside the van, tiny needles of frozen condensation hung in the air, a snowstorm in suspended animation. Inside I huddled beneath two sleeping bags, lying on a brown corduroy bed in a parking lot in the middle of town, wondering if I was going to freeze to death. My breath rose in tiny puffs and turned to frost on the roof of the van.

I wriggled my toes. Nothing. I unzipped the bags, grabbed my ankle and rubbed. A burning sensation returned, that wonderfully strange sensation telling me my foot wasn't going to fall off. I dove back into the bags, then lay still, watching my breath steam to the roof. The frost was twice as thick as it had been just moments before. It was going to be a long night.

It had already been a long day. At eleven o'clock this morning I had pulled myself behind the wheel of the van parked outside my apartment on DeGraw Street in Brooklyn. All I had to do was drive two blocks to Bond, turn left, and then make another left onto Atlantic about eight blocks later. Past the fifth light was the Brooklyn Queens Expressway. Get on that, take the Triborough Bridge, the George Washington Bridge, the Palisades Parkway in New Jersey to the New York State Thruway, then Route 87 north of

Albany to 73, and into Lake Placid. It was all outlined in green on my Triple-A Trip-Tik.

But I didn't want to go. I flipped on my tape recorder instead of the engine. "I am scared to death," I said. I rewound the inch of tape and played it back. "I am scared to death." Yes, I know. I looked around the van. Two cardboard chests of drawers, the brown corduroy chair that folded out to a bed, the rod across the back holding my clothes on hangers. A couple of flares for emergencies (but no tools; I wouldn't know how to use them anyway). Next to me was a box filled with food (granola, cheese, peanut butter, and fruit), notebooks, some extra tapes for my recorder, and a 35-millimeter camera. Everything was in place. I had to go.

I put the key in the ignition, and turned. The van groaned grudgingly. (This thing's going to get me around the country?) The engine caught. I flipped the heater to defrost and leaned back to wait for the blowers to clear the windshield. All too quickly they did. I could see everything in front of me. I put the van in gear and it lurched forward, ready to go. But was I? I pulled onto DeGraw, checking the apartment one last time.

I turned left onto Bond and left again onto Atlantic. The Brooklyn Queens Expressway approached. I swept to the right and up the ramp. The trip had begun.

Above New York City the sky was so clear as to be almost colorless. Snow along the highway grew deeper and the wind stronger, the cross gusts bouncing the van all over the road and too many thoughts bounced around inside my head. This idea had moved too quickly from the abstract to the concrete, and I wasn't sure how to grab hold of it. What does one do while attending sports events for an entire year? Perhaps I should have thought of that earlier. All I could do now was keep moving and find out.

Woodstock. A while later, Sleepy Hollow Lake. A sign advertised leisure living but all I could see were rows of mobile homes. I stayed on 87 around Albany, then headed due north, climbing up a six-lane interstate advertised as "America's Most Scenic Highway." I didn't argue—we could debate the claim in a year.

The sun set behind my left shoulder, turning the sky a brilliant orange and the Adirondacks into silhouettes. By the time I turned onto Route 73 for the final twenty-eight miles to Lake Placid it was dark. I remembered Jim McKay's warm and comforting introduction on ABC's Olympics coverage three years ago: "Welcome to the

1980 Olympics, when all the world comes to Lake Placid." According to my Trip-Tik, this narrow band of icy highway was the only way the world could have gotten there.

A few miles past Keene, still about fifteen miles from Placid, an orange glow materialized in the distance. The closer I approached, the less real it appeared. The lights from a thousand torches, it seemed, had transformed the mists and snows into a cauldron of slowly shifting orange vapors. And then, suddenly, right on top of it, mythic proportions vanished. It was the Mount Von Hoevenberg bobsled run, the mountain eerily reflecting the glow of the lamps that lit the area.

In Lake Placid I stopped at a café for dinner. The small restaurant had a long counter, tables with red-and-white-checked tablecloths, and three people—the cook, the waitress, and me. I ordered and tried to start a conversation with the waitress. My attempts were a total flop. "What's it like living in Lake Placid?" "It's all right." The best I did was learn that a couple of hours earlier the temperature had been 12 degrees below zero and falling.

That's why I figured it was at least 20 below now. I checked my watch. Three-fifteen. I'd fallen asleep after all. I unzipped the bags, crawled into my snow boots, put on my parka, and walked across the parking lot to the public restroom. Returning to the van, I noticed a layer of frost clinging to the roof. I decided to start the engine. It had been sitting in the cold for almost five hours. Last thing I needed was a dead battery and frozen oil pan. But the engine kicked over immediately. I sat in the driver's seat until the temperature gauge pushed into the normal range. The van was warm and so was I. I cut the engine and hurried back into my bags, praying the van would trap some heat. It didn't. Around five o'clock I fell asleep again, exhaustion more powerful than the cold, but I was awake with first light at seven.

I saw my first bobsled while standing on the bridge that crossed the finish line. Finish curve was maybe thirty yards in front of me. From there the bob run angled up and to the left on a long straight. I heard the sled before I saw it, and then I saw it hurtle down the straight, flash around Finish curve, and streak between my legs just fifteen feet below. The bridge shuddered. I clutched the railing. Why hadn't the sled flipped over? Why hadn't the two helmets (all that reminded me of people) been bashed about the ice? It seemed as if a giant hand had come out of the sky and whipped the sled onto the wall of the curve and then just as quickly slapped it back to the bottom of the run. I heard another sled coming at me, clamoring down the mountain as if it couldn't get here fast enough to scare me. A deep, low rumble topped by a high-pitched screech of steel on ice that sent shivers down my spine. I wanted to see it and I didn't want to see it. And then there it was. Through the straight. Into the curve. Up on the wall. Down on the track. Between my legs. The bridge shuddered, my throat choked, my fingers gripped.

I watched three more sleds, equal parts mesmerized and paralyzed, and then walked down to the offices of the U.S. Bobsled Federation, a small room the size of a large recreational vehicle. The view of the track from here was singular. Windows, level with the run, looked directly onto the track just a few feet away. You heard the sled coming, then felt it, and finally, if lucky, you saw it flash across the window past the electronic timers.

I introduced myself to a secretary, thankful that I could tell her I was doing a story for *USA Today* about the two-man championships. I didn't want to tell anyone I was traveling the country attending as many sports events as I could in one year. My year was all of one day long. "Man you want to see is right there," she said. "Les Fenner; he's the coach of our national team."

Les, a tall man with thinning brown hair, had been a member of the last U.S. team to win a medal in world or Olympic competition.

"That was a bronze in '69," he said, his voice equal parts pride and disappointment.

Back when he first got into the sport thirty years ago, Les told me, the idea had been just to get all that weight down the mountain as fast as you could. You didn't have to be an athlete. "Now it's all very technical. Push time is very important." In modern bobsledding, according to Les, the race is won or lost in the five seconds it takes bobsledders to run their sleds through the first fifty meters. "We're trying to get a physical training program going. We have to mold athletes. We can't take bobsledders and turn them into athletes anymore. We have to start with athletes."

Les offered to show me the track. He pulled up the top of his insulated jumpsuit, which had been dangling from his waist, and covered his balding head with a brown fur hat.

We crossed the bridge above Finish curve, and walked up the path paralleling the straight where earlier I'd watched my first sleds appear. Every so often a sled zoomed past, filling the air with its terrifying clatter. A long silence followed. To our left and farther up the hill, the luge run snaked down the mountain. Occasionally I heard the announcer talk a luger down the track; but most of the time there was just the silence of the hill.

We walked past curve 15. Above the curve was another, shorter straight, which began at the exit of Zig Zag, a combination curve of back-to-back 90-degree turns. We stood on the wooden stands built into the side of Zig Zag, and watched a sled flip-flop through the two turns, a sharp left followed by a sharp right. There was no margin for error here, Les said, and despite the fact that Mount Von Hoevenberg was regarded as the safest track in the world, Zig Zag remained the most feared corner in bobsledding. We watched another sled, this one an out-of-control pinball that banged into the lips of both the left and right curves before sliding out of sight. It was readily apparent how Zig Zag had earned its reputation.

Farther up the run the track was a series of straights connected by curves that seemed harmless enough, at least compared to Zig Zag. Straight ahead and farther up the mountain, however, I could see the tail end of what could only have been a mammoth curve.

"That's Big Shady," Les said, respect crowding his voice. "The sled drops 180 degrees around a $3\frac{1}{2}$-story drop inside a radius of 100 feet. This is where the race really begins. This is where you pick up your momentum."

We walked up the path, away from the run, to a semilevel patch of ground, the epicenter of Big Shady. Above me I could hear a sled approaching. I turned and faced the curve, a twelve-foot wall of ice that wrapped itself around me. The sled appeared above my left shoulder, corkscrewed down and across my body, and exited below my right hip. I watched the sled slingshot out of sight, my jaw left slack by the combined forces of power, speed, and noise.

"Too bad you're not going to be here next week for the four-man championships," Les said. "You get all that momentum sliding down the mountain, and this entire place starts to rock." Right.

Les pointed to the two men in red nylon USA jackets standing by the lip of the run in the middle of Shady. "You want to talk to a couple of drivers?" he asked. "There's a couple of the better ones.

Guy on the left is Tony Carlino; the other's Bob Wilkens. I got to get back down the mountain."

Tony and Bob were happy to talk. Publicity was scarce on Mount Von Hoevenberg. I asked if ABC Sports was going to cover the nationals. They shook their heads and chuckled throaty laughs of disgust. "No way," Bob said. "But you know what the really sad part is? Last year Jim Morgan got killed over in Italy, on a bob run. Do you think ABC showed that? Sure they did." He shook his head sadly. Tony, hands in his pockets, stared at the snow. "Poor dumb bastard had to get himself killed before he could get on television." We turned and watched a sled, ten feet away and directly at eye level, whip through Shady and flash out of sight. Tony backed up, almost involuntarily.

"Why don't we take a couple steps back, okay?" he said. "We're getting into some of the less experienced sliders now. No telling what might happen."

"How do you guys figure to do over the weekend?" I asked. They shrugged their shoulders, not willing to commit themselves. Tony was a six-time member of the world team. Bob, a four-time member, was older than Tony, about forty, I guessed. His hair was carefully coiffed in an old-fashioned Wayne Newton style. Must have pained him terribly every time he put on his helmet. His face carried a perpetual expression of urgent concern.

"A lot of it's going to depend on the weather," Tony said. "Not real well if it stays like this." The temperature was still below zero. The bright, cloudless day gave the mountain only an illusion of warmth. "The ice is brittle now. We're just praying it gets about 10 or 20 degrees warmer." I asked what kind of times I should expect. Anything about 1:01, they said, would be great.

"The thing is, though," Bob said, "they're having the world championships here next month, and for any of us to have a chance of winning a medal, one of us will have to jump a full second ahead of everyone else this weekend."

"What's the problem?" I asked. Tony let go with a smirk.

"We're talkin' politics and money," he said. What followed was the "Bobsledders' Lament," a song of frustration screamed at the cold, uncaring mountain. Les had hummed a few bars earlier, and I would hear it again whenever I talked to a slider. "There isn't a sledder on this mountain who isn't in hock up to his ears," Tony said. "A good two-man sled costs $7,000. More for a four. A couple of us spent $3,000 each to go to Wittenberg, Germany, in November to get in some runs. By the time we got over there the Swiss and the East Germans had already gotten in fifty, sixty slides. By the time of the world championships they'll have 350, maybe 400. You know how long we've been on this mountain?" Tony stopped.

Bob stared right at me and answered the question. "Nine days."

"It's like going to Indy the day before the race," Tony continued. So began the lament's second stanza: politics. Mount Von Hoevenberg was administered by the Olympic Regional Development Authority under the auspices of the state of New York.

"It's a government bureaucracy," Bob said.

We walked back down the mountain, Tony too disgusted to talk about it, Bob too disgusted not to. It was difficult to keep up with his train of thought, but the bottom line was that he was angry and frustrated. There was just no way the best drivers were ever going to be world class if they weren't given the time to slide down the mountain. The track was open from 8:30 in the morning to 4:30 in the afternoon—government time. All the sliders practiced together. The nation's best with the guys screaming down the hill for a Michelob Light. The maintenance crew was top-notch, but they were paid for an eight-hour day, no overtime, which meant no sliding at night.

"You know what they say to us," Bob said ("they" being the Olympic Regional Development Association). "They say they don't want us to slide at night because the lights might go out and then there we'd be at seventy miles an hour in the dark. I say let the sliders make that decision. It's our ass, not their's." His voice turned suddenly sarcastic. "We know how to get down this mountain. We'll figure something out." He shook his head.

"We're never going to get anywhere with the system we got," he said. By now we were standing near Finish curve. Clouds had begun to cover the sky, bringing with them the promise of warmer temperatures. The way things worked now, according to Bob, he was lucky if he got in four runs a day, four times a week. "That's sixteen minutes of practice time a week." He pointed a finger at me. "How old do you think Dorothy Hamill would have been when she won her medal if she'd only been able to practice four minutes a day, four days a week?"

I drove back to Lake Placid with but one priority: finding a warm place to sleep. I was *not* spending another night in the parking lot. According to *Where to Stay USA,* there was a hostel at 54 Main Street. But I couldn't find 54 Main, let alone any hostel. I asked a man—the only person on the street, save for a group of teenagers heading into a theater to watch *Tootsie*—if he knew any cheap places to stay. Try the next street, he said; there are a bunch of boardinghouses that shouldn't be too bad.

The one I found wasn't bad at all. Nineteen dollars a night, three meals included, in a house that had been lifted lock, stock, and fireplace from a Norman Rockwell illustration. The housemother said she generally reserved the place for athletes, but at the moment she had plenty of room.

I put my stuff on my bed and headed for the bathroom. Hot, hot, gloriously hot water. I stripped quickly and sat in the tub, warm for the first time in twenty-four hours. Twenty-four hours! The first day of the trip was complete. I relaxed for the first time since leaving DeGraw Street.

The Mount Von Hoevenberg bob run snaked up the side of the mountain for almost a mile. It rose 488 vertical feet through sixteen curves, and was frozen by thirty-three miles of refrigeration pipe. Saturday morning, before the championships began, I hiked to the top to watch the starts of the first few sleds.

The starting area was quiet, expectancy filling the air. In front of the warming hut was a large, level slab of ice with two grooves about two feet apart etched into it. The grooves extended about twenty feet to the lip of the run where the concrete walls of the track started and the run itself began. A wooden gate, like a railroad crossing, blocked the track. The gate could be raised and lowered by a drawstring attached to a pole. On that pole was a bell.

The bobsleds were stacked on the other side of the grooves in the ice slab. Lying on their sides to prevent their runners from icing, they looked ungainly, like a herd of multicolored whales beached on a frozen shoreline.

The bell rang, and the voice of the track announcer echoed across the mountain: "Clear the track to the mile start." The pilot sled had already slid down the mountain to test the track and cut the groove. The first sled was called to the line.

I watched four sleds take off, and the routine hardly varied.

The two sliders tugged and cajoled their beast onto the two grooves in the ice. They removed their rubbers, revealing light and flexible shoes with thousands of tiny needles protruding from the soles. They shook hands. The driver, on the left, bent over and gripped with both hands a bar that stuck out from the side of the sled. The brakeman, directly behind the sled, wrapped his hands around the grips of the push bars that rose from the rear on either side. Together they rocked the sled forward about a foot, gently, as if the power and speed had to be approached cautiously.

"Ready?" asked the driver. They pulled the sled back.

"Yes," said the brakeman. They pushed the sled forward again.

"Ready," the driver said, this time a statement of fact. But then, as if they weren't quite sure, they pulled the sled back again.

"Yes," said the brakeman. Encouraged, they pushed the sled forward again, this time a little farther.

The driver began the count as they pushed and pulled. "One . . . and . . . two . . . and . . . three . . . and . . . ." Driver and brakeman in perfect synch, the brakeman standing fully erect behind the sled, his hands wrapped tightly around the push bars, awaiting the final command.

"GOOOOOooooo." They leaned together, the driver into his sidebar, the brakeman exploding through the push bars until his arms were fully extended behind him, actually pulling on the push bars. A flurry of legs. Screaming. The few drivers standing outside yelling and exhorting, disregarding for a moment the competition, united by their brotherhood. Another sled was off to challenge the mountain.

The bob angled off the level slab and onto the track. After thirty meters the driver hopped into the sled, wriggled into position, and collapsed his push bar into the cowling. The brakeman continued to run. No longer in front of the push bars, he was, in fact, perilously close to being left behind. A final few strides and he swung aboard and tucked himself behind the driver. His job was complete. He couldn't use the brake until the sled was down and off the track.

Despite the tension hanging heavily around me, the start was an unsatisfying place to watch the race. The sleds invariably took their promise of speed and power and disappeared. I walked down the hill, following the course, stopping to watch when a sled shot past.

Once a sled was out of sight, its rumble growing weaker in the distance, workers inspected the two parallel slices the runners had just etched into the ice. There was only one correct "line" down the mountain, a line that was, strangely enough, perfectly straight. This was a concept difficult to grasp until a driver suggested I imagine the run as a piece of ribbon held between my fingers. Pull it tight, he said, and I had a straight line. Shape the ribbon into a series of curves and I still had a straight line because even where the ribbon curved there was a flat surface running widthwise across the ribbon. By running the sleds on this flat surface of the curve (the "wipe"), the shortest distance between start and finish remained that straight line. And any adjustment by the driver, no matter how necessary, destroyed that line. The perfect run could be accomplished only when the driver didn't steer so much as ride along, permitting the sled to be guided by centrifugal force and aerodynamics. The best drivers were the ones who had learned how not to steer.

When the workers discovered a new gouge, they dropped onto the run with shovel in one hand and a bucket of slush in the other and repaired the track. They also examined the evidence to decide what this particular gash, the result of a particular mistake, had cost the sliders in terms of milliseconds. Then they'd climb off the run, huffing and puffing over the side of the track and up onto the snow. (All the workers, it seemed, were friendly fellows of expansive girth.) They'd listen as the announcer talked the sled through the finish line and announced the finishing time. The workers were seldom wrong in their predictions. The evidence had been there for anyone to see.

As expected, Brent Rushlaw was in first place after his two runs on Saturday with a combined time of 2:02.86. Bob Hickey was second, just eighty-one hundredths of a second behind. But the New York Jets were playing the Miami Dolphins in the American Conference Championships, and everyone, it seemed, was more interested in that game than in this one. I wondered if Richard Todd, the Jets' quarterback, would be running home tonight after his game to check the bobsled results.

Sunday broke warm, gray, and ugly. A fine drizzle hung in the air, and dark clouds sat on the mountains. In case a quick getaway were needed, I packed before leaving for the run. The local wisdom I'd gathered held that today's weather meant (a) no change,

(b) storm, (c) clear tomorrow, or (d) all of the above. There'd been but one agreement: "Anything can happen at Tupper Lake," thirty miles from Placid on Route 3 west, my only road to Chicago.

The weather was of immediate concern for the sliders. Warm and wet translated into quick runs for as long as the ice could withstand the beating, but the real danger was the mist, which didn't seem to be falling so much as just hanging in the air waiting to collect all over the driver's goggles. I considered the prospect of a blind slide down the mountain. The risk was not unreasonable for the veteran driver. It was the inexperienced sliders, forced by regulations into the same pot with the top drivers, who were taking the gamble. They had to take their chances when they could, even when common sense argued against it. "You know what's going to happen, don't you?" a top driver said to me. "These new guys are going to get a crash course in driving down the mountain." I started to laugh, then stopped. No joke had been intended.

But there were no crashes. I was relieved, yet at the same time disappointed. I'd come to terms with the speed and power the bobsled generated, but watching sled after sled rush down the mountain had a hypnotic effect. I expected success and began to demand more from the sleds. More could be furnished in only two ways: spectacular speed or a spectacular crash.

I almost got both. I was standing at the entrance to Zig Zag when a sled clamored down the straight approaching the turn. It slammed into the wall, and for a moment the sled was in the air and coming right at me. My stomach jumped to my throat, my hands gripped the railing. Involuntary reactions. The sled bounced to the bottom of the run, somehow still on its runners, and fishtailed crazily through Zig Zag. The entire episode hadn't lasted more than three or four seconds, but it had left me weak-kneed with fear. I released my grip on the rail slowly. My stomach stayed in my throat. Who was I, standing here, to be demanding more from these drivers and their sleds?

I left as soon as the races were complete. The clouds had closed in, it was almost dark, and soon the roads would be freezing. I wanted out. I had to be in Chicago next weekend for the Women's Powerlifting Championships, and if a storm were on the way I didn't want to be anywhere near here. I could be stuck until early April.

As I waited for the engine to warm, I checked the final standings on the result sheets. During the races I hadn't kept score myself. Each run down the mountain had its own identity, and, with so much time between runs, it was easier to consider them individually than as participants in a race.

It had been quite a contest. At the end of three rounds Rushlaw was still the leader, but Hickey had narrowed the gap to eighteen-hundredths of a second with a 1:01.51 in the third heat. It was the fastest run of the day and the fourth fastest of the championships. On the fourth and final run Rushlaw had inexplicably clocked a 1:03.26. That left an open window for Hickey. His final ride was an unspectacular 1:02.49, but it had been good enough to win.

I put my hand over the defroster. Warm and getting hot. I checked the rest of the sheet. Tony Carlino finished sixth with a combined 4:10.79. Bob Wilkens was tenth, less than a second behind Carlino. They wouldn't be going to the world's.

* * *

January 27

The Women's National Powerlifting Championships were scheduled to begin tomorrow, but the battle lines were apparent Friday night in the Midway Room at the Rosemont Holiday Inn near O'Hare Airport.

Tonight was the annual meeting of the United States Powerlifting Association Women's Committee. Jan Todd, a competitor in the 148-pound class and president of the committee, presided. After her state-of-the-committee address, elections were held to fill the various positions for the upcoming year.

That's when the battle lines took shape. On one side of the room sat one faction. A compact woman with curly blond hair and a white sweatshirt seemed to be their spokeswoman. Near the stage a second, smaller group sat gathered around a woman in a green sweatsuit. Her name was Michelle. At one point she mentioned living in New England, which led me to believe that her last name was Greenspan and that she was the owner of the New England Women's Gym. It had been through correspondence with her that I'd learned of tomorrow's championships. The rest of the women—and a number of men too—had apparently pledged their allegiance to Jan Todd.

Todd's opening remarks mentioned "pulling ourselves back as a federation." Five years ago, she said, there were twenty-eight women in the nationals, and there were no qualifying standards. At this year's championships there were over a hundred women and all had qualified at regional meets. But then came the inevitable remark: "Growth means problems." Should the women's committee remain an arm of the men's association or should it seek autonomy? There was the perennial problem of finances. And there seemed to be a conflict involving drugs.

Todd favored remaining part of the existing federation while gaining control of the women's situation. Her reasons were in part financial: "If we go independent now, with only 800 members, we would have a budget of $8,000. Women want autonomy, but we need the men." She had also come down hard on the side of drug testing.

But I understood Todd's position only because she'd expounded upon it. The positions of the other two groups were not so obvious. Especially when the blond-haired woman nominated Michelle for president of the committee. (Todd was reelected easily.)

After the elections Todd introduced Dr. Mauro di Pasquali, the chairman of the International Powerlifting Medical Committee. The 1983 nationals were to be the first United States championships—male or female—in which drug testing for all world records were mandatory if the lifter wanted the record recognized. The test had been personally financed by Jan Todd. Since this was the first year, the test was optional. If a lifter elected not to test, the record would be listed as an American record, but not a world record.

Talking in rapid little bursts of words, the doctor listed the four main groups of drugs under scrutiny. He would be administering the same test the International Olympic Committee currently used. Over 400 drugs were on its banned list. "Caffeine, for instance," he said. "Almost everybody has a caffeine positive with regular intake." He admitted there would be many problems and more questions; the decision to test had been reached only two weeks ago. Most lifters were woefully undereducated about drugs. For those conversant with drugs, the two-week notification period probably caught them by surprise. He stopped talking, and stood with one thick arm leaning against the podium. A short man with a strong but not overpowering build, black hair, and beard, his voice had been warm and reassuring. "Any questions?"

It would have been easier to count the people who didn't raise their hands. Was such-and-such on the list? I'm taking a pill for my sinuses; will I test positive? When should I stop taking so-and-so? How sensitive are the tests?

The doctor answered each question simply, keeping a complicated subject to its most common denominator. This was the issue that had created the battle lines and divided the lifters. The doctor pointed to a woman sitting in a section of the room I had decided was politically nonaligned.

"How can I beat the test?" Pow. The other questions had just been dancing with the only concern that mattered: beating the test, not getting caught. Whether you took drugs or not, this was the information you needed to know. You had to know how to cheat or how to catch the cheaters. The doctor didn't shy from an answer.

"You can still use drugs and still test clean," he said, conceding that there was just no way they could test for everything. "Adrenalin, for instance, in small amounts is almost undetectable. The problem, though, from a user's standpoint, is that there is just no way of knowing how sensitive the test is going to be." He spoke briefly about long-term side effects and admitted again that for all that was known there was even more to be learned. "Think about this," he said. "There is a possibility that a man using steroids can inject them into a nonsteroid-using woman during sexual intercourse."

I sat in my seat after the meeting ended, my head swimming. This wasn't going to be just two days of watching strong women lift heavy objects.

Ruthi Shafer entered her first powerlifting contest as a joke. She weighed over 200 pounds and couldn't lose weight. Then someone dared her to enter a meet. She took the dare, and won. A coach asked if she was interested in serious training. Ruthi said yes, and on her first day in the gym she set a regional record and on the third day an unofficial world record. More important, at least at the time, Ruthi was losing weight.

We sat together in the back of the ballroom. The carpeted room was empty save for the workers constructing the stage for tomorrow's championships.

It was difficult to imagine Ruthi as a 200-pounder. She would be competing in the 132-pound class, and although built square and close to the ground, her body sported a trim efficiency that didn't suggest it had ever allowed any extra weight. Ruthi was the woman in the white sweatshirt. She was twenty-three years old, which jolted me—I would have guessed she was thirty-five—tiny lines had already aged the corners of her eyes and mouth. Red lipstick dominated her face. She smiled quickly and often, unabashedly enthusiastic about her sport and its possibilities. She would be lifting Sunday, and she could hardly wait.

"I'm hoping for some big things. I hope to have the heaviest deadlift ever," she said.

"In your weight class?" I asked.

"Ever in the history of women's powerlifting." I asked how much that would be, poundwise. "Five-oh-seven," she said.

"The highest total that a woman has ever gotten is about 1,060-something—that's not totally accurate—but that was for a 181-pounder. I'd like to get close to 1,200 pounds, which has never been done."

"How do you do it?" I asked. Ruthi's face went blank. "I mean, when you're out there on the platform, what do you think about?"

"Well, first of all, I've got the best coach in the world—Doyle Kenady, three-time world powerlifting champion. I used to be a very loud, aggressive, shout-type lifter on the platform. But I wasn't a winner. When Doyle took over my training—that was 2½ years ago and I haven't been beaten since—he taught me that aggression should be on the inside. Taking it outside detracts from your psyche and your concentration. You'll find the best lifters don't do it.

"That's the way it is in men's lifting. With women, we've found—and this is sexist—we've found that the media doesn't go for it, number one, and number two, I feel it detracts from the sport from a women's standpoint. I don't like it that way, but that's the way it is. We should all be equal, but I know we're not. You have to face facts. Not only are overly muscular women unattractive in this sport, but so is the aggressiveness, the yelling and the screaming." She returned to my original question. "I turn my energy inside. By concentrating only on the bar I never believe that I can fail. And I can never miss a lift my coach picks."

"Do you address yourself to the question, 'Is this an acceptable sport for women?' "

"Yeah, I do. And I feel it can be. Women's body building was very unacceptable for a long time. Now it's rather chic. Very beautiful women are getting involved. Unfortunately, we've allowed one person in particular to promote the bad side of our sport. Powerlifting has a bad side, but we're a terrific sport."

One person in particular. Ruthi's voice, upbeat and enthusiastic, had dropped its bounce, her words assuming an edge, her emotions boiling just beneath the surface. I guessed that person to be Jan Todd.

"Drugs hang over this sport like a cloud, don't they?" I said. Ruthi nodded, disgusted.

"We have a lot of coverage out in Oregon because the media likes us. We don't talk about the problems. People don't want to know about all the internal problems. They want to know the good things we're doing, the big lifts we're making. They want to know that some girl is going to pull 500 pounds. That impresses people. It doesn't impress people when you tell them, 'We're going to test for steroids.'

"It's not that big a problem," she said, matter-of-fact. "Less than 10 percent of the lifters in this sport take drugs. At least 30 percent has been proved in track and field. Why do we never hear about that? Because they don't want it out. If you know athletes are on drugs, NBC's not going to pay $50,000 to film them because it's too controversial. We're in the same boat. Downplay the problems."

Ruthi explained her reason for refusing to test here at the nationals. At last year's world championships she'd competed in—and had won—the 132-pound class while suffering from pneumonia. She was tested for drugs and found positive. "I had a cough syrup called Novahistamine DH and an over-the-counter cold tablet called Sudafed." She said she'd also had written permission from the meet doctors to use the drugs. But when she tested positive, the International Powerlifting Federation sent letters to all countries involved at the worlds, telling them that Ruthi had been using amphetamines. Six months later the case was dropped.

Ruthi leaned back in her chair. "I almost lost my title, and I spent six months not knowing if I was going to be able to compete again. It hurt my reputation terribly. So I'm not too anxious to take any more tests."

I ran into Michelle Greenspan in the lobby as I was leaving. She was wearing a shirt advertising her New England Women's Gym. I asked if we could talk. She said yes, and we sat on a leather sofa across from the front desk.

Michelle told me how she got involved in powerlifting. A guy she knew was into strength training and taught her the fundamentals. She continued to train after she left the army and went to college, and one day in the gym a coach approached her. I guessed her story to be more representative of the other lifters than Ruthi's do-it-on-a-dare beginnings. But if her origins were ordinary, her commitment was not. Not many athletes buy their own gym and publish their own magazine.

Michelle smiled self-consciously. "I'm the kind of person who, well, I don't know, is some sort of natural leader who likes to start on the ground floor and get right into policymaking." Her voice was a center of calm amid the excitement that buzzed around us. "I enjoy the creative end of things and moving in new directions. I think that is the basic part of me that has brought me to where I am now."

"Do you get the standard question a lot, 'What's a nice girl like you doing in a sport like this?' " I asked. Michelle looked past me, thinking. Her straight brown hair was pulled back off her face.

"No, I don't," she said after a while, "but that's because I don't put myself in that kind of situation. I can't be around that all the time, explaining to people all the time and justifying it. That takes too much energy."

"Is it an unfair question?"

"No, not at all. I think there is a real curiosity, you know, as far as femininity and mystique are concerned." She glanced around the lobby. "I think the really neat part about lifting is that it shows people there really is no boundary as far as what a woman can do in terms of strength. And that they can have any body size and shape. You just can't make assumptions. It's really important for people to understand that, because people seem to have this idea that we're all, I don't know, very muscular, or . . ."

"Brick shithouses?" I suggested.

"Right."

The problem, Michelle said, was that the introduction of testosterone, the male hormone, and steroids into women's powerlifting had placed the "feminine mystique" squarely in the spotlight. "I'm sure you've seen it here. You have these women who are really drugged up. Complete masculinization. But then at the same time they'll go out and . . . ," she hedged, wanting to say exactly what she meant, "and try to act, really, you know . . . . They'll let their hair grow extra long or they'll put on more makeup. It's really strange."

I asked how she'd managed to remain independent of the testing-antitesting factions. Drugs in powerlifting seemed to demand a for or against stand. Michelle admitted it was a fine line to tread. Her latest effort to maintain the balance was to sponsor the Natural Nationals.

"My own opinion on the subject is to try to offer everybody the options they want. If people don't want drug testing, fine, let them go to their nationals. But then also offer a natural nationals for athletes who are clean. I've never taken them and I never will, but anyone can do what they want. I think what will happen, though, is that if the Natural Nationals catches on in prestige these other lifters will try to get into it and win it. Then we'll have the same problems all over again."

Michelle planned to use lie detector tests as well as drug testing for all world records at her Natural Nationals. "I take it," I said, "that using drugs has nothing to do with ethics."

"Well, sure," Michelle said, gently chastising me. "There's always going to be someone who's going to do it. It comes down to wanting to win so badly you'll do anything. The more sophisticated the testing procedure, the more sophisticated the beating of the test becomes. The majority of the women do not take drugs. The problem is you have a small percentage, 5 percent—well, let's say 10 percent—of the women using drugs. The other women get completely frustrated. The women who don't take drugs are forced to compete against those that do, and they can't say, 'You are on drugs.' They could be taken to court for saying that. There's nothing they can do."

Saturday morning I drove to the Rosemont in Albert, a lemon-colored Volkswagen that was more rust and dents than anything else. It belonged to Irene Sullivan, a friend from Alaska now living in Chicago. As I whipped Albert into the passing lane of the JFK Expressway, I wished this old bug with the sheepskin-covered seat and snowshovel in the back could be my transportation for the rest of the year. Albert had everything the van never would have: a personality, a name, and Alaskan license plates. The van was a brown slug that didn't deserve a title. But the worst thing was the New York plates. Boring. Pull up to a group of people inside a car with Alaskan plates and it was instant conversation.

Albert found a parking place across the street from the Holiday Inn. I uncurled myself from behind the wheel, and, walking through a cold and dreary Chicago day, tried to figure out how to handle this "drug thing" here at the nationals. I'd heard a lot about drugs in weightlifting, but I didn't want to be swept along by the popular story simply because it was the easiest story to find. I thought back to my conversation with Ruthi, the pained look on her face, the deep hurt in her voice when she talked about the drugs and testing controversy. To change the subject I'd asked her what she would promote if given the chance.

"What would I sell?" she said, her face suddenly bright. "Oh, God, I'd have a great time." It was like I'd set up the cameras right there, pointed to her, and said, "Action."

"Number one, I'd sell the battle between Terry Dillard and Diane Raoul in the 105s. Two of the best competitors in the world. Go to the 114s and it's the battle of the century. My friend Vicki Steenrod, a fabulous bencher, going against my good friend Carol Peterson. Vicki's a very pretty girl, a body builder. Carol's a professional woman, an R.N." I tried to interrupt, but there was no stopping her now.

"The dedication. The concentration. I'd talk about what the women do. Most of us are professional people. I run my own insurance business. Some women are balancing family and career plus the tremendous amount of hours this sport takes, for what is quite literally no reward." Back to you, Brent. Ruthi sounded like she'd just received her degree from Cliché College for Color Commentators, but her ebullience made it work.

On the other hand, Ruthi had also said she could "prove" that less than 10 percent of the women were taking drugs. On the surface, 10 percent isn't too alarming a figure. Michelle had said the same thing. But there were two ways to control a sport: get 90 percent of the people to think your way at the annual meeting, or win all but 10 percent of the medals during the competition. And today the power struggle was moving to the platform. I would have to keep my eyes and ears open before making any quick decisions.

In the ballroom the lightest weight class had just begun the squat. Every couple of minutes a woman peg-legged onto the stage wearing a lifting suit. The outfit was grotesquely tight. It bound the waist and squeezed her body out of the top of the suit. Thighs, bulging from the bottom of the leggings, looked like pressed baloney because their knees were bound with ace bandages just as tightly as their bodies. The bandages caused the peg-leg walk, and the lifting boots clomped across the platform.

Once the lifters reached center stage, they stood behind the bar, which was suspended at shoulder length on a metal rack. They took their time gripping the bar, until it looked like their hands would adhere to the surface. At this point, styles changed. Some lifters continued methodically, gently positioning themselves under the bar, then standing upright and stepping back to clear the rack and await the referee's signal to begin. Others attacked, diving under the bar, lifting it up and stepping back in one aggressive movement. Spotters stood on either side, their hands just inches beneath the ends of the bar, waiting to catch the weight if the lifter faltered. The referee raised his hand, and then, with a quick flick of the wrist, said, "Squat!" The lifter took a deep breath and lowered herself to the floor, sometimes slowly, sometimes with amazing quickness. Everyone in the ballroom, meanwhile, started screaming.

The lifter's face was one color on the way down—red, usually—and another color—violent purple, with veins and arteries and tendons bulging wildly along her neck—on the way up. Once upright the spotters grabbed the weight, and, with the lifter still stuck beneath the bar, placed the weight back on the rack. There was a momentary pause as the three judges registered their opinions. A white light indicated a successful lift, a red light a disqualification. A lifter needed two white lights. If she got them she'd jump in the air, and peg-leg triumphantly off the platform. The unsuccessful lifter, adrenaline pumping, walked off defiantly, defeated yet unbowed.

My confusion began early. What, exactly, was a kilo (besides a stash of cocaine)? And what happened when the competition was reduced to a handful of lifters? (A lifter got three lifts in each discipline—squat, bench press, and deadlift—with the heaviest pull in each category recorded toward the aggregate weight lifted, which determined final placement. World records, however, are tabulated in each of the three lifts as well.) The announcer would scream that a competitor was about to attempt a world record. "*And she needs all the help she can get*!" The ballroom would go nuts. If the lifter made the weight and set the record, she pegged off the stage to a thunderous ovation. Meanwhile, the spotters would add a couple more kilos to the bar, the next woman would goose-step to the weight and squat virtually unnoticed. Even if she made it, she walked off the stage to a smattering of polite applause. What was going on here?

The bench press could not have been duller. One after another the lifters walked out, lay down on the bench, and took their turns pressing the weight. Down, up. That was it. All the lifters looked alike, and the announcer continued to ask for extra screams on world record attempts but then pointedly ignored the next lonely soul.

The deadlift was last. Its appeal was immediate. The bench had been boring, and although the squat did have a certain dangerous quality—the lifter had to pit her body against the weight—the object of the deadlift was wonderfully basic: Pick the sucker up.

The lifters walked out quietly. The knee wraps were gone, the clodhoppers replaced by, of all things, ballet slippers. They positioned themselves over the weight, their legs covered with baby powder and spread wide, their feet under the bar. They gripped the metal, one hand in front of the bar and the other behind it. Again, techniques varied. Some pulled in one quick motion until they were standing up, their backs arched and the weight at midthigh; others lifted slowly, their faces turning a deeper and deeper purple, their bodies quaking under the strain, until they too had lifted the bar to midthigh. A few placed the weight back on the platform gently, a defiant gesture demonstrating total triumph. Most, however, dropped the weight quickly, glad to be rid of the burden, and the bar thundered to the floor.

The deadlift proceeded as did the others, with three lifts and the heaviest being the one that mattered. And yet there was an added element. Because it was the final event, if the lifter didn't make it now she never would. "The meet doesn't start till the bar gets off the floor," a woman told me between screams. That's when I finally caught the excitement Ruthi had talked about last night. I suddenly realized why the announcer yelled for some and not for others: because two weight divisions were being contested simultaneously. The realization could not have hit me harder had I been clanked in the forehead by a 100-kilo weight. Two different weight classes, two different sets of records! I breathed a sigh of relief.

But I still had other questions.

Only the first of the four sessions of the two-day meet had been completed, but it was readily apparent that drugs and powerlifting went hand in hand. There seemed, in fact, to be two competitions going on at the same time (which had nothing to do with the two weight classes being contested simultaneously). There was an A championship and a B championship. The B championships involved the women who didn't appear to be using drugs. Once that competition was completed, the A championships began. The non-drug users were competing for third and fourth place, the apparent drug users vying for first and second.

I was walking into unknown waters, and I had to tread carefully. I knew virtually nothing about steroids or testosterone injections or any of the things Dr. di Pasquali had talked about last night. And yet, a number of things were just plain obvious as I walked around the ballroom. First, there was nothing inherently unfeminine about women's powerlifting. These were strong women who could lift heavy objects. And most of them were stunningly healthy looking. There was, however, a handful of women who just didn't look like women. There was no other way to say it. They looked like my younger brother—if I had a younger brother. I'd been told that TV, after covering women's powerlifting with an initial burst of enthusiasm, had shied away once some lifters began using drugs. It was obvious why: Their faces were rough, chiseled, even, with harsh features and strong masculine lines. Some had dark patches of fuzz on their upper lips, the kind of growth I'd shaved so proudly when I was sixteen. Others had thick hair on their arms, or well-defined musculature that started with powerful shoulders and dropped in a V to a narrow waist. This group of competitors was definitely the minority, but their presence was felt everywhere, starting on the platform (where they dominated the contests).

Of course, there was no way to determine precisely who was on drugs unless everyone took the test. Even that would be inconclusive as there were methods of circumventing the test. And besides, Dr. di Pasquali had said that only the steroids and the testosterone produced the virilization so apparent in a few of the lifters. The most feminine looking lifter here might be jammed full of pain killer or totally buzzed on a stimulant. If she didn't take the test no one would ever know, and maybe not even care. The general attitude I discovered talking to the lifters was that steroids and testosterone were the only real enemies, because they were the drugs that played such tricks with a woman's body. The novocaines and stimulants seemed to fall between the cracks into a less definable area that might just be acceptable to everyone.

The women whom I suspected of using steroids and/or testosterone would not, of course, admit to using anything. The closest they came was to state that drugs are a personal choice best left to individual discretion. There were even a few for whom drugs were just the new frontier of athletic excellence. "When you think about it," one person said to me, "it's really very exciting. I'd like to see how much we are capable of lifting with the right dosages of the right drugs." The horizons were limitless.

And there were those for whom all questions were political. They refused to be tested because it was an attempt by the international organization to undermine the United States dominance of the sport. Or as a protest against Jan Todd's leadership. A few maintained the continuing controversy was actually being shaped by Terry Todd, Jan's husband. This was his attempt, they said, to gain control of a drug-free lifting federation because he had lost control of the men's drug-dominated association. Everyone was pointing the finger at everyone else. But the pro-choice drug advocates always had the last word. "They [nondrug users] are just sore losers." Winning remained the bottom line.

Jan Todd had proved impossible to pin down for anything remotely resembling a conversation. Her job was to compete, administer the test, and hold together a fractious organization. So I talked to her husband, Terry, instead. A large man with a gray beard, he was a former powerlifter and currently a dominant force in the sport. He summarily dismissed the accusation that he was trying to "gain control" of anything.

Terry believed that if there were no drug testing now, in five years all the women at the nationals would be taking some sort of drug. The United States was dragging its feet because so many of the administrators within the sport used drugs themselves. In the men's game drugs were part and parcel of the sport ("*Everybody* takes 'em," everybody told me). This everybody-does-it attitude had created its own moral standard. Good versus evil was no longer determined by the decision to take drugs; it was determined by how much you were willing to take. "But," Terry asked, "is it right for a man to take steroids because they make him a hyper male, but wrong for a woman because they tend to move her away from her femininity?" The last unanswered ethical question involving drugs and sports.

I sat in the back of the ballroom to watch the second session. On the platform, a handful of women took turns breaking one another's minutes-old world records. To the right of the platform the lifters huddled with their coaches, deciding what their next weight should be. The strategy wasn't as simple as deciding beforehand that a lifter should go for 100 kilos on her first pull and follow it with lifts of 110 and 125. It wasn't enough to beat the opponent's previous lift. They had to be able to pull enough weight to keep their competition from beating them with *their* next lift. The result was that all the women grew stronger together, pushed by one another to new and previously unconsidered limits.

Yet despite the psychological sideline dramas and the real dramatics on the stage itself, one thought continued to intrude on my enjoyment of the event: What, exactly, was impressing me so much? The accomplishments achieved by these women on the platform, or the comprehensiveness of their medicine cabinet? The seed of suspicion, sown last night, had taken root. I decided to talk to Dr. di Pasquali.

I found him in the lobby. No one was taking the test at present, although a few women already had. I asked him to estimate the number of lifters using drugs here at the nationals. He hesitated before speaking, then said, "I'd guess between 25 and 50 percent." An estimate five times higher that any I'd heard previously. The doctor didn't limit his definition of drugs to steroids and testosterone, however, as did most everyone else. "People will use a painkiller or a cold tablet to get a little boost," he said, and then he ran through a quick list of the main categories of banned drugs.

Stimulants were number one, followed by narcotics, and then the anabolic steroids and testosterone. "It's complex, of course," he said, winding up. "I'm just trying to simplify it as much as I can.

"They're very dangerous," he stressed, talking of stimulants and narcotics. "People have died from excessive use of amphetamines in the Olympics. In the second group we're not looking for aspirin and that kind of stuff as much as we are for Percodan, codeine, Demerol, morphine, heroin. If you have an injury they can allow you to bypass it. That leaves you open to greater injury. I've seen people pull their biceps off completely. I've seen legs go out from underneath people. I saw a tendon snap. Things like that."

"The steroids and testosterone are for gaining strength?" I ventured.

"Right. Gaining bulk, building strength, increasing muscle size, decreasing fatty tissue. An anabolic effect." He listed the side effects of these drugs, effects readily visible in some of the lifters here.

"What about long-term effects?"

"That's under study," he said. The statement, short and clipped, chilled me. "There probably are long-term effects we're not even aware of. There are hepatomas coming out, primary liver cancers that may be the result of steroids people took quite a while ago. There are problems with increased cholesterol levels, which increase your cardiac problems. Stroke problems. People definitely become hypertensive when they're on them. And the doses people take in order to stay on top become more and more extreme. Eventually they're taking three, four hundred times the official allowable physiological dose. Daily.

"It has to be controlled," his voice was urgent now. He was convinced that for every athlete who used drugs as a training tool there was another athlete using them because he or she saw no alternative. "I think if someone were overseeing the problems, someone saying, 'Okay, we're going to have the test,' a lot of athletes would say, 'Whew! That's over with. I don't have to worry anymore. I don't have to worry if I'm going to get liver disease anymore.'

"You see, it's got to stop. We can't leave it up to the athlete. The athlete isn't concerned about things on a grandiose scale. They're concerned about how they are going to do in the next contest. 'I don't care,' " he said, placing himself inside the head of a world-class athlete, " 'what I'm doing two years from now. Right now I'm training for one contest. I want to get better. I want to win.'

"It isn't difficult to make the decision to do drugs in the heat of battle. But the battle will be cold in thirty years. Will they still have no breasts, deep voices, hair-covered arms, bad skin, and have to shave once a week? People are trying to reintroduce some sanity into all of this."

The story of drugs wouldn't go away. It was everywhere: up on the platform, etched into the lifters' faces, anchoring conversations. It was the best story at the nationals, and by Sunday morning it became the only story.

Everyone I talked to on Saturday had told me that the premier session would be the 60- and 67.5-kilo classes on Sunday morning. Ruthi Shafer would be challenging the 500-pound deadlift and a 1,200-pound total. At 67.5, four women would be locked in what *Powerful Times* billed as a "royal battle!" Diane Frantz, Angie Ross, Debbie DeWitt, and Jan Todd. That Todd was one of the four participants added the exclamation point.

Todd was the first women to peg-leg to the bar for her initial squat. One hundred sixty-five kilos. She squirmed herself under the bar, stood up, and backed away from the rack. She looked at the ceiling, her breath popping in little bursts. The referee raised his hand. Off the platform Debbie DeWitt slumped in a folding chair, looking bored and withdrawn. Diane Frantz, forty-six and still a contender, was a coil of nerves as she sat next to her husband, Ernie. "Squat." Todd stopped breathing and lowered herself, her eyes glued to the ceiling. She came back up cleanly and placed the bar on the rack. Three white lights. Her followers cheered mightily.

Frantz was next at 170 kilos, her face a violent explosion of purple as she brought the bar back up. She goose-stepped to the edge of the platform where Ernie caught her and carried her to a chair.

Angie Ross, the defending champion, squated 180 kilos, followed by DeWitt, who did 182.5 and made it look easy. Frantz did 182.5, too, but just barely pulled it. Todd went after 185, a 20-kilo jump over her first attempt, but didn't get it. Then DeWitt, instead of getting a record at 185, added 2½ kilos and squatted the weight as easily as she had her opener, to establish the first world record of the day.

That brought Ruthi Shafer to the platform for the first time. She was by herself in the 60K class. "She's going for a world record on her very first attempt!" the announcer screamed. Ruthi went down, came back up, and placed the bar back on the rack. Her first world record and the session's second. Angie Ross added another 2½ kilos, pushing the bar to 190, and set the day's third world record. Frantz tried to match it with her third lift, but missed. DeWitt then tried 192.5, but she missed, too. Now it was Todd's turn. She passed. If her strategy was at all muddied before, it was now clearly evident. The squat had been pushed beyond her capabilities; she could no longer win the title. But she could conserve her strength now and go for a world record deadlift. *And then take the test.*

Ross, then, was already the winner of the squat, and she still had a lift remaining. A big-boned woman with long brown hair, she was the most girlish looking of the four principals at 67.5. She elected to go for 195K. Every kilo counted when it came time to add them up at the end. Angie got under the bar, started her squat, and then suddenly collapsed. The spotters caught the bar; otherwise, she might have been crushed, accordionlike, into the platform.

That left Ruthi, sixteen pounds lighter and all by herself in the 60K class. She had the bar set at 200 kilos, and the crowd gasped. But she took the bar down and brought it up. Her second world record and the fourth of the session. "I don't understand this," the announcer said, "she looks like she has more trouble going down than she has coming up." According to the rules, Ruthi now had three minutes before taking her next lift. She used all the time, then squatted 207.5 kilos. World record number five. "That's 457 pounds," the announcer said. I thanked him silently for letting me in on their kilo secret.

To no one's surprise, Debbie DeWitt blew everyone away in the bench. Debbie was a body builder in addition to a powerlifter, and her shoulders and arms were massive, absolutely massive. They dominated her body and made her look top-heavy. Her opening press tied the world record, and her two subsequent presses were the session's sixth and seventh records. Her third lift, a 112.5K effort, pushed her into first place with 330 kilos total. She'd made up 32.5 kilos in the bench. Ross, who'd finished second in the bench with a 90-kilo press, was now second overall at 280. Frantz was third at 269, and Todd, waiting for the deadlift, fourth at 245.

The crowd was primed by the time the stagehands had prepared the platform for the deadlift. For the first time in two days the ballroom was reasonably full, an expectant buzz sharing space with the baby powder and chalk dust that hung in the air.

Ross opened at 180K. Todd followed with a quick snap at 187.5K, and DeWitt an even quicker snap at 190. That put Ross back on the platform, also attempting 190. She made it cleanly, and three minutes later was back on the platform looking at 195. Angie needed this pull. It was her final lift and Frantz still had all three of hers. Ross had to make this lift and then hope Frantz couldn't make up the difference. She squirmed her feet into the platform, her slippers covered with white dust. (Lifters wear slippers, I learned, to prevent themselves from rocking forward.) She positioned herself over the bar, squatted down, and began the pull. Halfway up she lost her grip. The weight crashed to the floor. In tears before she even straightened up, Ross walked to the edge of the platform where her coach wrapped his large arms around her and, with her head buried in his shoulder, escorted her into the warm-up area and disappeared. First after the squat, second after the bench, there was no telling where she would finish.

Frantz added five kilos to the bar and prepared for her first deadlift. Her face turned that violent, explosive purple, but she pulled the weight easily and set the bar down gently.

DeWitt pulled the same 200. Then Ruthi Shafer added five more kilos and hit it easily. As with her opening squat, her first deadlift had broken the 60K world record.

Now it was Todd's turn, also at 205K. A lift that would tie the 67.5K world record. She pulled the lift, holding the bar an extra beat for good measure, her back arched, the muscles across her neck and chest pulled taut. She dropped the bar triumphantly, and jumped into the air before it hit the floor. Turning to her husband, she punched the air with her fist and ran into his arms.

Her triumph was short-lived. Frantz broke the new world record with a 207.5K pull, and a couple of minutes later DeWitt popped 210K to break it again. I lost count of the world records, but

DeWitt's 210 had been her final lift. She was through for the day, unless she elected to take an allowable fourth lift that could count as a world record deadlift but not toward her overall total.

Todd huddled with her husband and a few close supporters. I tried to figure their strategy. DeWitt was already the overall winner. She was also competing on a sprained ankle. Did Jan and Terry know that? DeWitt probably wouldn't go for a fourth lift with the championship in the bag. And by declining a record attempt, DeWitt could keep her hand in the psychological game being contested. By "giving" the record to Todd she stripped away some of its luster.

Frantz posed a more immediate problem. She could wait for Todd to choose her weight, then match Todd's lift and be declared the winner on lighter body weight. Then it would be a question of who would take the test. Todd, of course, would, so she could still be the "winner" if Frantz declined. But that would produce a technical victory. For her purposes, Todd needed an undisputed world record. She had to go after a weight Frantz couldn't match, even if in the end it proved too much for her as well. Todd registered her lift: 215K, a 10-kilo increase over her last lift, a 7.5K increase over Frantz's second lift. The final gamble.

Todd hunched over the bar, the audience pressing forward, most of the spectators ready and willing to pull the lift with her. She took a deep breath and the pull began. The crowd screamed, wanting, begging, demanding that she make it. S-L-O-W-L-Y she stood up, the bar rising off the floor smoothly. Her back arched as she completed the lift, and again she held the bar that extra measure. When the weights dropped to the floor she turned to the judging lights. White. White. White. World record. She jumped in the air, and the crowd hugged itself in delight. Todd ran to the end of the platform and into Terry's arms. "Redeemed," she said, "redeemed."

Now Frantz was alone on the stage for her final pull at 215K. I remembered Michelle Greenspan's comment about last year's nationals and the "emotional destructiveness" these test-antitest confrontations had precipitated. How would the crowd react if Frantz made this lift? Worse, what might happen if she didn't? But Frantz missed convincingly, solidifying Todd's dominance. There was scattered applause as Frantz walked off the platform, but Todd's victory had already been internalized, the point made.

Besides, Todd had still finished fourth, despite—or perhaps because of—her world record deadlift. DeWitt was the winner with a 510K total and a world record bench. Frantz was second at 476.5K, and Angie Ross third at 470K. Everything had been proved; nothing had been proved.

"Don't go away!" the announcer reminded us. "We still have Ruthi." The spotters added two kilos to the bar, for a 217 total. Ruthi's assault on the 500-pound deadlift and the 1,200-pound total had begun. Ruthi's bench had been 95K. Coupled with her 207.5 squat, her total now was 302.5K (665.5 pounds).

Ruthi made 217, but for the first time she struggled with the bar. She walked off the platform and sat down in a metal chair. The strain was beginning to tell. Three minutes between lifts was not a long time. She grabbed her T-shirt with a thumb and forefinger and popped it up and down quickly to cool herself. "I'm starting to hyperventilate," she said. "I get so nervous . . . ." Doyle Kenady, Ruthi's coach, crouched down to calm her, the two very much alone in the middle of the crowded room. They talked quietly, then Ruthi shook her head firmly. Doyle registered the final weight. The announcer, God love him, read it in pounds.

"*Five hundred and one pounds!*" The crowd had been waiting all morning to hear that, but they didn't know how to react. First there was silence, than a gasp, then excited chatter. With a minute remaining in her rest period, Ruthi walked onto the platform and described a slow, deliberate circle as she paced behind the bar. Doyle stood next to the platform intoning a mantra of encouragement.

"This is your action. This is yours. All or nothing. Set yourself. Set yourself. This is your action . . . ."

Ruthi stepped to the bar. Doyle stopped talking. The crowd lurched forward. She squirmed her feet into place, gripped the bar, gripped it again, and then a third time before she held it for good. The bar was four inches off the floor when her legs began to shake. The quiver moved through her hips, up to her shoulders, and down to her arms. The weight swayed. Desperation contorted Ruthi's face. It was out of control. She dropped the bar, disgusted, and walked off. For Ruthi, the iron is the only competition. This time the iron had won.

* * *

Wednesday morning. Howland, Ohio. Gas $1.03 a gallon. I filled the tank and for the first time received green paper as change for my $20 traveler's check. Driving east on I-80, I wondered if there wasn't some way I could do this trip without leaving Ohio.

I was already a day late for the National Figure Skating Championships in Pittsburgh, but I knew that before I got there I had to find some resolution to the Women's Powerlifting Championships. I'd been in a blue funk since leaving Chicago. I was finding the "drug thing" difficult to shake.

The problem was that I was refusing to come down heavy on either side of the question. I couldn't join forces with Jan Todd. She was too much the white knight, too much the righteous crusader. The drug users were paying a heavy price for their decisions. They deserved more respect than Todd seemed willing to give them.

At the same time, I knew I could never embrace drugs as just one more route to the victory stand. The drug users were a handful of people, isolated and outcast, gathered around one another because no one else would have them. But despite a certain dignity of purpose, their perimeter status wasn't completely unwarranted. Their changed physiognomy had taken them past any standard definition of femininity. But femininity per se wasn't the issue (exactly what is femininity anyway?). The problem was that at some unrecognizable juncture the use of steroids and the changes those drugs produced in their bodies had taken some of the lifters past any workable definition of human. They become something else, although what that something else was I wasn't precisely sure. Athletic animals? Performance freaks? Everything sacrificed to the final outcome. They weren't *less* human; they just became something else.

The sun disappeared by the time I reached the Pennsylvania Turnpike. It looked like rain. I tried to place myself inside the mind of one of the lifters. If I were she, would I make that final sacrifice? Impossible to answer. I'd never stood at the outer limits of a sport, looking into the unknown and asking myself how can I get *out there.* I also never would. It would be naive to say I'd never use drugs as a means to push myself into those outer limits.

Yet I refused to give up my notion that sports should be pure. I want the athletes who thrill me with their feats of strength and beauty to do so without using drugs—even if that means their accomplishments aren't quite as strong or as beautiful. I want someone to do those wondrous things for me because I can't do them myself. And I want the people capable of such feats to be just as human as I am, so that I can say, as my heart pounds at the sight of yet another breathtaking achievement, that there is a part of me that I hold in concert with that wondrous human being, and because of that connection, we are, in some grand and mysterious way, doing all those marvelous things together.

Rain spattered the windshield. The noise brought me back to earth. I flipped on the wipers. Nothing happened. What to do: wait out the storm or drive to the next service area? No real decision to make. Figure skating would be the first event where I'd be a member of a bona fide press corps, and I was too anxious to be there to wait here.

I missed the Pittsburgh exit marked in the Trip-Tik and had to come into the city on Route 8. I followed 8 to the Allegheny Expressway. Pittsburgh was down to the left. So was the Allegheny River. I crossed the Highland Bridge, then pulled to the side of the road to check my map. I was planning to stay with a family friend from York, Pennsylvania, where we'd both grown up. He was a sophomore at the University of Pittsburgh now. He lived on Oakland Avenue, wherever that was.

The Fifth Avenue bus was crowded with rush-hour commuters; it was difficult to stay close to the driver to remind him to tell me where I had to get off. But at Fifth Avenue and Washington Street he stopped the bus, pointed up the hill to the right, and yelled, "Civic Arena!" I jumped off the bus, and walked up Washington Street, between the Hyatt Pittsburgh and the Epiphany Church, to the arena. A silver dome dominating the hill; a giant grain silo that had been buried until only its rounded top was exposed. Or maybe a giant thermos buried the same way, because it looked like you could screw off the top and peer inside.

I entered through the media entrance on the ground floor and signed my name: "Steve McKee—*Anchorage Daily News.*" (Back in September I had arranged affiliation with the *Daily News* through Roger Brigham, the sports editor. He loved the idea of the trip, and had asked but one question: "Are you a child molester?" After I'd assured him that I wasn't, he dubbed me his National Sports Correspondent.) I walked down a long corridor to the press room, hoping my abecedarian status was neatly tucked out of sight. Inside the press room I signed my name again. "So you're the one from Alaska!" a woman said, startling me. Was something wrong? Was my trip screeching to a halt right here, refused admission at the first major event? The woman smiled warmly. "I think it's just great that they sent you down here for this. Just great." I mumbled something to fill the space she had obviously left for me to fill, and gratefully reached for my press kit.

Still too nervous to risk conversation, I shuffled over to a table, sat down, and opened my press kit. A *Great Skate* handbook, a program, too much information about Campbell's soup, and the press pass. The press pass! A laminated, mustard-colored card the size of a driver's license. It had a place for my name, although in that space was already written "156." On the line marked "area" it said "Media." At the top in the middle was the symbol of the nationals, a trapezoid divided into two triangles. "Pittsburgh '83" was written in one; a pair of skaters twirled in the other. A black cord was attached, and the instructions said to wear this badge at all times. I put it around my neck, looked at it dangling on my chest and took it off immediately. I sat and watched members of the press enter, sign in, and receive their kits and credentials. They grabbed for them nonchalantly, like it was no big deal, like they fully expected to be given one. I waited half an hour before putting my credential around my neck again, until someone else hung his credential around his neck.

I ate dinner at the media reception in the Igloo Club on the second level. A bar stretched the length of the room, and pictures of hockey teams with gapped-tooth players mugging for the cameras covered the walls. Everyone else knew what to do. Clusters of people laughed and talked by the bar. Lots of complimentary drinks. Much free food. I ate by myself, still too intimidated by the media scene to risk talking to anyone. After dinner I decided to take a look around.

Drawn by bright lights, I walked up a ramp and into the arena. A wall of television lights banked one side of the stands, filling the stadium to the flash point with blinding white light. The arena was empty—it wasn't yet six o'clock—and the persimmon-colored seats glowed. The ice jumped up at me, a sheet of flat, shapeless white. My eyeballs ached. I blinked, forcing them to adjust. The ice metamorphosed from a flawless white into a soft, milky blue with thousands of white skate marks etched into it. The Zamboni machine was leaving the rink, and the ice was still covered with a microthin coating of glazed water.

Two skaters, a man and a woman, glided onto the rink, their bodies reflected in the ice, the images meeting at the skate blade. The four of them, two upright and two upside down, floated silently across the ice. I sat down to watch a short moment of the year that I knew would be worth remembering.

This evening's program began with the Novice Ladies' final and the Junior Men's short program before the Championship Pairs Competition—where the national- and Olympic-caliber skaters performed their compulsory short programs. The competition proceeded slowly, rhythms dictated by the need to keep the ice in as good a shape as possible. Four skaters skated a practice session, and then the Zamboni machine growled around the rink resurfacing the ice. Two workers carrying tin cans of slush then inspected for gouges. When the ice was deemed fit, the four skaters who had just practiced skated their programs, and the entire process started anew.

The judging was equally tedious. Nine judges, each sitting alone on one side of the arena, took their time deciding the skaters' marks. Two girls from the Pittsburgh Skating Club, the tournament host, skated across the ice to collect the scores, and then the results were punched into a computer and the numbers flashed on the scoreboard. As the 5.1s and 5.7s lit up the scoreboard, the crowd clapped and booed accordingly, and then the announcer read the scores for all of us who couldn't read them ourselves. He took his time, enunciating every numeral with excruciating accuracy. But no one seemed in a particular hurry to get things over with. The lady in front of me—obviously a veteran figure skating watcher—had brought her knitting.

When I first sat down in my press box seat, I was more than a little apprehensive. I was about to watch figure skating for the first time without Dick Button and ABC Sports to tell me what was happening. (That I had never understood what he was talking about didn't matter.) But as things turned out, I didn't need Dick Button. ABC Sports had been bringing an entirely different competition into my living room from the one I was watching now.

Here I had a new frame of reference. On television, the TV camera follows the skaters too closely. It's impossible to determine where the skaters are in relationship to where they've been and where they're going. Sitting in the arena I could see the entire rink. It was the frame of reference that really mattered, the focal point that gives skating its elegant definition. The scrutiny of the camera was gone and forgotten, the performance no longer so many individual components to be criticized or praised. I had the big picture right in front of me; commentary would have been an unwanted intrusion.

Watching the Novice Ladies and the Junior Men before the Championship Pairs provided an unexpected bonus, a touchstone for the comparison of good, better, and best. Each skater was the best skater I had ever seen, until the next skater took the ice. Whenever I thought I was beginning to understand the sport, another young and talented body would glide onto the ice and raise my "knowledge" of skating to a new level. To add to my delight, whenever I marveled at another series of jumps and spins, the woman next to me patted my arm reassuringly and admonished me with, "Nothing compares with pairs."

She was right. Throughout the night individual skaters had been dancing with the illusion of flight. The thousands of white skate marks sliced into the ice gave the surface a third dimension of cloudlike realism, but it wasn't until the pairs competition that this illusion fairly brushed reality.

The man would lift the woman above his head and then, with her arms and legs extended and back arched, they would glide the length of the rink. Pair after pair performed this maneuver as part of their compulsory short program, and time and time again they took my breath away. The pairs appealed to me in ways the singles could not. Two people who must make themselves one. That the two were a man and a woman only served to heighten the tension, injecting an undeniable sexual chemistry to the portrait they were creating on the ice, each working within the framework of his or her own role to produce the final image.

By the end of the evening, after five hours of figure skating, I still didn't want the night to end. I wanted the pairs to skate forever, to make those chills dance delightedly down my spine until they collapsed from exhaustion. I would never be sated by their beauty and elegance. And I would never be able to comprehend the quality of their courage, the absolute fearlessness they both must possess to soar so magnificently across their own private sky.

Thursday I returned to the arena early, anxious to watch the pairs finals. I leaned against a rail behind the press section, looking at the ice, that pale blue sky, that delicately spun glass. A man wearing a blue blazer with a Civic Arena emblem over the breast pocket walked over to me. "You know," I said, looking for an opening into a conversation, "after watching the figure skating last night, it's kind of difficult to imagine that they play hockey here, too."

"Yeah, yeah," the man said, but then he reminded me that the Pittsburgh Penguins played their hockey here. His name was Joe, a short man with round body, round face, and glasses. He was a program seller and had been at the arena for twenty-two years. "Since it opened," he said, his voice proud and full of cheer. He worked on 15 percent commission and he did all right.

"I guess you like it here, then," I said.

"Yes, very much. What's really nice about it is you get to see all the different shows. You know, a different type of people for every show: wrestling, boxing, basketball, hockey. We've had operettas here."

"You get to watch 'em?"

"Sure. We used to get real excited. We'd go down and see what the people looked like, the stars and all. Now I could care less. I've seen all the top entertainers. Frank Sinatra, Tom Jones, Humperdink, Elvis. Nat King Cole was here for one of them operettas. He was here for a week. When he sang on that stage you could'a heard a pin drop. People just stopped and listened. Of course, they did that for Perry Como, too, and they did it for Sinatra, but I mean, Nat King Cole was a black man, you know what I'm saying? Oh, he was good. Oh yeah, he was good."

Joe stood behind a short podium that raised him about a foot off the floor. Behind him were stacks of *Great Skate* programs, the covers an abstract painting by Judy Blumberg and Mike Seibert of the Pittsburgh Figure Skating Club and the current national ice dance champions.

"What's your best crowd?"

"Wrestling." No hesitation. "Those people are broke, they're a poor type of people, but they buy anything and everything. We always sell out of programs. Let me tell you, that wrestling? It's all fixed. But those people come in here and get excited. Oh, do they get excited!"

"How about hockey?"

Joe waved his hands, indignant or delighted I couldn't tell. "They're like schizophrenics, you know? Inside they want to see blood; out here, they're calm, normal people."

The two ushers working the turnstiles behind me unlocked the gates. "Well, gotta go to work," Joe said. I asked if he figured to do very well with the skating crowd. He looked at the people coming through the gates. Fur coats, ties, lots of jewelry. Joe shook his head. Not the kind of crowd that spent its money on programs.

The Championship Pairs final did not disappoint. My stomach tied itself in knots whenever a woman took flight. And that quality of courage I wanted so desperately to define remained as elusive, mysterious, and provoking as it had last night.

As expected, Kitty and Peter Carruthers (a brother-and-sister team) won their third straight national title with a factor placing (whatever that was) of 1.4. Bill Fauver and Lea Ann Miller, like the Carrutherses also from the Ice Skating Club of Wilmington, Delaware, moved from second to third, beating Jill Watson and Bert Lancon of Los Angeles by six-tenths of a point.

Lea Ann and Bill were the first pair to skate. Dressed in black, they contrasted sharply with the ice, their image as clear as two ravens silhouetted against the sky. Midway through their performance each skated to opposite corners of the rink, and then rushed toward each other and the center of the ice. The Civic Arena tensed, expecting to be thrilled. Lea Ann crouched while Bill, skating backward and totally blind, leaped over her and completed a 360 before returning to the ice. For the rest of their performance Lea Ann and Bill held the audience in the palm of their hands. They finished their routine by joining for a spin. Facing each other, one leg bent, the other extended beyond the partner, they crouched, looking like they were trying to crawl inside the same egg. When they finished the crowd roared and stood as one, pulled from their seats by the energy that Lea Ann and Bill had generated inside the arena. Flowers showered the ice. People screamed for encores. Lea Ann and Bill skated around the rink, wide, joyful smiles glowing across their faces, their bodies still heaving from the strain of their efforts.

The Carrutherses' performance was, to my untrained eye, flawless. Their lifts were held that extra second, their throws extended that extra inch. Nothing had been overlooked. Their routine had choreographed the smallest detail into perfection.

They did not equal Lea Ann and Bill's intensity, but they probably didn't have to. They were securely in the lead and were impossible to beat. The crowd reacted accordingly, its standing ovation not so much a spontaneous outpouring as a mandatory requirement for the national champions. This was a coronation, not a competition. The ovation served to annoint the fairest of our finest, a gesture of affection and support before they did battle on behalf of the United States at the world championships in Finland in March.

Jill and Bert were the final pair. Dressed in plum-colored outfits and hidden beneath too much makeup, they skated shakily at first but grew stronger as their four-minute program progressed. Jill, in fact, captured that illusion of flight more perfectly than her predecessors. She was a short blond with a firm, athletic body, and Bert was able to carry her the length of the ice. Although they had been together less than six months, the woman next to me, who had steered me so correctly to the pairs competition the night before, told me I was looking at future Olympians. "And remember," she said, "you heard it here first."

At the press conference afterward, the three medalists, still in costume, were ushered into the interview area, a corner of the press room cordoned off by curtains. The area was filled with perhaps twenty-five reporters. The skaters sat looking at the reporters; the reporters sat looking at the skaters. There was an awkward silence. Finally one reporter said, to no one in particular, "How do you feel?"

Peter Carruthers dominated the interview, not so much because he wanted to, it seemed to me, but because no one else would, and *somebody* had to say *something*. He went to great pains to compliment the other medalists, saying the right things about "working hard" and "great competition" and so on. He seemed immensely likable and down-to-earth. Possessed of a rare and exceptional talent, he held the world by the tail but knew that he did. Peter and Kitty's story was too implausible for even a Sylvester

Stallone screenplay. They were both adopted. What were the chances of two kids with such complementary talents winding up together and then going on to win the National Figure Skating Championships?

But it was Lea Ann Miller and Bill Fauver who intrigued me the most. Of all the performances, theirs alone had the electricity that is only rarely produced, and I knew I'd been fortunate to have witnessed it. Bill, at twenty-nine, had none of Peter's youthful bounce. He was much more thoughtful and introspective, unable, or perhaps unwilling, to take his talent for granted. Lea Ann was quiet and self-contained, not appearing uneasy, just not inclined to do much talking. In 1976, paired with a different partner, Bill had been to the Olympics. Two years later, after only six months together, Lea Ann had broken her back. In 1980 they'd missed Lake Placid and people told them to pack it in. But now here they were again.

I left the arena as soon as the press conference ended. The last bus to Oakland Avenue left at midnight. I ran down Washington Street and sprinted up the hill to Forbes, and got to the stop as the bus was pulling away. I ran it down, and had the bus to myself. I used the ride to think of questions to ask Lea Ann and Bill.

"We call girl skaters 'Bears,' " Lea Ann said. "That's the nickname we've given ourselves." She laughed. "Bears." Lea Ann sat in a chair in her room at the William Penn, an old, established hotel in the center of Pittsburgh's Golden Triangle, just down the hill from the Civic Arena. It was Saturday afternoon, two days after the pairs final and the day after the women's final. Lea Ann's parents sat on one of the beds. Bill wasn't here yet. He was tracking down their Team USA jackets to be worn next month at the world championships.

I told Lea Ann that my overriding impression of the pairs program—besides the fact that it appealed to me much more than the singles—was the absolute control over her fears that the woman skater must possess. Then I stopped, catching myself. Had I overstepped the boundaries? "Is fear something you don't talk about?" Lea Ann shook her head.

"No, no, I will. In fact, I talk about it openly. We go to a sports psychologist. We bring everything up. Fear is one of the things, the big thing we talk about. Especially in pairs skating for the girl. You just can't say you're not afraid to fly through the air and hope you land on one foot. I mean . . . ." She stopped and pulled a leg up underneath her. Her hair, blond and frosted, was pulled off her face in a tight knot at the back of her head. Her face was round and so were her eyes and cheeks. "I mean," she began again, searching for the correct words, "you're afraid of it. It *is* scary."

I mentioned that she and Bill had managed to make everything look extremely easy. Lea Ann and her parents laughed. "I guess," I said, "the point is to make everything look easy, right?"

"Right," Lea Ann said. And then, as if to put me more at ease, she said, "But you know, I've got to say that everything in the long program, except for a few things, really *is* easy. When you get to a certain level, it's in your head what you believe to be easy or hard. There wasn't anything in our program that really upset me. It really was easy. But that's because we've made it that way. We trained for it.

"We've been together four years now. This is our second year with this program. It takes you that long to get used to each other. There's not only the tricks of pair skating, there's the timing sense you have to have together. I mean, we've taken hours to figure out where our eyes should be looking. After a while it gets that nitty-gritty." There was a knock on the door and Bill walked in, carrying two red, white and blue jackets with USA across the back.

"Hi," he said, throwing the jackets on the bed. "Took me longer than I thought it would. He stopped in the middle of the room, collecting himself and restoring his calm. "How are you?" he said to me. Then he walked over to a chair across the room from Lea Ann and sat down.

I told Bill that Lea Ann had been discussing her fears of flying. "I would guess," I said, turning to him, "that you would have a fear of . . . of flopping?" Bill leaned back and extended his legs in front of him.

"It's indescribable," he said, "when you're skating across the ice at full speed and your blade suddenly sticks. There's a lot of twisting and a lot of torque, and you're deathly afraid of putting the lift down but you know if you don't do something you're both going to get hurt. We've been lucky. I think I've only dropped Lea Ann, out and out dropped her, twice. Luckily neither of us got seriously hurt."

"Who controls how long a lift lasts?"

"Everything is preset," Bill said. "We don't add anything, we don't take anything away." Bill was wearing a black turtleneck sweater and black pants, the same outfit he had worn Thursday night. He had dark hair and well-defined features. He was also rather thin and undeveloped across the chest. Had I not seen him do it, I would never have imagined that he could carry Lea Ann above his head with one hand while skating across sixty feet of ice.

I told them I thought they brought a mature quality to their skating that the other pairs had lacked. They both agreed. "I think it's an asset," Bill said, "but the American perception of sports is to do it young and get out. And I think that's where America has missed out on a multitude of talent and a multitude of would-be champions. I'm not saying we're going to be champions—we'd like to be—but if you look at the Olympics, the truly great champions are the mature athletes." It was, Bill insisted, the United States' demand for youth and titles that had burned out so many young and promising skaters.

"They aren't given a chance to mature," he said, a measure of frustration in his voice. "If I were to write down on a piece of paper all the wonderful skaters that could have been champions but were passed by by the system, it would take me all day."

"Is skating as cutthroat as TV makes it look?"

"Well," Bill said, hedging, "in some ways it is cutthroat. I'll be honest with you. There's been some packaging going on here that far exceeds the acceptable level."

"By whom? The press? The networks?"

"By the organizing committee," Bill said succinctly. "They've gone out of their way to single people out and support certain people. That kind of packaging isn't fair at all."

Lea Ann was more to the point. "We're talkin' politics," she said.

"You're not necessarily talking about the pairs, are you?" Mr. Miller asked.

"Oh, no, no," Bill said. "Actually I'm not talking about the pairs at all. It's just that this sport is such a neat thing to do, and if you can cut through all the rest of the strings and the bull and get down to it, it's really a wonderful thing to do. It's when everything starts getting messed up, when judges like certain people for certain reasons, that they lose sight of skating."

"You know, it's interesting," Lea Ann said. "When figure skating first came about, why did we automatically think in terms of competition?" Good question. "And that's what TV does to it all the time. You watch," she said, referring to ABC's *Wide World of Sports* and their scheduled broadcast later today of the pairs and women's competitions. "Just watch what they do to the ladies' competition. They're going to turn figure skating, this beautiful thing, into fisticuffs, a cutthroat sport. They'll probably put it on with boxing."

I asked how long they had been seeing a sports psychologist.

"We've been seeing him for what, over two years now," Lea Ann said. "It's becoming more and more the accepted thing, but Bill and I have been one of the few pairs that consistently delve into it."

"You've got to understand," Bill continued, "that Lea Ann and I are in quite a different boat than the others. We're dealing with several problems. Number one, I'm old, which isn't a problem for me, but it is for how we're perceived. They love to go with youth. We also left one program that we were very close to and moved across the country. Lea Ann broke her back. I hurt my knee. We've been down a hard road. It was very hard for us to go from fifth one year down to eighth. Everyone told us to get out. It's been hard to keep coming back. I guess it was all just something that we needed some help with. We needed someone to help us understand our relationship and how best to use our mental powers.

"You see, I had several partners. I had a reputation for going through partners, of being hard to get along with. I was in the '76 Olympics with one partner and she was already my third partner. She quit, and I took another partner for six months; that didn't work out, and then I had another partner before Lea Ann. So people, you know . . ."

"Had you pegged?" I offered.

"Yeah. Your attitude depends a great deal on your position on the ladder. Your perception of where you are. I was all the way down looking up. People were telling me to get off, to get away. Looking back, I really don't know why I kept going. I think Lea Ann . . . ," he stopped for a moment and then continued. "I just felt it was something I had to do.

"Lea Ann changed me. There's no comparison between what my skating was in 1976 and what it is today. It's a totally different thing. Lea Ann and I have, I think, in a very real way grown up together.

"I'm proud of the fact that we've matured together," he went on, "and that I've mellowed out and learned how to get along with people. And I think that Lea Ann and I are getting as much out of each other as we can."

Later, I watched ABC Sports present its version of the women's competition. It had been, in real life, a cutthroat affair, and ABC didn't have to stretch its point to create the proper air of competitive catharsis. It had also been a too-perfect example of Bill Fauver's lament that the system doesn't allow skaters to mature.

The gold medal contest involved two women: Rosalynn Sumners and Elaine Zayak. Rosalynn was the defending national champion, Elaine the defending world champion. An intriguing set of circumstances compounded by the fact that there was an unmistakable air of contempt swirling around the Civic Arena at the mere mention of Elaine Zayak's name.

I first saw Elaine skate on Thursday night during the Ladies' short program. As the defending world champion and a past national champion, she was more familiar to me than Rosalynn, who, to me at least, was the mystery woman of the competition.

Even so, I was completely unprepared for the Elaine Zayak that skated onto the ice. I had expected a bouncy, effervescent pixie. What I got was a hardened, unsmiling teenager with bleached-blond hair. The chubby athleticism of simpler, spunkier days hadn't yet translated into young womanhood. In 1981, young and cute and full of boundless energy, Elaine had blown the doors off the skating establishment. Her free-skating program had included seven triples, had dethroned Lisa-Marie Allen, and had positioned her as the very future of figure skating. Now, two years later, despite her world championship status, the crowd wanted nothing to do with her. In less than two years she had burned out her audience while simultaneously being burned out by them. At fifteen she had been wildly talented, the embodiment of raw athleticism brought to life on ice. But every triple she had drilled at her audience was one less triple she had left to give. She had wrung them out, and now they were throwing her away. Live by the triple, die by the triple. How quickly we eat our young.

Rosalynn, on the other hand, glided gently onto the ice and into a wide open, unconditional embrace. A graceful young woman with just the right dash of youthful ebullience, a flawless complexion, and—this was too good to be true—natural blond hair, Rosalynn was exquisitely feminine, totally elegant, and classically traditional. The arena skated every step of her program with her, no one more passionately than the woman sitting next to me. When Rosalynn jumped, she jumped; when Rosalynn pranced across the ice, a delicate flower come to bloom, she danced with her. And when Rosalynn fell, she fell too, then picked herself up and continued bravely on. She was out of her seat before Rosalynn's music had stopped, rising as if pulled up by the neck.

"She's still champion! She's still champion! She's still champion!" She screamed it over and over. The rest of the arena stood with her, adamantly reaffirming their choice of the nation's number one woman skater, restating, in case it needed restating, the direction they demanded women's skating take.

Rosalynn skated around the rink embosomed by the audience, filling her arms with the bouquets that showered the ice. She skated off to thunderous applause, deposited her flowers, then returned to the rink to collect even more, leaving Dick Button to twirl his microphone. That was the most telling moment of all. "Look, look!" the woman next to me pointed out with delight, "She's even keeping Dick Button waiting!"

At the press conference after the awards ceremony Rosalynn and Elaine sat side by side and together defended themselves as best they could against a press anxious to turn them into blood rivals. To portray the two skaters as mortal enemies was just too good a story to pass up, and the press pressed its case. But neither Elaine nor Rosalynn accepted the bait. At one point, Elaine suggested that maybe what the press really wanted was for her and Rosalynn to put on guns, take ten paces, and shoot each other.

Off to the side sat Tiffany Chin, the third-place finisher. Tiffany was a member of the world team now, but a decided spectator at these proceedings. Her fifteen-year-old eyes were open wide, trying to absorb everything at once.

"What do you think of all this, Tiffany?" a reporter asked, more polite gesture that the little girl not be ignored than a real question. But what a perfect question. What *do* you think of all this, Tiffany? Because right now your future is before you. Be wide-eyed while you can because you are next in line.

"I don't know," Tiffany responded, her braces flashing in the TV lights. "This is all kind of new to me." Indeed. Tiffany was young and cute. The whole world was waiting at her feet. And her being Chinese introduced an exotic flavor. Right now, Tiffany was actually newer than new. How long that would last was another question altogether. For an answer all she had to do was ask Elaine.

CHAPTER 2

* * *

Wednesday, February 16, 1983

Dear MacDee–

I thought you could do with a letter. Letters are always welcome in February, particularly when you live 120 miles north of the Arctic Circle.

I spent the past two days at Madison Square Garden watching the Westminster Kennel Club Dog Show. This Friday it's Boston for the Continental Team Tiddlywinks Championships. Not sure either "event" can be classified as "sport," but this is my trip, right?

The dog show was ridiculous. An Afghan hound named Ch. Kabik the Challenger (the "Ch." stands for "Champion") won Best in Show. Eight hours before the finals I was told that an Afghan would win. The Word was everywhere. And during the finals, with only seven dogs still in the contest, thirteen thousand dog-crazy people went bonkers every time the judge—a solitary, tuxedoed figure on the arena floor—so much as glanced in Kabik's direction. Would you have picked the bulldog?

The Garden is a tiny place when filled with 2,621 dogs. A terrier piddled on my sneakers, a bloodhound slobbered on my corduroys. I was forever dodging doggie doo-doo. There were more dogs than I could identify: Pomeranians (isn't that a fruit?), Rhodesian ridgebacks (not an armadillo with fur, just a short-haired, copper-colored dog with a cowlick running down its spine), Italian greyhounds (frightened, emaciated rats), borzois, salukis, Ihasa apsos, vizslas (bred for championship tennis?), and papillons, which once starred in a movie with Steve McQueen.

Even the dogs I know I didn't recognize. Like the Alaskan malamutes and Siberian huskies. The malamute is the classic work dog; big and strong and built to last a lifetime of eighteen-hour days. But these 'mutes were just too big. Small lions, really, for whom a hard day's labor would be finding a spot by the woodstove. I just couldn't accept that these dogs mirrored the best of their breed. They were larger than life, designed to attract attention, not define the standard. Westminster has turned the judging criteria upside down. A representative animal will never win because no one will ever notice it.

With the Siberians it was worse. That steely determination to pull a racing sled was conspicuously absent. And they had names like Virginia, Cinnamon, Cashmere, and even Candi's Dandy. Siberians should be named Rex and King and, of course, Buck. If life were a Disney cartoon, the Siberians at the Garden would be the eastern pansies who checked the temperature with their pawsie-wawsies before venturing outside.

Now the dog people, they didn't disappoint. For the record, not all dog people look like their dogs. But dog people *are* crazy. An observation proffered by the dog people themselves. Any number of people joyfully admitted that they were dog nuts working on getting nuttier. (We're doing major reconstruction; we're adding a dog room!") A self-fulfilling prophecy.

The Westminster was actually two shows. One show took place out on the arena floor. It was governed by civility and subdued good taste. The second show took place in the "benching area," the off-stage section beneath the stands where the dogs and the handlers waited their moment of glory, and where everything was happening, and all at once.

People scurried about carrying hot dogs (frankfurters),

Cokes, potato chips, and Alpo samplers. Salespeople and vendors lined both walls. I could have bought a computerized pet profile to help me understand my dog's behavior. Or an insurance plan "run by dog fanciers for the fancy," whatever that means. One display boasted a fourteen-piece canine toiletry kit. What was so wonderful, the salesman told me, was that the scent was consistent, and that I could use them too.

Most of the benching area was filled with rows of stalls. But at the far end was the styling area, a frenzied place hidden beneath a cloud of baby powder and sweet perfumes. I watched a woman wash her Afghan's feet and then polish its nails. Professional hairstylists worked on dogs in quick succession. Poodles were transformed into balls of cotton perched on top of four smaller balls of cotton. Parts were combed down the backs of Pekingeses that were so straight Vidal Sasson would have wept at the sight. Shih Tzus (tiny animals with flowing white hair that covers their faces) had their hair tied up on their foreheads with cute little ribbons, and looked like Peggy Lee with a mustache.

This was, of course, just the prepping and the preening for that moment in the ring. The dogs assembled within their breeds (there were 138 breeds). From each breed was selected a Best of Breed. These winners then got together in their groups (seven groups: sporting, nonsporting, herding, toy, hounds, terriers, and working). Each group selected its Best of Group. These seven winners then proceeded to Best in Show, where Kabik the Afghan was finally awarded the title.

At the end of each "best of" competition there remained one more ritual: taking pictures of the winners. If there's one thing dog people love more than showing their dogs, it's got to be getting their picture taken with their dogs. The owner would stand behind his or her dog, one hand under the mutt's chin to hold up the head, the other hand holding up the tail. The photographer would throw a bone in the air, the dog perking his ears at the sudden distraction, and then snap a quick picture of a person holding a dog by the tail.

This weekend, like I said, is the Continental Team Tiddlywinks Championships at MIT (makes you wonder what tomorrow's technocracy is learning today, doesn't it?). Keep your fingers crossed that I get good weather. Two weeks ago I raced a snowstorm from Pittsburgh to New York (I won), but last weekend here in the city we got twenty-two inches in twenty-four hours. Waiting out a blizzard camped someplace in the back of the van might make a good story, but I don't want to have to write it.

I've finally come to realize the enormity of what I'm trying to do this year. Reality struck in Chicago. After the Women's Powerlifting Championships I stopped in the bar at the Rosemont Holiday Inn (I seem to remember the front end of an Edsel protruding from a wall). The Super Bowl was on TV. I'd been so wrapped up in the drugs of powerlifting that I'd forgotten about it. As I walked in John Riggins was running off tackle, turning a four-yard gain into the winning touchdown.

In one year I'd be at the Super Bowl. The realization hit me as hard as if Riggins had run over me instead of the Miami Dolphins. And between now and then I'd be just about every place else, too, watching in person all those events I'd only seen on television. The trip was ten days old by then, but the magnitude of my undertaking had just registered.

That thought stayed with me through my stay in Pittsburgh. Will I have enough money? Enough energy? Will the van make it? In theory my plan had sounded like a grand idea. In practice it was hard work. Three hundred sixty-five days of sports was too cumbrous a task to comprehend. It was time to seriously consider bagging the whole idea.

Well, I have zero confidence in the van, and we do not have enough money. I *think* I have the energy, but at least I've solved the problem of a year on the road: I'm not going to think about it. While racing that snowstorm from Pittsburgh to New York two weeks ago, all I wanted was to get back to the city. With the prospects of a blizzard stranding me on the highway, I stopped thinking beyond the immediate goal. And I suddenly realized that was the key to my survival. My year's been planned as a series of swings that start and end in New York City. I don't have to think about the next twelve months. If I get myself back to New York City one swing at a time, the year will take care of itself . . . .

Steve

* * *

Room 407 in the MIT Student Center was old and tired and overworked, an empty space surrounded by walls that should have been painted years ago. A couple of folding chairs and one table sat in the middle of the room. This was the setting for the World Singles Tiddlywinks Championships.

Six people were gathered around the table. On the table was a gray felt mat a quarter-inch thick. On the center of the felt was a yellow cup the size of an egg holder. Scattered around the cup were green, yellow, red, and blue tiddlywinks. Some were clustered in piles; others were arrayed randomly around the table. The room itself seemed to be breathing, because everyone was breathing in unison and it was the only sound. The sixth game of the championships had just begun.

The competitors were two men. Both my age, they contrasted sharply. One had dirty blond hair, prominent eyebrows, and a set jaw. He looked at the table as though he were trying to stare through it. The other was rounder and softer and wore thick glasses. The spectators included a clean-cut preppy type, a hippie of late sixties vintage, a guy in worn jeans and bulky sweater, and a pregnant woman with blond, frosted hair.

It was impossible to decipher what was going on. The first guy would lean over the table and everyone else would lean forward expectantly. The breathing stopped. He would use a small disk the size of a quarter to move a wink about a quarter of an inch, the room would breath again, and everyone would straighten up. Murmured comments—"good shot," "perfect," "great position"—would be exchanged while the preppy one wrote on a piece of paper. Then the other guy, the one with the eyebrows, would peer at the winks. He'd turn around and walk away, clenching and unclenching his fists, the muscles along his jaw flexing. He'd come back to the table, stare again, walk away again, clench and flex again, and then finally walk up to the table and move a wink a quarter of an inch. Twenty minutes into the game the first guy flipped a wink in a small arc toward the cup. It bounced off the rim and landed on the felt. He hung his head, disgusted. Many mumbles of disbelief. Eyebrows then shot a wink from a foot away from the cup, and missed too. That brought the first guy back to the table, and he proceeded to flip the wink that he'd missed before into the cup. He straightened up and reached across the table to Eyebrows. "Well," he said, "it's about time."

"Eyebrows" was Dave Lockwood; "The First Guy," Larry Kahn. I learned their names an hour later when the six people who'd witnessed the world championships convened at Ken's Bar on Mass. Ave. for a postmatch wrapup.

Rick Tucker was the clean-cut one, Arye Gittleman the guy in the worn jeans. The pregnant woman was Dej, Dave's wife. They had met in Saudi Arabia where Dave worked for Pan Am and Dej worked for Saudi Airlines. Only "Sunshine" was missing. He was the hippie.

Dave, Larry, Rick, and Sunshine graduated from MIT in the late sixties and early seventies. Arye, from Ithaca, was twenty-two. He had attended MIT for a year, but now worked as a computer programmer in Boston. Larry lived in D.C., and so did Rick. Sunshine, they said, was sort of living here and there in classic freak style, although he'd once worked for five years as a programmer.

I felt very comfortable, sitting with them at Ken's drinking beer and eating potato skins. Warm and friendly, they were anxious to talk about Winks, and they did so in precise, animated terms. At the same time, I sensed a certain distance between them and me, a distance not fully explained by the fact that I'd walked into room 407 and dropped myself upon them. Their hesitancy, they said, was grounded in prior experience with the press.

"We entertain the media," Rick said, "but we don't seek them out." Dave, as world champion for the past 4½ years, had been a particularly easy target. On *Real People* he'd been portrayed as an outlaw gunslinger come to town to challenge the new kid. The audience, of course, didn't know the showdown would be Tiddlywinks, which only heightened the ridiculousness of the whole situation when they found out. No one came right out and said the show had made a fool of Dave, but they all agreed that it had made a mockery of their game. The bottom line, I was told, was that no one had bothered to look beyond the game itself—admittedly silly—to determine why people played the game. I decided now was not the time to tell them that yesterday I'd written a short article for *USA Today* about tomorrow's team championships. The article had begun, "Take heart. There is life after grade school."

Embarrassed that I'd fallen into so obvious a trap, I changed the subject by asking them to explain what I'd witnessed at the world singles. The crux of the matter, they said, was that Dave had entered the seventh game needing five points to send the match into another game. Both he and Larry had come out looking blitz. Dave tried an outrageous fourteen-inch squop, but missed. Larry then unbelievably, *incredibly,* missed a four-inch pot. Dave tried another squop, this one from thirteen inches, but missed again. Larry then calmly used his squidger to sink a six-inch pot to win the game and the match.

They were right, it really had been something, although it was more how they said what they said, and not what they actually said, that convinced me. I still had no idea what had happened. But I had two days to get the story straight.

Tiddlywinks was invented in 1888. That from Fred Shapiro, a librarian for the New York City Law School and an amateur lexicographer. A few years ago Fred and Rick Tucker had undertaken a historical research of Tiddlywinks and investigated the etymology of the word. Friday night, I had asked the group where I should go to learn about their game. Everyone, Rick included, had told me to talk to Fred.

I liked him immediately. A small, unassuming man with glasses and a bookish look, it was easy to imagine him in a library, totally at ease surrounded by all that accumulated knowledge. Owner of a wry, dusty sense of humor, he relished the incongruities of mixing and matching the seriousness of an academic pursuit to the workings of what was a very silly game.

We talked Saturday morning in the mezzanine room of the MIT Student Center, Fred walking me through the game's development. "I live for this question," he said, a self-effacing grin playing with the corners of his mouth. At the other tables the Continental Team Championship was being played by the twenty-five winkers who'd made it to the tournament. Beyond the winkers was a wall of glass that overlooked the MIT mall and a cold, bleak day.

Tiddlywinks, according to Fred, was invented by one Joseph Assheton Fincher in England.

"Where did the word come from?" I asked.

Fred smiled. "To me that is the much more interesting question, one that probably never will be answered. Well, that's not true. I can understand where he came up with it. The question is, where did the word ultimately start?" Fred related this story:

In England in the 1830s unlicensed pubs were allowed to sell beer. These pubs were originally called "kiddlywinks," although the K changed to a T rather quickly. "Tiddly," according to Fred, is a dialectic word for "small," or "baby word." Tiddlywinks, then, may have been the smallest kiddlywinks, although by all accounts all the kiddlywinks were tiny.

"Many people feel that this new game was played in these pubs. In the kiddlywinks they played Tiddlywinks. I believed that for a long time, but ultimately I don't believe it makes any sense." Behind us a group of winkers congratulated a colleague on an exceptionally fine shot.

"First of all," Fred continued, "you need a soft surface with spring to it. People say they flipped them into mugs; the winks would get all sticky. It just doesn't seem very realistic, and in fact we have no evidence that the game was played in the pubs. But we do have a lot of evidence that it was invented out of nowhere by this guy Fincher. Tiddlywinks was the name of these unlicensed pubs, and the word itself became a symbol of idleness, frivolousness. 'Tiddlywinks' was a generally silly word." Fred smiled. "So the idea right from the start was that this was a stupid game."

Tiddlywinks spread quickly, its advance assisted by the long arm of the British Empire. Fred said he and Rick had discovered reports of the game in Guyana in South America in 1889, and in the United States by 1890. But the game Fincher invented involved the flipping of winks into a cup by pressing on the edge of the wink with a second wink. This, as the winkers had been quick to observe, is the "children's game." Their game, "Tournament Tiddlywinks," incorporates a second maneuver, the mysterious squop shot to which I'd been semiintroduced last night. The squop is the flipping of the wink onto an opponent's wink, rendering that winked "squopped" and unable to be shot until it is freed.

The birthplace of modern Winks, the tournament game, is Cambridge University. Two students decided their résumés needed to include the fact that they had represented Cambridge in varsity competition against Oxford. They considered three sports—surfing, tree-felling, and camel racing—then turned to Tiddlywinks.

"They got together with a few friends and formed the Cambridge Tiddlywinks Club," Fred said. "They examined the rules of the existing children's game. The fundamental change they made was that you could get your wink onto another wink on purpose. This transformed the game. It is amazingly well set up. Everything works perfectly. It allows for a lot of room for strategy and physical skill."

The game was still a few years away from acceptability, however. For three years the Cambridge Tiddlywinks Club labored in anonymity. Then, in the fall of 1957 a headline of a story in the *Spectator*, a London newspaper, read: "Does Prince Philip cheat at Tiddlywinks?" The article satirized the current opinion that the royal family was wasting the taxpayers' money. The Cambridge Tiddlywinks Club took umbrage and wrote a letter.

"This is what made Tiddlywinks," Fred said. "They wrote to Prince Philip saying that his honor had been impugned. They suggested he play a Tiddlywinks match against the Cambridge team to prove that he didn't, indeed, cheat. Amazingly, they got a response from Philip's secretary saying the prince was very busy, but suggesting that the Cambridge team play the Goons, a popular English comedy team of the time, which included Peter Sellers, who would appear as the prince's royal champions. And that's what happened. It got a tremendous amount of publicity in England."

There were four teams in the continentals: Alliance, Chickens Courageous, Toads, and the MIT team. Each team consisted of two sets of winkers, and each pair on each team played all the other pairs (except their own teammates) in round robin fashion. Alliance, with Dave Lockwood, Larry Cahn, and Rick Tucker (plus Joe Sachs, the 1979 North American singles champion, and Fred Shapiro as a fifth-man winker), was the overwhelming favorite. Chickens Courageous was led by Sunshine and was the best bet to pull an upset, although before the tournament started the Chickens had announced that they would forfeit any play-off after the round robin. That left the upset factor to the MIT team, provided Arye Gittleman and Brad Schaefer played to their potential to offset their weaker teammates. Toads as a competitive force was out of the equation, despite the presence of Bob Henninge, one of the best winkers of all time (and one of the most respected figures in the game). The Toads were all members of a commune in southwest Ohio. Bob, a late sixties graduate of MIT and now a woodworker, had brought Tiddlywinks to the community, and the members played with a certain degree of enthusiasm, if not with any great degree of skill, Bob excluded, of course.

Winks is not a game easily fathomed. There was, first of all, that question of vocabulary, a problem I'd already encountered. (Blitz? Squidger? Squop? Pot-out?) But vocabulary was really the second half of my confusion. The first half was the game itself. The only obvious and recognizable action, flipping winks into the cup, isn't necessary to win the game, and it happens, at best, infrequently. Even when a winker said, "I'm going to blow it up," and I'd lean in expectantly, the ensuing action wasn't much more than a couple of winks moving a couple of centimeters.

Fortunately, Ross Callon, a superior winker of the early seventies, was in attendance as a nonplayer, and he offered to explain the game. What follows is, in abbreviated form, what he told me, plus some explanations lifted from the winkers' rule book.

WINKS: Each color has four small winks (three-eighths-inch diameter) and two large winks (one-half-inch diameter).

SQUIDGER: The plastic disk (one to two inches in diameter) used to flip the winks.

PLAYING AREA: A three-by-six-foot felt mat. A cup, or "pot," is placed in the center. Each corner is designated a wink color.

SQUOP: The covering of an opponent's wink with one of your winks.

SQUOPPED OUT: When all of one player's winks have been squopped. The squopping wink then receives free turns, the number corresponding to the number of their winks neither squopped, squopping, nor in the pot. After the free turns the squopped-out opponent has one wink "desquopped" and play continues.

BLOWUP: Flipping your wink onto pile of squopped winks, knocking pile apart. (Usually, however, when freeing squopped winks, the winker squops part of the pile—in which other of his or her winks are squopped—and uses next turn to free squopped winks by using the controlling, squopping wink.)

ROSS: When you are on top of a pile you have to touch your own wink first. On your follow-through you can hit any wink that is directly underneath. Sometimes, though, you can move your wink and get an opponent's wink underneath you and touch it on the follow-through. And of course the "touch" can be quite hard, and that is the real point of the shot.

Methods of follow-through:

BOONDOCK: Scatters enemy winks while keeping your winks in area.

DEBBIE BOONE: A double boondock.

PIDDLE: Freeing your wink while keeping your opponent squopped. *The* most delicate shot.

POT-OUT: When all the winks of one color have been flipped into the pot.

BLITZ: A winker attempts to pot out quickly.

COUNTER-BLITZ: Winker, sensing opponent about to blitz, attempts blitz first.

NURDLED: A wink whose edge is touching the base of the cup.

DENURDLED: Shot used to flip nurdled wink up and around the lip of the pot and *into* the cup.

BRISTOL: The movement of two winks, yours and an opponent's that you have squopped, over to a second opponent's wink, thus squopping two enemy winks.

ROSS: When the American team first went over to play the English, they amazed us by doing that shot. You need a specially designed squidger to do it.

SCORING: Seven points per game. Four for first, two for second, one for third. Partners or teams add points.

WINNING: If one color pots out, that color receives first-place points. All piles and squopped winks are separated. Play continues until a second color has potted out and then a third. If both partners pot out, they receive a bonus point while their opponents lose a point.

If the time limit (twenty-five minutes) expires before any color has potted out, time limit points are awarded. Play continues for five more rounds (one round consists of each color receiving one turn). After fifth round three points are awarded for each wink in the pot, one point for each unsquopped wink. Highest point total receives first-place points; next highest total, second place; third highest, third place.

Strategies:

DOUBLE-POT: Both partners blitz. All offense, no defense. Risky.

POT-SQUOP: One partner blitzes; other squops.

DOUBLE-SQUOP: Both partners squop. The tournament-level strategy of choice.

ROSS: Every free wink is worth one point. Every wink covered is zero. If you've covered your opponent's winks, it doesn't matter if you don't have any in the pot. Why take high gain–high loss [double-pot], when you can take high gain–no danger [double-squop]? What happens if you get five in the pot and then miss one? You're stuck.

Ross spread a felt across the top of a table and placed a pot between us. Using a borrowed squidger, he started flipping yellow winks into the cup. His long, thin fingers handled the squidger delicately, and he brought the winks to life one by one.

He removed the cup and handed me a squidger and six yellow winks. "We'll play a squop game," he said. "You use your six winks to try to squop my two winks." The odds were 3 to 1 in my favor, but in six moves my yellow winks were all beneath Ross's two red winks, neatly squopped and out of commission.

The squop was, as Fred had said, the shot that had revolutionized the game. Its introduction had transformed a mindless children's game into a strategic, complex activity that combined the best elements of chess with the fine motor skills of a microsurgeon.

Ross agreed with my observation, but not the comparison to chess. "Chess is all details and factors. Winks's strategy is extremely subtle. It's very hard to know what is going on." And in Tiddlywinks there are no guarantees the move itself will succeed. (Luck, in other words, although winkers referred to it as the "Heisenberg uncertainty principle," which states that an object's location and momentum can be predicted only to within a certain degree of accuracy.) In any event, for any given shot, there were an infinite number of outcomes.

"So," I said, attempting to wrap it all together, "in Winks you don't try to plan strategy, you just try to maintain a grasp of all the possibilities." Ross shook his head.

"All you can really try to do is get a feeling for all that is likely to happen."

Arye Gittleman sat down next to me. His MIT team was between games. I asked them if there was a certain type of person who was attracted to Tiddlywinks. Ross thought there was.

"To be attracted to a game like this you have to have two basic features. You have to be real, real smart in order to be able to handle what is going on, and you've got to be a little bit weird or you'll be too uptight to play something that on the surface looks so silly." Arye nodded agreement. "Anybody who has those qualities," Ross continued, "will probably be a pretty interesting person."

"Right now," Arye offered, "winkers tend to be computer people, so there are a lot of obvious similarities."

Tiddlywinks at MIT had blossomed in the late sixties, reached its peak in the early seventies, and had been in long decline ever since. It wasn't difficult to imagine college students in 1967 avidly pursuing a game that on the surface and to the establishment appeared so silly and so nontraditional precisely because it was silly and nontraditional. But times had changed.

"People are more serious now," Ross said. Neither lamenting nor indicting, just observing. "More people seem more worried about appearances. I personally was never inclined to worry about that. Obviously, you won't play this game if you are."

Tournament Tiddlywinks crossed the Atlantic in 1962 when winkers from Oxford toured colleges in the northeast United States and taught the game to interested parties. It wasn't until 1964, however, that Winks took root in North America. Severin Drix, a high school student from Ithaca, was visiting Boston. He heard that a Tiddlywinks match was being played at Harvard by a group of English medical students. A propitious encounter, as Winks was close to extinction in North America just three years after the Oxford tour.

Severin attended the match, was immediately intrigued, and wrote to England for a set of competition winks. He planned to attend Cornell in the fall and join the Big Red Winks team. When he arrived on campus and discovered there was no team, he formed his own. For competition he wrote to his high school friend Peter Wulkan (better known as "Ferd the Bull"), at MIT, and told him to form a Winks team so intercollegiate play could commence forthwith.

Ferd tacked up signs around campus. The notice caught the eye of Bob Henninge. In the spring of 1966 they traveled to Cornell. They were beaten seven games to one, but they were hooked. Sunshine got into Winks during his reading period for freshman exams that year, and together with Ferd, Bob, and Jeff Wieselthier, formed the original critical mass of Tiddlywinks at MIT.

At first, they didn't understand all the rules. They didn't play with a time limit, for instance; they played to a pot-out and their games lasted two hours and more. But they persevered. Their expertise sharpened, their confidence grew, and they refined their game.

Initially, everyone played pot-squop. Everyone but Ferd; he was the first to play double-squop. In the beginning this seemed more a tactic to bring him to the brink of annihilation than an actual strategy. The realization dawned, however, that more often than not Ferd's dramatic rescue attempts were successful, and soon double-squop was the tournament strategy of choice.

Bob Henninge and Severin Drix added color order as a strategic device. A good move by yellow, for example, also had to be a good move for its red partner. Sunshine advanced this strategy by advocating the multioption tactic, giving the opponent more than one thing to think about. By 1972, the year of the first American trip to

England, the Colonists were able to defeat the Royalists through tactical superiority, even though as technicians the British were clearly their betters.

As strategies grew more sophisticated, they also grew more conservative. In the early seventies position became all-important. Gain dominance of an area and take only the shots you know you can make. Bill Renke was the king of this Bobby Knight style. Renke owned winking in 1973. Ross was also a devotee of this style. His special twist was to play a negative game. Control the tempo by reacting to whatever the opponent tried to do.

This approach evolved into the noncommittal attack, a strategy that provided the winker with the greatest number of options on any given shot. Missing a shot no longer spelled automatic disaster. Ninety percent of the objective might still be gained, with the new position revealing another set of alternatives. Dave Lockwood is now the best at this. His game goes wherever it has to go, but he remains in control. And because he can grasp all the options all the time, he is also the best at suddenly, inexplicably, shifting tempo and direction. If a newer strategy is developing, it's a defense mechanism to this style of play. The subtleties have been sharpened to a finer edge. The only obvious shot is the only shot that isn't obvious.

Sunday morning the winkers reconvened. The continentals had been completed yesterday, but there were still a few hours left before people caught flights or hit the road. This, then, was quality time together. A reaffirmation of friendship and Tiddlywinks before returning to the larger world where winks and winkers ceased to exist.

Alliance had won the continentals, beating Chickens Courageous in the round robin 60.5 to 45. (Chickens declined a play-off.) MIT finished third with 39.5 points and Toads a distant fourth with 23.

Today, however, was designated a fun day. I was invited to play. Brad Schaefer offered to be my partner against Dave Lockwood and his wife, Dej. Our strategies were identical: pot-squop. Dej and I tried to pot out (to get out of the way), while our partners held each other at bay. Everyone performed admirably but me. Brad and Dave squopped each other, which left Dej and me free to go for the pot. But I was a shore battery bombing an aircraft carrier. First one long, next one short. I didn't get another chance because Dej then proceeded to pot out with world-class perfection. Flip. Flip. Flip. Flip. Flip. Five pots. One more and she would come in first, and then all her husband—the former eight-time world champion—had to do was figure out a way to dispatch me, and they would collect match points. All was well with the world.

But not according to Dave's eyes. They were crowded with intensity, dark and piercing beneath his brow. His wife could win with a pot-out in her first official game. And if he escaped from Brad and potted out for second place, the final score, with the bonus points for a double pot-out, would be 7–0. A washout. Then all would be well with the world.

Dej lined up her shot, flipped the wink . . . and missed the pot. But in missing, the wink blew up a pile of Dave's winks that Brad had squopped. Not a bad execution of a multioption strategy, however unintentional. Dej clapped her hands, delighted. Dave's jaw tightened. He would have to redouble his efforts if he was still going to make the game a washout.

I remember little of the rest of the game, except wanting it to end quickly. Brad and I (well, just Brad) countered Dave for a while before the game finally, mercifully, ended at 6–1. Dave smoldered. Dej scolded him gently but to little avail. I thanked Brad for enduring my incompetence, and then walked away shaking the tension from my shoulders.

There were a number of winkers at the continentals I'd placed in the "serious winker" category: Larry Kahn, Arye Gittleman, and Joe Sachs. Rick, editor of *Newswink,* was a serious player, too, and so was Brad. But these winkers shared a common trait, some variation on Fred Shapiro's thesis that Winks was, inherently, a silly game that could be taken seriously only if you remembered what it was you had started with.

Not Dave. As far as he was concerned, there was nothing funny about it. Walking away from my 6–1 drubbing, my T-shirt stuck to my back with nervous perspiration, I had to fight an irrational urge to turn around and challenge him again—with dreams of wiping his ass all over the felt. My first game of Tiddlywinks, that wonderfully silly game, and I'd succeeded in having no fun at all.

Fortunately, Sunshine, the sixties-style hippie, realigned my perspective. He hitched a ride with me to New York City; we talked the whole way and the miles flew past. After the tension of the afternoon, it was good to know there was room within the game for both a Dave Lockwood and a Sunshine.

"How come Chickens Courageous didn't want a play-off?" I asked.

Sunshine shrugged. "My team is a team because we're friends. Being friends makes the winks more valuable as a shared activity. And I'm in favor of less competition. Alliance is the best team; who cares who comes in second place?"

Had this been anyone but Sunshine I wouldn't have believed him. People play sports "for fun" only when they can no longer win. But Sunshine was, by general consensus, Tiddlywinks' consummate technician, fully capable of taking his game to any level he chose to play.

"Tiddlywinks is an art form as well as a game," he said, explaining his approach. "You can relate to Winks in a lot of different ways. It's a wonderful game that combines strategy, skill, and luck. There aren't many games that do that. After some shots you can almost feel the power; it's like electrical sparks are coming off the winks. Sometimes they have a personality of their own. The winks decide what happens. You can go on streaks where you know that's just the way it is. You cannot make the shots happen. You just have to ask the winks to do it, and then have wonderful things happen."

CHAPTER 3

* * *

Wednesday, February 23

Route 80, New Jersey, west to Wisconsin and the fifty-five-kilometer Birkebeiner Cross Country Ski Race in Telemark. The race was just three days away; there was little room for error: Warren, Ohio, tonight; Chicago on Thursday; and Telemark, Wisconsin, by Friday for the race on Saturday. I was worried about snow. Wisconsin and February is a risky combination.

Still, I had reason for optimism. The year had begun lightly, allowing me to get my feet wet before jumping into the heavyweight events. (It was one thing to say you're traveling the country, quite another to do it.) I'd been to six events—Knicks beat the Mavericks last night at the Garden—in four weeks. Now I was ready, I hoped, for the pace to quicken. From Wisconsin and the ski race to Pensacola, Florida, and the National Amateur Field Dog Trials. Then to Fairbanks for the North America Sled Dog Championships. Two weeks later, Easter weekend, was the NCAA Basketball Championships in Albuquerque, New Mexico. From there to Augusta, Georgia, for the Masters, which began on April 6. Six weeks on the road, but when I returned to New York City, 25 percent of the year would be tucked neatly into the glove compartment. I crossed the bridge between Jersey and Pennsylvania, the Delaware Water Gap spreading out beneath me. The trip was beginning, or beginning all over again.

The toll booth attendant took my money. I stepped on the accelerator, and the drive shaft fell out of the van. It was like everything from my earlobes back had slid out the back door.

I left the van by the side of the road, walked into Waring, Pennsylvania, and found the C.H.C. Garage, a body and paint shop. Posters of large-chested women cradling car refinishing equipment adorned one wall. The other wall was littered with newspaper photos of terrifying automobile accidents, the life's blood of the paint and body business.

I rode back to the van with a man with one arm. He tied the drive shaft to the belly of the van and hoisted its front wheels off the ground. Back at the garage an old man with gray hair crawled under the van.

"Your drive shaft fell out," he said. But yesterday I'd had the universal replaced and the drive shaft rebalanced. "Where'd you get it fixed?" he said, and then, before I could answer, "the City?"

"Yeah," I said. George, his name was George, harrumphed in disgust and spat on the ground.

"Figures." He crawled from beneath the van and disappeared behind the garage. He returned in a few minutes with a drive shaft. "If this fits, you're back in business." He slid under the van.

"Well there's your problem right there," he said. The old shaft rolled out and bumped my feet. Clearly printed in yellow paint was " '79 Chrysler New Yorker."

"This is not a Chrysler New Yorker." I know, George, I know. "Got this thing fixed in the City?" he asked again, and then he chuckled.

I was back on Route 80 an hour later. Total cost: $63.60. Spirits rose. A white-tailed deer darted by the side of the road. The trip was happening. All over again.

Or was it? I yanked myself back to earth. Fate could intervene at any moment. I clicked on my recorder and sang: "I think I better knocknocknocknocknock on wooooood."

The Telemark Lodge was outside Cable, Wisconsin, population 217. But there were 7,000-plus skiers jammed inside the lodge, a log-cabin labyrinth of mind-boggling proportions and 469 rooms.

Huge stone fireplaces made the place seem even bigger. Connected to the lodge by a long, sloping tunnel lined with souvenir and ski shops was the Coliseum, an all-purpose banquet room and indoor tennis facility. Through its doors oozed the wet, heavy smell of pasta. Seven thousand skiers need *a lot* of carbohydrates.

Directly in front of the Coliseum stood Mount Telemark itself. It would have been called a hill had this been any place but Wisconsin or maybe Kansas. Ski lifts lined the mountain and cross-country ski trails disappeared into the trees at several points. The lodge also had a heated swimming pool, two restaurants and bars, and plenty of parking. I was outdoors, in the middle of nowhere, and surrounded by everything I could ever hope to need. The Modern American Wilderness Experience. A Disneyland with snow.

The Birkebeiner is, technically, the American Birkebeiner. There is a race in Norway by the same name that started in 1932. In 1973, when Tony Wise started a cross-country marathon ski race in the United States, he looked to Scandinavia to provide the tradition the United States lacked.

The Norwegian race commemorates the rescue of Haakson Haakonsson, child prince, by a group of Viking soldiers who were forced to ski a long way with Haakson, Jr., in order to escape whoever it was they were fleeing. These soldiers were nicknamed "birkebeiners" because they wore birch-bark leggings. Of such do legends grow. It also explained the bronze statue in the middle of the lodge of a Viking with a pair of planks strapped to his birch-bark-covered feet. Behind a pointed shield he carried a baby wrapped inside his tunic, and he clutched a hatchet in his right hand. His beard—ribbons of frozen metal—trailed behind him, blowing in the wind.

The premier U.S. Birkie in 1973 had fifty-four participants and was won by Eric Ersson. The course, fifty-five kilometers long, starts in Hayward about twenty miles south of Cable, and follows a ridge of hills for thirty-two miles to the Telemark Lodge. The Birkie is part of the Worldloppet, a series of ski marathons held in ten countries. It is also one of the eight American races comprising the Great American Ski Chase sponsored by Maxwell House Coffee. In short, the Birkebeiner is a nationally and internationally acclaimed event, and next to no one in the United States knows anything about it.

The race statistics quoted by the PR people were impressive, although as I read the list the numbers lost their impact:

7,419 skiers as of February 23
1,000 people working the race
15 nations represented
40 states
10 skiers 70 or older
2 blind skiers

As for food provided:

Over half ton (dry weight) Maxwell House Coffee
Over half ton (dry weight) Creamette pasta
30,800 oranges
19,500 bananas
5,000 gallons of Gatoraide and Gatorlode 280
12,000 Shaklee Fruit Bars
10,800 Holsum Donuts
1,000 gallons Ekstern's Blueberry Nectar

One stat did astound: Ski tip to ski tip, skiers would stretch nearly ten miles single file.

Saturday morning I hopped a bus from the lodge to the starting line in Hayward, the only passenger not dressed to ski. Conversation was constant ("Turn down the heat!"), a nervous chatter that refused to die ("What kind of wax you usin'?"), because to stop talking was to start thinking ("I can't believe you talked me into this!"), and to start thinking was to get nervous ("I hear it's got a lot of ups and downs").

Inertia pulled us to the starting line. Past the tents where final waxes were being applied. Past a row of eighteen porta-potties, each with a line fifteen deep. Across an open field we walked and skied, pulled to the starting line by the strains of a band playing European circus music.

There were twelve starting lines. Elite skiers in front, the 25 percent club (skiers who'd finished in the top quarter of a past Birkie) behind them. Master skiers (competitors in the World Masters Championships held earlier in the week) were next. Filling out behind them like Moses's faithful in a frozen desert were hordes of people gathered behind placards that read "5 Hours," "6 hours," "7 hours," and "8 hours." Behind that was the holding area—it certainly was no starting line—for the rookies. Forty-three percent of the field. Go with God, my children.

The elite starting line was about one hundred yards wide, which left just enough space for the people who thought they could win to have a clear shot at the trail ahead. The course slid down a small hill and within three hundred yards funneled into a trail six tracks wide. It was obvious there was going to be a hellacious traffic jam once the first hundred skiers popped through. The elite skiers knew this, and jittered about nervously waiting for the gun, glancing behind them at the madding crowd, wondering if they would be swallowed by the inevitable onslaught and lose any shot at winning the race.

To see the start I positioned myself halfway up the first hill. The waves of energy created by the throng rolled over me, the excess exuberance of eight thousand skiers awaiting the command to march. But when the cannon boomed, very little actually happened. The crowd roared, its energy officially released. The elite skiers scrambled with absolute crazed abandonment down the gully, up the small hill, and onto the trail. They were past me in a flash, the power they generated astounding. Within fifteen seconds the tracks were filled ski tip to ski tip, the sound of waxed fiberglass on snow producing a mesmerizing rhythm. That lasted about ten seconds, and then the trail became a blob of skiing protoplasm as eight thousand skiers jammed themselves into the bottleneck.

I hitched a ride to the halfway point. By the time I arrived skiers were already flying past, the sound of skis on snow a steady hiss. The skiers looked like praying mantises, their skis and poles insectlike appendages, the race itself not so much a dash to the finish as an escape from the start, a furious exodus of bugs fleeing some unknown horror. To stop was to die. The effect was wildly exhilarating. I wanted to join the multitude, to flee with the rest of them as we tested ourselves against our unknown limits.

I missed the finish, the closest in Birkie history. Rudi Kapellar of Bad Schaalerbach, Austria, beat Sweden's Lars Frykberg by two-tenths of a second to win in 2:14:14.2. Ola Hassis, also of Sweden, was third just a half second behind. One hundred meters from the finish Frykberg held the edge. But he snapped a pole, and Kapellar caught him and won by a foot. I did arrive in time for the women's finish, although I didn't know it was happening and missed that, too. Jennifer Caldwell of Vermont beat Monique Wattereus of Whitehorse, Yukon Territory, by four minutes. Ruth Hamilton from Colorado beat Jay Jay Peot with a lunge at the wire for third place. I was jockeying for position in the crush of spectators—stocking caps having negated my six-foot eight-inch height advantage—and it wasn't until I heard the announcer say "Alaska's Jay Jay Peot" that I realized the women had even arrived.

There were, however, six thousand other skiers to watch finish, and I stayed to the bitterly cold end. As the afternoon wore on, the Birkie metamorphosed from a serious race into a serious athletic challenge, and from there it changed to a ski outing. A Mardi Gras on skies was its next transformation, before the race finally ground itself into a survival test that was at times painful to watch.

These various stages were easily identified by the costumes the skiers wore. The racers, of course, sported form-fitting racing suits. Thick, powerful legs rose into firm buttocks, the perfect foundation for well-developed shoulders. By the 4½-hour mark the first of the ski tourers waltzed across the line—skiers who looked like they could have gone another fifty kilometers had they wanted to. Woolen knickers held up by suspenders, high socks, and almost clumsy-looking boots identified them. And some of their skis were wooden and wider than the razor-thin fiberglass skis that had preceded them.

After the arrival of the ski tourers the race began a long, slow slide. Exactly when I couldn't say, but it was after the *Rocky* theme at the four-hour mark and before the *William Tell Overture* sometime after dark. Skiers coming home in five to seven hours were generally lucid. The race had been a giant if strangely perverse kind of party, and they were happy they'd invited themselves along. After eight hours things were different. For one thing, the giant Maxwell House Coffee balloon deflated at five o'clock. For another, it was mighty cold.

Levis coated to the knees with ice, flannel shirts wrapped around waists, stocking caps cocked at precarious angles, soaking wet mittens: this was the final uniform. Skiers crossed the line and compliantly allowed themselves to be directed through the finishing chute. The skiers' faces were devoid of emotion. They were standing in a place they'd probably never stood before, they didn't know how to act, and at that point were too tired to care. But these people were the Birkie's real victors, skiers for whom making the distance had been the only goal. A long day's journey into the night of their own limitations.

I spent the evening talking to Jane Parrish, a friend from Fairbanks. In addition to skiing today's Birkebeiner, Jane had participated in the World Masters Cross Country Ski Championships earlier in the week. She had won a silver medal in the thirty-five to forty age group in the 10K.

Jane sat on her bed, leaning against the headboard and nursing a glass of red wine. Brown curly hair framed her fine-featured face, and fatigue poked at the corners of her green eyes. And yet her eyes still danced and her face positively burst with health and vitality.

"I'm still having a hard time believing I skied fifty kilometers," she said, while at the same time quite willing to accept the fact that she had.

"What's the farthest you had ever skied before?" I asked.

"Forty-K, I guess. But I wasn't racing the Birkie very hard. I just wanted to finish. I had no idea on time. I paced myself. And I spent a lot of time at every feeding station. I was going to make sure I didn't hit the wall. I hit the wall once in the Midnight Sun Marathon in Anchorage and I had to walk it in four hours. I didn't want to blow the Birkie."

There was a knock on the door and Jay Jay Peot walked in, immediately replacing Jane's quiet happiness with an energy that filled the room. Jay Jay was tall and powerfully built, strong across the shoulders. She wore her hair in a pageboy, an easy no-care style for an athlete whose life was spent traveling the world in search of races. The only distraction was her mouth, which was filled with braces.

"I had jaw surgery this past summer," she said, straightforward and unself-conscious. "I had an underbite, so they cut my jawbone and moved it. I think that's had something to do with my performance all year."

Jay Jay was a member of the U.S. National Development Cross Country Ski team, which sounded impressive until she explained what it meant. She had missed making the World Cup team and hadn't qualified for the Marathon Ski team, placing her far down the totem pole.

"I'm on what they call 'Support-a-Skier.' I get private donations that go through the U.S. ski team and then are sent to me as I give them receipts. This past summer I made about $5,000 with it."

"What do you do?" Jane asked. "Just go up to people and ask them for a donation?"

"I put together a portfolio. It has pictures on the front, and inside are all kinds of results and stuff, a collection of what I'm doing. I took it around, said this is me, this is what I'm doing, this is what I'm trying to do, and can you support me. I even put on a promotional breakfast. It helps."

But being a quasi-team member had its advantages. Lousy snow conditions early in the season dropped her even farther behind everyone else, so with some money she had raised from Support-a-Skier she went to Norway.

"Norway is easily one of the most prestigious cross-country ski places I've ever been. They have tracks everywhere. And everyone skies on Sundays. It's great. In the United States everyone would rather sit and watch football. It's a cultural thing. Over here you have to go out of your way to become a skier."

"Doesn't that get a bit frustrating?"

Jay Jay frowned. "Well, yeah," she said. "This year all the races have been so different with the weather conditions. And I haven't been skiing well. But I'm up there." Her enthusiasm pulled her along. She said she'd won a half marathon a week ago, and before that had been leading two races before getting lost. "You know what they call me now?" she said, turning to Jane. "Jay Jay Wrong Way." She laughed at herself.

And, she added, today's fourth-place finish wouldn't look bad in her portfolio.

I mentioned the Olympics. The trials were in ten months. Jay Jay Wrong Way, not-quite-a-member-of-the-ski-team, and one second short of the bronze medal today, remained undaunted.

"You never know," she said. "The U.S. ski team isn't as well structured as, say, the Norwegian team. It's young. You don't know what to expect. So everyone has a chance. Everyone's right in there. You just never know."

"Do you think there'll ever come a point when you'll just have to give it up?" I asked.

Jay Jay laughed. "I should have done that this year. I'm flat broke right now. I don't have any money. But if you really want to ski, you will ski. You really just have to go out and hustle the money. You've got to be a wheeler dealer."

* * *

Overheard in Birmingham:

"Birmingham is dead on Saturday night."

"People up North think people down here are bein' bad to the Negro, all that hatin' and shit. And it was like that at one time. But you go out in this city today and you'll see as much sophistication in this city as you would anywhere."

"You know George Wallace is governor again? The word is he got elected by a coalition of young black people. All I got to say is they must got awfully short memories."

"Progress in the deep South? I think the South has, huh, I don't know if there is an attitude change or maybe the people are just better able to get along. Now unfortunately a lot of that had to be decreed by law. But that was a national law. The South was just picked as the place where it was first applied. We didn't have the riots like they did in California and other places. Maybe because of the influx of people from all around the country, this being the Sunbelt, maybe there's a mellowing or just better understanding between folks."

"The reason there's no NFL team in Birmingham is because people are afraid that if a team comes in here the players with the big money will move in, and some of them will be black, and you can't even begin to discriminate against them because they got the money."

"Birmingham wants the USFL; in all those other places, the USFL needs the cities."

"Birmingham is the only World Football League champion there ever was; the Americans beat the Florida Blazers 22–21 in 1974."

"If you want to get right down to it, people'd rather have white guys on the team. But they're not going to be players just because they're white. Alabama's been startin' five black basketball players for years. But you see, when they're out there with that football uniform on and they got that helmet on, you don't know what color they are. You just know if they be winnin' or losin'."

"I'm stayin' home. I'm not goin' out there and fight for a parking place when the game's on TV. Besides, I hear it's nothin' but a bunch of Negroes anyway."

"Birmingham, when Bear Bryant died, was like Memphis when Elvis died."

"You just can't begin to imagine what the Bear meant to Alabama. It was the things that had nuthin' to do with football that made for a really impressive individual."

"How important is God to the world? Bear Bryant was the best image factor the state of Alabama ever had. The winningest coach there ever was. When he died everybody thought they lost their grandfather. My goodness. Going to a bowl game twenty-four straight years. He was something. People from Alabama had something to be proud of. They were tired of hearing they were forty-ninth in education, forty-ninth in this, forty-ninth in that. Only Mississippi kept us from being fiftieth. But in one area, in football, by God, we were as good as anybody. We were number one."

"Birmingham is even deader on Sunday afternoon."

I had plenty of time to listen to Birmingham. To read its newspapers, sit in its library, walk its streets, talk to its people. Monday night after the ski race I was back in Chicago, watching Hawkeye and B. J. say goodbye. The day after catching the Sting against the Memphis Americans at Chicago Stadium in indoor soccer, I was on the road to Pensacola and the Amateur Quail Field Dog Trials. The van died Saturday night, drifting to the curb across from the Hilton when I stopped in Birmingham to get something to eat.

So I stayed till Tuesday to watch the first USFL Monday night game. The advertisement in the *Birmingham News* was hard to resist: "Be a part of history. Come see the Birmingham Stallions skin a Michigan Cat." Birmingham was making another stab at major league status. It was fun to be swept along.

I arrived at the stadium early, having exhausted the possibilities of downtown Birmingham. Legion Field was a giant skeleton of a stadium, all green girders and concrete. A utilitarian bowl that Bear Bryant had transformed into a shrine for 75,000 adoring fans to watch the pride of Alabama roll up and down the field.

I stood next to the field, the astroturf framed inside the silver-painted seats that rose around me. The stadium lights were on, but it was only five o'clock and an unnatural luminescence filled the stadium. Above, a clear blue sky was slowly turning navy. A few players were running the field, frisky colts shaking their legs and loosening up. Local TV crews had taken up stations around the field, readying themselves for the historic occasion. A black man wearing a green usher's bib leaned against the fence next to me. We talked about the obvious—will the USFL make it?—until he asked me where I lived.

"Fairbanks? Alaska?" The typical response. "Do you really have snow year round and igloos and . . ." He started laughing. "Listen to me. I'm thinking about Alaska the same way you're probably thinking about Birmingham."

"What do you mean?" I asked.

"You know, fire hoses and dogs and riots and all of that."

He was right. Twenty years ago, growing up in Pennsylvania, television had burned into me an indelible image of the South that I would never be able to discard: Black versus White, Bull Connor and Martin Luther King, "We Shall Overcome" and "Kill the Nigger." I told him that and said that after two days in Birmingham and given my Pennsylvania prejudices, I was finding it difficult to decide what had really changed. He nodded.

"I don't know," he said. But then he hesitated, as if he wanted to say things had changed, but he knew he couldn't come right out and say it.

"People don't kick dirt in your face anymore. They can't do that. There's laws against that. So it can't be on the surface anymore. But it's there. Now they sort of hold it in their hands and then rub it down your back as you walk by.

"Once integration became a fact of life, became the law of the land, they had to start paying what amounted to a decent wage. It used to be that you—well, not you, me—I'd be digging the same ditch as you and you'd be getting paid twice as much. But black people are making money now. Me and my wife are making enough to own our own house. Home ownership and money equals power. I don't think Birmingham knows exactly how to handle all that.

"I work as a fireman. If somebody white blows up, nobody thinks much about it. If I blow up, I got an attitude. Sometimes you want to scream and jump up and down and yell and push your fist down someone's throat. But you'll lose that way. You'll always lose. I do a lot of listening."

He was my age, which meant he'd grown up in the early sixties, when everything was happening. "What was that like?" I said.

"You just got to keep your character," he said, a phrase he used more than once. I wondered if, considering my suburban Pennsylvania background, I'd ever know exactly what he meant.

He had two little girls. He talked about them a lot, too, with obvious pride, and with a certain edge of hopefulness that was absent when he talked about himself.

"I didn't go to a dentist until I was twenty years old. How was I going to grow up wanting to be a dentist? That's why so many blacks are in professional sports. It's the only escape we can see. Now, one of my girls has been seeing a dentist since she was fourteen months old." And that paid a double dividend: Not only were her teeth just fine, but maybe she'd want to grow up to be a dentist.

The best thing to happen to the game—forget the dancing girls, the politicians, the skydivers who landed in the stadium to present Chet Simmons, the USFL commissioner, with the game ball—was that after Michigan kicked its second field goal it started raining like all getout. The ball sailed through the uprights and suddenly a vicious wind cut through the stadium. Then the rains began, pouring from a sky that had been clear just an hour before, the gods of the vernal equinox giving vent to their opinion of football in the spring.

But no one left. This was history. That the rain coincided with the Stallions' only scoring drive didn't hurt either. Starting on their own forty-nine, Birmingham reached the Michigan fourteen before stalling. Rollie Dotsch, the Stallion coach, sent in the field goal unit, but the fury of all 38,352 rain-drenched fans rained down upon him, so he called time-out. After talking to his coaches (and the team's public relations man, no doubt), Dotsch changed his mind and had Ken Talton run for the first down. The crowd loved it. Stallion quarterback Reggie Collier ran the ball three times, and finally scored from three yards out. The crowd, starting on its third beer, splashed in the aisles. Novo Bojovic hits his third field goal for Michigan, the half ended 9–7, and two quarters later, so did the game.

Watching a USFL game in person proved an interesting comparison to yesterday's ABC USFL Game of the Week. On television it had been difficult to decide what was good or bad, fast or slow, professional or only pretending to be. But the overall effect had been good enough. Television as equalizer. On TV, it didn't have to *be* the real thing, it only had to look like it was.

In person, things didn't look good at all. I had never seen a live professional football game before, and I wasn't convinced I was seeing one now. This was supposed to be the league for "all the football players who deserve a place to play" who were just "one lucky break" from the NFL. Those oft-quoted lines of the past two days suddenly seemed very suspect. However unfairly the NFL might have drawn the line, the "Established League"—as the USFL liked to call it—had created the criteria up to which a "good football player" had to measure. The question was how good is good? The answer had to be better than this.

But from the player's point of view, playing on *any* team in *any* league was better than not playing at all. Although as I walked through the locker rooms after the game, I realized that the players in this new league were incidental to the real action of the USFL. The USFL needed players to fill their rosters, but the league hadn't been created to give deserving boys a chance to play football. Owners and executives and assorted hangers-on patted one another on the back, telling themselves that this league was going to make it. The NFL had spent years building its own power pyramid, ensconcing itself inside layer upon layer of mythology. The effect was to render green with envy everyone who wanted to be on the pyramid. From what I could see inside the locker rooms, the USFL was just an attempt by bruised egos to create their own pyramid. If it wasn't as big or as powerful as the NFL, well at least it was all theirs. The risk was big, but the payoff could be tremendous.

I tried to talk to the players. This was my first big-league (more or less) locker room, and I didn't know how to act. But this was the first big-league locker room for most of the players, too, so it didn't really matter. They got naked while a bunch of older men crowded around and wrote down anything anyone said. But the players had been well coached, or they knew intuitively what to say so not to be fired by the pyramid builders. Their responses were uniformly bland. ("Me? I just want to play football!")

* * *

"Hey van! Get up van!" Awake immediately, early-morning brightness burning my eyes. Six A.M. "You in the van, get up." I pulled into the sleeping bag. If it's a cop he knows where to find me. If it isn't, well, whoever it is knows where to find me, too.

"Yell at 'im again." This not through the bullhorn.

"You in the van, we've got you surrounded." A zillion thoughts crowded my brain. I was parked across from the Hilton. Safe neighborhood, but why's a guy crashed in a van in a good neighborhood? And New York plates on the van. At the game, a police detective had given me some friendly advice: "In Alabama, if a trooper asks 'Where you from, boy?' it's downhill from there."

The bullhorn clicked on, but before anyone spoke I heard laughter. Friendly laughter, I decided. I pulled my head from the sleeping bag, suddenly brave. Car doors opened and slammed shut. I tensed. The voices trailed away. I peeked out the window. A couple of construction workers were walking down the hill. I fell back onto the bed, waited for my heartbeat to return to normal, and slept till ten.

I ate breakfast at a Steak & Eggs in Five Points above the Hilton, spending time with the *Birmingham News* and *USA Today*. The *News,* of course, had Stallion stories galloping all over the place. Before the game Chet Simmons had said the eyes of the nation would be on Birmingham, or something equally grandiloquent, and Birmingham was making the most of its moment. The Stallions had lost and the game was a bust, but it *had* happened, and that's what mattered.

In *USA Today* the headline read, "USFL Scores on Television," the only tally that was really important. "Early ratings show that up to 35 million of us watched opening day games of the USFL—three times ABC's prediction." Equally important, bettors were "intrigued." Meanwhile, National Football League officials were doing a fast dance around the USFL. They couldn't appear the bully and say the new league sucked, even if they wanted to. At the same time, they couldn't overcompliment lest they bestow too much credibility. So they said "announced" attendance figures were impressive and wrapped comments inside comparisons to the WFL. Leaving "and we all know how *that* turned out" unspoken.

I had already decided. Walking around Birmingham yesterday afternoon I'd determined that I didn't want the USFL to succeed. I didn't want football in the spring. Not just because football belonged in the fall, although that was reason enough. I wanted the USFL to fold because someone, somewhere, had conducted a marketing survey that determined we would watch football in the spring. Yes, it would be fun watching the USFL tweak the nose of the mighty NFL. And, okay, if a guy wants to play football, let him play football. I wanted the USFL to fold to prove that unknown, invisible, and almighty marketing analyst wrong. Power to the people. Go on a picnic. Just don't watch football in the spring.

By 11 A.M. I was on 65 south, sixty-seven hours after stopping in Birmingham for something to eat, two days late for the field dog trials. Birmingham disappeared quickly. I rolled over the hills to Montgomery. The sky was vast. Puffs of clouds dotted the expanse to create the perfect touch.

A turtle crossed the road. A sign told me to go to church or the devil would get me. A chain gang worked the highway, desultorily pushing rakes. Above Montgomery the world flattened. I crossed the Alabama River. Trees rose from the water, cobwebs of Spanish moss hanging from the branches.

Ninety-nine miles from Mobile grating sounds crawled from the right front wheel well. A metallic grinding that drilled into the pit of my stomach. I picked up my cassette recorder, wanting to retain my thought forever: "I think I can honestly say I hate this van."

The front wheel bearings were repacked at Windham's Auto Repair six miles from Evergreen, and soon I was back on 65, hooksliding around Mobile. The earth grew flatter and the trees greener. The clouds became wispy strands of angel's hair. On

Route 113 the color green acquired even more luster. Pine trees, born to be telephone poles, shot to the sky, their branches and needles reserved for the upper reaches.

The earth spread out before me. Freshly plowed soil, rich and brown. Silo to the right. Occasionally a house. A lonely suburban-style house, looking like it had lost the rest of its development. A quarter mile later a shanty sitting not-quite-straight on cinder blocks. The sun set, plummeting quickly, producing long shadows along the ground. I might hate the van but not moments like this.

The defending champion at the field dog trials was Music City Rex, a male pointer owned by George Olive, a physician from Missouri. On Wednesday morning I hitched a ride with him to the field trial grounds. On Tuesday, the day I'd arrived, Rex had been picked up because he'd been gone more than twenty minutes. According to the rules, the judges had to see the dog every twenty minutes during the dog's ninety-minute heat. Rex had been gone about twenty-five minutes when he finally showed.

"I couldn't see any sense in wasting the judges' time," George said, so he'd pulled Rex from the competition. The National Amateur Quail Field Dog Trials was a high-stakes game—in prestige if not money—and one mistake was all it took to make last year's winner this year's loser.

The trials were run in the Coldwater Recreation Area, about forty miles from Pensacola. The 6,000-acre area was reserved for trials and fox hunts. It was pristine forest, circa 1983. Not that the forest hadn't been touched. It had, in fact, been touched and retouched so much that a certain unreal quality hovered throughout. The longleaf pine trees were evenly spaced. Not in rows or in any pattern, just evenly spaced, almost equidistant one from the other. There was little undergrowth, and what there was was shinbone deep. From the road it was possible to see maybe a half mile into the forest. You *can* see the forest and the trees.

We arrived at the clubhouse as a small group of men and one woman were preparing for the morning heats. Most were on horseback, waiting for the judges to ride to the lead. Behind the pack a pickup truck pulled a dog wagon. On top of the wagon were foam-rubber chairs. I climbed aboard, joining a gray-haired man and the young woman. The sun was bright but the morning was cold, and the three of us comprised the wagon-riding gallery. The truck lurched forward after the horseback-riding gallery moved onto the trail.

Up ahead, two men released their dogs. The dogs sprinted into the forest and disappeared. The two men started yelling, mounted their horses, and gave chase. And for those of us who don't know what happens at a field dog trial, that's what happens at a field dog trial.

Back at the clubhouse after the morning session, I sought out Pete Mixson, one of the judges. We leaned against a station wagon in a parking lot covered with pine needles. Horse trailers and Blazers filled the lot. Off to the side, strings of pointers roped together formed a sort of fence. The pointers' ribs stood out in bold relief, their muscles tightly knotted wires just beneath the surface. A couple of them fidgeted, restless and edgy. Even those lying down and curled into little balls quivered with anticipation, their energy level set to a high-strung idle.

"What are you looking for in a dog?" I asked. Pete thought for a moment, shifting a giant wad of tobacco back and forth between his cheeks. A large man fleshy of face, if he'd been born a dog he'd have been a big ol' friendly bloodhound.

"We're lookin' for a big dawg that runs wahd," he said. He loosed a stream of brown tobacco juice on the pine needles. Apparently that was all one needed to know. But I needed more.

"A big dawg don't mean he's big," Pete said. "A big dawg can run flat out for the whole ninety-minute heat. A wahd-runnin' dawg covers the territory. He should be going as fast at the finish as he was at the start. He's always movin' to the front and coverin' the territory. Yeah. I want a big dawg that runs wahd."

I told him that from my position in the wagon I'd seen little of the trial, not much more than an occasional dog running past, and two men on horseback chasing after it. One was the handler, Pete said. Since this was the Amateur Quail, the handlers all had to be amateurs, and most of the handlers were the dogs' owners. But most of the dogs were professionally trained.

"The owner isn't usually the person who trains the dog?" I asked. Pete shook his head.

"Some of these guys come out here with a dawg they own but just picked up from a pro handler, and once they get up on a horse they can't do shit with the dawg."

The other guy was the scout. "You got to have a good scout. He's got to know where the dog is and where the handler is all the time. See that guy over there?" Pete nodded across the parking lot to a long horse trailer, where a couple of men were eating sandwiches. He pointed to the one in the middle, a large man in a white western shirt, cowboy hat, and jeans. "That's Pappy Keyes. Best damn scout in the bid-nit. He knows how to ride a horse. And he ain't afraid. If he's got to run to find a dawg, he'll run and find the dawg."

"You guys make any money at this?"

"You can make a living by boardin' and trainin' dawgs. A dawg costs $200 a month to board with a professional trainer. Now, a handler gets about thirty dawgs together and he's doin' all right.

"Another way to get your money back—I'm not goin' to say you're goin' to make any money—is by selling your dawgs. You got a dawg who wins, say, four or five stakes, and you can sell him. I gave a dawg away one time. The owner later sold the same dawg for $26,000. And I gave it away." Pete hit the pine needles with a second splat of juice. "Sheee-it."

The dog wagon was full for the afternoon session. Sixteen people sitting in the foam-rubber chairs, with me and two other guys standing in the back. Up ahead was the gallery on horseback, and somewhere in front of them two dogs being chased around the forest by the handler and the scout. The wagon followed as closely as it could on the rutted roads. Occasionally, we'd see a dog, and on even rarer occasions we'd see one go on point. It was like going on a pheasant hunt with Louis XIV.

The talk in the wagon was dogs, of course. Bloodlines and favorite dogs and places to hunt and breaking dogs and how wonderful this area was for trialing. But then William Jackson asked if anyone had ever seen a dog point fish. Jackson was the old man who'd gone out in the wagon with me this morning. A retired insurance broker, he trained and ran his own dogs, although not at this level. He seemed more intent on enjoying his retirement, and he looked to be succeeding.

"Did you ever see a dog point fish?" he repeated the question. It sounded like a bad barroom bet, but he passed the snapshot around. Sure enough, there was a pointer, up to its shoulders in the surf, head down, tail crackin', as they say, pointing a fish.

"That there is a mullet dog," William Jackson said. "Only dog I know that's a four-season dog."

The women next to Jackson looked at the photo a second time. "Can we borrow the dog? I love mullet. We used to go to a place where you ordered mullet and the man went out and caught it for you."

"You got to eat mullet fresh," someone said. "Fry it up in butter."

"Well I found a way to freeze it so it won't turn on you," Jackson said. Jackson was like that. He always seemed to have an answer, and you always wanted to hear it. "You fillet 'em out, see? Then fill a half-gallon milk carton with water and then stick the fillet in there and freeze the whole thing. You can keep them froze for a year that way."

"I like them with swamp cabbage," the woman said. "Water palm trees. Has a heart like an avocado. Season them up just right."

"And serve it all with grits," Jackson said, getting that last word. "Lots of grits."

The second brace of dogs was easier to follow. They weren't as big and didn't run as wide. One, Bronzini, was owned by a Doc McCall, who'd won the Amateur Quail twice. On the strength of the Doc's experience, Bronzini—who should have won on name alone—was considered a favorite. Bronzini had two "well-spaced finds," as the people in the wagon termed them, but on the third the dog went on point with its belly scraping the ground, more like a panther than a proud runnin' huntin' dog. Charlie Jackson, scouting for McCall, was the first to find Bronzini. He lifted the pointer's belly off the ground, then jumped back on his horse before waving his hat, the signal that he'd found the dog on point. Moments later, however, as McCall prepared to flush the birds, Bronzini jumped the covey. At least that's what the judges said. McCall's flush and the dogs jump were within milliseconds of each other, but the judges ordered the dog picked up.

"You know what the difference is between a southern Baptist and a northern Baptist?" McCall asked as he locked Bronzini in the dog wagon. "The northern Baptist says 'There ain't no hell,' and the southern Baptist says 'The hell there ain't.' Well, right now I'm a southern Baptist."

At the barbecue after the second session, Charlie Jackson took a full dose for styling up Bronzini's point. But no one seemed to mind the chicanery, and Charlie wasn't apologizing. The way he had it figured, there was no way a dog was going to win this thing pointin' on its belly, so what difference did it make if he got caught? That he'd gotten away with it just made the story all the more fun to tell.

As I worked on the ribs and cole slaw and corn bread, the trialers took turns telling me I had to talk to Doc McCall if I wanted to know what field trialin' was all about. Go to the Doc's house and it was wall-to-wall silver trophies, they said; he's forgotten more about trialin' than they'll ever remember, that sort of thing. Just keep one thing in mind, Charlie Jackson warned me, "When it comes to talkin' to these old guys, half of what they say is a lie and the rest is horseshit."

I found Doc near the stables, loading his horse into his trailer. I told him what the others had said, leaving out Charlie's advice for the moment, and that I was here and ready to listen. He looked at me, green eyes inside a leathered face reaching out to grab me. He was wearing a safari hat, the kind Stewart Granger wore in all those Africa movies, the brim rolled tight. His green shirt was soaked with perspiration and his khaki riding chaps were like second skin they'd been worn so long. He'd been huntin' quail for sixty years, still had a private ophthalmology practice after forty-two years, been bird doggin' for thirty-five years, and had logged nine thousand miles in the Rocky Mountains huntin' big game. He was old and crusty and wonderfully eccentric, and he played the part to the hilt.

The problem was he wouldn't tell me anything. Even after telling me he'd be happy to tell me anything. "Don't get me wrong," he said, "I'm not being ornery. I just don't want anything I say written up by someone who don't know nothin' about bird doggin'. People will read it and figure ol' Doc McCall got a shot too many of Jack Daniels in him and started shootin' off his mouth and tootin' his own horn. But I will tell you this. I'm the oldest man running dogs."

I asked about today's run. He had his opinion. "But I don't want you to think I'm comin' down on field trials. I've been doin' it all my life, and I think the world of it."

"What keeps you coming back?"

"The love of the dogs. And I'm very competitive. If I'm knocked down I'll get up again. You've got to take the kick below the belt." And he was still smiling through this latest kick.

"I always do, I never bitch. I may laugh on the outside but I'm crying on the inside. You know," he said. "I won't ever see seventy again. I'd like to win this one more time. I've won it twice, but nobody's ever won it three times. I'd like to do that, I really would."

From the minute I'd climbed aboard the dog wagon on Wednesday morning, it was obvious I'd have to ride a horse if I really wanted to see the trial. So on Friday afternoon I climbed aboard "Ol' Jake." I had a great view, but I didn't much care because I didn't know how to ride a horse. For forty-five minutes I fought Ol' Jake until he turned around and stared at me, looking like he was about to shake me from his back. I figured he knew more about this than I did, so I gave up trying and held on tight. (It wasn't until the next day that I learned I'd been set up on Ol' Jake.)

But if the view was better, I still didn't like it. A dog would go on point and the judges and the field marshals and the rest of us would ride over quietly and form a semicircle around the dog. In the center of this amphitheater the handler would perform the wing and shoot—the flushing of the covey and the shooting over the dog, who was to remain locked in place.

As a kid I had hunted with my father. As I remembered it, hunting was a solitary experience shared by hunter and boy and dog. This stuff here wasn't hunting. A man creeping up behind a dog he owned but didn't train wasn't hunting. A judge telling a man to pick up his dog wasn't hunting. Neither was riding around watching it all.

The second set of dogs was picked up early, which gave us a straight shot back to the clubhouse. I slowed Ol' Jake to the smoothest canter I could find and eventually caught up to Charlie Jackson, who was walking in an effort to warm up.

Charlie was the owner of Nitch—rumor said she had the inside lock on the championship—and the head cowboy of the self-proclaimed Texas mafia here at the trial. Pappy Keyes was from Texas also, as was Jack Herriage, Charlie's professional trainer. I had enjoyed their company all week, and was glad now for Charlie's companionship as I bounced the final few miles to the clubhouse. A friendly, expansive sort, Charlie had played some ball in the old

American Football League. Now he owned a successful cement business in Dallas. His face was deeply tanned, his mustache charcoal-gray. His sideburns were white and his hair turned dark gray as it reached the top of his head. He kept his eyes hidden behind aviator sunglasses and his head covered with a tan cowboy hat. The first time he took off his hat, I half expected the top of his head to come off with it.

Pappy joined us when we reached the clubhouse. We sat on the tailgate of Charlie's black Blazer drinking apple juice and vodka. The evening sun turned the sky a faded orange, and a chilly wind swayed the trees. Pappy was a former high school principal and football coach. He'd met Charlie through field trialing, and was now in charge of Charlie's southside Dallas cement operations. He'd been running dogs for years.

"Everybody says you're the best damn scout in the business," I said. Pappy shrugged and sipped his drink. He was bigger than Charlie, a bit fleshy around the jowls and the beginning of a belly around his belt. He did indeed ride fearlessly, just as Pete Mixson had said. Where other scouts picked across the grounds, Pappy was off and charging. "How can you ride the way you do?"

He shrugged again, not embarrassed, just understated and low-key. "The dog's not going to stand still waitin' on you," he said. "If I don't run, the dog will be twice as far away."

I asked if they could define for me the allure these "all-age dogs," the very top field trial dogs, held for them. "I like to quote John O'Neil, he's one of the most outstanding field trial men and breeders in the country," Pappy said. "His definition of an all-age dog is 'A dog that runs off, almost.' I like to turn a dog loose knowin' there's always a chance I'm going to lose him. But the thrill is finding a dog a quarter mile or a half mile away, standing on point, waiting twenty minutes for you to get there. That's something everyone looks forward to. I know I do. The dog is hunting. He's out there doing what he's supposed to do."

That was Charlie's cue. "One of my dogs had the prettiest point you'd ever want to see in an all-age dog," he said. The dog had run just three days ago, but Charlie's story already aspired to the stuff of legend. "I'd gone past the area a couple times, then found the dog about thirty feet from where I'd been lookin'. Instead of lookin' down at the ground I'd been lookin' out on the horizon. Anyway, it was pretty. I mean, she had those birds froze." It was those kind of moments Pappy had been talking about.

An older man with gray hair and mustache walked over, zipping up a green down jacket. "Hey," Charlie said, "How's that old dog of your'n? Still screwin'?"

Gene Casale laughed. "He's been screwin' his brains out for the past two weeks." Standing a dog at stud was one of the few methods an owner had to get some money back from field trialing. "I haven't had him out for two weeks. But not now. I figure I got to leave something in him for tomorrow."

"I don't blame you at all for gettin' your dog on stud." Charlie handed Gene and another man drinks. "I don't blame nobody when they get their dog on stud."

The conversation shifted from dogs to land. Or the lack thereof. An all-age dog needed room to run, and there just wasn't all that much room left anymore. That lack of space spelled a dwindling supply of game. Which in turn meant it was impossible to shoot and kill over the dog very much anymore, but without the occasional kill even the best dogs lost their snap.

But the conversation returned, as it always did, to dogs. Bloodlines and training and stories about the-best-damn-dog-I-ever-did-see. Charlie told his tale, of course. One story begat another. The process was infectious. At one point, between stories, Charlie folded his arms across his chest, leaning back, and looked at me. A self-effacing smile flashed brilliant white teeth against his face.

"Steve, you better get out of this field trialin' shit while you still can." The others agreed, and the stories continued.

Guard Rail, Gene Casale's pointer, lasted thirty minutes in Saturday morning's heat. None of the dogs lasted very long, and we were back at the clubhouse by 10:30. There was plenty of morning available to run the afternoon dogs now, but to be fair to the luck of the draw the final dogs waited till the afternoon runs at 1:30.

Few people hung around. Even if the judges weren't talking, the trialers realized their chances as soon as their runs were completed. It was too expensive to stay unless you figured you had a shot. "All that's left now," Pappy said, surveying the empty parking lot, "is the wishers and the wanters."

The Texas mafia was sticking around. Charlie Jackson's Nitch was still the odds-on favorite. The only dog with a real chance to challenge figured to be Pete Frierson's Addition's Go Boy. Go Boy had run on Tuesday, a hot day, and had been the only dog to find any birds all day.

The afternoon dogs were picked up quickly, which suited the wishers and wanters just fine.

Jack and Pappy rode the wagon back to the clubhouse. The week had worn them out, and they had been happy to give their horses to people in the wagon who wanted to ride the trail. Jack looked especially weary. Watching Jack work last night while Charlie and Pappy and I sipped our vodka and apple juice destroyed any lingering notions I might have harbored about the romance of the hired hand.

Yesterday, riding the trails, Jack had slowed once to give me some pointers on riding a horse. I tried to implement his suggestions—to little avail—and continued my hanging-on method of riding. During a lull in the trail I asked Jack if he enjoyed the life.

"Well, you're never going to get rich doing this," he said.

I asked which he preferred, working for one man or owning his own kennel. He grimaced, indicating that it didn't much matter.

"When you work for one man there's that security you don't get when you're on your own. But let me tell you, the guy who owns the dogs is sitting up there in his office wishing he could be out there in the field with you. Meanwhile, you're out there doing what you want to be doin'. Now I ask you, who's the richer?"

"Anything else you'd rather be doing?"

"Noooo. Not a thing." He smiled. "How many people can say that?"

Once the last dog was picked up and Pappy and Jack were in the wagon, we took the dirt roads back to the clubhouse.

"Hey, Steve," Jack said, sitting in the seat behind me. "You think you could tell people what a field dog trial is all about now?" I said I didn't have a doubt.

"All I got to do," I said, reaching for the thickest southern twang I could find, "is say, 'Ah wont a big daawg that runs waahd.' That says it all." Jack doubled over with laughter.

"You know," he said, "it does sound kind of stupid to call the dogs we use 'big,' don't it? In fact, when you think about it, most of what we're doin' looks pretty hilarious: Runnin' around out there with some half-wild dog, settin' him loose and then seein' if we can find him."

"I just got one more question. The only thing I can get you guys to agree on is that overcast skies make for the best hunting." Once more Jack doubled over.

"Tell you what, Steve," Jack said, "when we get back to the clubhouse, ask around what people think the ideal point looks like." He stood up, feet spread wide for balance as the wagon bounced about. "Some will go like this." He crouched a bit and put one hand in front of the other, index fingers pointing straight ahead, his head cocked to one side.

"Others will go like this." He leaned forward but pulled his arms close to his chest, thumbs up like a pug fighter. He stuck out his tongue and screwed his face into mock concentration. Then he broke point and laughed. "Everybody knows exactly what the perfect point looks like, and none of them looks the same."

Back at the clubhouse the timing seemed inappropriate for testing Jack's theory. The final decision was expected any moment, and the friendly, easygoing casualness of the past few days disappeared into the trees. Everyone assidiously avoided the company of Charlie Jackson, who hung around his horse trailer in the pine-needle parking lot, as well as Pete Frierson, owner of Addition's Go Boy, the other contender, in the screened-in clubhouse. That left the judges caught somewhere in the middle, and the rest of us down by the stables for a final go 'round of scuttlebutt.

Everyone at the stables agreed it was an open-and-shut case. On Monday the three judges, Mixson, C. C. Spears, and a Mr. Carter, picked a "winner." On Tuesday, a dog would have had to beat Monday's winner to become the new winner, and so on through the week. A series of championship fights, with the rest always compared with the best.

Nitch had run on Monday, and as far as this stable gang was concerned she'd stood the test every day since. Frierson's Go Boy was just a dog to fill in second place. But the judges were taking their time coming to a decision, and the more time they took the more time the stable gang had for speculatin'. Most of it centered on the possible wheelings and dealings. Not much could be agreed upon, except for one thing: nobody owned Mixson. Never mind that he spent much of the down time between runs shootin' the shit and chewin' tobacco with the Texas mafia. Mixson was his own man.

We watched Mixson talk to Frierson, then go down to Charlie and talk to him. Next he talked to Leslie Anderson, secretary of the Field Trial Club for twenty-seven years. "I ain't never seen anything like this," one of the old guard said. Then he stopped and said, "but I've seen everything."

Mixson talked to Frierson and Jackson again, and then once more to Leslie. "Well," someone opined, "at least if we've got a controversy we've got the president of the club here to straighten everything out." That produced some derisive chuckles.

"Who's the president?" That from me.

"Frierson."

"Oh."

After another round of talks, Leslie Anderson called everyone together under the pavilion. She cleared her throat and proceeded to explain the situation the way the stable crew had already figured it out. The vote had been 2 to 1, and since the vote was usually unanimous, a runoff between Nitch and Go Boy had been discussed. But Frierson had already flown Go Boy to a stakes in Georgia, and the earliest he could have the dog back was late tonight.

Then, fighting tears, Leslie continued, "And I think it was one of the . . . I don't know what I think. I want to cry if you want to know the truth. But he said under the circumstances of having to bring his dog in and wait until tomorrow and all, that he would graciously accept the runner-up. And I think he had done more than his share." She turned to Charlie, her body shaking with emotion.

"And so the winner, Charlie. I'm sure you feel the same way."

Charlie later took great pains to say Leslie had everyone's best interest at heart during her little speech, but his championship had been tainted nonetheless. The 1983 Amateur Quail wouldn't be remembered as the championship Charlie Jackson won, but as the year Frierson "conceded" a decision he'd already lost. Charlie extended his hand above the trophy to Frierson.

"That's mighty magnanimous of you, Pete," Charlie said.

* * *

Charlie Champaine placed a giant pot of coffee on the table, poured a bucketful for me and one for himself, took a drink, set the cup down, and wiped his thick brown mustache. He leaned back in the chair, stretched his legs in front of him, and shoved his hands into his pockets. He looked at me, a pleasant, inquisitive expression wanting to know who I was and what I was about.

I told him. The North American Sled Dog Championships up here in Fairbanks had been my eleventh event of the year. Then I looked at him with the same expression he'd just given me.

"Well, let's see. I grew up in Maine. I'm thirty-three. Moved here in '68."

"Come up to 'escape' the Lower 48?"

"Not at all. I was drafted. I went to Alaska to win the war! Keep Communist aggression out of the States!" Mock enthusiasm faded quickly. "I didn't even like it when I first came up here. I skied for the army in Anchorage, which didn't work out too bad."

"Better here than Vietnam."

"Oh man, let me tell you. I had direct orders for Vietnam as a combat medic.

"In 1970 I moved to Talkeetna, on a homestead. We lived about a mile off the road, couldn't drive in in the winter. I had three dogs. All I knew was they could pull a sled a little better than I could. I didn't know anything. But they pulled me and my groceries.

"I met this guy in Anchorage who raised a kennel. Bob Lee. He was a dog racer, a sprint racer. One day he showed me his dogs; these forty-five-pound wiry little things. I thought, 'Oh no, man, the bigger the better.' So Bob said, 'Okay, let's take 'em out.' Now Bob's about 220 and I'm 170. He said, 'Let's go,' and I thought, 'These little devils are going to pull us?' Well, it was white knuckles for the next four miles. Then Bob said, 'Okay, you're on your own.' He stepped off and, geez, away we went. Ten miles. When I came in it was, 'Shucks! I got to have me one of these! This is fun!' I'd skied all my life—downhill—and this was a bigger thrill.

"And, you know, one thing led to another over the next couple years, and I wound up with seven or eight or nine dogs. I moved to Johnson River and did everything with the dogs. I built a place off the road, hauled the logs with the dogs, trapped with 'em, hauled the groceries and the water with 'em. It was a utility operation. I left them in harness all day long.

"I really started racing in '75, and then in '78 I decided to run the Rendezvous in Anchorage. I had always wanted to do that. I finished in the money. Just. That was a real eye-opener.

"In '79 I didn't run. I completely changed my dogs. I was also gettin' divorced, which didn't help my energy level. I regrouped the whole kennel—I saw what I needed for dogs—and in '80 I raced the Rendezvous again. Came in sixth. Then in '81 I raced the Rendezvous and came in second; raced the North American and came in second. I didn't win a race, but you name it and I came in second. This is my first year I've really started to win any major races, which is kind of nice."

Charlie finished second (again) in the Fur Rendezvous, the world championships, in February, and last weekend finished third in the North American, the final major event of the mushing season. He broke his collarbone a couple of weeks ago in Valdez, the end-of-the-line city for the Alaska pipeline, which helped explain his third-place finish in the North American. But a better explanation was Gareth Wright. By common agreement, there was just no beating Gareth Wright this year. Harris Dunlap, the defending champion, finished second. Curtis Erhart from Tanana, a small town at the fork of the Tanana and Yukon rivers, finished behind Charlie. And George Attla, a six-time winner, was fifth.

Wright, Dunlap, and Attla were the heavyweights of Alaskan sled dog racing. Their stories were well documented. Dunlap was from upstate New York, and for eleven years had been driving north with his dogs, racing in towns along the way. Wright had been around forever. He first won the North American in 1950, and through constant breeding of his stock had created the quintessential sled dog, the Aurora Husky. Attla was better known as *The Spirit of the Wind,* the title of a movie a few years ago about his life as an Athabaskan Indian growing up in an increasingly white world, his childhood bout with tuberculosis, and his eventual rise to superstardom as a sled dog racer. It was a wonderful little film, unself-conscious and without pretense, totally honest in its portrayal of life in Alaska. Of Charlie and Curtis I knew nothing. Reason enough to seek them out. Spending the Wednesday morning after the race with Charlie was arbitrary; he lived in Salcha, forty miles from Fairbanks on the Alaska Highway. I couldn't find Curtis.

"Which driver do you respect the most?"

Charlie didn't hesitate. "Gareth Wright. I like his philosophy, his reason for being here, the way he does things, the way he conducts himself. He's a competitor, but the guy's always got a smile. Some guys are okay to be around when they win, but just miserable to be around when they lose.

"Dog racing brings out funny things in people. Around here we're surrounded by dog mushers, so I talk to a lot of dog people. And there are some real sour, dour, bitter, sad people racing dogs. The dogs, Jesus! The dogs are bringing them down. Why do it? It's meant to be a pleasure. Gareth and I have talked about this a few times over several bottles of gin. He has a real good philosophy of life, in my opinion, he really does.

"Gareth's a competitor. If you beat him he's the first to come shake hands, congratulate you, buy you a beer. If he beats you," Charlie stopped and smiled, giving movement to a very real admiration, "boy, he's the first to run over to get his hand shook and buy you a beer.

"I have a lot of respect for Harris. Harris is a nice fellow. And he's done a lot for the sport Outside."

"Which musher do you fear the most at race time?"

"Well, Harris, of course, over the last year or so. But you can never count George Attla down and out, just because of his sheer personal drive and experience." I'd noticed throughout the week a reluctance among the mushers to talk about George. I'd also been warned that his personality was, at best, enigmatic, a condition I'd discovered firsthand when I'd interviewed him for an article for the *Anchorage Daily News*.

"I take it George is a lot more complicated than *Spirit of the Wind* portrayed him." I said.

"Oh, yeah. Yeah, yeah, yeah." Had I stated the obvious?

Charlie shrugged. "I've had some good, bad, and indifferent experiences with George.

"He's a winner. That's his primary goal. That's how he approached the North American on Sunday. He knew damn well before the race that he might blow up at the TV camera spot—the twenty-three-mile mark—and never really be able to get by there. He knew that.

"I think that's why he is more of a winner than I am. It would bother me to blow up there. I don't like to have things like that happen to me. But he's going to go out and run: 'I'm going to win or die,' that kind of approach. George has the ability to drive dogs and make them do things I don't. He's capable of making them do things I can't. That's his style. This time he died. Every year it gets more difficult for him to do that, to just go out and pull out all the stops and win. It's getting harder for him to replace dogs. He uses them up faster than a lot of other people."

The North American was three days of racing. Twenty miles on Friday, twenty on Saturday, and thirty on Sunday. On Friday Wright posted the fastest time, 65.73 minutes. Saturday Harris and Curtis beat him, but Gareth remained in first place overall. Sunday he again had the fastest time, 99.60 minutes, and after the race no one argued when he exclaimed that no one could catch him now. A great big teddy bear of a man who really was always smiling, it was obvious why Charlie—and everyone else—held him in such high regard.

The races started on Second Avenue downtown, snow trucked in to cover the street for five blocks until the course swept onto the Chena River. From there the trail looped north across Creamer's Field and over the Fairbanks Country Club golf course before winding up again on Second Avenue.

Sled dogs are by reputation mean. I didn't test the theory and kept my distance. But once in harness the dogs jumped to their task, leaning and pulling, anxious to run. Waiting his turn, each driver held his sled, as did five or six handlers who dug their feet into the snow to prevent the sled from taking off down the street. Every two minutes a sled left the gate. The dogs, suddenly released, bent low to their task in bursts of enthusiasm. The front of the sled popped into the air; the driver, standing on the runners behind the sled, hung on; and away they'd go. A straight line of speed and power.

Their return was less impressive. Played out by the distance and a sun too warm for racing, each team was a bedraggled, wandering pack of dogs as they trotted up the street. Dogs crossed the line, tongues dragging, and fell to the ground refusing to move another inch.

"I was real pleased with the North American this year," Charlie said. "I evaluated myself before we went there, and after seeing how everyone else stood, I made a realistic appraisal of the race.

The best I could have hoped for was third. Which isn't the goal you want to have, but I knew I couldn't function to my normal standard." And a broken collarbone didn't help.

"I also lost a main leader on Friday, which was a real disaster. Daisy. She's the one I used all three days in the Rendezvous and she's the one that helped me win the state championship. She was a key dog. I've never had to drop her. Never, ever. But she just happened to get hurt. So things were a little more scabbed together.

"We trained differently because of my injury, just for safety's sake. It lowered my confidence considerably. I worked with their minds more than anything else. And I went out real slow. I did that for my own safety more than anything else. And I was less than 100 percent capable of dealing with a problem."

"You must have been really worried about getting tangled with another team."

"When I passed George on Sunday I really held my breath. Last thing I needed was to be sitting in the middle of his team. Especially with a leader in heat and a male beside her.

"Anyway, though, it worked out fine. I'm real pleased with the dogs. They just did real good. Real good."

"What's the difference between the twenty- and thirty-mile heats?"

An impish gleam covered Charlie's eyes, but he didn't give me the smart-mouth answer.

"Quite a bit. It's right about at the eleven-mile point in the trail that the ten-mile extension breaks off. On Friday and Saturday they've been going by that. On Sunday you put them on that ten-mile extension and they really like it. Trail's fresh and it really sparks the dogs. On their own they shift gears. Boy, you turn them onto there and they just start runnin' for all they're worth. They run like that for, gee, five or six miles before they get back into their normal pace. That can wind them. They run ten miles and pop back out in sight of the main trail where they left, and it pisses them off. You can see it. I'm never quite sure if they understand what happens to them. But there's that . . . it's just sort of a look they give: 'Hey wait a minute! Wait a minute now!'

"Then they're headed for the golf course. Now the golf course and that TV tower at Creamer's Field are places where the dogs are apt to quit. They've been runnin' in the brush for ten, twelve, fourteen miles and then, flap! All these people. It's an easy place for them to shut down."

I looked out a window of the log house. Beyond the parking lot Charlie had his twenty dogs chained individually to posts. Each dog had its own house. To the right of the kennels were a garage and barn, from which Charlie ran his dog food business. In the distance, somewhere beneath the snow and ice, was the Tanana River. A bright spring sun bounced whiteness in all directions.

"What's the name of your business?" I asked.

Charlie thought for a moment, then laughed. "We don't have one. Just 'meat business.' "

I asked him if his life revolved around dogs. He looked at me: You don't know the half of it.

"There's dog people coming by all the time. That stimulates the dog-related conversation. Got to go look at this dog, sell feed, all that. My feed business is really starting to take quite a bit of the burden off my income, though. It's working out well. I feel good about it, too. We're doing something good for dog mushing. People aren't trying to scrounge up a dead horse and that sort of thing anymore. For the ol' mutt it's not worth the trouble to buy fifty-pound bags of frozen meat, but for any type of athletic animal, it's cheaper than feeding them commercial feed. Figure thirty-five cents a pound. That's $17.50 a bag. And that's all meat.

"This business was a goal for me. I really enjoy it. We started doing this as a top-of-our-head idea to get inexpensive dog feed out of Seattle. One thing leads to another. But if I ever stop racing I'll stop doing it. I have my meat business because I race dogs, and I race dogs because I have the meat business. After I win a race, boy, I'll sell a lot of meat. Never fails."

Charlie's dogs barked all at once, their yelps comfortably muffled by the thick logs of the cabin. A knock on the door and a man and a woman dressed heavily for the trails entered awkwardly.

"We're here for meat," the man said. "We also want to know if we can extend ourselves just a little bit longer." Charlie shook his head.

"Nope, nope. Get the hell out of here," he shouted, and then laughed and lowered his voice. "Just get what you need and let me know. You need liver?"

"Yeah."

"It's up by the garage. "You're gonna get liver and chicken, right?"

"Yeah. We're gonna fill up for the summer and then we'll catch up with you."

"Take what you need. I mean, if you run out of dough, at least you'll have the dogs taken care of. Don't worry about it." They thanked him and left. Charlie turned to me.

"Turkey is getting really expensive. About a year ago we had a real good deal, but now it's all packaged for human consumption; they sell that stuff to prisons." He stood up to get the coffeepot. I was about to ask a question when he cut me short.

"You know, I was just thinkin', you were asking before about independence and the independent lifestyle?" He sat down and leaned back again, his hands once more going into the pockets, his long ponytail hanging down the back of the wooden chair.

"It's very comfortable for me to live in the state of Alaska. It's very easy for me to make a good living without having to work five days a week year round. I don't mind working. I do a lot in terms of energy expended, but the routine of the same job would burn me out. We don't stay here in the summertime. We go back to our place down on the Johnson River. It's a nice break. I'd find it real difficult to move back to Boston and work nine to five in a drafting office." He fell silent for a moment, thinking.

"I can tell you what I do, how my lifestyle operates. You can make of it what you see fit. There is a lot of independence. I like doing things the way I want to do them. I like getting around. I like going to the small towns. That's an important part of the racing for me.

"I consider myself wealthy up here. It's easy for me to be comfortable and still have an adequate income and still have time. Time is very important to me. Time to spend doing what I damn well please, time to spend with my daughter. Without being broke or worrying about where the next meal is coming from."

"Does it bother you that you're one of the best in the world at your sport but there's close to zero recognition?" Charlie just sat for a moment.

"I've thought about that a lot," he finally said. "Zero recognition and very little financial reward."

"But you're as good at what you do as, say, Herschel Walker."

"True. But those sports are recognized differently. There's a lot more money involved. But ours is getting recognized a lot more. There's more public input and financial input." He shrugged. "I don't really care. Dog mushers are nobody special."

Talking to people during the North American, I'd gotten the impression that big-money sponsorship was right around the corner. Bigger purses, more competitors, greater recognition. Good news and bad news. The good news was obvious: bigger purses, more competitors, greater recognition. But many people feared the dogs would suffer. Individual dogs and even entire teams suddenly expendable when the prize money outstripped the value of the animals. Race them into the ground and buy a new set tomorrow.

"Right off the top of my head I disagree with that," Charlie said. "The availability isn't there. There's a limited resource of premium-quality dogs. They are not mass-produced. It won't happen unless we start cloning dogs. Those kind of dogs are few and far between, and they're worth a lot."

"So what's the future for Charlie Champaine in dog racing?" I asked, shifting subjects. It was getting late. I had to get to town and Charlie had to run his team.

"It's real limited," he said. "I'm going to change one of these days. Get interested in something else."

"Are you really?"

"Oh, yeah. I like racing dogs. I just have a few other things in my life that I'd like to do. I'm buying a sailboat. This month, actually. Last summer my daughter and I delivered a boat to Whittier from Seattle. That kind of gave me the bug again—I used to live on the coast of Maine. I don't care to sail off into the sunset and never be seen again; I'd just like to take a year or so of my life and do a little sailing. I've had some very close friends my age getting cancer and dying. That's really kicked me in the butt to do some of the other things that maybe I've been putting off."

The conversation shifted to the weather. It was getting warm. The dog food would have to be packed in the freezer truck soon. We talked about his plans for the business and his prospects for next year's season.

"I take it you're not real interested in changing your lifestyle right away," I said.

"No, no. But when I do, I'll do it abruptly. That's been my style. I skied since I was five years old, seven days a week. I skied for a living and it kept me out of Vietnam. There was a time in my life when I could never have conceived of not skiing. Then I changed, abruptly, and it was a very comfortable change. No regrets. I just felt like it was time to do something else and I did. And I really believe that one of these days I'm going to do the same with the dogs."

* * *

Alaska Airlines
Fairbanks to Anchorage
Thursday, March 31

You can't be a traveler in your own hometown. Learned that the hard way the past couple of weeks. I thought I could return to Alaska, attend the North American, and just fit this northern leg into the rest of the year. But I couldn't.

The last event where I'd been hesitant to ask the stupid question was women's powerlifting. Since then I've used ignorance as both shield and weapon to learn about the event, to find out where I was and what was going on. But in Fairbanks I knew where I was and what was going on. In Alaska the answer to the question "How long you live up here?" makes or breaks credibility. I have six years' seniority. To have asked the stupid question would have meant relinquishing those six years. I couldn't give them up.

But if maintaining conversation was difficult, collecting first impressions was impossible. Everything was too familiar. Two weeks back in Alaska, surrounded by friends and standing on well-known ground, and my senses have dulled. I need to be someplace new, where everything is happening for the first time, where brand new events are happening faster than I can comprehend. I need to reconnect myself to that series of new moments I'd been passing through. I need to get someplace where I can be stupid.

Western Airlines
Salt Lake City to Albuquerque
Friday, April 1

I've picked a great event to practice my ignorance. I'm on my way to Albuquerque for the NCAA Basketball Championships. Georgia–North Carolina State in tomorrow's first semifinal; Louisville-Houston in the second. According to the *Salt Lake Tribune,* there are no hotel rooms, tickets are going for $1,000 a set, and if you don't have wheels you're dead in spread-out Albuquerque.

The van is in Dallas, where I left it to fly to Fairbanks. I'll pick it up after the NCAAs. Thus: no place to sleep and no transportation. I can only hope there is a press credential waiting. My "affiliation" with the *Anchorage Daily News* is about to get its first real test of the year.

Albuquerque, New Mexico
Friday, April 1
10 P.M.

Sitting in a darkened room of the Albuquerque Rescue Mission. Twenty-two bunkbeds in a room designed for ten. Room filled with smell of Lysol. Most of the guys look like regulars. Man in the corner has his possessions stacked on the table next to him. Stuff takes up half the desk. The only light is the glow from the TV. I don't anticipate sleep. Guy next to me is softly wrenching out his chest, one cough at a time. There is a young Indian in his jockey shorts slowly walking up and down the aisle created by the beds.

First things first: got no press pass; got no ticket. All I gots is the rescue mission blues.

I thumbed from the airport to the "Pit," home of the University of New Mexico Lobos and site of the NCAAs. Inside, 10,000 people were watching North Carolina State shoot around. From there I hitched to press headquarters at the Marriott to pick up my credential. "Steve McKee. *Anchorage Daily News.*" I said it like I expected it. The man looked through the file.

"Don't see it," he said. "Next."

I waited for a break in the action and asked him to check again. He did, but still nothing. I explained who I was and what I was doing. He didn't much care, and kept talking about setting a precedent. The deadline was March 1 for credential requests. No exceptions. I think he enjoyed telling me to beat it. I asked if he had any tickets. He laughed.

From the Marriott I went to the Hilton where the National Association of Basketball Coaches was holding its annual meeting.

Back in Fairbanks I'd talked to the coach of the University of Alaska at Fairbanks. He'd said he'd be here. Maybe he had some tickets.

The Hilton was filled to the rim with basketball coaches and ticket scalpers, everyone hanging out talking basketball and trying to buy and sell tickets in a feeding frenzy of American capitalism.

Most of the coaches were gray-haired men in sports jackets. The rest were the young and the hungry. They wore tailor-made sweatpants and T-shirts with school emblems. They were so fresh-cut they squeaked, and they spent their time shaking hands with everybody.

The first two groups of scalpers were the first and second group of coaches. Group three was outlandishly costumed black men in wide-brimmed hats and shiny jackets. Group four was the white scalper, which was further divided into two substrata. Subspecies one had huge bellies, baseball caps, football jackets, and a rolled-up program in one hand. The second subclass was trying to pass itself off as a group of young conservative businessmen.

I found the Alaska-Fairbanks coach. He has tickets for tomorrow's and Monday's games, but I told him I'd let him know. Because I'd already talked to "Nicky from Newark," and from what he said maybe I can save some money.

Nicky from Newark—only name he'd give—was a cross between the two subspecies of white scalpers. Jock-type clothes but white-collar attitude. When I told him what I was up to he said he didn't want to talk, that a magazine had done a story on him a couple years ago and he'd gotten into trouble with the IRS.

"But I'm the man you want to talk to," he said. He'd paid his way through college scalping tickets, and once he graduated figured he could make more money scalping than he could with his degree. "I'm one of eight men in the country who can get you a ticket to anything, anytime."

We ate in the hotel coffee shop. I had a hamburger. He had a lot of beans. I asked if there was any truth to the reports of the $1,000 tickets.

"Three quarters of what the media says about scalping is shit, babe. Rarely do we get the prices they say we get."

He said he had 18 "hustlers" working for him. "The problem

with a hustler, though, is they always need a stake," he said. "Five hundred dollars and they can get some tickets and try to scalp them. A good hustler can make fifteen hundred a night. That's not too bad for a nineteen-year-old kid who's too stupid to know any better. But hustlers deal in cash. Cash is a revolving door. They drink it or put it up their nose.

"Now me, I'm a businessman. The whole system is shit, babe. Coaches scalp, the front office scalps, players scalp. *Everybody* scalps. I didn't create the system, I just work it. The real crooks are the ones who get their tickets legit—complimentaries, even—and then turn around and start to scalp." He put down his fork and drank some Coke.

"You won't see many students in there tomorrow. And this is *college* basketball."

"How much money can you make at this?" I asked.

"I got $70,000 worth of jewelry," he said.

"Where do you get your tickets?"

"Georgia's a football school. They got 1,600 tickets from the NCAA and sold 400. Where'd the rest go, babe?" He laughed. "They sure didn't send them back to the NCAA."

There were other avenues of procurement, he said, but he wouldn't say much about them. "But I'll tell you this, I sell whole blocks of tickets to companies. They write the whole thing off. Now for some companies—say it's the Super Bowl in New Orleans—the ticket price includes a quail shoot in Mexico, all the pussy and booze they can eat and drink for three days, and then they fly them up to the game. And they write the whole thing off."

"You supply the whole package?"

"Well, let's just say I know people who can."

One of Nicky's hustlers stopped for a quick hamburger. Tickets weren't moving, he said. Nicky seemed unperturbed, even as he predicted cheap seats tomorrow. "I'm a gambler. I'll eat it if I have to. Anything else is bad for business." The hustler, a scraggly sort with blond hair sticking from beneath a baseball cap, finished his hamburger and stood up.

"You can get into any event you want to for free if you've got the guts and the patience," he said. Nicky agreed with the assessment and watched him walk away.

"He's an all right guy," Nicky said. "But as a ticket man, he's shit."

Inside the Pit
Saturday Afternoon, April 2

I'm one lousy ticket scalper, but I'm inside the Pit! The Georgia–N. C. State game is about to begin.

Everything is red—Georgia, N. C. State, the trim around the court, the foul lanes, the center jump circle. Louisville and Houston are red, too. Everyone is wearing red. I am already sick of red.

The Pit is dug into the ground. I'm way up in the corner of the Georgia section and right above me is a balcony. It cuts off any sensation of being in a large arena. It's all just very far away.

Nicky was right. There aren't many students here. Each school has been given a thin sliver of seats that fans out slightly up each corner of the court. The media dominates one side, foul line to foul line and maybe twenty rows deep. Immediately above them in the prime seats are the coaches I saw yesterday at the Hilton.

Game Time: Georgia versus State for the B Championship

- Spectators are just that. Very little participation. Very little of the ol' college spirit. Effect is quite dull. I don't have much feeling for BEING HERE. It's like I'm watching on TV, if you can believe it.
- Georgia fans are terrible. Louisville fans in the next corner are standing up now, giving Georgia a lesson in how to cheer for your basketball team.

Second Half

- Houston players just walked in, dressed and ready to go. Took seats behind the State bench and completely upstaged the game. Just wanted us to know what was coming.
- 1:42 to go; State up 59–52. Georgia making comeback and place alive, sort of.
- State won. Yawn.

Houston-Louisville

- Word is Houston should win, but Denny Crum, coach of Louisville, will find a way to beat Guy Lewis of Houston.

- Now these two teams know how to cheer!
- Opening tip. Ball in the air and Pit exploded in flashbulbs.
- Second half. Houston on the move! Block by Akeem! Slam by Drexel! Place goes nuts.
- 57–55. Houston back in on three straight slams! Crowd begging for more.
- We got it! Houston takes a four-point lead on fourth straight stuff. We're over the edge! We're getting full! This game is *great*!
- Houston outscored Louisville 16–1. Houston talent pins your ears back!
- Akeem started rebounding on the defensive boards and Houston started dunking and that was all she wrote.
- I can't believe it—1:33 to go and people are leaving. Why leave an NCAA semifinal? Especially this one?
- Final 94–81 Houston.

Albuquerque Airport
Saturday Night, Late
April 2

I'll be sleeping in the airport lounge tonight. Beats the Rescue Mission.

The Houston-Louisville game was awesome. When it was over, people poured from the Pit, all that talent pushing us out the doors and halfway down the street. Will it be remembered as one of the best college games ever? Should be.

There were tons of tickets available. The New Mexico attorney general or some such personage had announced that scalping was legal and to have at it. Everyone did. Nine-year-old kids selling tickets and giving the money to dad. Busloads of people wearing red sweaters and clutching fistfuls of tickets purchased back home from people who couldn't make the game. The law of supply and demand whipped to frenzy. By noon tickets were down to $20, their face value.

True confession: surrounded by all this unfettered American capitalism, I still managed to blow it. I bought at noon for face value. An hour later I heard some guy yell, "I'm buying tickets for $5." I did some quick calculations and sold my ticket. It wasn't until I no longer had the ticket and was holding a $5 bill instead that I realized I'd done it backwards. Bought high and sold low. I'd been bitten by the fever of the marketplace.

With game time approaching, the scalpers tried to hold the market at face, so I had to buy another $20 ticket. That's $35 for one $20 ticket. To salvage my dignity, I talked a guy into selling me a Monday ticket for ten bucks.

After the game I went to the Regent Hotel. Louisville headquarters. Their consolation party was in full swing. They'd been beaten by a more talented team that possessed superior firepower. Can't be ashamed of that. Their only regret was that the luck of the draw had prevented what would have been the ultimate championship final from ever taking place. N. C. State had no business in the NCAA final.

Downstairs, Denny Crum, the Louisville coach, ate a quiet dinner with family and friends. No one bothered him at all. Nice touch, that.

I ran into Nicky from Newark at the bar. "Hey, babe," he said, "What'd I tell ya? They were selling 'em for two bucks at game time. How'd you do?"

"Fine," I said. Just fine.

"You know, after the game one of the local TV stations wanted one of my boys to go on the air and say tickets were going for $500. My boy told them to talk to me. I told them to get fucked. They don't want to tell the story of the $2 ticket. I had an NCAA commissioner come up to me asking what tickets were going for. I told him the truth, too. Two dollars, game time. I don't think he wanted to hear it, either."

"How can they report the $1,000 ticket at game time?" I asked.

"There's only one person I know who ever sold a ticket for $1,000 at game time."

"Who was that?"

Nicky looked at me. "A certain TV announcer. I don't know if he sold it or had someone else sell it for him, but he sold it so he could go on the air and say tickets were going for a thousand at game time. It makes the broadcast look good."

"Who'd buy it?"

"Hey, babe, there are plenty of people who'd love to be able to say they got their ticket from a certain TV announcer."

"You going to be able to make up your losses on Monday?" Nicky remained as nonplussed as he'd been when he told me tickets were two bucks today.

"With Houston in the finals the big money will be coming up from Texas. They love to pay the big coin. I'll talk to them while they're still getting out of their Lear jets."

Monday Morning
April 4

I'll be glad to get out of Albuquerque. I miss the van. Well, that's not true. I NEED the van.

And the weather has turned. It is winter again. Cold and windy and sloppy with sleet and snow.

I'd also like to strangle whoever coined the Houston Cougar "Phi Slamma Jamma" slogan. A great throwaway line, it's been bonked over our heads mercilessly for the past two days. It's such a great line that everyone is afraid *not* to use it.

But what I really mean is I'll be glad to get away from the NCAAs.

When I walked into the Hilton on Friday, into the coaches' convention, I'd unwittingly stumbled into the epicenter of the NCAA. Walking through the corridors, past the rebounding machines and exercise displays and between the two groups of coaches, I realized why the NCAA exists: as a showcase for the coaches. And with the television networks, this group comprises the sun around which everything—and everybody—revolves.

The first outer circle is the press. The next orbit contains all the boosters and supporters and assorted hangers-on. Then come the players. (They, in fact, seem incidental to the real goings-on. Their faces change too quickly year to year to establish any real identity.) Finally, orbiting on the periphery, so distant from the sun as to receive little light and less regard, are the college basketball fans who just want to see the game. It's a series of concentric circles designed to insulate the event inside as much mystery and mythology as possible. The idea is to create an aura of importance, both for the event itself and the Inside Group, to make the event appear more significant than it really is, thus ensuring its existence. And all us fans, who just want to see a good game, believe it. We've bought the act, and now we're paying for it.

Airport Lounge
Monday Night, Late
April 4

Ohmygodohmygodohmygod!!!!

That's all I could say when the game was over.

N. C. State 54—Houston 52

An unbelievable game. The definitive argument for telling television to blow it out its picture tube and disavowing a shot clock in college basketball.

State was outmanned and outgunned, but they were never outgutsed or outcoached. They took an eight-point lead into the half, were outscored 18–2 at the start of the second, and Houston looked to be really cooking. Then Houston, on a roll, slowed it down. A decision that will be forever second-guessed. Slowing the tempo put the ball back in State's hands. Jim Valvano, the State coach, started fouling early. The gamble worked because Houston missed. He also used three six-foot guards at the same time! Ballsy! It became a question of who would rattle first. Would State hang tough in their slowdown game? (They never actually stalled.) Could Houston play without their vaunted (dare I say it?) Phi Slamma Jamma? Answers: Houston cracked, State hung tough, and Houston had no game but the slam.

With forty seconds remaining and the score tied, State had the ball and a time-out. After the time-out Dereck Whittenburg dribbled around out near center court, not even looking to do anything with the ball. And then he launched a prayer from downtown as the clock ticked off. Only it wasn't a shot, it was a pass! That was the consensus of the fans in the stands around me. It was a fuckin' pass! Akeem and the rest of Houston had waltzed out from underneath the basket while Whittenburg danced around out front, freeing Lorenzo Charles to catch the pass and slam the lid! Akeem collapsed in the foul lane and Valvano started running around like a crazy man.

What a play! What a play! It was generally agreed in the stands that Valvano should die and go to heaven right now, to be remembered as the mastermind of the single greatest basketball play in history.

I returned to the AmFac Hotel, Houston headquarters, after the game. The ballroom had been rented for the victory party, and everyone was trying to have the kind of party they had thought they were going to have before they left for the game. The band played and the cheerleaders shook all over the place. I found Tom and Jeannie Adkins, whom I'd met this afternoon. They were taking defeat gracefully. Tom was even detached enough to observe that the "party" was a "necessary cathartic experience."

Tom and Jeannie's friends were taking the loss a bit closer to heart. The woman took solace in the fact that never in the history of sport had a team provided its fans with such a roller coaster of excitement in one season. Heady stuff. Her husband, Charlie, looked like his dog had died on the way to his girlfriend's funeral. He was stricken. Life had ended. Charlie suffered every sling and arrow thrust at Guy Lewis's coaching ability, and after tonight's inexcusable loss the slings and arrows were razor sharp. He looked so pathetically desolate that I didn't even try to say I was sorry. Words just weren't enough.

It was generally conceded in the ballroom that Houston would still be ranked the number one team in the nation. They had beaten number two Louisville. Virginia and St. John's hadn't even made it this far. There was no way unranked N. C. State could jump all the way to the top spot in the polls. It just couldn't happen. Besides, everyone knew State made postseason play only because the NCAA tournament had become a giant sideshow staged by the networks. It didn't mean a thing. Which made some sense. Prior to the game an air of embarrassment had hung above the Pit. (*This* was to be the national championship game?) Don't include a team in the tournament if you're afraid they might win it. By yanking an upset out of thin air, Valvano had pulled CBS's and the NCAA's fat from the fire at the same time. Still, Houston fans were talking through their shorts when they screamed "We're still number one." Had Houston won tonight, they'd be annointing that TV-concocted tournament as the ultimate crucible of athletic competition. The Cougars had lost the one game they never should have lost. That's all there is to it.

Western Airlines
Albuquerque to Dallas, Texas
Tuesday Morning, April 5

When last we left the van, before departing the Lower 48 for Alaska, it was dead on its wheels in the parking lot of the American Airlines corporate headquarters ten miles from Dallas Airport. Still, I look forward to getting back to the van. Putting the miles on the road, and having a place to sleep right behind me.

The Masters starts the day after tomorrow. I'll have to move quick.

* * *

The plan was to put distance between me and Dallas. Cruise late into the night. But sixty miles from Dallas the five days in Albuquerque hit me. I pulled into a rest stop about 7 P.M. to take a nap. But I took off my shoes and socks. You nap with your shoes on; you hit the sack with your shoes off. I slept until ten o'clock the next morning.

Wednesday was power-drive. Louisiana, Mississippi, Alabama, and past Atlanta, Georgia, before I finally admitted I couldn't make Augusta in one day. Perhaps I could have, but in Alabama a cow fell out of the back of a truck in front of me—I'd just pulled out to pass—and I stopped to help the driver.

Augusta National is removed from the rest of the world by an impenetrable wall of trees and bushes. The main entrance was on Washington, and on one side of the street it was 1983; Piggly Wiggly, Kentucky Fried Chicken, Norman's Electronic Galaxy, Billiard Emporium, Green Jacket Prime Rib and Seafood, and all the one-shot souvenir stands hawking Masters memorabilia. On the other side of the street it was 1935. Augusta National exists of and for itself, an island of gentility amid the commercial storm.

At press headquarters I picked up my credential, pinned the button to my jacket and walked between the scoreboard and the pro shop. The first fairway was in front of me, sweeping left to right. Behind the tee was the eighteenth green. People were wearing brightly colored slacks, even brighter Perry Como sweaters, two-tone golf shoes with flaps hiding the laces, and carrying multicolored umbrellas that could have doubled as parachutes. I walked to the eighteenth hole, where a large crowd had gathered. Arnold Palmer was on the green, holing out to finish at 68. He was 4 under par and tied for second.

Friday, play was canceled. When the rain subsided, I decided to tour the course. A slate-gray sky had rendered the course's many shades of green a deeper, richer luster, and the whole place seemed alive and inviting.

I walked between the pro shop and the scoreboard again (Jack Renner, Ray Floyd, and Gil Morgan shared the lead at 67; Palmer, Seve Ballesteros, J. C. Snead, Charles Coody, and Jimmy Hallet, an amateur, were tied for second at 68), and out to the fairway of the first hole, Tea Olive. I stood in a small ravine, the tee up and to my left. To my right the fairway extended uphill to the 400-yard, par-4 green.

I walked in the rough that paralleled the fairway, the difference between rough and fairway an extra half inch of grass. The fairways looked more like greens. Until I arrived at the green. An immaculately, impeccably, and excrutiatingly manicured, contoured, and sculpted expanse of oval-shaped carpet. I fought an impulse to take off my shoes and run across the green, just to see what it felt like. I didn't because I feared reprisals. Like maybe I'd be spirited away and shot.

In front of the green and just to the left was a bunker. (Sand trap's too mundane a word.) Every grain of sand in place. It looked like rough-poured concrete. Behind the green were spectator mounds, and behind them longleaf pine trees producing that just-perfect touch.

From the tee at Pink Dogwood the second hole swept downhill in a par-5 dogleg left. Pink and white dogwoods lined the fairway. I pushed through their thick fragrance as I walked to a large bunker that cut the fairway in half 216 yards from the tee. A triangle-shaped green was 260 yards down the hill.

Flowering Peach, the third hole, was boring. A par-4, 360-yard straight shot uphill between the trees. Four was much more interesting: a 220-yard par 3 etched into the trees and bushes. The fairway ran down quickly into a little valley and just as quickly popped back up again. Dogwoods rolled around one side and a cluster of bamboo stood to the right of the P-shaped green. The hole looked to have been included as an afterthought, the architects forced to work with what they were given instead of bending and shaping the land to fit their august designs.

The rain returned as I walked up the hill to the green, so I stood with the security guard underneath a TV tower. "This is the best place to be," he said, looking at me through a pair of thick bifocals. I figured he meant to watch the golfers, not to be here underneath the tower waiting out the rain. A cigar, stuck on the left side of his face, slowly disappeared into his mouth as we talked.

"You can watch them hole out on three, drive four, hole out here, and drive five. I see the same people come here year in and year out. There's seven, eight, nine doctors that come here every year. They sit here all the time. They go down and get their drinks and bring them up and watch everybody go by. It's a good group we got. Look around here. The people haven't been through to clean up yet, but the only mess we got is a couple peanut shells."

When the rain stopped I continued my tour. Number five was a monster uphill even though it was a par 4 at 440 yards. Six, Juniper, was another par 3 and simply gorgeous. An elevated tee with a fairway that plummeted straight downhill. At 180 yards, the green looked farther down than it did away. Just to the right was the sixteenth hole, with a pond flat against the green. Picture perfect.

Walking down the hill the rain returned, slowly at first, and then in torrents. End of tour. I cut between the seventh tee and the sixteenth green, running toward a tent behind the fifteenth hole. My ark was a CBS television tent packed with electric equipment and thick black cables. The plywood flooring was about six inches off the ground, and it was already underwater. I sat in a metal chair, very aware that it was a great conductor of electricity, and waited out the storm.

The skies turned off the faucet early in the afternoon, and after drying out at a laundromat across the street, I walked back onto Hallowed Ground. Jack Nicklaus was at the practice range down near the clubhouse, hitting 250-yard ropes one right after the other. A large crowd, perfectly quiet, sat in the stands behind the tees.

Jack was wearing a raspberry-colored sweater and blue pants, his yellow hair a beacon on this still gloomy day. Shot after shot he repeated the same motion, as if he were running the same piece of film over in his mind, projecting it onto a screen for him to study. He planted his right foot first, shifted his left foot into place, jiggled his weight on both feet, and jerked the clubhead back a couple of times. With the wood's face addressing the ball, he slowly turned his head to the right, his body followed, and the club was pulled back through its arc. His face furrowed with concentration as he swung through the ball, and a little white dot followed the same trajectory as the one before it, at the same time describing the path of the white dot to follow.

Gary Player arrived. When first compared to Nicklaus, he seemed an awkward Sunday afternoon duffer, too uncoordinated to be a champion golfer. But the more balls he hit the more powerful he became, his shoulders tensing through his sweater as he ripped through the ball. Nicklaus stopped and watched for a couple of minutes, and then the two traded tips, giving each other quick little lessons. Nicklaus walked over to Gary's tee. In slow motion and without a club, he pantomimed a swing.

"Watch my hips," he said. He brought the club back, and then swung through an imaginary ball. "My hips shouldn't get beyond my feet." He finished his swing and Player checked Nicklaus's hips. Nicklaus looked at the four range boys, kids in their early teens, who stood waiting to retrieve balls, hand him a towel, wipe a club face, anything the Golden Bear wanted.

"Got that, fellas?" Jack said. The four boys looked at Nicklaus, mouths opened, too stunned to talk. Finally they mustered a mutter that yes, indeed, they had gotten that. "Good," Nicklaus said, a grin spreading across his face. "Because I don't know what I was talking about." The boys stood there, waiting. Then Jack laughed and so did they, hitting each other with their elbows as they shook with laughter and relief. They would relive this moment for a long, long time: Remember the day we shared a laugh with Jack?

Seve Ballesteros and Jimmy Hallet were incidental to the action I followed on Saturday. Because their third playing partner was Arnold Palmer.

In truth, I hadn't planned to join the Army. I had wanted to follow an unknown my first day, a quiet way to acquaint myself with the course. Besides, who hadn't followed Arnie? But Thursday's round had changed my thinking. Arnie was in second place and this was the Masters. And I wouldn't just be tripping down memory lane. History might be in the making, and I couldn't take a chance on missing it.

They teed off at 12:36 P.M., the thirteenth threesome to go out from number one. Ballesteros and Hallet walked to the tee greeted by polite applause. Arnie arrived, the masses parted, and I was lifted off the grass by the enthusiasm that ignited the crowd.

He was wearing a pair of steel-rim glasses, and I realized with a shock that he was old. I suppose I expected him to look like he had on the cover of *Sports Illustrated* all those many times and years ago. He walked kind of slouched over, as if maybe the years of carrying his Army had started to wear. Yet it was apparent that the Army sustained him, that playing a round of golf alone would be difficult. He accepted the applause and encouragement—a gush of childlike love, it was so pure and unconditional—as if it belonged to him by preordained right. At the same time, his expression suggested that after all these years he was still trying to figure out what he'd done to deserve all this. He didn't rule majestically nor govern imperially. He was that rare king, the truly humble servant, and there was something about him that suggested he understood how lucky his life had been.

It was difficult now, twenty-five years later, to discern which came first, Arnie or the Army. Perhaps it no longer mattered. They supported and gave each other life. For seven hours, through rain delays and lousy conditions, Arnie fought the course and the Army remained steadfast. The famous Arnie charge was no hyperbolic public relations ploy. I could feel it, I could see it, and it was impossible not to become part of it. Twice Arnie fell from the leader board, and twice he clawed his way back on. I spent much time talking to Army regulars as we walked along, asking them if they could explain Arnie's enduring mystique. One loyal follower observed that Arnie was the Everyman of Golf. As good an answer as I was likely to get. Because, as one person told me, if I had to ask the question, I would never understand the answer.

Number fifteen possessed the necessary ingredients of the classic golf hole. A great name: Firethorn (number eighteen, for all its legendary finishes, was innocuously titled Holly). Wonderful setting: tucked into a hollow with the sixth and sixteenth greens and the seventeenth tee, a tiny enclave backed by a high, lush cliff.

Demanding: a par 5 at 500 yards, with second shots taken about 200 yards from the pin, up a long sweeping hill near a series of mounds that broke the fairway in half. (The pond in front of the green posed a special problem; the pin was reachable with the second shot, but then again maybe it wasn't.) Most important, number fifteen had history: In 1935, during the second Masters, Gene Sarazen scored a double eagle when he hit a four wood over the pond and into the cup, thus bouncing into a tie with Craig Wood. Sarazen then won in a thirty-six-hole play-off. The bridge to the left of the green was named in Sarazen's honor.

All in all, a perfect place to watch a Sunday afternoon of golf.

The cavalcade of players started at 1:49 P.M. with Shearer and Nicollette. Stadler and Floyd finished the field. As pair after pair played through, the story of Firethorn played itself over and over, but never even approached dull. Most of the players laid their second shot on the fairway side of the pond, and then chipped over the water to the green. Time and again the ball hit the green crazy with backspin on the far side of the pin, and rolled toward the hole while the crowd went crazy urging it into the cup. Usually the ball had too much backspin and rolled past the pin. That was the cue for everyone to shout at the ball to stop. It almost always did, at which point the crowd cheered, its decibel level corresponding to the ball's proximity to the flag. Occasionally, however, the ball took off when it hit the green, a whirling top hell-bent for the pond. That signaled total pandemonium, everyone begging and pleading and beseeching the ball to stay on the green. If it stopped there wasn't applause so much as a collective sigh of relief. When it landed in the drink there was an immediate groan followed by consolation applause. It was all great and ridiculous fun. Talking and yelling and screaming at a dimpled little ball.

But it was the long hitters who provided the ultimate drama. They appeared on the crest of the hill 220 yards distant, lone gunslingers riding the green sage of Augusta. By the time they stepped to the ball the gallery was on its feet waiting the Big One. It was Dodge City, 1885, a shootout in the street, the townsfolk too afraid to watch but more afraid not to. A split second of anticipation that rivaled Dereck Whittenburg's desperate pass at the NCAAs. Going for broke, taking the gamble; cashing in the chips knowing there'd be hell to pay if it didn't work. Bob Gilder, Dan Pohl, Tom Watson, and Ballesteros were the only four to go for it.

Gilder hit to the right. Pohl actually went over the green. Watson hit dead-on, and Ballesteros just missed the front lip but was closer to the pin than Watson.

The arrival of the golfers reaffirmed the opinions stated earlier by the people around me. Watson was, of course, smiling. Crenshaw tossed his iron disgustedly after laying up poorly, which was immediately considered a representative pique of anger. It was decided that Gay Brewer should change his name, and everyone missed Chi Chi Rodriguez. When Lee Trevino appeared at the top of the hill everyone leaned forward, hoping to hear something funny from 200 yards away. Determining the best-looking golfer was the exclusive domain of the woman behind me. She had very definite ideas and talked a great game about testing her theories with some undercover action. Ballesteros was numero uno, followed by Tom (James Caan) Weiskopf. When Andy North appeared she stood up to get a better look, and used the time to adjust her tight, white jeans.

Palmer's arrival at the top of the hill brought the immediate, requisite response. The crowd buzzed, sensing the magic. But the buzz changed quickly to an audible gasp when his tout board came into view. Arnie was 3 over. This morning he had finished up yesterday's suspended-play round by bogeying the eighteenth hole, an ignominious ending to his glorious charge through the rain. And yet it didn't matter. The crowd at fifteen rose to its feet and paid homage to their king.

It was Calvin Peete, however, who engendered the most conversation. He had started the day 2 under, but had ballooned to 12 over by fifteen. Which suited the people around me just fine, and thank you very much.

Since arriving on Thursday I'd sensed an undercurrent of apprehension whenever Peete, one of the few black golfers on the circuit, appeared. Accompanied by his supporters, most of whom were black, Peete represented a patch of difference, his presence an obvious threat to the established order. It did not go unnoticed, and the battle was waged with whispered comments and innuendos.

Augusta National was an island unto itself in more ways than one. Fiercely bound to the Old South gentility I'd noticed the first time I'd walked onto the grounds was the belief that men are white and blacks are boys. The groundskeepers, the locker room attendants, and concession personnel were all black. But more than that, the attitude was everywhere and pervasive. This year, for the first time, the touring pros were allowed to use their regular caddies. This rule change was, apparently, a large concession by the tournament committee and was treated as major news. According to a guard, Thursday was the first time a white had ever caddied on this course. He had said it as a matter of fact, but an edge of trepidation played with his voice.

Exacerbating the attitude regarding Calvin Peete was a newspaper article in which Peete had said he would not play Augusta were it not the Masters. Peete's left arm was noticably withered, and he was not long off the tee. He was deadly accurate, but that counted for little at Augusta, a long ball course where even the rough under the trees was groomed. Peete's comment acknowledged the significance of the tournament, but his remark had been interpreted by those around me as a direct insult to the Masters. Shouldn't he be more grateful?

Now, his game had exploded, and Calvin Peete was getting his. The people around me were loving it. What did Peete know? Ten years ago he didn't even know what a golf club was. Didn't he know how lucky he was to be here?

"You know, you've got to hand it to him," someone said. "You got to give him credit."

Peete holed out, and walked to the sixteenth tee. From the moment he'd come into view his expression had been fixed. He exhibited, in fact, little expression at all.

CHAPTER 4

* * *

Thursday, April 21, 1983

MacDee–

You'll be glad to know the weather is awful. It snowed and rained the whole way home from Boston the day after the marathon. Some consolation as you wonder if spring will ever come to your little town of Noatak above the Arctic Circle.

Masters update: Seve Ballesteros won with an eagle on the second hole of the final round on Monday. I missed it. I was back at the press hut wondering if I should follow the leaders or camp at eighteen to have a good view of The-Putt-That-Wins-The-Tournament when I heard a roar from the middle of the course. That was Ballesteros, icing the tournament with sixteen holes to go.

Now, Boston: I stopped in Natick to visit your family Sunday night on my way to the race. Norman Rockwell spent his life drawing your house over and over again. And Natick is beautiful. Quintessential New England, just like you said.

Your father gave me a great tip. Told me to hit the Elliot Lounge in Boston if I wanted to be where the action was, runningwise. I'd been considering Natick to watch the race—

what is it, the 10.5-mile mark?—but decided to head into the city and check the Elliot.

It wasn't hard to find. There's a painting of Bill Rodgers pasteled on the sidewalk outside. Sort of gives the place away. "Boston Billy" is even wearing those white painter's gloves he made famous. They make him look like Mickey Mouse.

Have you been to the Elliot? Probably. Modern American Sports Bar. Upstairs, black-and-white pictures of Larry Bird and Kevin McHale. Downstairs, pictures of many runners. There's also a blowup of some columns by Ray Fitzgerald. One is called "A Christmas Story, 1973." Tells of Tony Staynings, English runner. Staynings was on his way to Western Kentucky U. when a car went through a window of the Post Road Motel and pinned him to the bed. Broke his pelvis. He was on crutches for nine weeks, and it was going to be a year before he could think about walking, let alone running. But that's where the story ends. I asked around if anyone knew what happened to Tony Staynings, but nobody did. Too bad, the story cried for a coda.

There weren't many people in the Elliot the night before the race. And those that were probably didn't run the next day. But up the street at Steve's Ice Cream the line wound halfway round the block. Last minute carbo loading. After the race, the line to get into the Elliot wound halfway round the block. More carbo loading.

I parked the van on Arlington Street, Boston Commons on the left, Ritz Carlton on the right. I pulled the left wheels up on the curve to compensate for the slope in the street and that's where I slept both nights. Was I in a safe area? On second thought, don't tell me. I've still got too much trip to worry about things like that.

I didn't have a press credential, but I didn't need one. I talked my way onto a press bus heading to Hopkinton before the race, and with a little help from a friendly official got inside headquarters (in the parking garage under the Prudential Building) afterward.

Hopkington was a carnival of potential energy. As the start approached, the energy level burst with twitching, nervous people. Most runners hung out in Leigh D. Hughes Square. Anyone who wasn't running was trying to sell something to those that were. There were as many balloons caught in the trees as there were tied to children's wrists. But the hot item was white painters' hats with "1983 Boston Marathon" in green letters. At 11:00 the loudspeaker played the *Chariots of Fire* theme and wired everyone a little tighter. Planes circled overhead, trailing tales of advertisement: "N.E. for Jesus Rally Bost. Common May." "Main Street Ford Waltham Bargain Town." Across the street the First Congregational Church conducted a sidewalk prayer service. The minister ran through all the clichés: "I'm running in circles," "the Heartbreak Hills of life," and, of course, "the Race of Life."

About 11:30 the pack began serious assemblage at the starting line, which is painted green (of course) and is right next to a bronze statue of a World War I doughboy who—for purposes of the race—was marching in the wrong direction. The news helicopters arrived as the multitude assembled. A pounding of the air to beat everything into a final fury.

The start of the wheelchair race fifteen minutes before the start of the running race presaged pandemonium. Something big was going to happen, and it was going to happen *now*.

Elite runners filled in the front rows. I was at the starting line, across from the doughboy, being pushed by the people behind me against the storm fence that lined the street. After one heavy-duty surge I turned around. Bill Rodgers was right behind me. Boston Billy fighting his way through the crowd, trying to get to the race. We lifted him over the fence. Johnny Kelly, the old and venerable long-distance runner, took his place a couple feet behind the starting line, standing on a manhole-sized green and white shamrock that has his name on it. That seemed to be the official signal that the race would begin.

Allison Roe, Joan Benoit, and Jackie Gereau were the only women in the first row. Benoit won in 1979, Gereau the year Rosie Ruiz said she had won. Allison won in 1981. Benoit and Gereau don't look like runners. Benoit especially. There was nothing about her to suggest that in two hours and twenty-two minutes she'd blow the doors off all the women and most of the men.

Now Allison . . . . Her profile suggests a hawklike quality, but that description doesn't do her justice. Her face sweeps back from her nose, past exquisitely high cheekbones that buckle your knees to windcut blond hair suggesting movement even when she's standing still. The prototype woman of speed and elegance. Loooong legs and precise symmetry complete the image.

Meanwhile, back at the race: Right before the gun the racers stripped off their warmup suits and threw them to the crowd. A Punch-and-Judy show as all these dummies popped into the air. The final scenario before this carnival turned sporting event. The crowd loved it and everyone grabbed for the Sweatsuits of the Stars.

By the time the 6,000-plus runners cleared through Hopkinton, Main Street looked like the inside of a giant goodwill box for very healthy poor people. Plastic garbage bags with arm and head holes cut in them were everywhere. So were sweatpants, shirts, extra socks, gloves, stocking caps, and jars of Vaseline. And one brassiere. Maybe I watched the start from the wrong place.

I hitched back to the Prudential Building on the press bus, and spent the ride talking Boston with race official Seamus O'Leary (I think that's his name—if not, it should be). He was responsible for the little things no one wanted to do, like taking the gym bags of the elite runners back to the Pru. None too glamorous, but he was content, fully aware that the little things do add up. Talking to him confirmed my suspicion that I'd come to the Boston at a pivotal time. The basic scoop is that last year the Boston Athletic Association sold the race to a promoter, which horrified the starch out of the traditionalists. Prudential rescinded its sponsorship, and it looked like the race wouldn't end at the Pru. But Prudential came back after the promoter was bounced. Right now things are in a holding pattern, which means the whole mess is tied up in court. Who owns the Boston and all of that.

Bottom line is that the traditionalists don't want Boston to go commercial, and they don't want to pay people to run. They figure the pull of Boston should be enough to attract a quality field. A race-or-die mentality. What saved Boston this year is that it's the American qualifier for the world championships in August. Next year is the Olympic year and the Olympic Marathon Trials are a month after Boston, so the only people running Boston will be those still searching to qualify for the trials.

Which means it will be 1985 before Boston has another chance to prove it can still pull 'em in on the strength of its eighty-nine-year mystique.

Seamus said Boston has to change, and quick. He mouthed "has to, has to," lest any hide-bound traditionalist overheard and threw him off the bus. "The Chicago Marathon has a half-million-dollar budget," he told me. "Beatrice Foods is the big sponsor. They have the money to put on a race. That marathon could easily wind up being *the* marathon in the country." To save Boston, he said, the race had to move to Sunday (again the whispered "had to, had to"). Sunday means television and television means money. Period. The churches in Hopkington will yell and scream, but the hell with 'em, so to speak. "If they scream we'll just move the start of the race." Like it or not, things were going to have to change. There should be a marathon, it should be in Boston, and it should be in April. Everything else had to be negotiable.

Seamus was for offering prize money, in a manner similar to professional golf. Don't pay anyone to show up, just put all the marbles on the table and let the chips fall as they may. I asked if he thought Boston might die someday, victim of its own race hauteur. He said "no," but then switched immediately to "hope not." With a little luck, he said, the amateur—the real amateur—will keep Boston going even if big bucks pull the heavyweight runners into some other race. A runner must qualify to run Boston. You're a good runner if you get in. Not great, but good. Runners around the country know that. That's what made the unofficial runner a big Boston asset. This year there were 6,000 official runners but who knows how many "scabs"? Twenty-five hundred? Probably more. The scabs proved Boston was the prestige race everyone insisted it still was. The more scabs the more prestige. But can Boston draw the scab if another race buys the elite runner? More to the point, can Boston afford to learn the answer? The only solution is marbles for the winners. Big marbles.

A ramp led directly into the bowels of the Pru's garage, the place thundering with the rumble of baggage carts as workers tried to get 6,000 gym bags into their numbered bins before the racers arrived. At the base of the ramp was the official interview area. It was decorated with bunting, which effectively masqueraded the fact that it was just a couple tables and some plywood partitions. The rest of the garage had been converted into a maze of corridors and rooms and tunnels separated by red and blue tarps hung from the rafters. Signs directed runners to various areas: "Triage," "Ultrasound," "Bone Fatigue Study." Under "Podiatrist," seventy-five cots had been set up, each with an aluminum space blanket. Behind "Medical" were one hundred cots, each with an IV bottle strung from low-hanging pipes. A man was giving final instructions to a group of people wearing "1983 Boston Marathon Medical Team" T-shirts. "Kind of looks like the 4077th, doesn't it?" Seamus said. Farther back, in front of a red tarp separating triage from the toilets was "Test Area." Sounded ominous. Behind more tarps were temporary showers.

Above the din I could clearly hear the voice of the announcer. Joan Benoit is on her way to a 2:18! Two-fuckin'-eighteen! (I said that, not the announcer.) She wouldn't get it, but her 2:22 knocked a couple of minutes off the women's record, as well as the socks off the racing establishment. Greg Meyer, meanwhile, was already at Heartbreak Hill, "and if he can maintain five-minute miles we'll have a new world record!" The BAA must have been licking their collective chops at that point. Two world records in the same Boston Marathon. Need we say more?

But Meyer slowly lost the world record, then the American record, and finally the Boston record. He finished in 2:09:54, certainly a creditable time. I went outside to watch Benoit's triumphant and astounding 2:22:42. I also watched the stream of runners thicken from 2:25 to 2:30. Once Benoit came through, the crowd's response, while good, became automatic. The only way to grab attention was to collapse into a wheelchair.

By the time I ducked back under the Pru, the heavy smell of damp cement had replaced the smell of dusty concrete. Water cups, so neatly stacked thirty minutes ago, were all over the floor. The debris they created would grow exponentially as the afternoon wore on. Sweat and liniment fought for space with a heavy billowing of steam from the showers. Confusion was everywhere—people wanted clothes, a shower, something to eat, something to drink, a place to lie down, a place to get warm, a place to stretch, space to cry and space to rejoice. All at the same time.

Crinkling aluminum became the dominant sound as more and more people staggered down the ramp and wrapped themselves in space blankets. In triage few people used IVs, but the cots quickly filled with cold, exhausted runners. An attendant would come by, take a temperature, tape the reading to the victim's forehead, and move to the next patient. Occasionally a mound of glimmering silver would burst to life in a paroxysm of agony and shout obscenities as a muscle suddenly cramped.

In the men's changing area women changed, too (I didn't check the women's area). The talk was light and heavy, happy and sad, joyful and full of regret. Runners found their friends and told each other how wonderful they were for having made it, then turned to people they would never see again and told them they were wonderful, too. And over in a semiquiet corner Erma Bombeck conducted a chatty interview with a recent finisher. He looked confused sitting there, the camera's glare shining upon him, talking to some woman in a full-length fur coat.

Your dad was right, MacDee, after the race the action was at the Elliot. Bill Rodgers dropped by. So did Alberto Salazar, I think. Greg Meyer was there and so were Jon Anderson, the 1973 champion; Dave Gordon, the Honolulu winner; and Don Kardong, who missed a bronze medal at the Montreal Olympics by 3.2 seconds.

I talked to Kardong, Gordon, and Anderson for quite a while. Kardong was covering the race for *The Runner* magazine. Gordon and Anderson had both run. Gordon finished eighth and Anderson in 2:16, about what he'd won it in ten years ago. All three were blown away by Benoit's performance. Totally. There was much discussion as to whether her accomplishment would get her on the cover of *Sports Illustrated.*

Gordon is a little guy. Kardong and Anderson are tall, at least as marathoners run these days. Kardong's about six feet four inches and Anderson six feet two inches. Anderson was wearing a brown sports coat and blue sweater with a red sport shirt and tan cap. His hair was dark and so was his mustache, which had a hint of the handlebar to it. He looked like a matinee idol, with dark, penetrating eyes, the dashing movie star type who saves the heroine from being run over by the train. The race had beaten him up. He said long legs work against themselves up and down hills, and he hadn't done enough hill work in preparation. "Ten miles from the finish my legs felt like they should have been finished the race already," he said. "That's when I knew it was going to be a long day." Since when is two hours and sixteen minutes long?

I asked if he thought top-quality runners and the four- and five-hour joggers like myself shared a common experience. He looked at me like I'd said something he'd been asked before and was tired of answering, or else I'd asked a question for which he still hadn't found a suitable reply. Finally he said, "We do have something in common, but I don't know what it is. But one thing you have over me is the stamina to run for four hours. I don't think I could do that. You have a different kind of stamina that I don't have." I took that as a compliment. He also thinks the four-hour marathoner has a different mentality for the running game. I took that as a compliment, too.

Not surprisingly, these upper-crust guys take a different tack to Boston "going commercial." They welcome commercialization and hope it happens fast. But their reasons are more altruistic than I'd have thought. They maintain that *unless* the Boston goes commercial, the little guy will get trampled. If someone comes up with megadollars for the big boys of running to race in Podunk, Iowa (Anderson said that, not me), on April 18, the media will follow the elite runners to Podunk, Iowa, and the Boston be damned. Boston won't mean jackshit, and the little guy will be trampled by lack of attention. On the other hand, put the marbles on the table as prize money at Boston, and all the elites will show up. The little guys can still run their four-hour Boston Marathons and rub elbows with the crème-de-la-run at the Elliot. Offer prize money in the big races we've already got, or else a professional golflike circuit will supplant everything else, which these guys said they didn't want. Anderson in particular. He is a past champion of the Boston Marathon. He wants that always to mean something. Right now Joe Average can say he ran the Boston with Bill Rodgers. How many Sunday duffers can say they played the Masters with Jack Nicklaus? Granted, the logistics are different, but by refusing to move into the twentieth century, the

BAA is cutting off its nose to save an old face. They can keep Boston the way it used to be, but they'll be sponsoring a race for their own benefit because no one will want to be in it.

I left the Elliot about midnight, the wood floor sticky and the carpet thick with beer. A layer of crushed plastic cups covered everything. I walked down to the Pru. Up a flight of steps from the starting line, "Quest Eternal," an imposing bronze of a man—half runner, half ballet dancer—continued his attempts to touch the top of the fifty-story Prudential Building. The storm fences that earlier had delineated where spectators could stand were rolled up and stacked on top of the finish line. The scaffolding was still up, but with the bunting stripped away the scene had a skeletal, half-up–half-down feel.

I walked down Ring Road and into the garage. A faint smell of atomic balm lingered in the air, but the tarps were gone and it was impossible to remember where all the rooms and tunnels and corridors had been. The toilets still lined the back wall, looking ridiculous exposed like that, as did the copper tubing of the showers, now looking like a shiny brown spider's web. Huge bags of trash were stacked in the middle of the garage, and everywhere there were giant balls of aluminum foil, like so many asteroids that had crash-landed in the Pru. I felt like an old soldier returned to the battlefields of his youth, trying to locate something I'd lost a long time ago but unable now to find it. As I was walking up the ramp a guy in a blue Corvette asked if he could park in the garage. "Pretty soon," I told him.

I drove to NYC the next day, through the snow and sleet. I'll be here until May 4 before taking off for the Derby. This Saturday I'll catch the Yankees against the Twins, and next Friday if I can talk my way into the Felt Forum I'm going to watch the Friday night fights.

After that I'm back to the road. The Derby on May 7, National Volleyball Championships in Memphis May 17–21, the 500 in Indianapolis May 29, U.S. Fencing Championships in San Francisco June 6–11. From there to Colorado Springs for the Sports Festival the last week in June and the first week in July. Then the All-Star Game in Chicago on July 6. Then: New York and I'll be halfway through the year. Or I'll still have half to go.

Noreen continues to study apace on her Master's and work

a couple of days a week. Starting in May I'm going to have an article a month in *American Way,* the in-flight magazine of American Airlines. The dollars are good and will help keep me on the road. Also, I'm going to be on National Public Radio's *Morning Edition* occasionally, which should help some more. But basically Noreen and I are paying the bills with hidden wires and two-way mirrors. But we haven't gotten divorced, so we must be doing something right. Right?

Steve

CHAPTER 5

* * *

Twin spires stood like sentinels above the entrance to Churchill Downs on Central Street, proud and silent guardians of the many images the Derby evokes. Respectability, gentility, decorum, and propriety—they could all be found between the steeples, a palpable presence thick enough to register on film. Outside the spires, things were different. The backside of the grandstand looked like a landlocked battleship, and all around the track were people mining the riches before this mighty albatross sailed. Everyone was selling everything to anyone who would buy it: T-shirts, rose-covered shoelaces, collector's item Coke bottles, laminated, uncirculated $2 bills on a plaque with a picture of a horse and a copy of a $2 ticket, day-glow colored spaghetti strands, straw cowboy hats spray-painted bright yellow and orange and blue and green, yard-long foam-rubber lizards on stiff wire "leashes." And Grow Your Own Kentucky Bluegrass kits ("complete except for soil, water, and sunlight").

But all I bought was an eight-ounce cup of lemonade—with ice—for twenty-five cents from two six-year-old kids whose stand was the back of their wagon. The buy of the weekend. Theirs was a competitively priced, quality product. Or so they told me, albeit not in so many words. But they'd been down this road before. They knew where the money was and how to get it. As the leader of the bunch told me, "We've been workin' for the Derby for a long, long time."

"Just call me 'Art from Connecticut,'" he said. He was a T-shirt salesman, one of seven forming a line on Central and Rodman Streets on Friday afternoon across from the main entrance of the track, and one of perhaps a couple of hundred working the crowds that circled the Downs. He was thirty years old, round of face and rounder of belly, his entire body about to burst at the seams. A real chatterbox, his voice snapped out rat-a-tat-tat. He used to be a teacher, and for a while sold stainless-steel surgical buckles. Then he went on the road selling souvenirs.

"I worked the NCAA tournaments between North Carolina and Georgia," he said. "Didn't make it to Albuquerque. I'll be workin' the 500, and then a bunch of parades up and down the East Coast. And of course the World Series.

"The way I got it figured, my business is economy-proof. I don't care if there's a nuclear war the day before the Super Bowl, people are still going to want to see the game and I'm still going to sell my shirts. You know, if the Russians were smart they'd attack us during the Super Bowl. You know that guy all the way down in the bottom of the hole? The one guy in charge of pushing the button? He don't care; he's watchin' the game."

Right now business wasn't so good, but Art didn't mind. It was early, and people liked to buy their souvenirs after they left the stadium—the "blowout," Art called it. "This weekend I'll make as much money as most people make in a month. You can't beat that."

Three hours later Art was still in position across the street, the blow from the afternoon's racing card in full gorge. Cotton sundresses and madras pants and seersucker sports jackets spewed from the entrance, pushing aside the halter tops and cutoff jeans that had till then been the uniform of the street. "They're too well dressed," Art said, surveying his new clientele, "too classy. They lose $20 a race but they can't afford an eight-buck shirt. The lower the class of people, the more they spend."

Farther down the street, far from the blow, two women were selling shirts for a higher price at a furious clip.

"They good-lookin'?" Art said. The shirts or the women?

"The women."

"Very." Particularly the blond. Tall and thin, the T-shirt she wore would never look better. Art shook his head.

"Yeah, yeah, if I could get twenty chicks working for me I'd do it in a minute. Girls trust other girls and will buy from them. Guys think if they buy a shirt from a chick they're going to get in her pants, too." He looked at me, disgusted. "Tonight will be the key. If the people gettin' here tonight buy, I'll be okay."

At midnight I found Art again. He was standing by himself in the middle of Central Street, eating a sandwich. He'd put his shopping cart away. People were too far into alcohol-induced craziness to buy T-shirts. And business had been lousy anyway.

"I don't know where these people are at," Art said. "Everyone is into playin' guess-your-fuckin'-weight." He was right about that. A minicarnival had materialized in a parking lot on Central, and the guess-your-weight booth was the hot item.

A man walked up and pulled a key chain from his pocket. "Hey man," he said to Art, "you got to start selling these." He showed us the key ring. Cast in pewter, it depicted a man standing behind a woman. Both were naked. By moving a lever the woman bent over while an enormous penis rose from between the man's legs and disappeared into the woman. Art burst out laughing.

"How you doin' sellin' these?" he asked.

"Shit man," the key-chain vendor said. "I brought ten dozen with me and sold out yesterday. Yesterday! I had to go get more." He gave Art the key ring and walked away, cackling. Art looked at me. Guess your weight and fucking key rings. How was a man supposed to know what was going to sell? He twirled the key chain on his finger and popped the rest of the sandwich into his mouth.

"Tomorrow at three," he said, jaws working, "I should know if I'm gonna get beat or not."

Central Street on Friday night was a long-playing album spun over and over into early Saturday morning. Consume alcohol and make noise. One begat the other. One demented soul would scream. His yell would cause those around him to yell. Their chorus would generate a rival scream at the end of the block, which trapped the people in the middle, whose only defense was to start yelling, too. Then it would all stop, as if on cue, until another demented soul started the chorus anew.

Well after midnight I dropped myself onto a grassy strip between the main parking lot in front of the Downs's entrance and Central Street. Next to me a bunch of guys were sprawled on the grass taking in the scene and drinking beer.

They were from Grand Rapids, Michigan. At least they all used to be. One had flown in from Denver to meet up with the rest. They'd gone to school at Calvin College back in the early seventies, and were continuing a practice that had started back then, of coming to the Derby to escape the winter. The tradition was long established and always practiced, although no one could now remember how it had started or why. But it was of obvious and paramount importance that it be continued. The motor home had been rented and filled with beer and the pilgrimage undertaken. As they drank beer, lulls in the conversation were easily filled with, "Boy, it sure is good to be back at the Derby," to which there would be a chorus of nodded agreement.

A guy in a Yankees' cap opened his arms to embrace his friends. "What you see here," he said to me, "is the end product of a liberal arts education." He pointed to a specific buddy. "He's a lawyer, the rest of us are fuckups." No one seemed inclined to argue.

A long motor home evaded the roadblocks and drove down Central, horn honking, the people inside throwing beers to the crowd. That precipitated the loudest scream of the night, and everyone participated. When that subsided a group of guys walked past us screaming, "Tits! Tits! Tits!" to no one in particular. Behind us thirty cops in riot gear stood by their squad cars, ruling the mayhem with intelligent and benign neglect. One of them walked over and asked if we had any bourbon. We all looked at him, but no one said a word.

"Come on," the cop said, smiling, "I get off in ten minutes and I want to start partying, too." He was told to come back in eleven minutes, which he did.

"You know," the guy in the Yankees' cap said, "I can deal with all this diversity because I have the background of a liberal arts education."

But collectively, the boys from Grand Rapids were having a hard time dealing with the Derby. It just wasn't what it used to be, although no one could say exactly why.

"You should have seen this place four or five years ago," one of them said. He pointed to the parking lot behind us. "This whole place was just jammed with people, everyone partying at 100 miles an hour till they fell over and that's where they spent the night."

But things were different now. No one partied at 100 miles an hour anymore. "There aren't as many tit wars as there used to be," he said, as if to lament the demise of a grand and glorious culture. "Used to be you'd get four or five chicks sitting up on guys' shoulders, and they'd take turns flashing their tits and the one with the biggest applause was the winner." Now you had kids walking up and down the street yelling "Tit!" for no good reason.

"Who's got the keys to the motor home," another asked. Keys appeared. "I'm going back and get some sleep." This wasn't like the old days, either, but half of them left, leaving the Styrofoam cooler for those who remained. By the time I departed an hour later, only two were left, drinking beer and telling each other how good it was to be back at the Derby, but asking each other why it wasn't quite what it used to be.

A blast of wind shook the van and woke me up. So did a police siren and the thumping of a helicopter. A bright, clear Saturday with lots of clouds and even more wind. I dressed and ate a huge breakfast of pancakes and eggs, sausage, bacon, and toast. I expected the day to be long.

I got to the infield entrance about noon and stood in line for almost an hour, waiting to be checked through the narrow front gate, and was then herded through the tunnel under the track to the infield. Walking through the tunnel, jammed together with the rest of the low-life riffraff (no madras pants and sundresses here!), I expected to be squirted onto the infield and set free on the grassy expanse, but that didn't happen.

The infield was crushed and exploding with sixty thousand people. Everywhere there were packs of guys screaming for tit. One group must have numbered five thousand. Few women complied. Betting windows, some permanent refreshment stands, and many tents erected for the day were scattered around the infield. There were long lines to go anywhere or to do anything, which explains why I never placed a bet and went to the bathroom only when I really had to. There were also giant, Romanesque flowerpots about eight feet tall and five feet wide dotting the grounds, and I think the macadam paths were designed with symmetry in mind. At the moment, however, landscaping hardly mattered. For every four people standing up, there was one person passed out on the ground.

I saw one horse the entire day, and when I did was more surprised and shocked than anything else. Horses had nothing to do with the serious business of getting plastered on the infield. I was not at a horse race. I was not even at the Kentucky *Derby*. I was, at best, someplace in Kentucky, and getting drunk.

The grandstand across the way was incidental. Although I couldn't help but wonder if the sundressed, madras-pantsed patricians of the grandstand set weren't observing the bacchanalia of the infield with a certain sense of detached bemusement. But the chances were good the grandstanders were bacchanaling just as hard as we were. A mint julep, after all, is merely an excuse to drink massive quantities of bourbon and get away with it. Styles between grandstand and infield might be different, but results were the same. A drunk is a drunk, no matter the uniform.

And that, sports fans, is the Kentucky Derby as far as I could see.

The tit contest I'd witnessed by a lady's restroom had shifted to one of the giant flowerpots by the time I'd picked my way through a tour of the infield. The setting here was more intimate, if that be the term. A row of pine trees and bushes enclosed it on two sides. Standing on the flowerpot was a guy with his pants around his ankles holding a girl (fully clothed) over his head. The guy with his pants around his ankles threw the girl into the crowd (she lived) and then jumped down himself.

It was now 5 P.M., thirty minutes to post. It started to rain, just as the weather forecast had said it would.

The rain crowned this saturnalia with its final, most hedonistic touch. A drunk assumes an added aura of dementia when his or her T-shirt is hugging every contour of the body and the hair is twisted in thick cords across the forehead. And on the infield, there was no place to hide.

For me, the rain, coming in sheets and driven sideways by the wind, presented another dilemma. Yesterday I'd arranged with a guy named Jimmy to watch the Derby from the porch roof of his apartment, which was on the second floor of a house across the street from the track. Throughout the day there had always been people on the roof watching the races. Now the roof was empty.

Stay or go? To stay meant seeing a glimpse of the race. To go meant gambling I might not see it at all. I opted for the gamble.

I was almost to the tunnel when I noticed him. Part of the Derby was getting drunk; the other part was watching the drunks. This guy looked to be the day's champion drunk, and that was saying something.

I wasn't alone. A small crowd of spectators huddled under a sheet of plastic cheered his every attempt at standing.

But then all of a sudden it stopped being funny. What we had was the serious result of a controlled substance. People backed away. Within minutes he had cleared an area thirty or forty feet in diameter—an immense amount of infield to call your own on Derby day.

He fell next to a Styrofoam cooler and pummeled it into little pieces. He stood up but fell again, this time head first on the macadam service road. And then he just stopped moving.

The race was minutes away. Most of the people who'd been watching this guy turned to find a place along the fence to watch the race. Four or five people walked over to the immobile body.

Two guys went off to find the cops while the other three huddled above the body. The race went off. A huge roar rolled over the infield, and for the first time I was aware of the presence of the grandstand. I looked up. Sixty thousand infielders, plus or minus a couple of thousand passed-out souls, pressed themselves against the fences. I watched the jockeys float above this crowd down the back stretch. As the horses approached the wire I once again felt the roar from the grandstand.

A while later the two guys who'd searched for the cops returned. Neither had had any luck. The race was over, it was still raining, and all around us people were screaming and shouting. And the guy on the ground was trying to stand up. Mild at first, more violently as the people tried to restrain him.

And then all of a sudden some guy wearing a red "Let's Get Naked" T-shirt appeared. "This guy hasn't gotten any help yet?" he screamed at us. "I've been looking for help for over an hour and I can't find anybody." He was enraged, his face as red as his shirt, the cords on the side of his neck bulging. Who was this guy?

"Goddamn! Motherfucker! Shit! Fuck! Cock . . . suckle,"—he said "suckle"—and then he just sputtered incoherently. "I'm *pissed*! Goddamn it! I've been looking for somebody to help this guy and I can't find anybody to help 'im." His voice cracked on the second "help."

"Goddamn it! I don't know who this guy is. But what if that was me? I'd want somebody to help me.

"You know what it is? It's the Communists!" Who *was* this guy? "It's the fucking Communists. Nobody cares about anybody in this world anymore. Nobody gives a fuck! This whole fucking world! Nobody gives a fuck!

"I'm gonna write my congressman. They should have the whole state of Kentucky out here helping this guy. Damn it, if that's going to be me down there, I want to make sure someone is going to take care of me!"

He relaxed after that, his rage spent. He'd been of no help to anyone, but his tirade couldn't have had a greater impact had he scraped his fingernails down a chalkboard. We were surrounded by sixty thousand people, all of whom were drunk, we couldn't get any help, and *what if that was me* lying on the ground?

I wanted out. Immediately. To be as far away as I could get. I joined the crowds crawling toward the exits. The rain, at first a final dash of craziness, in the end had only served to sober everyone up and turn a drunken, out-of-control mob into a mean and dispirited one. Inside the tunnel it was cold and dark. Broken beer bottles and Styrofoam coolers grabbed at our ankles, the crush of people so intense all we could do was stumble forward and hope no one fell over.

Outside, I hustled back to the van, my clothes dripping wet, my fingernails blue, my teeth clenched to fight the shivers. Once inside I stripped off my clothes and jumped into both sleeping bags and shook for two hours. When finally warm again I changed into dry clothes. And then I climbed behind the wheel and got myself back on the road and away from the Kentucky Derby.

I drove up I-65 through a rain and lightning storm. Intermittent flashes of straight white light joined earth to sky and lit the world with a frightening incandescence. I didn't stop until I reached Indianapolis, where I parked in the back lot of a Howard Johnson Motor Lodge and slept the night.

The new day, although clear and sunny, didn't dawn bright for me. I still swirled with emotion, tugged in two directions at once. I'd left Louisville too hastily; I never wanted to see the Derby again.

I ate at a Denny's Restaurant, read a newspaper to find out who won the race (Sunny's Halo), and decided to drive back down to Louisville. I was being unfair to the Derby, and I had a week to spare before the volleyball championships next week in Memphis. But the van wouldn't start. That sealed it. Fuck the Derby; fuck the van. I had the van towed to a Triple-A garage—the problem was minor—and continued to Chicago. Irene Sullivan was at work when I got to her apartment, so I let myself in with the keys she'd given me. When she got home I told her all about the Derby. (You wouldn't believe . . .)

Then I relaxed.

* * *

> *In rugby we play for two reasons. One is individual. It keeps you fit, you're active, you enjoy the game. It's wide open; it's running. In football you're controlled by a coach who sends in the plays and shuttles people in and out. In rugby you got fifteen people playing two 40-minute halves and they've got to do it. So secondly it's the team. You play for yourself and the team. No one else. There's no coaches and no on in the stands.*

I found the National Rugby Championships by accident. On Thursday before the tournament I paid homage to the game of baseball by going to Wrigley Field to watch the Cubs against the Phillies.

I sat in front of three generations of salesmen who should have been at work. The young guy was big and round. The middle-ager had thinning gray hair and wore glasses. The first-generation salesman was the other two guys' distributor. He sported a handlebar mustache and a plaid driving cap. They were arguing when they first sat down, each trying to find the best rationale for being at the game and not at work. I turned around to commiserate, hoping a conversation might develop.

"He's been good to us," the young one said to me as he motioned to his distributor. Like if he could convince me then they'd all be off the hook. "We figured we'd take him to a game, buy him a couple of beers. You pat my back, I'll pat yours, you know?" Sounded good enough for me. The middle-ager laughed.

"When I got up this morning I put on my sweater. No suit coat today. Boss is out of town. This is a Cubs day." The truth confronted, the rationales ceased and they ordered their first round of Old Style beer.

The middle-ager was Bill. He was the one who told me about the rugby tournament. Right after I told him where I was from and what I was doing and he came back with the standard reply.

"Fairbanks? Alaska? No shit! You know, if you're really traveling around the country like you say you are, the thing you got to see . . ." That, too, had become part of the Standard Reply: the recommended sport, the one event I *had* to attend.

"If you're really doing what you say you're doing," Bill told me, "then you can't miss rugby. Those boys are nuts." I wanted to see the Bucks against the Sixers in the play-offs in Milwaukee, or if that was impossible head down to Indianapolis for the first day of 500 qualifying. Still, it was a good tip. I filed the information.

I turned around and stood for the national anthem. Susan Anton, opening at a local club that night, did the honors and ran through the song in less than a minute. Then Pete Rose stepped into the batter's box.

"I hate that fucker," Bill said. "But I'll always pay money to see him play." Bill stood up. "Hey Pete, how's the Grecian Formula 44? Lettin' your hair turn gray because your wife's got you back in court? Tryin' to show the judge you're too old to be makin' the big money anymore?" He sat down, cackling.

"We're what Elia called the five-and-ten-cent fan," Bill said, slapping me on the back. At the end of April, Lee Elia, the Cubs' manager, had blasted the fans. "He said the people who come out and boo are all the people who are unemployed, the bums who don't know any better. They just come out to the park every once in a while, get drunk and boo. He's still payin' for that remark."

In the second inning Bo Diaz hit a solo home run to give the Phillies a 1–0 lead. The third and fourth innings passed quickly, forcing the salesmen to gulp their Old Styles to keep pace. I spent the time falling in love with Wrigley Field. The brick walls behind the plate. The people watching the game from the roofs beyond the stadium. The ivy-covered outfield walls were so many brown sticks this early in the season, but that hardly mattered. This was baseball the old-fashioned way. During the seventh inning stretch eight thousand people stood, turned around, and looked up at the press box where Harry Caray sang "Take Me Out to the Ball Game" with all his heart and soul. I was experiencing the game as it was meant to be played.

"We've never come to a bad ball game," Tom, the young one, said. "This place is a salesman's paradise. Our customers love to come to Chicago. Who wants to see a game on a Sunday afternoon? Play the game during business hours. I wouldn't want to live in city with a team that only played at night." Bill choked on his beer.

"There ain't no fuckin' way we shouldn't have a domed stadium in this city," he sputtered. I considered moving quickly lest Wrigley Field rise up in swift retribution and kill us all with a falling column. "No way am I going to go out and watch a football game in three feet of snow. But you know why we don't have a dome? Politics. Goddamn politicians. Politics are changing in this city, but the machine still controls everything. I'll bet you there's been fourteen commissions to study a dome and we still don't have one. Eight million people in the metropolitan area and we still don't have a dome. That's shit."

"Why don't the Sox have the same kind of following the Cubs have?" They looked at me askance.

"You haven't been to the south side yet, have you?" Tom said.

"The south side is why the Cubs are Chicago's team," Bill said. "What happens when you first move to Chicago? Like me. I wanted to go to a ball game so I went with somebody I knew. Naturally they're going to take you to a Cubs game. Chicago needs a dome if for no other reason than to get the Sox out of the south side."

Keith Moreland walked to open the bottom of the fifth. Ron Cey doubled, but Moreland stopped at third. Bill was disgusted. Jody Davis hit a sacrifice fly to right. Bill watched Moreland cross home plate, then muttered obscenities to himself. Ryne Sandburg scored in the sixth to put the Cubs up 2–1, but no one was writing home to momma.

"This town wouldn't know what to do if the Cubs started winning," Bill said. "But if they ever do this town will go nuts. Crazy. Pack this place every day."

Al Holland relieved for the Phillies in the seventh inning with the Cubs leading 3–1. "That catcher's going to earn his money now," Bill said, pointing at Diaz as he warmed up Holland. "He's going to feel every pitch. I remember when I played baseball as a kid . . ."

"Wait a minute," the distributor said, breaking a long silence he'd been filling with beer. "They played baseball before World War I?"

"World War I? Shit! Abraham Lincoln was the pitcher!" They all cackled. "There was a kid I played with whose catcher's mitt was so worn out there was a hole right in the middle of his hand. If he didn't catch the ball in the pocket, watch out. Back when they wore *mitts*."

"Yeah," the distributor said, wiping beer from his mustache, "just little things. Paper. That's all we had."

"Now what do they got? These goddamn baskets. How can anybody make an error these days wearing those things? And with all the money they make, too. Cey hasn't done shit this year. He's too busy trying to figure out how to invest all that money. He's not worth it."

Cey had already doubled and singled and scored a run. In the eighth he blocked a Gary Maddox line drive with his chest.

"That's exactly what Cey needed," Bill said, not missing a beat. "Get the confidence back up. You know," he said, suddenly solicitous, "it must be hard coming over from the kind of team he was used to playing on. A winner. Now he's with the Cubs. They're paying him all that money but they're finding that he can't bee-bop alone. Who else on this team came from that kind of winning attitude? Larry Bowa? Last year he sucked, too."

The Phillies scored twice in the eighth but the Cubs won 6–3. Teachers from the Michigan Christian School rounded up their charges. They'd been sitting in front of us keeping the ice cream vendors busy.

"I think that's great," Bill said motioning toward the students. "Every kid should get to see at least one baseball game in his life. Get to see some real entertainment. Wrigley Field is the perfect escape. I mean, you come out here, eat a couple of hots dogs, drink a couple of beers. Hey, Susan Anton sang the national anthem; that was a nice surprise. Baseball is the perfect entertainment."

In rugby a big hit doesn't mean that much. In football one yard can make all the difference. In rugby, unless you're right down by the goal, what's the big deal if you give up a couple extra yards when you make a tackle? In football coaches tell you to put your nose in the guy's numbers. They go crazy over the big hit. After the second week of the season I'd have two black eyes for the rest of the season. In rugby you tackle with your shoulders and go with the man. Again, what difference does it make if he gets an extra yard or two? The idea is to make the stop, not make the big hit.

Saturday afternoon was a miserable day to watch two games of rugby. The rain was unrelenting. Twice I returned to the van to change into dry and warmer clothes. The wind buffeted the left side of my face and I had an earache by the end of the day. Yet I was glad I'd taken Bill's advice: Ya don't know nothin' about rugby, but what the fuck, right?

Right. And I couldn't get into the Bucks-Sixers play-off game, and Indy qualifying had been rained out. So I looked in the phone book under rugby. Sure enough: Rugby Football Union. I got a recorded message: "The Michelob National Rugby Championships will be held this weekend at Winnemac Stadium located at Damon and Foster Avenues in Chicago. The four participating clubs are the Chicago Lions, Dallas Harlequins, Boston Rugby Club, and the Berkeley Blues. Games start at 1 P.M. Saturday and 11 A.M. Sunday. A block party Saturday night at 6 P.M. Live band, food, and drink. Free admission."

The block party sold me.

Dallas beat Boston in the first semifinal. The Old Blues of Berkeley beat the Lions in the second, a game everyone told me was the de facto championship because only the Lions could come close to the Blues. I was also told that both semifinals involved much more kicking than usual because the rain made ball handling difficult. I could only nod and take people at their word. My familiarity with rugby began and ended with the scrum, surely the strangest invention of sport. Ten players on each team formed themselves into a locked unit by wrapping arms around shoulders and sticking heads between thighs and arms between legs and grabbing hold of each other's shirts. They then bent over and rammed heads with the opposing team, which was similarly intertwined. The scrum became a forty-legged spider with a life of its own as it crawled around the field. And then suddenly the ball popped out and those not involved in the scrum took off running while the scrummers tried to untangle themselves one from the other.

> *In rugby I'm in better shape. In football, what lineman do you know who can run all out for two 40-minute periods? None. In rugby, I can't lift as much and I only weigh 200, down from 220 in football, but I'm in better shape. In football they have to have oxygen on the sidelines.*

Rugby must be a game of infinite subtlety and precise delight. Why else do nations risk international censure by playing the South African Springboks? But watching my first game I was struck only by how obvious and brutish and devoid of finesse the game appeared to be. The object, of course, was to cross the opposing team's goal line. How that was accomplished I couldn't say. Except that the Old Blues were obviously the best at doing it.

The program offered scant assistance but was delightful reading:

> The forwards deliver the ball to their backs, who advance with speed and cunning, passing it from one to another, or not, as the passion takes them. . . .
>
> If you want to appear to know what's going on when someone questions a referee's call, mumble "advantage" and shuffle away thoughtfully. . . .
>
> Armour is prohibited; there is nothing under a rugby shirt but steaming flesh. . . .
>
> It is, you see, a handling game. Rugby is an amateur sport played for its own sake. The beer is incidental.

Certain elements did make sense. Players were numbered consecutively one through fifteen, which permitted quick identification of positions: props, hooker, lock forwards, breakaways, scrum half, centers, wings, and fullback. (Not that I knew what they did.) When players crossed the goal line they scored a "try," which said it all. They were also required to touch the ball to the ground, a nice bit of dramaturgy integrated into the flow of the game and not just so much dancin' in the end zone à la American football.

In essence, what I'd gotten was a quick vacation to Mother England. Even the weather cooperated. The skies were dark with rain and heavy with wind. Winnemac Stadium was old and dank, a red brick structure in a working-class neighborhood of red brick row homes. Across from the stadium was a large red brick school with a huge smokestack that shot into the sky. The school became a factory and the stadium's environs a hardscrabble industrialized city in northern England. While all around us howled a vicious blow off the North Sea, we enjoyed a spot of weekend sport—cheering mightily for our boys to fight fiercely for pride and honor—before returning to the grim realities of weekday factory life.

The block party furthered these intentions. The Chicago Lions, tournament host, seemed intent on out-Britishing the British, if such was possible. The clubhouse was painted black, the color of the Lions Rugby Club. Even the aluminum siding was black, a syrupy coat laid on thick and heavy. Inside, the walls were covered with framed photos of past Lion teams. A television played a videotape of today's games. Rugby was all the TV was allowed to play, a woman told me, unless the Cubs ever made the Series. Behind the bar were mementos of the Lions' international sojourns. Up on a shelf was an old wicker-backed wheelchair. At the end of the year it was awarded to the Lion who'd accumulated the most injuries. And despite everyone's insistence that rugby was safer than football, there were plenty of contenders. One guy's leg was encased in a jointed plastic cast. I counted five guys with their arms in slings nursing the classic rugby fracture, the broken collarbone. Three more guys had broken arms, and one guy, completely bald—difficult to grab hold of, I guessed—looked like he had a good-sized onion stuck under his left eyelid.

The atmosphere of the club was relaxed comaraderie based on an equality created by the shared love of rugby. It didn't matter if a Chicago Lion played on the club's first side or the fifth, all the Lions talked of today's defeat in the first person. And players from all four teams in the tournament mixed easily, drinking beer and talking rugby, everyone wearing shirts and ties and blazers in team colors with emblems on the coat pockets. A gathering of well-groomed, young white professional gentleman. It was *Chariots of Fire* in Chicago, with music by the Blues Brothers.

> *I spend so much time on rugby that it better be pretty important to me. If I thought about it I'd probably quit playing. I wake up Sunday morning after playing and I'm pretty beat up. I spend a lot of time training. My social life ends up revolving around it. The parties are here, the people I know are here. It's a real good group of guys. I like being a Chicago Lion. It sounds kind of crazy, but it's very important to me. I'm proud of it. I was changing jobs this year. I work in finance and most of the opportunities are in New York. I thought about going, but one of the reasons I stayed was because of this club.*

Sunday, the weather broke. It was, in fact, so clear that as I turned onto Lake Shore Drive on my way to Winnemac, the view of the city skyline was so sharp and precise it literally took my breath away.

The weather also changed the nature of the championship round. Today's games exhibited more of the ball handling that rugby professed to be all about, and less of yesterday's kicking strategy. A player would carry the ball, and then, on the verge of being tackled, he would lateral it to a teammate. And so the ball proceeded across the pitch, the action sweeping as much right to left as it did up and down the field. All of which didn't conceal the fact that the championship game was everything it was promised to be: lousy. The Old Blues pummeled Dallas, 23–0, "propelling the ball," as the program put it, across the goal line seemingly at will.

After the game, I returned to the Lions' clubhouse to drink more Michelob and eat the best Polish sausage this side of Krakow. The Boston and Berkeley teams departed for the airport, which left the traditional postmatch rugby bash in the hands of the Chicago Lions and Dallas Harlequins. The old saw about "losing the match but winning the party" was, however, vociferously denied by all participants as a bad rap promulgated by college rugby "kids." To add teeth to this contention, a number of Chicago players talked some Dallas players out of mooning the crowd while singing a song rich in rugby lore and full of filthy lyrics.

But if these ruggers disavowed the party line, they embraced fully and defended staunchly their position as the last bastion of true amateur athleticism. "We receive no compensation," is how they liked to put it. This attitude made the *Chariots of Fire* imagery all the easier to accept. They played their sport and sacrificed their bodies for the love of the game. Nothing else. A quaintness that would have been embarrassing had it not been so passionately professed.

> *In football, it's the pyramid thing. At each level more players get eliminated. From high school to college, players get eliminated. By the time you're twenty-two, if you're not a superstar you become sedentary. Your idea of sports is to pop two beers and watch the NFL on Sunday. In rugby, you can compete. It's a good outlet. It's a competitive sport played at a very high level. It's pure sport. In football, I never touched the ball. All I did was tackle. In rugby I tackle and run with the ball. I wish when I was little I'd learned to play rugby instead of football.*

* * *

It was Monday afternoon by the time I left Chicago. Volleyball started tomorrow and I could delay no longer. Illinois 57 was a table with bushes on either side, so flat that all I could see right in front of me was what was right in front of me. It wasn't until late afternoon, just south of Orchard Lake and one mile north of Lick Creek Road, that I finally came over a hill. The sudden appearance of a real vista after all those monotonous miles made me shout out loud.

To pass the time, I counted the cardinals that zipped across the road in front of me, gossamer strands of red light that flew past and disappeared. The last twenty miles of 57 into Cairo the seams between the pavement were filled with macadam, which produced a rhythmic pounding in the van that kept knocking my foot off the gas pedal. There were thirteen cardinals in the final thirteen miles to the Missouri border.

By the time I reached the Mississippi River the sun was a red rubber ball framed inside the passenger window. In Missouri, Route 55 was lined by gravel flood levees. A helicopter crop-dusting a field flew next to me ten feet off the ground and matched my speed. When it reached a line of telephone poles it jerked itself into the air and spun around on its own axis, the rotors going so slowly I could almost follow them one at a time. Then it started back down the field away from me, a giant dragonfly tracking the field.

Arkansas in darkness. (Welcome sign: "Home of Miss America and Miss USA.") Everything flat, an occasional cluster of lights in the distance. Twenty-three miles north of Memphis, Route 55 was coconut brown. Not pavement brown, coconut brown. And then I crossed the Mississippi River for the second time and drove into Memphis, Tennessee.

Too much heat, too much humidity, too much volleyball. And too many good-looking women. Who's complaining?

Most of the volleyball games were played at the Millington Naval Air Station, thirty miles north of Memphis. In a converted airplane hangar, six games were played at the same time, the courts separated by huge fishing nets. The games started at 8:00 in the morning and weren't over until after midnight. It was the only possible method of selecting national champions in five divisions totaling 157 teams in just five days.

The two large doors at each end of the hangar were kept closed because of glare and wind. So to walk inside was to crawl inside a warm sponge. With six games being played simultaneously, there were seventy-two players on the courts, another seventy-two warming up, and a third set of seventy-two cooling down. All the time. Players' shirts soaked with sweat before they even took the court. The air was heavy and I never figured out how the players were able to breathe. And yet the place never smelled. Or maybe I just got used to it quickly.

The space not occupied by all that humidity was filled with the sounds of all that volleyball happening all at once. The squeal of rubber-soled shoes on varnished floors, the shriek of skin peeled against wood. The slap of hand on ball, the smack of ball on floor. A permanent hum of people talking, shouting, celebrating volleyball. And the thunderous ka-doink of the monster smash: hand hitting ball and ball hitting floor as two parts of one sound. I'd turn in time to see six players standing on the court, frozen in place, while the ball rocketed off the floor between them and drove itself to the ceiling.

The tournament was broken into five divisions, men's and women's open, men's and women's seniors, and men's Golden Masters. There were forty-eight teams each in the men's and women's open. The tournament format was logical and orderly, but impossible to follow, especially in the early rounds when everyone was playing all the time. So I melted into the bleachers and immersed myself in all that heat, humidity, and volleyball.

And all those good-looking women. There must be an ordinance or something that permits only extremely attractive, wildly athletic-looking women to play volleyball. Or maybe it's the game that makes them look that way. Anyway, the Beach Boys know whereof they sing.

It was also easy to believe there was a law mandating that everyone look like everyone else. All those California-type gods and goddesses cut from the same mold. A white-bread homogeneity that had sprung everyone from identical suburban backgrounds. This made it easier to think there was also a law prohibiting participation by black volleyball players.

Volleyball is one of the last bastions of white athletic dominance, a fact not lost on the participants at the air station. It was generally conceded that blacks were better athletes than whites. "Us whites just aren't as good in athletics," was the way it was phrased, but it worked hard to denigrate the relative worth of being an athlete. Being an athlete was fine, but the implication was clear that "our best athletes," as blacks were euphemistically labeled, were chasing after the only goal they were capable of achieving. "Blacks may be stupid but they sure can jump," that sort of thing. I'd discovered this attitude throughout the trip, but with the color ratio so obviously reversed here, it was given a much louder, more confident voice. (That I was in Tennessee was incidental; the hangar was filled with people from all around the country.) The goal of athletic superiority was deemed inherently inferior, and was attainable only by those who could achieve nothing else. That this thinking was a defense mechanism to explain the dominance by blacks of athletics was ignored. "Us whites" had loftier ambitions and possessed the wherewithal to achieve them.

The subject of more black volleyball players appeared to be an open-and-shut case. A few more black women to increase the talent pool, but that's it. People seemed content to preserve volleyball as a glorified amateur sport played by white suburban boys and girls. Keeping it amateur was the key. Reducing the economic incentive guaranteed that America's Best Athletes would stick to basketball, which was okay because hoops had been lost to the blacks a long time ago anyway.

At the same time, some people fairly salivated at the thought of Our Best Athletes playing volleyball. The prospect of a Julius Erving or a David Thompson soaring over the outstretched hands of a Russian block was just too wonderful a thought not to consider. Of course, as one guy noted, "You could only put five blacks out on the court at the same time. You'd still need one white setter to do their thinking for them."

Of course.

Thursday night after the first round was completed, I decided to pin myself to one team for the second round. I needed an anchor. I chose the California Junior Girls, although it wasn't until midway through their second second-round game that I realized the lecherous implications of my following a group of sixteen- and seventeen-year-old girls. I stilled those thoughts by maintaining that I'd chosen them with the hopes of seeing future Olympians in action, which was the truth.

That I'd chosen a women's team over a men's team was, of course, no accident. From a spectator's standpoint there is no better team sport to watch than women's volleyball. Period.

The game of volleyball is the quintessential team game. In most instances, a team can establish no dominance over its opponent until the ball has been touched by 50 percent of its team members. There can be no big hit without the perfect set, and no set without the well-placed pass. In basketball, one person can control a game. The better the supporting cast the better that person will be, but in basketball one player can take charge of a game and shape it in his or her own image.

Not so in volleyball.

Of course, all this held for men's volleyball, too. But the men suffered the onus of being almost too overpowering. All the best men's teams had at least three players capable of putting the ball on the floor at 100 miles per hour. When a team had its back against the wall, the big whips took over. These plays received my undivided attention, but the cumulative effect was anesthetizing. When the very best teams squared off, the scores remained close, but the games crept forward by increments, the action a staccato series of serve, bump-set-spike, side-out repetitions.

Not so the women. For once the athletic stereotypes that plague female athletes worked to their advantage. Their game wasn't as fast or as powerful, the ball wasn't hit quite as hard, it didn't travel quite as fast, and there were few big whips capable of putting down the sure thing. But there was more passing, more blocking, more finesse, more all-around athleticism. There was more going to the floor to attempt the impossible save—and more making it, too. Defense was a precious commodity. There could be no success without a total commitment from all six women. Rallies were long and play continuous. Rarely did a spike overwhelm the opposition, but time and again incredible saves and unbelievable recoveries would be strung together. I delighted in these moments, wishing they could last forever. That only one team could receive the point after these agonizingly long exchanges seemed decidedly unfair.

Steve George was the coach of the California Juniors. I found him Friday morning sitting on a rolled-up wrestling mat in the corner of the hangar. The Cal Juniors were on the court warming up. Across the net was a team from Hawaii, the defending national champion.

"If their middle hitter was here I'd say our chances would be zero," he said. But their middle hitter was still in Hawaii. "Without her here our chances are pretty good. Actually, we've already reached our goal. We wanted to get to the second round. I'd say our chances of getting out of the second round to the final eight are about 30-70. Our chances of winning the tournament are about 99 to 1 against us. But you never know. I figured we had a 50-50 chance of getting this far, so who knows. We could go 0-3 in the second round but if we play well, then this week's been a success.

"The big problem with the Juniors is inexperience. You just never know how they're going to do. We can probably beat any team here. But we can also get blown out by any team here, too."

Hawaii jumped to a quick 5–0 lead on poor serve reception by the Juniors. At 6–0 the Juniors finally got to serve, but the ball hit the net and Hawaii served again and picked up another point. At 7–0 the Juniors got the serve back again, but once again the ball hit the net. Then they started to rally, although they remained unsettled. With the score 11–7 Hawaii, the Juniors built some momentum but then served into the net again. At 13–8 Steve called time-out. They lost the first game 15–8 on a soft spike that caught the whole team out of position. They lost the second game 15–7 but played much better, a couple of times making the big save or getting the big block when all seemed lost. Steve was pleased. After all, Hawaii was the defending national champion.

"If we play that well in our next two matches I'd venture to say we'll beat both teams," he said.

The Juniors' second match was played at Millington High School, another tournament site where a few games were scheduled. After four days in the hangar, the high school gym was like walking into a stiff breeze after a week in a steam bath.

According to Steve, his job was to take good high school volleyball players and turn them into some of the very best players in the nation, fully capable of starting as freshmen on the best college teams in the country. From this year's team, one girl would be going to USC and another to UCLA. All but one of the rest, he figured, would start as freshmen wherever they went.

This was Steve's second year with the Cal Juniors after two years coaching at a junior college and one year each as an assistant at USC and Arizona State. He was only twenty-eight, which surprised me. That seemed extremely young to be coaching one of the high-powered junior programs in the nation. There was only one other junior team at the nationals, the Orange County Juniors. The rest of the teams were thinly disguised college teams and powerful club teams with a sprinkling of former Olympians and national team members and pros from the now defunct International Volleyball League.

"This tournament is easily the most prestigious in the nation," Steve told me. "First of all, so many teams come here, and secondly, the team that wins this can probably beat the NCAA champion.

"I work closely with Arie Selinger, the coach of the women's national team, developing the same kinds of skills he works on. I haven't coached any future members of the national team yet, but someday I think I will. I coached Tracy Clark last year, and she went to USC and was the MVP of the national tournament as a freshman. Arie says right now she's the only girl playing in college who has the skills to play on the national team. She's amazing. She's a man in a woman's body. She can do things no other woman can even come close to doing."

The Juniors were crushed 15–3, 15–3 in their second match. Steve remained expressionless and impassive on the bench, in part because international rules prohibit bench coaching. But it seemed to be his style anyway. During the games he just sat and watched, his chin resting in his hand, his elbow resting on his knee. He maintained the same position throughout the third match of the second round, another shellacking that left the girls looking to be the juniors they really were.

"Sometimes I think I'll be quitting coaching in two days," Steve said. And then he apologized for his team's performance, saying I'd seen them play two of their worst games they'd played all season.

"Was that the problem?"

Steve wasn't sure. "We play in a power league against open players and we go to a lot of tournaments. By the time we get here the competition shouldn't be a problem. We've seen it before.

"What is a problem is being away from home for more than a weekend. I try not to have too many rules, but they can't go anywhere unless I know where, and, of course, they can't drink because they're underage. I'm not checking up on them every minute, but if they break the rules and get caught they don't play anymore."

"Where do you take them from here?"

"Our big tournament is the junior nationals," he said. After that tournament in June, their season would be over. There would be a graduation—a picnic, actually—for the girls leaving the program and going off to school. Come September, it started all over again.

"I do try to build rapport with the girls. I try to develop the whole person. There are a lot of things that are more important than volleyball. I'm always telling them they have to be aware of the outside world. I have an eighteen-page booklet that I give all my players that tells them how to pick the right school. They're picking their school for volleyball, of course, but all my players have gone to good academic schools and have gotten good grades, except one.

"Sometimes I wish I could be closer, just be their friend. But I have to make demands, get down on them when they're not playing well. If I'm too close to the players, they'll think I'm getting down on them personally and not just the part of them that is a volleyball player."

We walked outside. It was early evening, and the sun had turned the sky a soft magenta, the last light before darkness descended. Steve's girls were in the van waiting for their coach to drive them away. "They come to me hoping to become one of the best volleyball players in the nation," he said. "It's my job to do that. If they don't hate my guts at least a couple times during the year, then I'm not doing my job."

I left Memphis Monday morning. The finals on Saturday had played according to script. The Outrigger Canoe Club of Hawaii shocked Nautilas Pacifica in the first game, 15–9, but in the next two games form reverted to shape and Nautilas overpowered the Outriggers 15–11 and 15–4 to take the title. The women's open final was, of course, a pure delight. Syntex, from Stockton, California, beat the Fish Market of Palo Alto, 15–11, 11–15, 15–10, and 15–11. It should have been the featured match.

Leaving the Holiday Inn parking lot, another of those undefinable van noises appeared, this time a mysterious knocking noise from somewhere deep inside the engine. I looked for a service station and found Elrod and Son at the corner of Crump and Mississippi. Eddie, a short, round black man wearing a straw hat with a brown band, listened to the engine.

"That ain't nothin'," he said. Music to my ears. "That's just a lif'. Just a lif', a little valve down at the bottom of the engine. Probably just lost its prime. How far you goin'?"

"Indianapolis." The 500 was Sunday.

"Far enough. You travel about a hunret miles at high speed and you'll get it right back up. Get it up. No problem."

Eddie was right. The knocking noise was gone before I hit the interstate.

Only I was on the wrong interstate. North on 55 instead of 40 and then 65 to Louisville. To remedy that I'd have to take the Kentucky Parkway, but that was a toll road. So I paralleled the parkway to Route 65, taking 155 to 51 in Tennessee, then 45, 80, and finally Route 68 in Kentucky before hitting the interstate again.

An unexpected bonus, an opportunity to see the America I'd been missing as I cruised the interstates in my haste to be getting there all the time. In South Fulton, I bought a quart of grape juice. West Hardin High School was holding its graduation. Between Brewers and Hardin, I counted twelve guys on riding lawnmowers. They became the same guy, cutting the same lawn, riding the same red lawnmower and wearing the same yellow shirt and red hat. I gave Stephensburg an extra salute for spelling Stephen correctly, with the "ph" instead of a "v."

I had a few days to kill before the 500, so I stopped in Louisville to write an article about the Golden Masters Volleyball Tournament for *American Way* magazine. And give the city a second chance. But the first morning a sharp pain in my right side woke me up and grew worse as the day wore on. I didn't have the money for a doctor, so I decided to hang on until I got to Chicago.

I spent the time writing the article and reading *Five Seasons* by Roger Angel. At night, I slept in the parking lot of the Holiday Inn south of town. Worried about stumbling barefoot into the lobby at three in the morning with a burst appendix, I wrote a note and stuck it in the shirt pocket of the hospital greens I wore for pajamas.

In part it read:

> I have Blue Cross and Blue Shield. . . . My wife is currently living in New York. . . . I own a brown Dodge van, license plate 7238ARF. . . . I was sleeping in your parking lot . . . sorry about that. BUT I AM NOT A BUM. Call Roger Brigham, sports editor of the *Anchorage Daily News,* for reference. My wife's phone number is . . . . Only call her if I can't later.
>
> Thank you.

* * *

I survived Louisville. And once in Indianapolis I wanted to be back in Louisville. Back at the Derby, even. Because the Derby is a genteel, southern picnic compared to the Indianapolis 500.

I got to the Speedway Friday night. The famous "rounded rectangle" had already assumed its position as the center of the universe, and the rest of existence was affixing itself in orbit around it. Sixteenth Street, a six-lane highway that fronted the short straight between turns one and two, was being transformed into a two-day souvenir shop.

I tried to walk around the Speedway but stopped halfway down Georgetown, the road that paralleled the front straight. There were too many people and too many cars. Besides, the track was a $2\frac{1}{2}$-mile oval. So I hung out on Georgetown, joining the ranks of people leaning against the recreational vehicles that lined the road, drinking beers as they were offered to me, and watching the passing parade.

The 500 scene begged comparison to the Derby, but the 500 was the Derby times ten with a harder, steelier edge, the entire atmosphere charged and hovering near the flash point. Cars had an importance all their own, their throttled power pouring high-octane energy into everybody. And then there were all those bikers. And all those cops. They were everywhere—cops and bikers—an irrefragable presence that invited confrontation.

I walked back down Georgetown to the White Castle Hamburger Palace stuck on the corner where Georgetown and Sixteenth Street came together to create a traffic jam. There were cars going in all directions at once, it seemed, and I decided they were driven by people under very heavy influence. When I reached the 500 Center, a shopping plaza across from the Speedway, I retreated into the parking lot to get myself as far from the street as I could.

And found Art from Connecticut. I had to laugh. The last time I saw him at the Derby he'd said, "See ya in Indy." Yeah, right, I'd said, you and a million other people. Now here he was again hustling T-shirts. I helped him round up the shopping carts he'd collected for his workers tomorrow. He had the carts hidden down a side street behind a truck. When we got there a guy was trying to steal them. Art chased him off.

"How'd you make out at the Derby?" I asked. The torrential rain must have washed away the final blowout.

Art laughed. "I got arrested." he said. "Remember those fuckin' cops givin' me a hard time?" I did. I also remembered Art giving the cops a hard time, too. "They arrested me for not having my cart up on the curb. They took me down to the station and kept me there till the race was over, then let me go. This one guy says to me as I'm leaving, 'I told you we were going to get you.' 'You got me,' I said, 'and you left at least two hundred sellers out there breakin' the law. Big fuckin' deal.' I was supposed to go back for my hearing but I blew it off. I guess I'm an outlaw in Kentucky now."

Late Saturday morning I went into the Speedway looking for Gasoline Alley, and nearly missed it. I walked through most of it before I realized I was there. It wasn't what I figured Gasoline Alley would be. Two long rows of stables, white with green trim, that could have been borrowed from Churchill Downs. Each driving team had been assigned one stall with two sets of double doors. The only engine I heard was the gentle chug-a-lug of an air compressor. It was all so clean it was almost antiseptic, the crews bedecked in team overalls that they must have laundered every night. There was no gasoline smell, either. And it was all so quiet. Hushed, even. All those spiffy mechanics going about their business with workmanlike efficiency.

I also never saw a car, at least not one whole car. Most were up on lifts, fiberglass skins peeled off and standing in a corner, leaving the insides all exposed. Few had their wheels on. Perched there with their guts hanging out, they reminded me of the old "visible man" plastic models we used to put together in grade school science class.

Once past Gasoline Alley, I walked to the track through the main entrance, the area through which the cars would be pushed tomorrow. There were terrace stands on either side of me. Across the track was the main grandstand. I looked for my seat on the terrace side, down to the right of the starting line.

It was near the pit entrance and close to the top of the stands, which meant I'd see the cars coming out of the fourth turn and all the way down the front straight. I wouldn't lose them until they were well into the first turn. The starting line was maybe a quarter mile to my left, and the large black pole that kept track of laps and car positions was clearly visible. Not a bad seat and pretty close to great. The only problem was that the pits were right in front of me. An exciting view, unless there was an explosion, at which point I'd be fried in a matter of seconds. An eventuality I didn't want to consider, but my proximity to the pits and the large fuel tank for each car made it hard to ignore. I mean, I was right on top of the pits. The stands ended, there was a narrow walkway, a low retaining wall I could have jumped over, and then there were the pits. Right there. *Ka-boom!*

I wasn't the only person scoping the seats for tomorrow's race. Up and down the terrace, people were repeating the process I'd just completed: glance at ticket, locate lettered section, walk up steps onto terrace, glance at ticket, locate aisle. Walk into aisle, glance at ticket, find seat number, turn and look at track. Pass judgment on view, sit down, squirm around a bit, and claim seat. Anticipation built as the ritual progressed step by step until, finally seated, people would rub their hands together, anxious for the race to start.

I climbed to the top of the terrace, turned, and walked toward the finish line. About a hundred yards from the three-foot-wide brick strip of original track that marked the start and finish I stopped, put my hands in my pockets, and leaned against the top rail, content to begin building toward tomorrow. So were the nine guys down on the walkway.

They were scoping for their seats, too, but one guy was holding all the tickets. That didn't matter. They took off running across the terrace seats like grade school kids let out for recess, everyone heading more or less in the same direction as the guy with the tickets. He performed the discovery ritual in a row about three quarters of the way up the terrace. "This is it," he said, and everyone came running.

Their seats were great, and they roared triumphantly. Each received their ticket and then together they stood and surveyed the track, then sat down to stake their claims. And, just like that, it seemed to hit them that they were at the Indy 500. "We are here!" "We are here!" "We are here!" Times nine.

"We're not home watching this one on TV," one of them said, standing up to slap palms with the guys next to him. "We are here!"

"Yeah," another said. "We are here! We'll always be able to say, 'Yeah'—real casual-like—'I was at that one.' "

They were a bunch of guys from Rochester, New York. Most were here for the first time. All but one worked for Xerox. He was the one wearing the Xerox T-shirt. They built the copiers the scientists had put together on paper. They'd rented a motor home for the weekend and were about to take the bus tour of the track. I went along for the ride.

The track was narrow—frighteningly so—and the curves more steeply banked than they appeared from a distance. Heavy black skid marks were etched into the pavement and slid along the track for hundreds of yards before disappearing into the white of freshly painted walls. Each tire mark screamed its own story, a frozen reminder of a moment of terror. That they disappeared beneath a spotlessly clean wall seemed a total disregard for the history of the track.

But it was that claustrophobic confinement between the walls that impressed me the most. The thought of three cars side by side flying down the straight and jockeying for the line into the curve was simply impossible to conjure from inside a bus crawling along at twenty-five miles an hour. Being on the course in this bus seemed an act of sacrilege.

I didn't belong on this track, and I wasn't convinced I was worthy enough to witness those that did. The Indy 500 had captured me completely.

Saturday night, Sixteenth Street was closed. It had been converted into a three-lane parking lot extending from the Speedway entrance, under the railroad overpass and down Sixteenth as far as I could see. The idea was to party all night, drive onto the infield in the morning, and keep on partying till you dropped.

By midnight, the hardness I'd noticed the night before had been sharpened to a razor's edge. The fuse was lit and the world was about to explode. Bikers lined the street, hanging out, waiting, for what I wasn't sure, but I knew I didn't want to find out.

The 500 Center was locked solid with cars; so was the field next to it, where the Rochester copiers had parked their motor home. I walked away from the Speedway, past a bowling alley and under the overpass, past Mike's Place on the right, heading toward the van, which I'd parked for free down a side street.

"Hey, buddy, ya got any beer in that blue bag?" I had a blue and yellow bag. Whoever was asking was talking to me but I couldn't locate the voice.

"Hey, buddy, ya got any beer in that blue bag? Anything but Bud, cain't hardly stand Bud." I looked around.

"*Hey!* Down here. I said, you got any beer in that bag of your'n?"

I looked down. Sitting cross-legged on the curb in front of a chrome-studded motorcycle was a biker. Behind him, face down on a green sleeping bag, was a comatose woman with blond hair and dark roots. Behind her was a gang of choppers, all chrome and shiny paint, parked wheel to wheel in the parking lot of Speedway Auto Parts. "How you doin', buddy?" he said, looking up at me and smiling.

I had no beer but he invited me to sit down anyway. His name was Tim Lyons—"my nickname's Pigmy"—an Irish pug with button nose and ruddy complexion, red beard, and red curly hair. On his head sat a Daniel Boone–style possum hat he'd made himself. He was wearing jeans under a pair of black leather riding chaps. The woman behind him was his old lady. "I should say my wife," he said. "Been married about a year. She'd kill me if she heard me call her my ol' lady."

Tim had been a biker since he was fourteen years old. His daddy had been into motorcycles and turned his son onto the open highway. "I'll tell you what," Tim said, "bein' a biker is freedom. It's freedom all the way. I don't owe nobody nothin'. I got my paper on my bike, I got my paper on my house. I don't owe nobody a dime.

"I'll tell you what." He said that a lot, I'll tell you what. "Once you start, it's like getting sick every year. I just got to ride a motorcycle. There ain't nothin' in the world like gettin' out early in the morning, rollin' up your sleeping bag and throwin' it on the back of your bike and headin' on down the road, lettin' that sun—those heat rays—hit ya right in the face. And all you're doin' is dreamin'. You ain't got nobody there to say hey. Nobody there to say nothin'. You're your own man."

"You ride alone?"

"I've been in three motorcycle clubs. But to me, clubs, all they're doin' is fightin' over their jackets. That's all it is. Hell's Angels, Banditos, Outlaws. They got this conflict to see whose the baddest." So he'd retired, and was now a member of the American Motorcycle Club, a loosely organized clan of other independent bikers.

"There's two types of bikers," he said. There's the Outlaw Motorcycle Association and the American Motorcycle Association. That's something that really needs to be specified."

He was on the road, he figured, six, seven months a year. His wife had two kids from a previous marriage, and they went to school here in Indianapolis. He liked to ride by himself, but he also liked to take the old lady with him whenever he could. "She rides her own," he said. "Like last night, I was wasted over there and I couldn't ride, so she had to ride me home."

I asked how her children liked having a biker daddy. "The last year we've gotten really close as far as family is concerned," he said. "Now the kids, I love 'em like they was my own. They wouldn't even get on a motorcycle before we got married. But they're real proud of what their daddy does now. They got shirts that says: 'My daddy is the biggest and the baddest biker in town, so please, don't fuck with me.' Well, it don't say 'fuck,' you know? It says 'mess.' "

He turned around to check on Lana Turner, which he said was his wife's name. "I got to keep my eye on her," he said. "People around here are gettin' fucked up."

They'd met about fifteen years ago at an A&W Root Beer stand not far from the Speedway. Tim reckoned the year to be 1967 because he was driving a '65 Mustang.

"We ain't been together the whole time we've known each other. I think we always loved each other, off and on for those fifteen years, though. It was just that we was both young then and she wanted to sow some wild oats and so did I. Last May, we met again. Got reacquainted, you know?"

He turned back to the street and crossed his arms around his knees. "Everything a girl can be on the nasty side, she's been it. She's been down the line."

He reached into his wallet. "I'll tell you what," he said. "This will probably be hard to see, but we had a write-up in the paper when we was married. It was all over, cable TV and everything." He handed me a folded clipping from the *Indianapolis Star.* The wedding had been quite the deal. Three hundred independent bikers from three states watched as Tim and Lana "tied the knot" in a driving rainstorm.

"You got married in the rain?"

"Yeah. But that didn't stop none of the bikers."

I read out loud: "The ceremony shattered the usual serenity of the working-class neighborhood."

"There was about a dozen cops come bustin' it up," Tim said. "But we wasn't causin' no trouble at all. Hell, two girls beat the shit out of some guy, that's all that happened."

I wanted to follow up on that, but just then a guy walked past carrying a case of Miller. Tim swapped a couple of hits of Jack Daniels for a bottle of beer. As he was unscrewing the cap, a little kid walked past hand in hand with his father. He was staring at Tim's possum hat but was too shy to come over. Tim took off his hat and placed it on the little kid's head. The hat was way too big, but the two holes where the eyes would have been were perfect for the kid to look through, like it was a furry Batman mask.

"Now you're lookin' good," Tim said, his voice soft and full of tenderness. He took the hat off the little kid's head and steered him gently toward his parents, who'd been smiling bravely as they watched their three-year-old hang out with a biker.

"I think the hell out of my name," Tim said, watching the little boy walk away. "I'll probably want a kid of my own someday, where I can carry on my name, you know?"

The prerace festivities were interminable. I sat in my terrace seat, waiting. There was a snap in the air and the wind was gusting. Few clouds in a blue sky. Good. Zero chance of rain delay.

Rick Mears and Al Unser, Sr., were the race favorites at 5 to 1. Teo Fabi, the Italian rookie, was sitting on the pole, having qualified at 201.395 miles per hour. But Roger Mears, Josele Garza, and Scott Brayton occupied the pit areas directly in front of me, so I passed the time reading about them. They would be my hometown favorites, three to keep tabs on because I had the advantage of watching their particular dramas unfold right before my eyes.

The best of the three was Roger Mears. He'd qualified at 200.018 miles per hour and was starting in the middle of the third row. He was a 23 to 1 shot, according to the *Indianapolis Star*. It labeled him a "sleeper." Garza was his teammate. He was the Mexican driver with the impossibly great looks. In 1981 he led the race for thirteen laps and was named Rookie of the Year for finishing twenty-third. He'd be starting in the sixth row. The *Star* had him at 30 to 1. The odds on Scott Brayton were even worse. He was listed at 40 to 1 and would be starting in the second to last row. "Not a good bet to finish."

So much for hometown favorites.

The parades ended and the bands stopped marching and the cars were finally wheeled onto the track. Jim Hebert sang the national anthem and then Jim Nabors sang "Back Home in Indiana," which was what everyone wanted to hear.

And then everything happened too fast to write it all down:

- "Gentleman, start your engines!"
- "They're all moving!"
- Parade laps slow! The total agony of speed frustrated.
- Green flag!!!
- First lap. Cars out of fourth turn and into straight. No roar. A scream. Screeeeeamm. Pinned me to my seat.
- Teo Fabi through the straight on first lap. I turned to pick up the next car, but the pack was right there. Right there! Seven cars together at 200 miles per hour! Screeeeeamm!!!!!!!
- Third lap: Teo Fabi, the leader, is already at back of rear pack trying to get through.
- Can't focus on one car. Focus on one, lose ten others.
- Teo Fabi just always seems to be there. Every time I look right into turn four there he is.
- "Unsers right together. Father and son."
- A.J.'s in pits. Out of car, out of race.
- Yellow flag. Unser, Sr., no pit stop, takes lead. Yellows are long. Not like on TV where they say, "We'll be right back," and you come back to the race.
- Roger Mears crashed! Crew hanging out, waiting. Announcer says Roger's OK. Crew drifting away. One favorite out.
- Garza: Safety marshal pointed at something on car. Josele back out on course, but back in on next lap. Crew took off top. Josele out of car. Race over. Scott Brayton, number 37, my last favorite.

- Andretti out. Parsons got down low, veered right. Andretti right behind him hit Parsons and went into wall. Another yellow flag. Lap 82 (or is it 92?). Cars bunch together and slow down. Out of sight for so long you forget there's a race.
- Sneva takes lead on lap 107.
- Lap 171. Sneva, Unser, Sr.: one, two. Both into pit on yellow. Guy next to me: "This is it. They'll be going from here on what they got left." Unser out first. Sneva out in thirty-two seconds.
- Lap 178. Order: Unser, Sr., Unser, Jr., then Sneva. One behind other. Jr. is one lap down. Guy next to me: "Jr.'s runnin' interference for the old man."
- Sneva closing on Jr., but can he get to Sr. after that???
- Ten laps to go!!!!!!!!
- Sneva passed Jr.!
- "Sneva—on back stretch—takes first!!!!"
- Jr. passed Sr.! Guy next to me: "Dad's going to have to make it on his own, now."
- Sneva four seconds up. Unser, Sr., won't be able to catch him. Move on lap 190 was the race.
- Last lap!!! Announcer talking Sneva around track: "Turn two . . . Back stretch . . . Three . . . Four . . . Straight . . . *Sneva*!"
- Announcer describing scene in victory lane, but could be describing action in Brayton's pit. Lots of celebration. "Not a good bet to finish" had finished eighth.

I was in no hurry to leave. I had just witnessed the single greatest thrill of the year and I wanted it to last. Everything I'd witnessed in the past few months paled by comparison to the experience of being absolutely welded to my seat in the terrace section of the Indianapolis Speedway a little after noon on Sunday, May 29, 1983. After Teo Fabi had screamed down the front straight at the end of the first lap, I'd turned to my right to pick up the rest of the pack. Only the rest of the pack was all over me and inside my head, jamming me down with the sounds and sensation of power and speed.

During the race I tried to imagine a human being inside the cars as they screamed from right to left in front of me. But I never could. Tom Sneva was a maroon and white number five Texaco Star March-Cosworth racing machine. I had no conception of him as a human being. And yet, I never forgot there was a man inside and slicing past me at 220 miles per hour. The men who raced these cars possessed a quality that would remain forever alien to me. There was something about them that I couldn't, wouldn't, perhaps shouldn't attempt to define. It was their particular gift to push a car at 200 miles per hour around a 2½-mile rounded rectangle of terrifyingly narrow dimensions. My particular duty was to sit there pinned to my seat, struck dumb.

My lack of coherence persisted even after I left the terrace. I talked to Scott Brayton and asked him all the questions he'd been asked a million times before. I know this because he told me so. But I didn't care. This event demanded that those questions be asked: What's it like? Aren't you scared? Sitting in his motor home after the race, Scott didn't seem to mind my pestering, and I was pleased and a bit surprised when the first thing he said about all that speed was "unbelievable." I didn't think racers talked like that.

I walked through the big fence gate one last time, through the alley between the terrace stands where the cars had been pushed to the starting line. The track was deserted, save for an ABC *Wide World of Sports* crew setting up their delayed broadcast. The wind had stiffened. Papers swirled around the track and beer cans clattered down the steps in the stands. The place seemed lonelier than it actually was, because it was impossible to forget how jammed with people and full of drama it had been just a couple of hours before.

Outside the track, I stopped at the Rochester copiers' motor home. They were in a severe state of aftershock, too. The race, for all its buildup, had been over almost before any of them knew it. Now they were desperately trying to party but failing miserably. Two bodies were asleep in the captain's chairs in front, and more bodies were sprawled on the sofas in back. The rest were playing cards. They debated driving to Rochester tonight but gave up that idea quickly. The place reeked of stale beer and shelled peanuts, and there was much discussion that perhaps it would be easier to buy the motor home than clean it up. But mostly they talked about the race, wistfully, as if maybe they hadn't really been here to see it.

"Wait a minute," one of them said, his voice filled with an excitement the others lacked. "Wasn't somebody back home going to Betamax this for us?"

"Yeah, that's right!" All they needed to hear. The race wasn't over. It hadn't even begun. Life breathed itself back into the motor home.

"We can have a party. We'll all get together and have everybody come over who wasn't here and tell 'em what it was like to be there." They'd been given a reason to live again. More important, they'd been give the energy to drive back to Rochester. And they would all be back next year. No question. A tradition had been born. And next year it was $40 tickets.

"What the fuck, $70 tickets."

"Yeah, and a bigger motor home, too."

Good idea.

Friday, June 3, 1983
Amtrak
Denver to San Francisco

The van's parked at Regis College in Denver. I'm on the rails to San Francisco and the U.S. National Fencing Championships. I'll be staying with the mother of friends from Fairbanks. (As added bonus, the friends, Bob and Claire Murphy, will be visiting.) Fencing will last a week, June 6 to 11. I'll stay in northern California till June 19, then head back to Denver, pick up the van, and drive to the Sports Festival in Colorado Springs. I'll leave before the festival is over and bomb to Chicago for the All-Star Game on July 6. Then it's New York City again, after two months on the road. Too long.

That's the plan, but nothing is guaranteed. Roger Brigham is having trouble getting the *Anchorage Daily News* accredited for the festival. I need fencing as subject for an *American Way* article, but if I don't get in the festival, I'll lose June, sportswise, because my train ticket ties me into specific dates.

So right now I'm trying to persuade myself that this "year-in-sports" isn't a dumb idea. I fight this battle periodically, usually after I've been away from home about 3½ weeks. Suddenly, I don't want to be getting to the next event. I want to bag it completely, hang it up, blow it off. I convince myself the trip isn't do-able, that there are too many outside forces conspiring against me. That I'll run out of money or energy or both. That getting into events is left too much to the whim of public relations offices. That the van will finally die.

I'm tired and lonely and feeling sorry for myself. That I've been lucky thus far counts for nothing at times like this. It's still eighteen hours to San Francisco, and the lady across the aisle keeps telling me her husband is sixty-eight today and they're on their way to visit their son in the air force and would I like to see pictures of the grandchildren . . . .

Wednesday, June 15, 1983
Western Airlines
San Francisco to Denver

Begin at the end. Fencing is over. I'm in the air to Denver, on my way to the National Track and Field Championships in Indianapolis. Murph and Claire paid for the flight to keep me on the road.

No credential for the Sports Festival. Roger did everything by the book, but there was no getting in. I think our Alaskan identity worked against us. I'm not convinced public relations people mean it when they say, "How can I help you?" What they're really asking is, "How can you help me?" We can't. The *Anchorage Daily News* is about as far west as Honolulu and 3,000 miles north. Stories that make its pages are too far away to make an event's PR people look good. Unless the idea of coverage by an Alaskan paper strikes their fancy (that worked at the Masters), I've always gathered that they'd just as soon not bother with me at all.

Last week I asked Roger to call Track and Field and request a credential. They said fine. Just one problem: Track and Field is June 17, 18, 19, this weekend. But because I was tied to a train ticket, that meant I could be at an event I couldn't get into (Sports Festival), or I could get into an event I couldn't be at (Track and Field). But then Murph and Claire came to the breakfast table yesterday morning and offered to pay for this flight, and here I am now, overcome by their kindness.

From the Sporting Green of the *San Francisco Chronicle:*

> *Houston Wins in 12th*
>
> ASTROS OUTLAST GIANTS
>
> Garner's Double Keys 3–2 Victory
>
> By Bruce Jenkins
>
> With the fog rolling in, the winds gusting near 40 miles per hour and the Candlestick fans hanging in there, the Houston Astros scored an appropriately dismal-looking run in the 12th inning to beat the Giants last night, 3–2.

Everything they say about Candlestick Park is true. It's a terrible place to play the "summer game." I sat in the upper deck, and from there could see San Francisco Bay. Whitecaps lapped at the foundations of the park, or so it seemed. The fog didn't roll in; it clawed over the top of the stadium and buried us (Carl Sandburg never saw the Giants at Candlestick Park). Seven rows behind me sat a lone spectator. I never saw him move, I never saw his face. He sat inside an old army parka, the hood up and the drawstring closed, peering out at the game through the tunnel created by the ruff.

But we hung in there. Murph and Claire and Murph's brother Billy and Jim Gross, a friend from Omaha visiting California, Karen, a friend of Claire's from Santa Clara, and Meg, a friend of Billy's. And because we did we received the "Croix de Candlestick," the greatest promotional gimmick ever.

All fans who stay to the end of an extra-inning night game at Candlestick receive the Croix, an orange button with the SF logo covered with snow and "Veni, Vidi, Vixi" printed across the bottom. It's presented because "Loyalty and devotion above and beyond the call of fandom have earned you this badge—wear it with pride. Thanks for hanging in there." A tacit admission of how horrible Candlestick can be, a playing to weakness to create strength. Like Colonel Potter said about a scam by Klinger to get out of the army: "It's got a lot of reverse topspin."

Watching baseball in a stadium where pitchers get blown off the mound demands a special devotion. You've got to want a Croix to get a Croix. During the sixth inning, the scoreboard welcomed Jim Smith and party to the sky boxes. The sky boxes, of course, are indoors. Meanwhile, we're outside huddled under blankets. Meg read the board out loud and then shouted, "Well fuck Jim Smith and his party," which pretty much said it for all of us.

Meg wanted the Croix the most. Tom, her husband, had decided not to go to the game, and when Billy picked her up she told Billy that it was a Croix night, that she could feel it. "And I won't let Tommy even touch it." In the eighth inning we wanted to move down lower to get out of the wind (well, sort of out of the wind), but Meg wouldn't let us. "If you want the Croix we've got to stay where we are. We've got to hang in there."

But it was Billy who provided final inspiration. Billy, a red-haired Irishman, isn't so much a baseball fan as a San Francisco Giants fan. He knew all about his team, plus all about everyone on the Astros who used to be a Giant. It was like the whole universe swirled around Candlestick Park, and given prevailing conditions that wasn't difficult to imagine.

In the bottom of the ninth the score was tied and Lee May was at the plate with a chance to win it for the Giants. But what to do? The Croix was within our grasp, and, for the moment at least, I'd had enough beer not to mind the cold. "Never cheer against the Giants," Billy said, slowly and with great care, not so much suggestion as edict. Then he turned philosophic: "If the Croix is to be, the Croix is to be." So we cheered mightily for some Lee May heroics. He flied out. Billy was right. The Croix was to be, but never cheer against the Giants.

* * *

Just two days out of Denver, but I felt like I'd been driving forever. Colorado, Nebraska, Iowa, Illinois, and Indiana. The road in front looking like it did a mile ago. The only monotony breaker was joining a caravan of silver and black corvettes tooling across Nebraska.

Friday night in Indianapolis I picked up my credential at the Atkinson Hotel and was out to the stadium a little past eight o'clock. The stadium looked like an erector set, designed for participation but not much spectating. The west end was dominated by a large scoreboard and clock, and only down the front straight did the stands rise to a height of about thirty rows. The rest of the track was ringed by stands not more than four or five seats high. To get into the stadium, I walked behind the scoreboard. Mary Decker was running away with her trial of the women's 3,000 meter. I could see only half the track, and after she passed it was a good twenty seconds before the rest of the pack came into view.

I walked up into the stands by the finish line. Tonight's activity was heats and trials, so there were plenty of seats. I sat down behind the ABC *Wide World of Sports* booth, which occupied prime real estate halfway up the stands and directly in line with the finish. Jim Lampley, the ABC announcer, and Marty Liquori and Dianna Nyad, the color commentators, were lounging across a couple of rows, spread out with the rest of their crew, watching the early rounds. I decided to try for an interview with one of them, and after the last event I chased down Lampley. We talked for a couple minutes in an ABC trailer. I told him what I was doing. "Oh, sort of like a kaleidoscope, right?" Jim said. I had no idea what he meant but said yes anyway. He told me to meet him tomorrow morning at the Hyatt for breakfast.

Super. An interview with a network broadcaster. I could only hope that ABC Sports would be picking up the tab at breakfast. There were no provisions in my budget for brunches at the Hyatt.

Jim Lampley didn't set out to be an ABC *Wide World of Sports* broadcaster. He graduated from the University of North Carolina with a graduate degree in mass communications and an eye toward politics. He worked as a press aide during a senate campaign for a North Carolina congressman, but while talking to a man in a bar he was offered a radio sports show. At first, Jim said no. "Then he said, 'Fifty dollars for a fifteen minute show,' and I said, 'Yes, absolutely.' "

In 1974 Roone Arledge, the president of ABC Sports, came up with a "gimmick idea"—Lampley's words—to use a close-to-college-age commentator on the Saturday afternoon football telecast.

Jim was chosen in a talent hunt that auditioned 430 people. He was twenty-five years old. "So all of this is accidental."

We met as planned at the Hyatt. The dining room was packed—fortunately—so we sat outside a ballroom. It was 9 A.M. and Jim hadn't shaved yet, but the growth added character to his smooth good looks.

I asked the questions and he answered them, each response totally articulated and impeccably complete. He was knowledgeable but not opinionated, while at the same time obviously comfortable expressing himself. He was also disarmingly candid. I didn't expect that from a network type. The topics ranged wide. Memorable moments: "The Great American Bike Race; I could get five Emmys for that show and that would mean nothing compared to what I already feel about it." Ambition: "If we carry the Olympics in '88 and I'm not the host, I'll be disappointed." Celebrity: "For my own sanity I try not to think of myself as a star."

But mostly we talked about television.

JIM: There are a lot of misconceptions as to the degree to which television controls sports. We are portrayed as the enemy, but I don't think it's fair to paint television as the villain. That's a bit odd when you consider that the so-called power—I prefer to call it influence—that television exerts has in every instance been given or sold to television by the organizers. You can't lay the blame at our feet for something that sports organizers have willingly and eagerly gone along with in pursuit of the almighty dollar. At our best we are simply the most effective medium—to use the word properly—by which the viewer can consume the event with the people in the stadium. A lot is written about the rights of the spectators and how television fouls up their opportunity to enjoy the event. But is it better for 70,000 people to derive 100 percent enjoyment from an event to the exclusion of any enjoyment at all for the 200 million sitting at home, or for 70,000 people to derive 90 percent enjoyment while the 200 million at least have the opportunity to enjoy and understand the same event? If I was a sports organizer I think I'd make the bargain. Particularly when you see how much they're paid to make that bargain.

Q: How would you define yourself?

JIM: In the best of all possible worlds, I'm a sports journalist. And there are times when I get to exercise legitimate journalistic practices and instincts. That's the orientation I bring to my business. But it really wouldn't be honest for anyone in my position to claim that he is always in the position to exercise his best journalistic instincts and practices. There are too many times when we're limited by time considerations; or there are stories which a newspaper would report on a daily basis but which we can't find the proper posture to cover during our programming. When I first started working in sports television, I wanted to believe that American sports fans were intelligent and objective and analytical, and that they wanted to be exposed to issues and controversy and substantial subjects on sports telecasts. Every shred of evidence I've seen in nine years would lead you to believe that that's not the case. When network television executives–jaundiced and jaded though they are–tell you people want action, and see sports events as an escape from real life, I think that's largely true. You have to recognize the commercial motive inherent in sports television: to get as big an audience as possible. If the way to get the biggest audience is to mine the escapism and entertainment value of an event, then that's obviously what you should try to do.

Q: What's your responsibility to the TV viewer?

JIM: To provide the viewer with every shred of information necessary to maximize his enjoyment and understanding of that particular event. But not much more. By and large I agree with people who say the play-by-play man should achieve a limited role. Part of my responsibility is to leave enough breathing space between me and the event and the viewer that he has the option to appreciate it on his own.

Q: On TV are we seeing the real Jim Lampley? Or is that an unfair question?

JIM: No, I think it's fair. I think it's the single biggest pitfall of on-camera television people.

Q: What becomes "real," the image or the off-camera person?

JIM: I think I've always been able to be myself on the air. And I've never felt terribly hamstrung about what I can or will say. I'm doing what comes naturally given the circumstance, recognizing that I have to work within specific limitations. But within those limitations, yeah, I think what you're seeing on the air is the real me. If I think an event is dull, I'm likely to tell you so.

Q: What do you think of the USFL?

JIM: I'd rather not.

Q: Is that a no comment?

JIM: No, no. I'll tell you the truth. I had to cover some of the games, and I don't think I was unfair to the league the first week when I said, "I'm going to have to be shown that this country wants football in the spring."

Q: It sounds like you were asking the viewer to go out and play golf.

JIM: In the back of mind I probably was. I like to see the players get more economic opportunities, but it perplexes me to turn on my television set and see football in the spring.

Q: If the USFL makes it, will that prove that TV does tell us what we want to watch?

JIM: I don't think it will prove anything, necessarily. What it will suggest to me is that in the world of mass media and mass man the natural clock has been blurred, and that traditions can be destroyed. But it's impossible to say if it's the viewer demanding the event or television looking for something to fill hours that's destroying that tradition.

Q: If the USFL makes it, will there be other USFLs?

JIM: Yeah. It will provide more grist for the mills of those who take the limited view that economics is everything.

Q: How important is sports in America?

JIM: Very. Sports nowadays is a very graphic and emotionally important reflection of society. A microcosm of society's values and society's ills. And certainly economically it's a huge business.

Q: How important should sports be in America?

JIM: Oddly enough, I'd say we've got it pretty well in perspective. I think it was out of perspective twenty-five years ago when athletes were treated completely as white knights and heroes. An unrealistic, nonobjective view presented by the mass media and swallowed by the public whole-cloth. Now that we recognize and examine the seamy side as well as the glamor side we've got it in the right perspective.

Q: Despite the fact that the harder-hitting news is difficult to get on the air?

JIM: It's in the papers. It's not covered to the same degree in commercial network television and to a certain extent I don't think that's our job, because it's not what the public demands. There's a large segment of the population that wants their cocaine stories in here [pointing to a daily newspaper] and their tears and glamor on the air.

Q: Standard question: What's your favorite sport to cover?

JIM: Track and Field.

Q: Why?

JIM: Variety, for one thing. You have all sorts of different athletes involved in this sport. At the world-class level we're talking about very, very fine margins making the big difference. The pressure produces a breed of athlete that's high on narcissism, high on hypochondria, and very high on standard athletic neurosis multiplied to the *n*th degree. But also high on athletic intelligence; understanding their own bodies; trying to think carefully about what they're doing and how to go about it. These people are much more individual and much less programmed than, say, figure skaters or swimmers or gymnasts. They are much more deeply self-analytical. They lead a harder, more nomadic life. When the game is over they have to fend for themselves. They lead their own lives.

Q: Can the average sports fan appreciate the kind of life these athletes lead?

JIM: No. And I don't think the average fan is terribly interested, either. There are sports fans who find social conditions and the way an athlete leads his or her life interesting, but not the great masses. But that's the thing that always fascinated me, because to me that's an integral part of sport. To me, unless you understand why Carl Lewis chooses to run and jump where he chooses to run and jump and where the money comes from and why the money goes to him in the ways in which it goes to him—unless you examine all that—you don't really know who Carl Lewis is. To judge that you know who Carl Lewis is because you watched him jump 29 feet 2½ inches is wrong. You don't know him until you've examined all the conditions in which he exists. The great masses are interested in whether he jumped 28 feet 9 or 28 feet 10. That's the limit of their interests. They have a level of interest in personality, but it's superficial. I think they just want to turn the TV on and be entertained.

Everything happened at once. Running, jumping, throwing, hurdling, vaulting, putting, disking.

The field was crawling with officials in blue and white hats. Four for the high jump, eight for the long jump, ten for the javelin, ten for the 100-meter dash, and twenty (I think) for the 110-meter hurdles. Photographers wearing fluorescent orange bibs (ten to thirty, depending upon the significance of the event). And, of course, all those athletes: black and white, big and little, men and women; the variety was exhilarating. Everywhere there were athletes of one shape or another: the shot put circle, the long jump pit, the pole vault strip, the track and the infield. If not competing they hung out in the medical tent getting rubdowns, or behind the scoreboard warming up or cooling down, putting on sweats or taking them off.

Back in San Francisco, I'd seen *Personal Best,* the movie about women pentathletes. The physicality of the track athlete's life as portrayed in the film had overwhelmed me, but I realized now it had been the perfect primer for my seeing the national championships. These were athletes who existed of and for their bodies. They performed very fundamental, very elementary tasks: run the fastest, jump the highest, throw the farthest. The human animal displayed in its purest form. And Lampley had been right when he'd spoken of the track athlete's independent approach to life. Walking around behind the scoreboard I was surrounded by individual entrepreneurs (have body, will run) brought together only briefly by the present challenge of the national championships. When this weekend was over they would disperse in as many directions as there were track meets willing to pay them. Indeed, the dominant topic of conversation behind the scoreboard wasn't tactics or strategy, training techniques, or even injury prevention. It was travel arrangements: the best way to get to Paris, the cheapest hotel in Frankfurt, the easiest way to get from Stockholm to Milan.

The Sunday session, a parade of finals in twenty-three events, started quietly and built momentum slowly. It began with the hammer throw at 2:30. At 4:15 the men's long jump began, and by 7:30, we'd seen or were seeing the women's shot, the men's discus, pole vault, high jump, triple jump, and javelin, as well as the men's and women's 200-meter dashes, 400-meter hurdles, and the women's 1,500-meter run. The final event, the women's medley relay, didn't go off until after 9:30, and it was after 10:00 by the time Willie Banks bounced his way to a triple jump title and Dwight Stones flew over the bar at seven feet six inches to win the high jump.

Keeping pace with all this action was, of course, impossible. But I was lucky. I wound up sitting in front of the editors of *Track and Field* magazine, plus other assorted track and field aficianados who got their kicks wearing digital stopwatches around their necks to time the tries of all the men and women running around the track. ("Who's got the splits on Marsh?") No one was assigned to watch any particular event ("Shot put!" High jump!"), but taken en masse they affected total coverage of the entire field. ("Pole vault! Pole vault!") All I had to do was listen ("Beyers!" "Scott!" "Sidney!") and then look in the direction of their shouted commands and remarks ("Petranoff! Petranoff!"—that meant javelin).

It's the only way to watch a track meet.

The stadium emptied quickly after the 5,000 meter. I sat behind the ABC booth again, and watched Jim Lampley and Marty Liquori call the 1,500 meter, which was being replayed on a monitor. They threw themselves into it energetically, matching the fevered pitch the race itself had generated more than an hour ago. Lampley handled the play-by-play. Facile and precise, and never at a loss for words, he pointed at the screen when making particular points, as if he were standing in everyone's living room highlighting the action for the people sitting next to their coffee tables. Liquori came in with the color, never missing a beat, usually when Lampley put his arm around him. Together they bent down close to the monitor, working off each other to keep their energy levels at the same pitch as the race. And then it was over and they clicked off the television, and with it went their energy. They shook hands and smiled.

"Good call," Lampley said.

CHAPTER 6

* * *

Back in New York City ahead of schedule. I'd planned to stay in Indianapolis until Monday, but Sunday night I was in the rear of the van straightening up the perennial mess, when a man peered through the windshield. His sudden appearance shook me, and I crouched, motionless, as his footsteps circled the van. When he reappeared he was walking more slowly and peering more intently than the first time. Then he disappeared, the crunch of his footsteps only slightly louder than the pounding of my heart, which had suddenly acquired residency in my throat.

I locked the van and hurried into the Howard Johnson Motor Lodge. I hung inside for about an hour. Then I went to the men's room. And there he was again. At least I hoped it was he—Indianapolis doesn't deserve two guys with greasy hair and scraggly beard lurking in the shadows. I split quickly. The last I saw him he was across the street at the Holiday Inn, peeking through the windows of the rooms behind the restaurant.

So it felt very good to be back in New York City. Eight events in seven weeks had proved long enough. I'd pushed myself hard. It was good to be off the road.

But now it was Sunday, June 27, and I was at the National Synchronized Swimming Championships at Yale in New Haven, Connecticut.

The meet was in the Kiphuth Pool of the Payne Whitney Gymnasium building, an imposing rock fortress that looked a hundred years old, but was only fifty-two. The pool was inside a labyrinth of corridors that were interconnected by stone arches, the pool itself at the bottom of a huge hall with steep sides and dark brown, high-backed wooden seats. An appropriate atmosphere to hear a lecture by Dr. Frankenstein, perhaps, but an incongruous setting for an event that smacked of everything Californian.

I arrived in time for the semifinals of the eight-woman team competition. I was immediately disappointed. I'd hoped synchronized swimming would be figure skating with the ice melted, but that was obviously a comparison the swimmers would always lose. In synchronized swimming there were none of the spectacular skating throws that had taken my breath away in Pittsburgh. In New Haven, the chills never splashed down my spine, the physical evidence that what I'd just witnessed was indeed spectacular. The swimmers were locked in the water, looking like they wanted out.

And Kiphuth Hall, with its strong sense of time and place, exuded more character than the women in the water. Everyone looked precisely like everyone else: hair pulled back, impeccably applied waterproof makeup, an aura of excruciating femininity, thirty-two-tooth smiles that refused to quit. That the point of synchronized swimming is for everyone to look alike didn't help at all. Or maybe it helped too much. As far as I could tell, the same eight women were performing all the routines, with but a quick change of bathing suits between each performance.

This quality of sameness intensified on Monday. The women who'd made it to the finals of the solo, duet, and team competition performed their individual, required moves in the afternoon. All the women wore black racing suits, white Speedo swim caps, and goggles. I watched for a while but grew bored quickly, and wasn't the least bit upset when I had to leave to put more money in the two-hour parking meter (is it possible to park in New Haven for more than two hours?). By the time I returned the compulsory event was over.

I wound my way back out, through the gothic hallways connecting the pool to the rest of the world. I was looking for Paula Oyer, the executive director of the United States Synchronized Swimming Corporation. Last night, we'd made arrangements to talk, but today every time I'd see her she was off to yet another meeting. This time she found me.

"Don't go away," she said. "I've got a meeting with the people from Red Lobster and then I'll be free."

"Red Lobster?"

"Yeah. They missed the sponsorship boat when it came time to getting directly involved with the Olympics. Now they're looking for a way to cash in next year in L.A. The next best thing to being involved with the Olympic movement is to be involved with an Olympic sport."

Paula Oyer wasn't what I'd expected of an executive director of a national amateur sports organization. For one thing, she was way too young—twenty-four, and on the job two years already. Even more surprising, she wasn't a synchronized swimmer. In fact, before she accepted the position she'd asked to see some synchronized swimming to see if she'd like it. She did, and she became the first paid staffer of the new corporation.

"I really think they made a wise decision to go outside synchronized swimming," she said. "I know the others could have done a great job, but it would have been different. Their focus would have been on one aspect of the sport, whereas my position is apolitical. I don't get involved in changing rules, I don't say someone is scoring funny. I report to the board of directors like any corporation."

We sat on a bench outside Whitney Hall facing Tower Parkway. A stiff, pleasant wind blew away the heat but kept blowing a few strands of Paula's brown hair into the corner of her right eye. The collar on her Izod shirt was turned up. Her tan midiskirt must have been insufferably hot. A graduate of Indiana, she'd worked for Pepsi-Cola in New York, promoting the Diet Pepsi 10,000 Meter Series before landing with synchronized swimming. She was young, confident, and ambitious, a combination that's not always an asset when you're also female. But she seemed to have found the correct balance. Her ambition reached beyond herself to encompass sports in general and synchronized swimming in particular.

"I went out of my way to be overly competent," she said, "and I think I did a good job in the area they hired me for. I work with publicity and promotion. My philosophy was to set up the organization on an administratively sound basis. We run an efficient organization but our product is a sport instead of, say, soap."

A bigger problem was that she wasn't a synchronized swimmer. "I think there were resentments at first. All of a sudden this young kid comes in and gets to go to Hawaii for the senior nationals—and they're paying her! Meanwhile, all these other people had been giving blood to the sport for twenty years. But I think I've been well received because I'm nonthreatening. I'm not taking over anybody's area.

"I'm also the first staffperson to work with the volunteer organization. That was quite a niche to carve. I couldn't deal with it like it was Pepsi-Cola, where if you're incompetent, get out. That was my attitude when I first got here. Sink or swim." We both groaned at the bad pun.

"You have to work with the volunteers."

"Right. And they're working for the love of their sport. In our sport the people are in it for the right reasons."

I switched the conversation to the business of synchronized swimming. "How'd things go with Red Lobster?"

So-so. "The big frustration is people gear up for the Olympics but then drop it because all they were interested in was the advertising and media potential.

"A lot of companies are just trying to get a piece of the action because they can all look so great through the Olympic Games. But if they want to be synonymous with the gold medal when we win it, it's going to take a couple of years of investment. The Olympics are every four years. Both parties have to realize it's a working relationship that is built over a period of time."

"Anyone amenable to that?"

"Some are, some aren't. You can usually smell them out. Elizabeth Arden is interested long term. We have a very real skin care need so we can build a product tie-in with them. We also have gorgeous females, and cosmetics and athletics is glamorous right now. It's an honest reason for Elizabeth Arden to be involved with us over the long term."

"What angle are you pushing, a 'tasteful' sex appeal?"

"Most amateur sports are hitting their heads against the wall trying to figure out why they aren't getting coverage like *Monday Night Football*. They can't understand why not because they're so emotionally tied up in their sport. I think we all have a lot to sell. But we have to look at our own unique selling position. I think archery has a certain snob appeal that could attract a men's cologne.

"We have three unique selling points. We have the entertainment value of Esther Williams. We have newsworthiness because we're a new Olympic sport, and we have attractive, young females who are marketable. People can identify with us. We're youth, we're career-oriented, college-bound, very attractive, feminine-shaped, and very tan. We look great in bathing suits. We're the girls in *Savvy* and *Vogue* and all the major women's magazines. The intelligent, attractive woman who has it all." She put on the breaks and laughed at her own enthusiasm. Then she continued. "Not only that, she's a world-class athlete, too, and can't you identify with her because she's the ultimate?

"We're using all that as our unique selling point, and it's working."

"Don't the purists within the sport cringe when they hear you talk like this?"

"No, they don't."

"That surprises me."

"I know, it amazed me, too. But they love to hear it. They tell me, 'Finally, finally, someone is showing people what we love.' They really believe in their sport. And what we do is done in a very tasteful way. We don't abuse the qualities we have. But they are marketable."

But the key to all this sales expertise was the inclusion of synchronized swimming in next year's Olympics. Without Olympic credibility, synchronized swimming would be dead in the water.

"No matter how neat synchronized swimming is, we weren't going to get the exposure until the sport was voted into the Olympic games. Period. The other thing we hadn't done—because we didn't have the resources—was promotion. Catch-22. Until you get television nobody's going to be interested, but how do you get television without somebody's interest?

"We need to maximize our exposure. We have to do everything in our power in this, the pre-Olympic year, to maximize our exposure. Next year the Olympics are going to come and we're going to get a lot of exposure and little girls are going to be tugging on their mothers' skirts saying, 'I want to be like Tracie Ruiz and Candy

Costie,' our duet national champions. Right now we don't have the structure or the programs to support that."

Paula's prognostications were a familiar anthem I'd heard throughout the day: Synchronized swimming was the next great sport. Next year's Olympic coverage was going to make the little girls of America forget all about Olga Korbut and gymnastics.

"There's a lot of things we're doing with the sport that are going to shock the world. We're going to pull off some things we have no business pulling off."

"Such as?"

"Well, this year we're launching 'Classical Splash,' the U.S. synchronized swim team performing with some of the finest symphonies in the country. It's a major risk, but there's never been an event like it of this caliber."

"Whose idea was it?"

"It was my idea."

"She said proudly," I added, and we both laughed. Paula grew more enthusiastic as she talked of next year and its world of possibilities. And she was very convincing. There had to be an unknown number of women out there who had athletic talent and wanted to be athletic, but who still harbored fears of the lady-jock syndrome. Title IX and the women's movement notwithstanding, being a woman and being an athlete were not necessarily synonymous. For many women being an athlete still involved a perceived loss of femininity.

"Exactly," Paula said. "And that's what's so perfect about synchronized swimming." And this was the first event I'd attended created by, administered by, and involving only women.

"You know what I like best about our sport?" Paula said. "It's that we aren't 'I am woman, hear me roar.' When we talk about our athletes we just say 'athletes.' We don't say our 'women athletes.' Nobody is carrying any women's libber banners. In fact we have a lot of very conservative people involved who don't want anything to do with women's lib. I mean, they aren't saying: 'Isn't this great, we have women athletes, and here we are women in a man's world.' They just say, 'Here we are, we're glad we're a part of it, and we think it's lovely.' "

"You're putting a lot of energy into developing a sport," I said, playing devil's advocate. "How do you justify that?" Paula looked at me, her face blank. "How important is it that the United States have a strong synchronized swimming program?"

"You mean, why don't I develop my energies elsewhere? Or that sport shouldn't be taken that seriously?"

"The latter."

"Well," she said, smiling, "I think you can put it in God-Bless-America terms." The smile turned for a moment to a small, self-conscious laugh. "This is going to sound corny, but when you go to Russia or a Third World country and you meet other athletes who can't comprehend your sense of freedom—this goes way beyond sports—who can't comprehend your standard of living, well, sports gives you that . . . ." She stopped, searching for a word. "Medium," she finally said, but obviously not pleased with her selection. She paused for a moment and then continued.

"Sports did so much for me—I played soccer at Indiana and ran track and field all my life—sports is just so much a part of my life that I really believe in it. I see little kids playing soccer and I think that's great. Those kids will grow up and they'll know how to handle rejection. They won't get devastated. They learn how to bounce. You don't always make first string. Sport and fitness and competition does a lot for you. I think it's a great vehicle to fulfill your potential."

The feminine mystique of synchronized swimming was exquisitely refined for the finals. Potted plants sat in each corner of the deck. Begonias and geraniums framed the pool. The door to the ladies' locker room had been transformed into an elegant entrance by a trellis of plants and flowers and pink bunting. At the opposite end of the pool a large bouquet of mums graced the deck.

I sat down next to Peter Ulrich fifteen minutes before the event was scheduled to begin. Peter lived outside Washington, D.C. He was a very young-looking forty-six with blondish hair, sharp features, and a trim, fit body. He used to be a runner, he said, but now he was into race walking. Less pounding on the legs. Peter was here with his wife, Jeannie, and their daughter, who was on a synchro team that hadn't made the finals. The weekend had also been a homecoming of sorts as Peter was a graduate of Yale, class of '61. He and Jeannie had a son, a student at MIT and a former national synchronized trampoline champion. Their daughter was, too. Jeannie was a synchronized swimmer and a triathlete.

Jeannie walked into our aisle. Like Peter she was wearing a yellow T-shirt and blue shorts. And, like her husband, she looked much younger than her years. "This guy here," Peter said, pointing to me, "doesn't know anything about synchro. I told him you wouldn't mind if he asked you questions during the meet." Jeannie turned and looked at me.

"A lot of questions," I said. She laughed and sat down.

"Not at all." She pulled a video camera up onto her lap, fiddled with the dials and said, "Did you know Benjamin Franklin was one of the original synchronized swimmers?" No, I didn't. "I know that because we were just at the Swimming Hall of Fame. When Ben was over in England, he took a swim in the Thames that's become famous.

"I also learned that synchro used to be a man's sport. There was one man early in the sport whose notable accomplishment was turning somersaults underwater while tied in a folding chair." She laughed again. I was glad I'd sat down where I did.

"What happens," I said, "if a swimmer loses her suit?" This question had popped to mind early last night. It seemed like a really distinct possibility.

"The rules say you can't stop," Jeannie replied. "It's a throwback to the days when they wore these real elaborate suits with hats and skirts and the costume itself was much more important to the routine. Now the suit is just something to wear and look good in. I once saw a girl swim right out of her suit. But I've also seen a girl hold the straps of her suit in her teeth and complete the routine."

"Next question: How do they get their hair like that?" The swimmers wore their hair slicked into a bun, every strand cemented to their head and held in place with about a hundred bobby pins.

"Knox gelatin," Jeannie said. "You use two packages with a half cup of water. It forms a real thick paste that you work into your hair. We used to use Vaseline. At long competitions like this we'd just leave it in and walk around with our hair stuck to our heads for a week. Knox washes out with warm water and it's good for your hair."

The competition opened with the duets, and was won by Tracie Ruiz and Candy Costie, the defending champs. Their movements—always mirrored images—had that extra snap and finely etched definition that separates the merely spectacular from the truly great. It's the finest of lines, but you know it when you see it.

But it wasn't until the solo competition that I finally came to appreciate synchronized swimming. Solo synchronized swimming demonstrated the sport in its purest form. The solitary swimmer was in synch with the music and in synch with herself. Alone in the pool, freed from the restraints of partner or team, the solo artist was at liberty to create and define her own character. My fear that synchronized swimming was cloning the youth of America dissolved.

More important was that of all the elements the swimmer was synching with, none was more important than the water itself. Because the swimmers belonged in the water, and the water defined their sport. Without their specific medium they were lost. Between the duet and solos I had walked around the halls of the gym. The swimmers were all rehearsing their routines. But without the water their dances looked ridiculous. They looked like, well, fish out of water.

Tracie won the solo and Candy finished second, which explained their dominance in the duet. They made for an interesting pairing: Tracie a doe-eyed beauty, reserved, and rather mysterious; Candy more the spunky girl next door, full of life and effervescence. An interesting chemistry that coalesced perfectly. That they both looked absolutely smashing in their bathing suits didn't hurt either.

Few teams in the eight-woman team competition used the classic kaleidoscope move, where the swimmers form themselves into a circle while floating on their backs. Like the June Taylor dancers seen from above. Last night during the semis one of the teams had created such a flower and then dissolved it by collapsing it into its center, as though someone had pulled the plug and sucked them down the drain.

"They're too easy," Jeannie explained. "Because they're easy, they're low-scoring moves so nobody uses them. Teams only use them if they need to get a break in the action during a difficult routine."

Too bad, I decided, because they were extremely enjoyable moves to watch. Jeannie admitted that could be a problem. Some of the most technically difficult moves weren't all that much to look at. But because they were tough moves they were also big point getters, so teams loaded up on them.

"But I don't want to watch the technical stuff," I complained, "I want to watch what looks good." That's where the problem started.

"We can't lose our audience in an effort to perform the difficult moves," Jeannie admitted. "We can't afford to lose our audience because right now we don't have an audience. We have to capture the audience, educate it, and then we do the technical stuff. The audience has to learn when and why to clap."

The Walnut Creek Aquanuts from California won the team competition, but it was Ohio State Synchro that put together the best routine, at least so far as this East Coast crowd was concerned. An East Coast team had never won the team event, and everyone had high hopes for the Ohio State club. And I think they deserved it. They were the only team to perform a routine that produced chills up and down my back. That was good enough for me.

Their music was an eclectic mix that included the Alleluia Chorus, music from the *Nutcracker,* and some futuristic synthesized computer stuff—strange combo, but it worked. They were also the first team that had some of its members dive into the water to start the routine. But it was their finale that put it all together. The entire team was underwater, and then slowly one girl broke the surface. All night long women had been propelling themselves out of the water past their waists, but this woman just kept on going, until she was standing about ankle deep in the water.

"That's the third time I've seen that, and I still don't know how they do it," Jeannie said. "Did anybody see a wire come down from the ceiling? You know, like in the Esther Williams' movies, the way they used to pull her out of the water and slowly float her away?"

That was as good a description as any. Only I was surprised to hear her make it. I'd gotten the rather strong impression from more than a couple of women that synchronized swimming could live just as well without comparisons to the water princess. Esther was too obvious and too marketable for Paula Oyer not to use her, but the rest of the synchro community held her at arm's length. As one woman said: "Synchronized swimming is a sport. All Esther Williams ever did was swim around while music played in the background."

I left Kiputh Hall before midnight. I considered sleeping in the van and driving back to New York City tomorrow, but I was wide awake and New York was only two hours away.

The next night at my apartment, I turned on News 4 New York and learned that a section of bridge on I-95 had collapsed around 1 A.M. Eight people had been killed. The way it looked on TV, an entire section of the bridge had been sliced out with a razor. I stared at the television. I'd been on that bridge. For the rest of the night, I could think of little else. I'd been on that bridge. I searched for a reason to explain why I'd made it home and eight people hadn't, but the answer escaped me. The next day I learned that only the northbound lanes had collapsed, but by then that didn't matter.

* * *

Sunday, July 3
New York to Chicago
Go Greyhound

I'm on the express bus, bound for the Windy City. Greyhound costs less than gas and tolls if I took the van. And I'll be staying with Irene (again), so I won't need the van, which is fine with me.

This will be the Golden Anniversary All-Star Game, back in the city and the park (Comiskey) where it all began in 1933. An aging Babe Ruth won that game with a two-run homer into the right-field grandstand off Wild Bill Hallahan in the bottom of the third. And in the top of the eighth with the score 4–2 Americans, he saved the game by crashing into the right-field wall to steal a two-run homer from Chick Hafey. All that was fifty years ago this coming Wednesday, but today at Comiskey Park the bases are still ninety feet apart and the grass a natural green. Life as we know it goes on.

July 4
Hyatt Regency
Chicago

I'm sitting in a downstairs ballroom. Just attended the Old Timers' press conference with the nine surviving members of the 1933 American and National League All-Star teams: Joe Cronin (Senators), Charlie Gehringer (Tigers), Lefty Gomez (Yankees), Rick Ferrell (Red Sox), Earl Averill (Indians), Ben Chapman (Yankees), Wally Berger (Braves), Dick Bartell (Phillies), and Hal Schumacher (Giants).

From left to right, across the dais. Lots of clear blue eyes and loud plaid sports coats. And nostalgia so thick you could hit it with a bat. The boys of summers past are gray-haired men.

"This brings back great memories," Cronin said, then added, "I've been praying I'd live to see this day." That's what this was all about. Fifty years after the fact and they were still alive. No better fact to celebrate. Each was called on to speak. What they said didn't matter. All anyone asked was a funny story, a sweet remembrance. Not so much a trip down memory lane as an opportunity to share the game they'd played fifty years ago that was still, like them, surviving today.

Hal Schumacher: "I've been asked what is my most vivid memory of that 1933 game. Well, I'll tell you. I was fifty years younger."

Wally Berger: "I looked at three very good pitchers—the best in the American league—[Lefty] Gomez, [Alvin] Crowder, and [Lefty] Grove. Chapman robbed me of a hit."

Ben Chapman: "It's good to meet old friends here. Like Wally Berger. The first thing he said to me was, 'Why did you rob me of that triple?' "

Lefty Gomez: "My most vivid memory? Driving in the first run. Eight hundred people fainted when they saw me cross first base. I had one weakness as a hitter: the pitched ball. My age? You hear pitchers say, 'I lost three inches off my fastball.' Hell, I've lost sixty feet."

But the best comments were by Dick Bartell and Rick Ferrell. When Bartell stepped to the microphone he pulled his old baseball mitt from the pocket of his sports coat. "I thought you fellows might like to see this. It's the glove I wore during my pro career, a Bill Doak model." It looked like an old piece of black leather, and wasn't much bigger than his hand. "I may have booted a few, but I caught a lot more than I booted and once I got the ball in there, it stayed." He slipped his hand into the glove and pounded his other fist into the pocket. Old black leather snapped to life. "It still has a good pocket," he said, eyes sparkling. Then he pounded the pocket again. "I wonder what would happen if they used these gloves today?"

Rick Ferrell had been the starting catcher for the American League, and had played the whole way in front of Bill Dickey.

"It was no big deal," he said. "A lot of great players, like Jimmy Foxx, didn't get into the game. Connie [Mack] told me that if a left-hander started for the National League I would start. Bill Hallahan started and I was in the lineup. Mack said that as long as we were ahead there wouldn't be any changes. So we got a couple of runs early and stayed ahead, so I played the whole way. It was no big deal."

"The hell it wasn't!" That from Joe Garagiola, sitting a couple seats away from me, said more to himself than anybody else. Then he spoke up. "Hey, Rick, how many pitches did Lefty Grove have?"

"He had a fastball," Rick said. "That was it." Garagiola laughed. "Well," Rick continued, "he had a curve that broke about this much." He held his thumb and index finger a couple of inches apart.

"How many curves did you call?" Garagiola asked. Catcher-to-catcher conversation, but also more than that. Garagiola was a kid in a candy store. Once a player, now an announcer, always a fan.

"I don't think I called for any," Rick said. Garagiola gasped in amazement.

"Hey, Rick, they've got radar guns and all this electronic stuff to time pitchers these days, and Nolan Ryan's been clocked in the nineties and all that, but how fast do you think Lefty Grove was?"

Rick didn't hesitate: "A hundred."

"Who was the greatest pitcher you ever worked with?" Garagiola said.

"As a left-hander, I'd have to say Lefty Grove. He threw as hard as anyone I ever saw. As a right-hander, my brother Wes." Rick, as phlegmatic as ever, walked from the podium and sat down. Garagiola squirmed in his seat, still excited. He leaned forward and nudged the man in front of him.

"He caught the whole game," he said, his voice eager and high-pitched. "With Dickey on the bench. Jeesus Ku-rist! And nuthin' but fastballs! Can you imagine that? Nuthin' but fastballs!"

Monday, July 4
Late Night
At Irene's

I spent the evening at the Hyatt. At the Old Timers' reception, up to the top of my strike zone in legends.

They sat and talked and drank and ate. Members of America's most select and certainly most envied fraternity: the men who'd been permitted to play the game of boys. Except for one group of men at a table in the middle of the room—they held themselves apart, and were in turn, it seemed, held apart by everyone else. Here sat a small clutch of the old, old men of the Negro Leagues. Amends had been made, past injustices corrected. But they'd been denied inclusion when they could play the game, and there was just no making amends for that.

Outside in the hallway, a small group of autograph hounds stood watch over the exit door. Most were professional traders. There was nary a starry-eyed kid among them, and they all knew exactly what they were doing. Some had collapsible files filled with *Sports Illustrated* and *Sporting News* covers. Others had briefcases of baseball cards. And everyone, it seemed, had a Kodak photo-paper box filled with eight by ten, black-and-white photos of the stars.

This was serious business. They worked in teams, they worked alone. Strategies varied. It did not appear to be fun. Most of the seekers harbored a swaggering disdain for the names they were trying to collect. And no one used more than a glance of triumph once they got the name. There were always more names to get.

A player walked out and was immediately engulfed. He signed patiently, the woman with him acting as secretary, pointing him to the next card or ball or picture. When they left the seekers compared scribbles. A small man carrying a leather bag filled with collapsible files walked into the group. His baseball was blank. "He wouldn't sign for me," he said, voice indignant. "He got everybody else and missed me."

I turned to the group. "Are you guys collectors or do you sell?" Silence. Then, "I just collect." "Me too." "Yeah." So nobody sold. Sure.

Two guys working together were Jack and Bill. "Who's the toughest guy to get to sign?" I asked.

"Jim Rice," Jack said.

"Steve Carlton," Bill said. Other seekers had their "favorite," but they all agreed George Hendricks of the Cardinals was the nastiest of them all. He just won't fuckin' sign. A dubious distinction, but probably by design.

Buck Leonard walked from the reception, a huge smile across his face. "See you tomorrow, see you tomorrow, see you tomorrow," he kept saying, still smiling, and made it to the escalator. I turned to Bill. "Doesn't it bother you to have to walk up to somebody and stick a pen and piece of paper into his face?"

Bill shook his head breezily, totally dismissing the question. "It's part of their job. Listen, they're making six hundred grand a year for workin' two hours a day. They forget what it was like when they were rookies, when they were first comin' up. The worst, though, is when they ignore you. When they put their heads up in the air and keep on walkin' like you aren't there."

A man in a Hyatt uniform chased us to the end of the hall, through a set of double doors, and up an escalator. "The celebrities want to have their party in private," he said. The seekers, not a particularly rowdy crowd, just obnoxious and always there, gave ground grudgingly. They were out of touch now, and they were pissed.

Upstairs I talked to Fred. He hadn't involved himself with the downstairs brigades. He said he was a collector only, and I could see no reason not to believe him. Perhaps because he admitted that he felt "like an asshole" every time he asked someone for an autograph. He had 150,000 signatures. He pulled a baseball bat from a gauze protector.

"This is special. This belonged to George Brett. I'm going to get it signed by Hall of Famers only." He also had a briefcase full of baseballs. He wanted one signature per ball.

"I have a display case at home," he said, then smiled. "Actually, it's more like a whole room. I've got everything arranged real nice. It's a good way to get the anxieties out." That seemed to be true, too. Fred had apparently discovered the secret of collecting autographs for fun, a pursuit that had eluded the boys downstairs.

"There was a time when collecting was my whole life," he said. "I've been collecting since I was eleven, any big name. I can remember when I used to come to these events and be absolutely crushed when I didn't get an autograph from someone I really wanted. It would ruin my entire weekend." He shrugged his shoulders a bit and smiled. "I'm not like that anymore. I'm thirty, and I've been married about a year and that's kind of, well, you know. Now, it's just fun to see who will sign and who won't."

Tuesday, July 5
Old Timers' Game
Comiskey Park
Auxiliary Press Box

Press "box" is a misnomer. I'm in section 237, row E, seat 2. Across every other row are composition boards for desks. I'm in the upper deck, above third base. I hope that tomorrow the outcome isn't decided by a great catch in the left-field corner, because if it is I won't see it. But the seat's great, and with the makeshift desk I've even got a place to rest my elbows.

The National League just won the Old Timers' game 6–5. Billy Williams, former Cub, stroked a pretty-as-you-please line drive, two-run homer into the lower right-field deck, much to the joy of the local crowd.

I didn't watch the game from my press seat. I was the only person in the entire section, and, feeling lonely, I walked along the left-field line in the upper deck until I found Nate, an old black man eating a hot dog, who motioned for me to sit on down. He didn't have much to say after that, but he was very friendly and seemed to enjoy the company. He had three teeth, near as I could tell, a gray goatee, and short gray hair, and watched most of the game through binoculars. Down on the field the surviving members of the 1933 team were being introduced. Dick Bartell and Rick Ferrell were the only two to trot onto the field. The rest managed as best they could, walking or shuffling or being helped along.

"Looks like ball players outlive everybody, don't it?" Nate said, choking on his words. He choked on almost everything he said. "Everybody 'cept me. I'm seventy-five."

"You go to the '33 game?"

"No, no. I've lived in Chicago and been following baseball for sixty years, but I was on the road for that game. I worked for the Sante Fe Railroad for thirty-one years. I was a dining car waiter. I used to have season tickets. When I was on the road, I'd send my wife."

"Where you from originally?"

"Came up from Uniontown, Alabama, in 1907." I wanted to ask a million questions, but whenever I tried they sounded trite and hollow. There was a whole lot more to Nate than I was ever going to learn. Or that he was ever going to tell me.

"You go to the old Negro League games?"

"Hell, yes. Hell, *yes,*" he said, answering the first of my stupid questions. "I seen 'em all. Now, Josh Gibson, he could hit a home run with one hand. And the American Giants down at Thirty-ninth and Wentworth. Stadium held about fifteen, twenty thousand people. Downtown. It's a projects now."

"I guess things have changed quite a bit in Chicago since you got here, huh?"

"Hell, yes. Hell, *yes.*" That's all he said about that. In fact, that was all he said to most of the questions I asked. An answer that spoke volumes I would never completely comprehend.

"Was there much of a problem in the old days with blacks getting into White Sox and Cubs games?"

Nate kept his eyes trained on the field.

"Not here, not up north." He pointed to the right-field line. "I was right over there in Wrigley Field when Babe Ruth pointed to right field and then hit that home run. But he wasn't pointin' to the stands or sayin' he was going to hit one. He was pointin' at the flag. It wasn't flappin'."

He pointed to the right-field bleachers. "I was right over there when Bob Feller pitched a no-hitter on opening day in 1940. A no-hitter!" His voice punctuated the sentence.

"Cool Papa Bell," the announcer said. Nate put the binoculars back to his eyes. Down on the field an old, old black man in an ancient flannel uniform was being helped up the steps of the dugout.

"Cool Papa Bell," Nate said, his voice raspy but filled with affection. "Cool Papa Bell!"

When Juan Marichal came in to pitch, Nate wondered if the former Giant would kick his leg like he used to, raising his left foot well north of his head before bringing his leg toward the plate. On the first two pitches he didn't. I turned to ask Nate a question, but as I did he nudged me and pointed to the field. I turned in time to see Marichal's foot above his head. Tony Oliva hit a deep fly to right center. And there was Willie Mays shagging it down. He caught the fly basket-style and threw to second. Nate handed the binoculars to a little kid a few rows behind him. "Say hey, Willie," Nate said, a big smile creating lines all over his face. "Say hey!"

When Billy Williams stepped to the plate, there was much warm applause. When he punched Hoyt Wilhelm's first pitch out of the park everyone stood and applauded some more.

"Who was that, Steve? Who was that?" The little kid still had the binoculars.

"Billy Williams," I said. "Two-run shot into the lower deck."

"Billy Williams?" Nate said. He scrinched his face, happy, and all the lines returned. "Billy Williams!" he repeated, this time nodding his head. "Hell, yes. Hell, *yes!*"

July 5
Late Night
At Irene's

I spent today rubbing elbows with the press at Comiskey Park. My credential got me into both clubhouses, the interview room, and down on the field during the National and American League All-Star team workouts.

The managers' press conference was insufferably dull. Nothing was said, except what the reporters wanted—and needed—to hear. My first indication of what lay ahead. The day was well scripted, as though all six hundred reporters were driven to get the same story as everyone else or they would be branded incompetent. It was readily apparent why ballplayers quickly learn to dislike the press.

It was also clear why reporters like any player who says anything resembling an insightful comment. These men can play baseball better than everyone else in the world; they don't have to ask themselves why. So the reporter must try to get interesting quotes in an atmosphere that abhors perspicacity (If you were a ballplayer, would you reveal much of yourself in front of six hundred pushing, shoving, sweating reporters?) from a group of men who don't have much to say, anyway. Then, staring down a deadline, he turns to his mini-word processor and writes the same story as everyone else. Because tomorrow that will be the story we want to read. And he only has so many minutes to do it. It has all just got to be there. Right now. The words just have to come.

No one left the stadium early despite the rote monotony. It was as if everyone involved, players and press and spectators alike, had been assigned specific functions. The concentric circles I'd noticed at the USFL game and experienced again at the NCAA Basketball Championships have assumed clearer definition.

The all-stars taking batting practice were the center of this particular solar system. The next orbit, just behind the rope barriers, were the press and the various bigwigs with the proper-colored field passes. Beyond the press, held behind the railings of Comiskey Park, were all the fans screaming and leaning and wanting so badly to get down there on the field to hang out with all the rest of us. Had there not been six hundred media people milling around on the fringes of the infield, the envy of the people in the stands would have had no clearly defined target. The press understood this. Its role was integral, and no one left until they had to. And that included me.

I visited each clubhouse. The noise was the same: a constant chatter punctuated by the plunk of baseballs dropping back into their little boxes after players autographed them. After touring the Nationals' locker room, I walked through the coaches' area, where Tommy Lasorda and Whitey Herzog were trading stories, through a dark corridor, and into the dugout and sat down. When might I get another chance to sit in a major league dugout? Although "bunker" would be a better word, because you sit down, way down, like you're somewhere deep inside the ground with the rest of the park towering over the top of you. Very claustrophobic. The left-field wall disappears. So does center field, and so does second base. A baseball diamond from the dugout looks like a giant mound of grass. It's the lousiest seat in the house. How can a manager contest a call? He can't see the game!

I watched a lot of batting practice, standing just outside the cage as the players jumped in and out of the box playing home-run derby. You get a very good idea of how far the ball travels when standing that close to the plate. The player leans into the ball and gets full extension in his arms, and you can feel the power. The crack of bat on ball is clean and instantaneous. And then the ball is gone. Just gone. It disappears. You pick it up again as it rockets toward the stands where it seems to hang, stuck in the air as it completes its parabola, and for a moment you don't know if it will land on the field, in the stands, or maybe even over the roof. And then it drops, and disappears. The players played their game in little groups, each player taking one swing at putting the ball over the roof. One smash demanded another, which the next player usually provided.

But for all the talent that trooped to the plate (George Brett, Fred Lynn, Jim Rice, Cecil Cooper, etc.), only one man looked like he truly belonged in the batter's box holding a bat and attempting to hit a baseball with it: Rod Carew. The realization was astounding. In a gathering of his peers, he managed to stand apart. To call him The Natural is to diminish the aura he carries with him. He looked like a cat when he stepped to the plate, light and lithe, holding the bat so delicately it was a wonder it didn't fall from his hands. There was nothing wasted in his movements or his motion, and when he whipped the bat around his body he was all over the ball all at once.

DATELINE CHICAGO, July 7

With one swing of the bat last night Fred Lynn of the California Angels blasted his way into the record book and erased eleven years of American League frustration in All-Star Game competition. In the third inning of the fiftieth anniversary installment of the midseason classic, Lynn lined a slider off San Francisco Giant pitcher Atlee Hammaker into the right-field bleachers of Comiskey Park for the first grand slam in All-Star Game history. The shot into the lower deck lifted the American League into a commanding 9–1 lead on the way to their 13–3 thrashing of the National League.

It was a night for the record book and the partisan crowd of 43,801 cheered every minute of it. In addition to Lynn's premier grand slam, the thirteen runs scored by the American League were the most since they scored twelve runs in the 1946 All-Star classic in Boston. Hammaker's seven runs on six hits in two-thirds of an inning was also a record for a single pitcher. The American League tied the record for most extra base hits. Its three doubles, two triples, and two home runs matched the output of the 1934 American League team.

Pitcher Dave Stieb of the Blue Jays started for the Americans and picked up the win. Despite the hammering Hammaker sustained, it was Mario Soto of the Reds, giving up two unearned runs in the first two innings, who absorbed the loss for the Nationals.

Lynn, a thirty-one year-old former Rookie of the Year with four home runs in nine previous All-Star outings, was a unanimous selection as the game's MVP. "We just happened to get on one of their pitchers for a change," Lynn said. "That's what we have not been doing in the All-Star games I've played in. We've chipped away at them but never had the big inning."

Tonight's "big inning" was the biggest ever. Jim Rice of the Red Sox started the fireworks with a solo home run, followed by a George Brett triple. A single by Dave Winfield scored Brett, and after a single by Manny Trillo, Rod Carew drove in Winfield, moving Trillo to third. Carew then took second when Winfield drew a throw to the plate. With two out Hammaker walked Robin Yount to load the bases and set the stage for Lynn's dramatic shot. With two strikes against him Lynn passed on a high slider that just missed before connecting on his historic round tripper that sent Hammaker to the showers.

"To put it bluntly, it's probably the worst exhibition of pitching you'll ever see," Hammaker said. "And I couln't have picked a worse spot for it either, my first All-Star Game and in front of all these people. I have no excuses."

National League manager and St. Louis Cardinal skipper Whitey Herzog was more succinct about the 13–3 pummeling. "It was just a good old-fashioned ass-kicking," he said. Herzog's American League counterpart, Harvey Kuenn of the Milwaukee Brewers, was more upbeat. "This is certainly a highlight of my managerial career," he said. "This game is gone, but it won't be forgotten for a long time."

Ironically, the two innings before the historic third gave no indication of the fireworks to come and probably are best forgotten. Dodger second baseman Steve Sax opened the game with a tap to Stieb, who threw the ball over Carew's head at first base. Sax stole second and scored when Tim Raines of the Expos tapped a second chance to Stieb. Carew lost the ball in the sun, allowing Sax to score.

With Raines on third after the error, Stieb struck out Expo Andre Dawson, walked Al Oliver, also of the Expos, and then struck out Dale Murphy of the Braves and Mike Schmidt of the Phillies to get himself out of the inning.

"The first inning was typical of me," Stieb said. "I got in some big jams but was able to get out of them. If I don't get them right there it usually gets out of hand. Usually I don't get out of it with three strikeouts, though."

In the bottom half of the first Carew atoned for his error with a single. Yount then struck out, Lynn walked, and Rice bounced to Schmit at third. But the gold glover misplaced the ball and the bases were loaded. Brett then scored Carew with a sacrifice fly to Dawson. After setting the National League down in order in the second, the Americans picked up their second run when Winfield doubled down the left-field line and advanced to third when Sax's throw on a Trillo grounder pulled Oliver off first base. Yount later scored Winfield with a sacrifice to Dawson.

The Nationals scored one run in the fourth and one more in the fifth, but managed only three hits against American relievers Bob Stanley, Bob Young, and Dan Quissenbury over the final four innings. The Americans, meanwhile, added two more runs in the seventh and another pair in the eighth.

In the fourth inning Oliver scored for the Nationals on a single by Dale Murphy after reaching second with a hit down the left-field line. An inning later the Nationals picked up their third and final run when lead-off hitter Ozzie Smith singled to right. Dickie Thon advanced Smith to second with a single, and the Cardinal shortstop scored when Sax singled to left.

The American League scored two runs in the seventh when Ron Kittle beat out an infield hit and then scored on a Lou Whitaker triple to center field. Whitaker later scored when Willie Wilson doubled. In the eighth Brett scored from third when Pedro Guerrero of the Dodgers dropped Whitaker's fly to left field. Cecil Cooper, who had singled earlier, moved to third on the error and scored when Rickey Henderson grounded out to Thon of the Astros.

Although it was Ron Kittle, the rookie sensation of the White Sox, who collected the longest applause, both Johnny Bench and

Carl Yastremski received sustained ovations in their final All-Star appearances. Bench, playing in his twelfth All-Star Game, popped up to Oriole Cal Ripken, Jr., in the eighth. An inning earlier Yastremski, appearing in his eighteenth classic, was set down swinging by Pascual Perez of the Braves.

Thursday Morning
July 7
At Irene's

I wrote the news story. Sitting in my press seat during the game I'd gathered or been given forty-one legal-sized sheets of paper containing every fact I would ever need to know about the game being played. Quote sheets and note sheets plus a complete play-by-play breakdown delivered to my seat every three innings. By the time the game was over I felt rather obligated to produce an official account.

It was indeed a night to remember. The entire game was a highlight film of ups and downs, highs and lows, winning and losing, triumph and disaster. Had this been a regular season game the crowd would have been gone by the seventh inning, but this was the Golden Anniversary All-Star Game. Fred Lynn punching the air with his fist as the first All-Star grand slam rocketed into the stands where 43,801 fans were going absolutely berserk was placed immediately in my memory bank of special moments of the year. In fact, the entire night belongs there. The thrills and chills were never-ending. Even the errors—real bonehead plays—were memorable.

There was no escaping the game's historic significance, either. During the break in the fifth inning, George Burns stepped lightly onto the field and sang (well, talked) "Take Me Out to the Ball Game." Then he said, "See you in another fifty years." What a wonderful thought! We were celebrating fifty years of All-Star games, saluting the surviving members of the first "Classic," while, in the present, cheering grown men in striped pajamas as they ran around a green expanse trying to hit a small ball with a wooden stick. To consider the future was most appropriate. Does anyone doubt that we'll be playing the hundredth anniversary game in 2033? Much has been written about the demise of the game, but some things don't change. Of greater interest is speculating about who among us will be there to see the hundredth game. Will an old and hobbled Fred Lynn be called to the mound to throw out the first ball? Or perhaps it will be Atlee Hammaker, his terrible hammering elevated to the stuff of legend, but the man himself wholly revered for having survived not just the defeat but the next fifty years as well.

After the game, I went down to the American League clubhouse and shoehorned myself into a room full of moving, steaming flesh comprised of equal parts naked athlete, TV camera, microphone, tape recorder, lights, and reporter. Everyone was asking everyone else the same question: "How does it FEEL?" And all the players, despite their pregame protestation that the game was a meaningless encounter, admitted that it felt pretty damn good after all.

And yet none of this is what I will remember best about the fiftieth anniversary All-Star Game. It is the very sound of Comiskey Park that will remain forever with me. The pregame show had been a whiz-bang production, but then the Oakridge Boys walked out to the pitcher's mound and began singing the national anthem. Just like that. No buildup, no fanfare, it appeared deliberately underplayed. The crowd caught their understated mood quickly, and soon everyone was singing softly—quietly even—until by the end of the anthem the stadium itself seemed to be singing and I felt myself surrounded by the song.

The game, of course, was noise personified, with new sound barriers broken with every heroic. The sound so completely enveloped me that most times I felt it was starting from somewhere within me and emanating outward. There was no escape. When Lynn teed off on Hammaker, the fireworks began in earnest, and after the game the display was even more ferocious. The noise was so mighty and fearsome I could feel the cuffs of my pants vibrating against my ankles. I wanted to hold onto something, *anything,* if only I didn't feel the entire stadium was about to disintegrate around me.

* * *

The green room for contestants at the National Juggling Championships was the organ room, a large, cinder-block cubicle down a short hallway from the main stage at the State University of New

York at Purchase. A row of mirrors completely banked one wall, and across the back was a giant pipe organ that overpowered the entire room.

The championships would be starting in a couple of minutes, and most of the entrants were back here running through their five-minute acts one last time. One guy was juggling three yellow Ping-Pong balls in his mouth. Another was juggling three blue and gold baseball bats (not in his mouth). A guy in a red vest was trying to catch one club between two other clubs, only he kept missing the catch. He tried once and missed, twice and missed, three times and missed again. He stopped trying and waited. A man in a white sleeveless T-shirt and red gym shorts reached for three 8-foot cue sticks. That got everyone's attention. He threw one cue stick into the air, then the second, and then the third, each cue stick describing a lazy circle.

"Do you think it looks good?" the man asked, his forearms flexing and bulging with every heavy-handed flick of his wrists.

"Yeah," someone said, truly amazed, "it looks good."

"I've been keeping this under wraps. Nobody in the audience has seen it. And this is harder than it looks. And more dangerous, too. It would be real easy to take out an eye doing this." He stopped juggling, collecting the sticks in one hand. "And to think that people said I had an eye-cue problem!" The organ room groaned.

"Listen up everyone," said a judge as he walked into the room. "I'm going to have to be really tough on the time limit. If you hear the whistle, please just walk off the stage."

"What happens if the audience is really applauding?" That from Edmund Jackman, a juggler with a real shot at the title. "Can we suck their blood and stay out there and the judges will have to take that into account?"

"The judges stop judging when I say time," the judge said, and walked out of the room.

"Yeah," Jackman said, "but we can still suck their blood." From what I could gather, that might be more important than winning the competition.

The National Juggling Championships in the middle of July was, like Tiddlywinks, one of those events I simply had to attend once I learned it existed. That the Juggling Federation's national championship and annual convention was scheduled for

SUNY-Purchase, just north of New York City, was an added bonus.

Most of the convention activity was centered inside the gymnasium. The weather was hot and humid outside—95 degrees and 95 percent humidity—and twice as bad inside the gym. I walked through the doors and the familiar, wet-heavy embrace I'd experienced at the volleyball and the fencing championships reached out and enveloped me again. I had once again walked into the center of the universe, into a gymnasium filled with hot and sweaty people going about the happy business of enjoying an activity that unlocked the secrets of their solar system. No one had to tell me that. Being in the gym, with the perspiration rolling down my face, I understood intuitively that juggling was absolutely and positively the greatest activity the Great Juggler in the Sky had deemed to bestow upon the human race.

The convention was unrehearsed and Felliniesque. There were at least three hundred people in the gym, and every one of them was throwing at least three things into the air. That's nine hundred objects, minimum. Balls of every pursuasion, beanbags, clubs, plates, rings, tennis rackets, cigar boxes, sticks, and hats. Some people were throwing these objects back and forth between each other. A couple were riding unicycles *and* throwing objects back and forth between each other. Some people, standing on the wrestling mats, were throwing *people* back and forth between each other. There was no rhyme or reason to any of it, none was intended, and none was needed. There was just a sense of total exhilaration.

Alan Howard, the guy who couldn't catch one club in the notch created by two other clubs, was the first contestant in the tournament. I watched from the side of the auditorium so I could also walk backstage. Out front, on stage, and with the pressure on, Alan made his catch.

The next juggler was Linda Gobbe of Australia, the only woman in the competition. She started with two plates, then three, then four. Next she took two beach balls, one larger than the other, and tried to spin the larger one on her finger. But she missed. She tried again, missed, tried a third time, and missed again. She turned to the audience, assumed the guise of femme fatale, and moved to put the balls back in the box. But she stopped herself and with renewed vigor tried a fourth time to spin the ball. No go. She put the balls away and spun a soccer ball from foot to foot to finger, across her arms, around her neck. Two tennis rackets were next, which she spun using wooden dowels. She finished by spinning one racket into a blur.

For a finale she put a small saucer on her right foot and proceeded to kick it up onto her head. She followed that with a cup, which she kicked up onto the saucer. Then another saucer, followed by another cup. She turned to the audience, mouthed "One more?" while giving a coochie-coochie wiggle, and then, one by one, kicked four more saucers and cups onto the stack. With, of course, the coochie-coochie wiggle between each one. And then, the whistle blew. She shrugged her shoulders helplessly and walked off stage.

Backstage someone whispered "very good" to Linda as she dropped the saucers into her prop box. Out front the audience was booing her low marks.

"I was awful," she said. "I missed the trick with the balls. I've been doing that trick since I was twelve years old." She was more upset than angry. "And I usually kick a sugar cube and a spoon into the final saucer, too.

"Watch this, I'll do it now." Linda pulled out the two balls. She spun the larger ball defiantly and placed the smaller one on top of it, looking like she'd been doing the trick since she was twelve years old. Out front, the audience was still cheering.

Thursday afternoon was better than Wednesday. It was impossible not to be swept along in the enthusiasm generated by eight hundred jugglers in a confined area.

"In juggling you get a lot of adventurous types," Gene Jones told me. He was the outgoing president of the IJA. We were sitting behind the gym, watching a diablo class. A diablo is sort of like a yo-yo. You work it by holding a stick in each hand. Tied to the end of each stick is a length of string. The diablo, which is made of wood and has a dumbbell shape, is made to spin back and forth along the string. The instructor made it sing and dance and all but tell a story.

I asked Gene if there was a certain kind of person who became a juggler. Most of the jugglers I'd asked had mentioned enjoying computers and mathematics, spatial relationships, and configurations. But Gene added a new dimension to the equation.

"I think you get a lot of people who enjoy an unstructured lifestyle," he said. "They are an alive group, very spontaneous, and fun-loving. I'd say a group that is warm and friendly and really isn't all that interested in monetary things. They're not possession-oriented. We have a lot of people here who learned their values during the sixties or learned them from those that did."

I couldn't argue his observation. The festival possessed an air of joyful innocence. A time out of time.

Gene was an actor. His best credit was the movie *Can't Stop the Music,* in which he'd juggled a ball, a tambourine, and a chicken. He had curly dark hair, olive skin, and a permanent five o'clock shadow. He was Italian, or Jewish. Or maybe Armenian, Turkish, Algerian, Mexican, Israeli, Arabian, Palestinian, or French. He wouldn't say but took great delight in my trying to guess. He could be whatever the casting director needed, except, perhaps, a Swede. His manner was light and exuberant, as if he were saying everything for the very first time and discovering it along with me.

Gene had learned to juggle while working in a vaudeville show. His story seemed typical of the how-I-started-juggling stories I'd already heard. He saw someone juggling, was immediately captivated, and had to learn himself. He especially wanted to learn how to bounce a ball on the ground and catch it while still juggling three balls.

"That to me was just the neatest trick," Gene said. "I said, 'I must learn that trick.' It was one of those things you really can't explain. It was like falling in love. I fell in love with the idea of learning that trick."

"Can you make a living juggling?" I asked.

"If you are good, yes, you can make a good living. The people who work the clubs in Reno and Las Vegas, the big clubs in Manila and Tokyo, or the Lido in Paris, these people are very well paid. We're talkin' six figures. And they're working every day. But that's a small, elite group. Then again, in the streets you can make a few hundred dollars a day, which is nothing to sniff at either."

Gene estimated that only a small percentage of the eight-hundred people at the convention made a real living working the streets. But he figured a good number made a "side living" working the streets from time to time. The rest, probably about 60 percent, were recreational hobbyists.

"But don't assume the recreational hobbyists are the jugglers who don't have a high degree of skill. There are people here with technical skills that are incredible. They just aren't professional. They don't have an act.

"The key word is 'entertainer.' A performer performs a feat of skill. An entertainer entertains an audience. Sometimes the performance itself is so great it becomes its own entertainment. But let's say you drop a club. What happens at that moment marks you as the entertainer. Because if you can still hold the audience—whatever your comeback—then you are an entertainer.

"I think one reason for juggling's growing popularity is that it has become more relatable. The presentation of juggling has really changed. In the past a juggler would come out and do what's called the 'flash act.' Six or seven minutes of the audience holding onto the edge of its seat being nervous for the poor guy because he might drop something and then my gosh, we'd all be embarrassed. Now we have some people doing very difficult tricks but also making very light of it. And I think that's to the delight of the general audience."

Anthony Gatto was on stage. He started with four balls, then bounced a ball on his forehead while juggling four rings. The four rings wound up around his neck. He juggled seven rings, which again ended up around his neck. He balanced a six-foot stick with a Wiley Coyote stuffed animal at the top on his forehead and juggled five rings. This time the rings wound up on Wiley's nose. He juggled five balls while balancing another six-foot stick—this one with little nets placed at various heights—on his forehead. The balls wound up in the little nets. He juggled three clubs—behind his back, off his feet, on his head, between his legs—and then while bouncing a ball on his forehead. Then he juggled five clubs, starting with four while balancing the fifth on his forehead. When he dropped the fifth club into the pattern the only sound in the auditorium was the slap-slap-slap of Anthony's hands hitting the clubs. Then he stopped, bowed to the crowd, which had risen to its feet as surely as if Anthony had pulled them on a string, and walked off stage.

For the past two days I'd been hearing all kinds of things about

Anthony Gatto: he was ten years old, cute as a button, a certified juggling genius, and the future of juggling. I realized now that all I'd heard was true. Without doubt I'd witnessed the single greatest athletic performance of my year on the road. I couldn't imagine anyone else coming even close.

None of the jugglers in the championships had missed Anthony's routine, and when he walked backstage he was swamped by praise from his fellow jugglers. Edmund Jackman shook Anthony's hand and said, "Nice goin' kid, but give me a break, will ya?" Anthony shrugged and said thanks a lot. It was Nick Gatto, Anthony's father, assistant, and manager, who did the talking.

"If somebody's going to beat Anthony," he said succinctly, "he'll need to juggle eight clubs and eight rings. And nobody can do that."

Daniel Holzman, an outside contender for the title, was next. He spent quite a bit of time trying to put on his hat, then switched to a three-ball act. The balls were alive in his hands. Sometimes less is more. Three-ball juggling is the essence of the art.

That opened the door for Edmund Jackman, the self-proclaimed and self-deprecating macho-man of juggling. He was nothing if not spectacular, incredible, and completely, hilariously overdramatic. Everything he did, from the most insignificant gesture to the most elaborate gyration, looked to be his last act before he died, right there on stage, having given himself completely to the audience.

He started with a three-, two-, and two-ball ankle-toss routine. By gripping the balls between his ankles, he threw them in the air and caught them in midjuggle. By the time he finished, he was juggling seven balls. Then he spun a large ball on his finger, and placed a smaller ball on top of it, completing the trick that had eluded Linda Gobbe. He juggled three clubs, then three clubs and a ball. He threw three pins into the air and caught them in midjuggle. He threw them in the air again, pirouetted, and caught them. He did it again with two spins, and again with three. From there he went to three balls, throwing them into the air and somersaulting before catching them. For a finale he balanced a ten-speed bicycle on his forehead (on his forehead! by the rear wheel!) and juggled three clubs. With Jackman, I was told, everyone expects the outrageous, but no one had expected anything as out-fucking-rageous as this! When his act was finished, Jackman stood at center stage, the sweat streaming down his face, his chest heaving. And sucking the audience's blood.

Backstage his energy didn't dissipate. "That was fun, that was fun, that was fun," he kept saying. Then he pulled himself together, or at least tried to, and waited for his scores. They were mostly 9s, with just a couple of 8s. Jackman bounced to his feet, clapping his hands. "I'm in the running. It's a horse race." Anthony Gatto's father walked past and stuck out his hand.

"I think you beat him" he said, and continued walking.

There were only two contestants in the latter half of the competition who had a realistic chance to stay with Anthony Gatto and Edmund Jackman: Steve Mills and Alan Jacob. But before we got to them we endured five minutes with Bob Nickerson, the guy with the "eye-cue" problem. His act was awful and his jokes were even worse, but it worked. He knew it was bad but refused to apologize. He started with three hatchets, then progressed, relatively speaking, to bouncing three basketballs between his legs while in the background played the song "Red Rubber Ball." It was so bad it was good.

The real tragedy, however, was that the whistle blew before he got to the cue sticks. He disappeared behind a screen, only to reappear moments later with the sticks slung over his shoulder. The audience defined new levels of pandemonium, only to be denied final gratification when the judges insisted on the five-minute time limit. The audience worked up a healthy chant for the judges' throats. The judges relented—wisely—and the audience went totally bonkers cheering for the worst act of the night.

Steve Mills's performance was superb. He started with three gold pins, then spun a soccer ball on his finger, and then bounced it on his forehead. While still bouncing the ball he juggled four rings and—while still bouncing the ball—wrapped the rings around his neck. He then juggled the ball on his face, rolling it around his head to the back of his neck and back and forth across his temples. Then he juggled four clubs, and when he dropped one executed the best "cover" of the night. A dropped object was an automatic half-point deduction, but a good cover could win the half point back. Still juggling three clubs, Steve walked over to the club on the floor and cradled it in his ankle as if to execute a dramatic foot flip to reestablish the club in the pattern. But at the moment of truth before the Big Trick, he meekly bent down and picked the club up, leaving the crowd to laugh at itself for having been taken, and me to wonder if maybe he hadn't dropped the club on purpose.

Two jugglers later it was time for Alan Jacob. He was the crowd favorite. His performance was much different from the others. Whereas those before him had crammed their routines with tricks, Alan created one overriding image. In one sense there was really nothing to his act: two minutes of club swinging followed by three minutes juggling three clubs. But it was a seamless whole in which nothing was missing and no detail had been neglected. He grabbed the audience and held them with style and flair and a subtle yet overpowering athleticism. It was all there, from beginning to end. There was no way he could lose. And he didn't.

Later there was much discussion concerning the final placements. Alan had won with an 86.5, Jackman was second at 86, and Gatto third at 85.5. Everyone was pleased Alan had won but was also feeling quite guilty that Anthony Gatto had lost.

Anthony was close to being the best juggler in the world while still a preteen. Someday he would be the best juggler in recorded history. That was a given. Since he was already making $10,000 an appearance, his losing made little difference to his professional development, but his defeat could be seen as an embarrassment to the event itself. How could someone that good not be champion? The problem, if such be the word, was the scoring system. It gave as much weight to technical skill as it did to presentation. Performance versus entertainment. Alan Jacob won with consummate presentation. Jackman kept it close with a wild combination of everything. Anthony had lost because his only presentation was himself. All he could do was juggle better than anyone else in the world.

There was no consensus—except to reiterate pleasure that Alan had won. As for Anthony, he was only ten, and he would probably win the title for the next twenty-five years. But there were some larger questions. The spectators wanted Anthony to push back the boundaries of juggling, to accomplish the unimaginable. And they wanted to be there to experience every inch of the Gatto explorations. I understood that desire. I considered myself fortunate to have seen him juggle. But as anxious as people were to witness the progression of Anthony Gatto, Juggler, they seemed equally as apprehensive about the development of Anthony Gatto,

Person. "Is Anthony really happy?" was a question I had heard more than once. No one had a ready answer.

Anthony had no act. When you're ten years old that's probably good—who needs a kid with an "act"? But Anthony juggled whatever his father gave him, handed it back and waited for his father to give him something else. When he was finished, he bowed stiffly and walked away. A toy soldier. No emotion, no nuthin'. He seemed to take no joy in his amazing ability. He just did it.

I walked up to the dorms and joined a large group of jugglers milling about in the steamy, midnight air. In the middle stood Nick Gatto, Anthony's father. A vaudeville performer, Nick had appeared on all the famous stages of the world. Now he was his son's coach and manager. And at the present moment asking everyone to tell him why Anthony hadn't won. Nick was completely flabbergasted. Why had his son lost? How could he lose to some guy who swung a couple of clubs?

Listening to Nick demanding answers no one would give him, I understood what the jugglers had meant when they asked if Anthony was happy, and what they were really saying when they wondered aloud if Anthony liked to juggle. Nick continued to ask the same questions, over and over, until Anthony appeared and suggested to his father that maybe they should go down to the gym and juggle.

Chapter 7

*　*　*

New York, New Jersey, Delaware, Maryland, Washington, D.C.

No motivation. After seven weeks in the city, getting back to the road the sixth of August wasn't easy. It was too damn hot to be cruising the highway in a van with a broken air conditioner.

Tampa Bay Rowdies 4, Team America 1 at RFK Stadium.

Maryland, Virginia, North Carolina, South Carolina, Georgia

In Virginia the van turned over 100,000 miles. In North Carolina, John McDermott, a friend from Alaska hitching a ride to Dallas, christened the van when be bought gas. "You know," he said, his $20 bill changed into a couple of coins by the attendant, "You should call this thing 'Jabba the Hutt.' It's big and brown and ugly and eats everything in sight."

Jabba. After seven months of decidedly dubious service, the van finally had a name.

Atlanta Braves 4, San Francisco Giants 1 at Fulton County Stadium.

Georgia, Alabama, Mississippi, Louisiana, Texas

All night power drive after the Braves game. John had a plane to catch and the Outdoor Speed Roller Skating Championships were only two days away. We alternated behind the wheel and lying on the corduroy bed. But sleep was impossible. A clammy haze seeped into Jabba and clung to the cardboard insulation.

Sixteen hours later we arrived in Ft. Worth at the Will Rogers Coliseum, the roller skating site. I picked up a credential, and then we found an air-conditioned motel. MacDee watched the Red Sox play the Rangers up in Fenway. I fell asleep at seven.

The next morning John caught a bus to the airport and I went roller skating. An event best forgotten. (Outdoor speed roller skating is deadly dull; the 10,000 meters—to mention one race only—was 9,900 meters of skaters hiding behind each other, followed by 100 meters of hell-bent-for-macadam sprint.) And the heat! One-oh-four by 9 A.M. At night I lay on the corduroy bed in a Quality Inn parking lot, pools of sweat collecting on my chest. I didn't move, I didn't sleep. I just promised myself that I'd never try this year in sports again, or if I did that I'd go to the All-Star Game and then sit in an air-conditioned room until Labor Day.

Texas, Oklahoma, Missouri, Illinois

I read the schedule wrong and arrived in St. Louis forty-eight hours before the Cardinals were to play the Astros. I stayed at the Huck Finn Youth Hostel (no AC, but a couple of fans), and watched the Cardinals beat the Astros in ten innings on Thursday night. After the game I returned to the road. I wanted to put some distance between me and St. Louis before stopping for the night. I could drive the final miles to Du Quoin, Illinois, and the waterskiing championships tomorrow. But there were no rest stops on I-64, and Route 51 was deserted after midnight. No time to change my practice of camping in crowded motel parking lots. Safety in numbers. I stayed on 51, pointed to Du Quoin. The moon was a tan egg sitting to my left, lighting the road. On either side were walls of corn. A rich, loamy smell filled the van and kept me awake. At 2 A.M. by the Du Quoin National Bank clock, an Illinois Central freighter stopped me in the middle of town. The train was 129 cars long.

I'd expected a Cyprus Gardens setting for waterskiing but didn't get it. What I got was a thin brown lake in the middle of a field. Oak trees bordered one side, as did a fleet of recreational vehicles parked elbow to rearview mirror. Bleachers were set up, but the first rows of the "grandstand" were beach chairs in the water, from where spectators watched the skiing and escaped the fireball sun.

The National Waterskiing Championships were the kind of competition that included the Pepsi Taste Test (I chose Pepsi, giving it a 15,792 to 9,501 vote lead over Coke in the Du Quoin area). Taking my first tour of the grounds, I clicked on my recorder and said: "I have met middle-class America. It water-skis and wears a tiny bathing suit." Waterskiing, more than any sport I'd encountered, occupied the very center of all that America strives to be: affluent and possessed of its accoutrements (boats, skis, Winnebagos, etc.).

The nationals were a five-day, family affair with competition in thirteen divisions starting with the boys and girls under twelve, and continuing through men forty-five and older. The operative word was "family." All the promotional material trumpeted waterskiing as the finest "family-oriented" sport in the world, and it was not unusual for one family to be represented in two, three, even four divisions.

But the nationals were more than just a family outing. For the kids under twelve, the nationals were a chance to stay up way past normal bedtimes. For teens it appeared to be an elaborate mating ritual. For contemporary adults, five days in Du Quoin was the perfect opportunity to display that newfound affluence. And for the men of the veteran divisions, the nationals offered a fine opportunity to congratulate one another on still being in such great shape. Which they most definitely were.

As for the tiny bathing suits, yes. If waterskiing was the perfect family sport, it was even more perfect for getting into shape while developing a uniformly even tan. There are only so many bodies in the world capable of wearing the bathing suits fashion designers tell us we should, and here I was surrounded by every last one of them. Women *and* men, young *and* old. You know the suits: cut down to here and hiked up to there, and never in a million years would you dare to put one on. But here, by the side of a dirty brown lake in southern Illinois, were all the people who could and did.

Then there was me. Six feet eight inches and 195 pounds of translucent Irish Catholic skin made even more anemic by seven winters in the Land of the Midnight Sun. I hid from the 100-degree heat as best I could, wearing green hospital pants, my long-sleeve Team Alaska Volleyball shirt, and the White Sox cap I got at the All-Star Game. All the while running through a couple of squeeze bottles of Sun Block 15.

The Men's I slalom was under way when I took my first walk around the lake Friday morning. It was a mesmerizing event to watch, an intricate combination of power and precision, speed and delicate balance. The slalom course was 900 feet long, with three buoys spaced at equal distances about 40 feet on either side of the centerline of the course. While the boat drove the centerline, the skier, balanced on a single narrow ski, maneuvered around each buoy. He entered the course through a starting gate four feet wide, then swept to the right and around the first buoy, crossed the wake, and swept to the left to ski around the second buoy. And so it went, the skier snaking down the course as the boat pulled him through. If the skier completed the run, he was pulled through the course a second time at a slightly higher speed. This procedure was followed until the boat reached maximum speed for the category of skier being pulled. Once speed had been maxed, difficulty was increased by shortening the tow rope. Physics prevailed and the skier's speed increased around the buoys. It was all rather confusing at first because everyone talked in waterskiese ("3½ at 32 off"), until I realized that the idea was to ski around as many buoys as possible with the shortest possible rope.

The skiing itself was a joy to behold, the skiers describing patterns of lyrical symmetry across the water. Approaching the buoy and holding the tow bar with both hands, the skier dropped his outside hand, leaned into the curve, and then, fully extended, hung himself just inches over the water as he swept around the buoy, the ski slicing the water and throwing a giant wall of spray in the opposite direction. There was no margin for error, the fine line between absolute disaster and total success drawn with razor-sharp exactness. Once around the buoy, the skier righted himself, grabbed the bar with both hands again, and bounced across the boat's wake to perform the same maneuver around the next buoy.

The cumulative effect was hypnotic and poetic, with the walls of water the skier produced providing an added punctuation.

There were 524 skiers competing in the thirteen divisions. To reduce the field to a more manageable number I decided to interview the three women members of the U.S. National Water Ski team—Deena Brush, Camille Duvall, and Cindy Todd. I'd ask them the same questions and see what happened to the conversations.

I met Deena at the HO Ski booth. She was a new HO representative and was required to spend time near the booth signing autographs and talking skis with prospective buyers. She handled her chores with considerable aplomb, genuinely interested, it seemed, in whomever she was talking to. She was in wonderful shape, her arms perhaps a bit overly developed compared to the rest of her. She had sun-drenched brown hair, brown eyes, and prefectly straight teeth that she displayed frequently in an easy smile. A genuineness that suggested both strength and vulnerability. During a lull, she suggested we retreat to an air-conditioned Winnebago, an invitation I accepted immediately.

Like most skiers, Deena had started young. In Deena's case, at 3½. Her father had held a broomstick over the edge of the boat and Deena held onto it. "I can remember it really clearly," she said. "I don't remember being scared; I just remember seeing my mother driving the boat and my dad holding the back of my jacket."

By the time she was ten, she had definite goals. Members of the national team wore red, white, and blue Team USA bathing suits. She told herself that someday she'd be wearing one, too. In 1977, she made the team for the first time. Now, at twenty-three, she was an eight-year veteran, the defending national Open Women's slalom champion and number four overall in the world.

"What's your favorite event?" I asked.

"I used to say slalom because I was afraid of crashing in the jumps." I'd yet to see any jumping, but I'd seen the ramp out on the lake. It sat quietly in the water, like it was daring somebody—anybody—to take a chance on it. "Lately I've been doing well in the jumps," Deena continued. "So right now, it's hard to pick between the slalom and the jump. I like them both." I asked about her fear factor in the jumps.

"I don't particularly like to talk about that," she said and fell silent. I was mulling ways to restart the conversation when she spoke.

"There is a big fear factor. In the back of your mind you're always thinking there's going to be that jump when you don't come in right. When you're coming into the ramp, you're going fifty-five, sixty miles an hour and there's a lot that can go wrong. I crashed here last year. I was really lucky I wasn't hurt. So I'm kind of scared to go out and jump. I've had a really good season in jumps—I've won my last two tournaments—but it's just this jump here. There's something in the back of my mind saying take it easy."

Deena's entire disposition had changed while she talked. Sitting on a chair next to the kitchen table, she'd curled herself into a tight little ball and wrapped her arms around her legs. Her hands fidgeted, and she talked faster, as though she wanted to get this part of the interview over with as fast as she could.

I told Deena about the pairs skating in Pittsburgh, and how the women had such control over their fears that they could be lifted eight, nine feet in the air and carried the length of the ice. "That didn't terrify me so much as it just left me awestruck," I said. "I think that's what's going to happen when I watch the jumps."

"It's probably better to be out there jumping than it is to be on the shore. I'm scared when I watch my friends jump. I can't tell them to keep their arms in, their head down. I don't like to watch."

"Then how can you do it?"

"You have to respect the ramp," she said. "You have to have a lot of technique. Everything has to be right. You just can't let it all hang out."

The talk turned to money. Deena was a professional, but from what I could gather there was little money to be made waterskiing. There were rumors of a pro circuit, but I was hearing the same old song: no television, no money. Deena at least had a comfortable salary with HO skis.

"Being with HO is a good way for me to give something back to skiing," she said. "You see, I feel really lucky. I come from one of the poorer families in waterskiing. Not poor like we were on food stamps or anything, but my parents were divorced when I was five years old. The people in waterskiing have just been so good to me. From the time I was little I was given all my skis. I was given a boat in '76. There are a lot of richer families who sent their kids to ski school after ski school, but I'm the one lucky enough to have the skill to make it to the top. My mother gave up clothes so I could ski and have nice clothes to go to school. Now she says, 'You made it to the top and you won the world jump championships and you've gotten to travel all over the world. It was all worth it.'

"Early in May, I got a letter that said my contracts were up and I cried and cried and told my mom I was going to have to quit skiing because we wouldn't be able to afford it anymore. But then I tried HO skis and we worked out a contract. It's the best contract I've ever had; the person I'm working for is the best and the skis are the best I've ever ridden. And my mom said, 'Now look at you, look how fortunate you are.' And I swear," she stopped suddenly. I looked up from the table. Deena's eyes were filled with tears, and for a long moment she was unable to speak. "Every day," she said after a while, "I think, 'I'm so lucky, I'm so fortunate.' " She paused again. "It's just like everything has been going my way."

Jumping in one of the boys' divisions had begun by the time Deena and I finished our conversation. I applied more sun block and walked to the shore to get a better view.

As expected, I wasn't as terrified as I was just plain dumbstruck. How can people *do* this? Although the actual flying through the air looked to be the easy part. It was the stylized ritual of approaching the ramp that created the larger agony.

The approach was, of course, paramount. As Deena had said, everything had to be done right. The boat appeared around the corner of a dogleg in the lake about five hundred feet from the ramp, the skier out of the wake to the left of the boat. As the boat pursued a straight course intended to pass just to the right of the ramp, the skier shot across the wake and swept wide to the right away from the ramp. So wide, in fact, that the skier almost passed the boat and came to a stop in the water. Then began the crosscut. The skier dipped his left shoulder hard toward the water and, gaining momentum and speed, raced over and out of the wake back to the left of the boat and up the ramp. The impact crushed the skier down hard on his haunches and produced a screech similar to that of fingernails across a blackboard. At the lip of the ramp the skier straightened up, looking to "pop" one, and took to the air. Centrifugal force slowly turned him as he reached the apex of the jump, and it was important to get straightened out again before landing. As for the landing itself, anything that didn't result in a dumping was considered success.

I positioned myself on the bank close to where the crosscut began. It was this moment in the approach ritual that intrigued me the most. (It wasn't the Moment of Truth; that came later, sometime after the skier had zipped across the wake and before he was actually on the ramp. But that moment happened too fast. Zip-zap and he was up the ramp.) The beginning of the crosscut allowed more time to think. There was a particular moment when the skier was quite close to me ("setting up wide to the right of the boat"), when I could watch him run the situation through his mind—his position, the boat's position, the angle of the ramp—and quite consciously make his decision to go for it. The calm before the storm, if cliché be permitted. The moment the shoulder dipped certain decisions had been reached, bridges crossed, and die cast. I found myself dipping my shoulder and bending my knees with each skier, and then standing up straight in anticipation as he whipped across the wake.

Saturday afternoon, I found Camille Duvall sitting at the end of a short dock watching members of a men's division pop their jumps. These guys were going as fast and as far as the open women would be tomorrow, and she wanted to get a feel for the ramp. We'd met last night at the auction to raise money for the U.S. national team, and she'd agreed to talk to me today. I told her my story, and asked her to tell me hers.

"Well," she said. "I'm twenty-three. I've been competing since I was six. I won my first overall title at fourteen and won five in a row. And then I retired at age eighteen. I was burned out. This is my third season back. But quitting was the best thing that ever happened to me. When I came back I was mentally a lot more prepared. Before I was just out there skiing and not really thinking about anything."

"You just bagged it?"

Camille nodded, long blond hair brushing her shoulders. Her manner was straightforward and to the point. Tall and strikingly attractive, she had bright, beautiful green eyes cut from crystal.

"Did you quit with the idea of eventually coming back?"

"No. I quit for good. I said, 'This is it; I don't want to ski anymore.' I was tired of training, I was tired of freezing my ass off practicing all winter."

She stopped to watch a skier pop a jump, following his flight through the air, taking mental notes, it looked like, to be remembered. I asked about the fear factor in jumping.

"The fear factor is crashing," she said, very matter-of-fact. "But if you're skiing here you've got the technique.

"Maybe I wanted to be domestic," she said, returning to the subject of her three-year hiatus. "I got married, I learned to cook, to garden, to do all those things. And for me, at that point in time, it was all worth doing. I'd never had that life."

"What brought you back to skiing?"

"I went to see my brother at his ski school and he said bring your slalom ski and run the course just for fun. So I did, and I ran four at twenty-three off, which I still think is pretty amazing for not having been skiing all that time."

She started working as an instructor at a friend's school. "I started skiing again in June of '81. At that point, I still had it within me but it needed a lot of nurturing. I needed a lot of confidence, and that's what my friend gave me. Once I knew I could still do it and I enjoyed it, I said, 'I'm going to take the ball and run with it.' "

"As opposed to when you were younger and you weren't enjoying it?" She stopped to watch another skier, and didn't come right back to the conversation. Then she said, "I think some of the reason for before is because I was skiing for my parents. My dad really wanted me to be a skier, and my parents really forced me into it. When I came back I did it for me. My parents didn't put any pressure on me at all. They were just very supportive in every way they could be."

"What made them change?"

"I don't know, I really don't. I guess they were just glad to see me back skiing. If it took a softened attitude for me to come back, then that's what they were going to do.

"I think a lot of parents push their kids too hard here," she said. "But a lot of kids need it. I know I needed it—to a certain point."

"It can be tough to find that fine line."

"Yeah, I'm sure it is, and I don't envy parents. I know I won't envy myself when I get to be a parent. I mean, I'm not going to make my children ski. Oh, by the way, I'm divorced now, so a family isn't in the immediate future."

"Was the divorce . . . ," I stopped, looking for the right phrase. Camille laughed and found it for me.

"The fact that I started skiing again?"

"Yeah."

"One followed the other, I'd say that. He wanted someone who spent all her time taking care of him. Then all of a sudden I was doing something for myself, working real hard and spending a lot of time away from him." Again she stopped to watch a jumper. Then, "I don't know how a professional athlete can be married. It's not a traditional role for a woman. Cindy Todd's married and she's got a little boy. But her husband is very supportive." No hints of envy. "It takes a certain kind of man to withstand the pressure."

During her time away Camille had worked at a health spa, but she had also done some modeling, an experience that stood her in good stead now that she was back in the sport and looking for endorsements. In front of the O'Brien Ski booth was a full-size cutout of Camille in two-piece bathing suit holding an O'Brien ski. It was, she said, a way of giving back to skiing something skiing had given her.

"You know," I said, "a lot of people think you probably lead a real fantasy life."

Camille laughed. "You want reality? Reality is going home after five weeks on the road with a suitcase full of laundry. I'm basically working from nine to five. When I get home, I'm burned out. People don't realize how hard it can be. They come here and ski a little bit and think that's all there is to it. But we've got to be on top of it all the time. There are a lot of sacrifices you have to make. This is my job. That's the way I have to look at it."

Another skier crushed himself on the ramp and popped his jump. Camille fell silent again and watched his ride.

Sunday, Deena won the first Open Women's event, the slalom. When the men's slalom began I talked to Cindy Todd, the third member of the national team.

At twenty-seven, Cindy was a grande dame of waterskiing. She'd been skiing since she was four, but despite winning two national titles as a teenager didn't really commit herself until she was twenty.

"I rededicated my life to the Lord," she said. She also got married. "Lester, my husband, has been really good for me. We've made a great team. I think our combination of God, me, and Les, is what I needed."

That was in 1975. In 1976 she'd won the national title. Since then she'd won a couple of national slalom and jumping titles, plus three overall titles at the world championships. In 1977 she'd participated in the Superstars competition, and she was the current women's world record holder in both slalom and jumping. And in 1980 she'd had a son, Benjamin.

"Being pregnant was super," she said. "I was just so happy and so peaceful. I thought I could spend the rest of my life just being pregnant, but I guess the Lord had other things in mind for me." Three weeks after having Benjamin, she competed in a tournament.

"From '76 to '80 when I had Benjamin I was skiing every bit as much for me as I was for the Lord. But after Benjamin it was a lot less for me and a lot more for God and Les and the people who had put so much time into me. I wanted to give them back something that they had given me."

For a person in the middle of a national competition, Cindy seemed remarkably relaxed. I asked if maybe she shouldn't be off someplace being nervous.

"When my faith is low, that's when my fears crop up," she said. "When my faith is strong and I know He's with me, I don't worry at all."

"Not even when you're jumping?"

"I've never been seriously injured," she said. "I make sure I'm doing all the right things and leave the rest to the Lord."

Cindy had been a late replacement in the '77 Superstars. She'd had only two weeks to train, but was still pleased with her performance because she placed in every event.

And the Superstars had been most instructive. "I realized how lucky I was to be a waterskier," she said. "It seemed that the girls from the other sports overdid everything. They were overly confident to the point of being egotistical. I'm not saying they were all like that, but some of them—most of the them—seemed kind of stuck-up. And I usually don't call people that. When I met those girls, that was the biggest thing I felt, that I was just so happy to be around the kids I'm around.

"I think the nature of our sport has a lot to do with it. If we get a lot bigger that may change. You start adding money and pressure and you may see it change. I just hope it doesn't."

At the same time, however, Cindy felt the sport had to change. Waterskiing had experienced a couple of years of growth but was holding steady now, which was tantamount to falling backward. Cindy's solution was to draw clear lines between amateurs and professionals, and separate the organizations. And clean up the rule book. There were too many gray areas and it was too easy to cheat. Until the rule book was tightened, the Olympics wouldn't touch waterskiing with an eighty-foot tow rope.

But in defense of the book, Cindy said, "We've always prided ourselves that very little cheating does go on when actually there could be a whole lot." Not a bad comment to be able to make.

"That's what I like about our sport. I can't explain it, but the people in it are people of high moral standards. It's not everybody out trying to get all they can get."

"But that's because there's so little to get."

"Exactly. And that's why I worry about the money coming in. It could change everything."

Cindy was not a liberated woman—her comment, not mine—but that was because she didn't believe she had anything to be liberated from. "I don't feel there is anyone holding me back," she said. "I feel absolutely free and I can do everything I want to do."

"By some definitions that would make you a liberated women."

"Independent," she said, correcting me. "I'll tell you what. I think it takes a lot more for me to be a skier than it does for the other girls because I'm married. I have the responsibilities of a household and a baby, plus I have a lot of church responsibilities. But the thing that would go first is waterskiing. And that doesn't frustrate me."

"If you were a man, you wouldn't have to make that choice." Cindy was willing to accept that.

"Being an athlete costs a woman more, but I don't think I would ever want to be only an athlete. Women have lot more to offer, and I think you can be an athlete and a lady. That's important for me to try to do. Those liberated-women types spend too much time worrying about being equal to men rather than worrying about being the best woman they can be.

"Someday I'll quit waterskiing. But I won't go through some big emotional crisis. I'll have plenty of things the Lord will want me to do after I quit. They may not be as exciting, but I'll do whatever He asks me. And I'll be satisfied."

Cindy turned in the most patently athletic performance in the tricks event. Her lean, wiry build served her well. Deena, on the other hand, approached the tricks with more artistic flair and feminine grace. And Camille had been right yesterday when she'd said tricks was the hardest event to regroove. She was also too tall. In the slalom, her height had helped create a series of rides both powerful and elegant, but in the tricks her height slowed her down and seemed to get in her way.

The tricks event itself didn't impress me. The spins and flips demanded obvious athletic talent, but the event seemed more a stunt than a test of skill. Something to do to impress the gang during summer vacation. After the superior athleticism of the slalom, I just couldn't take the tricks seriously.

In any event, tricks was won by Karen Roberge. Karen was the defending national overall champion, as well as the defending world overall champion. She was not, however, a member of the national team, which had been selected earlier in the summer. Karen was an alternate, but her absence from the starting team put the National Waterskiing Association behind a rather sticky wicket, especially when Karen finished third in jumping with a 134-foot effort. (Deena won with a 136-foot jump.) Combined with her third-place finish in the slalom, Karen accrued enough points to win the national title.

Illinois, Indiana, Kentucky, Ohio, West Virginia, Pennsylvania, New York

Monday: Rainstorm in Ohio. I'd seen it coming for miles, a flat cloud with a column of water pouring from beneath it. The rain came in waves, large chunks of water pounding on Jabba's hide. And the lightning. I could see the streaks and hear the sizzle, the thunder bouncing around inside the van. I grabbed the steering wheel with both hands and hoped the wipers didn't quit. No Cleveland Indians game tonight. I kept Jabba on I-70 east. Pittsburgh was playing Houston in a doubleheader tomorrow. Fine. I'd enjoyed myself in Pittsburgh during the figure skating championships, pleasantly surprised how unlike "Pittsburgh" Pittsburgh really was. A lovely city, actually, a San Francisco in blue work shirt.

I arrived at Three Rivers Stadium with a full tank of gas and two $20 traveler's checks. Mistake One.

The parking lot attendants on Lacock Street wouldn't touch the checks. I finally talked a guy into letting me leave the van by promising I'd break a check and come right back. He said okay, but hurry up. Bill's Lunch was closed. The adult threater seemed inappropriate. I walked down Federal toward the Sixth Street Bridge and into Castellano Bros. Deli. Mistake Two.

I grabbed a pint of chocolate milk and a hostess cherry pie, plunked them on the counter and waited till the kid at the cash register rang up the sale before saying, "You take traveler's checks, don't you?" (Dirty pool, but I was desperate.) The kid looked at me, looked at the check, shrugged his shoulders, and said why not. But then he turned to a big, meaty-looking guy sweeping the mat by the front door.

"We don't take checks," the meatman said, not looking up.

"This isn't a check, this is a 'cheque,' " I said, trying to keep it light. "You know, 'Don't leave home without 'em!' "

"We don't take fuckin' checks!" A sudden rage. "We don't take nuthin'." I looked at the kid behind the counter.

"I think you better leave," the kid said. He was either on the meatman's side, or he was imparting sound advice because he'd seen this all before. I decided on the latter. I left the milk and pie on the counter (on purpose) and started for the door. Mistake Three.

"Put your fucking stuff back," the meatman said. Macho time. Foolishly, I didn't heed the call but continued walking. Mistake Four.

The meatman blocked the door, holding the broomstick across his chest. I was probably a foot taller than he was, but the last time I'd thrown a punch in a fight I was in the fourth grade. I think the meatman knew that. I turned around to replace the milk and pie, but the kid did it for me. The meatman stood aside to let me by, the broomstick still crossing his chest.

"Asshole," he said as I walked past. Well, maybe. But so was he and I told him so as I walked out the door. Mistake Five.

Before my foot hit the pavement, his broomstick hit my left shoulder and clipped me behind the ear. It didn't hurt and didn't surprise me, either. Somehow I'd known it was coming from the moment I'd opened my mouth.

"You come in my store again and I'll have you arrested," the meatman said.

"Arrested? You hit me!" That forced him to think for a moment. I used the second to finally think, too. Why had I needed that last word? From now on the meatman could say whatever he wanted.

"I'll have you arrested for, for, aggravating me. Now get out of here." We'd drawn a crowd. I turned and walked away, unleashing a string of invectives at the meatman, but this time with my mouth shut.

And I still hadn't broken the check. I tried a few more stores. When I showed the check to a man in North Shore Cigar & Tobacco, he backed himself against the wall like he'd just seen the monster in a bad horror flick. "If I take that the boss'll kill me!" Maybe this *was* a bad horror flick. Finally, I walked into the Apollo restaurant. Yes, they would break the check, but only if I ordered something. I got the all-you-can-eat salad, paid immediately, and told the waitress I'd be back to eat it later.

The van was still in the parking lot. "Gee," I said, "sure is difficult to get a traveler's check cashed around here."

The attendant nodded. "Yeah, well, this ain't no suburban neighborhood around here. One thing you got to remember is nobody around here trusts nobody else."

I told him I'd remember that, and went back to the Apollo to eat my salad. Sitting in the booth, applying ice to the welt growing behind my ear, I listened to the radio as Karl Malden told me not to leave home without 'em.

For all of that, the doubleheader should have been anticlimactic, but it wasn't. For one thing, extricating a Three Rivers Stadium hot dog from it's foil bag is a real adventure. The rolls are moist and limp and stuck to everything.

But it was the guy in front of me who provided the real entertainment. He was dressed in summer uniform: Pirates' cap and black shirt, gold Pirates' shorts, black knee-length socks with gold stripes. Throughout the game he kept pulling hot dogs and beers from what looked to be his wife's hair-curler bag. He was having a grand old time shouting and yelling and second-guessing Chuck Tanner, the Pirates' manager, until the Astros put together a very serious rally to win the first game 6–4 in the top of the ninth. Much to the displeasure of the man in front of me. He alternately yelled and screamed and then fell silent, slumped in his seat, totally despondent and beyond hope. Then a burst of energy would revitalize him and he'd pound the seat beside him. By the time the game was tied, he had pretty nearly lost his voice and was threatening to go home if the Pirates' didn't get their fucking act together and real goddamn quick. Of course they didn't. So the Pirates became a bunch of clowns in the wrong suits. He ripped off his cap and refused to wear it again, lest anyone mistake him for a Pirate. When Houston scored the go-ahead run (I have no idea how, I was watching the man in front of me), he stood and, with hands on hips, told the Pirates, the city of Pittsburgh, and most of the Monongahela valley to go to hell. He then raised his arms and flung them toward the Pirates' dugout, washing his hands of the entire fucking sorry lot of 'em. And his pants fell down around his ankles. He was wearing no underwear, but that didn't matter. He finished his tirade, standing there butt-ass naked from the waist down, swearing off his season tickets and vowing never to return. Then he reached down, calmly pulled up his pants, stuffed his radio and baseball cap into his wife's curler bag and left. He had warned those clowns once already and that was it. And he wasn't comin' back till they learned to play the game of baseball.

Chapter 8

* * *

September 4

Third round, U.S. Open, National Tennis Center. Johan Kriek versus Roscoe Tanner. Kriek won 6–7 (5–7), 3–6, 7–6 (7–4), 7–6 (7–5), 7–6 (7–2), in three hours and forty-two minutes. But no one should have lost, and no one should have won. I'd stumbled on one of those rare moments when sport transcends its usual boundaries.

The evening started inauspiciously. Hana Mandlikova dispatched Kathy Cummings in less than an hour. Then at 8:31 Kriek-Tanner began. Picking a favorite—a practice I'd adopted to make matches more interesting—was difficult. Kriek was delightful, a Lee Trevino with tennis racket. Tanner reminded me of a friend from the midwest: even-tempered, gentlemanly, and seemingly unflappable.

By midway through the match, picking favorites didn't matter anymore.

Tanner jumped to a 3–0 lead on the strength of his rocket serve. Nobody could see it—that means it must be good—including "Cyclops," the electronic eye used to detect serves up to fourteen inches long. Anything longer the line judge had to call, but

Tanner's serve moved so fast the line judge couldn't tell when a serve was a foot and a half over the line. Kriek complained, making the referee jumpy, who then started second-guessing the electronic eye and calling in serves that were out. I think. The stadium lights glared hard off the green surface, and the only way I could follow Tanner's serve was to watch Kriek and hope I picked up the ball coming off his racket. Tanner, of course, complained when the referee started calling in serves out, so Cyclops was turned off and a linesman positioned to make what is surely the most difficult call in all of sport.

Kriek got back into the set after that, and at 6–5 Tanner, broke serve for the first time to send it to the tiebreaker, which Tanner won with an ace. Tanner won the second set, too, 6–3, the only set that lasted less than thirty minutes. In the third set service held to 4–4 until Kriek broke Tanner to go up 5–4. Tanner countered with two straight games before Kriek tied it at six to send us into the second tiebreaker. This time Kriek won and Tanner led the match two sets to one.

Tanner came out smoking in the fourth set, broke Kriek twice, and held his own serve to go up 3–0 before Kriek could get untracked. At 5–3 Tanner, Kriek reeled off three straight games to wrest the lead from Tanner, but Roscoe tied it again and the crowd rode into its third tiebreaker, close to delirious from all this impossibly wonderful tennis. The tiebreaker mirrored the set. Tanner jumped to a 5–3 lead before Kriek rallied for four straight points to win 7–5.

By now it was 11:25—the fourth set had taken fifty minutes. The night was hot and steamy, a funky gray haze hung over the stadium. Kriek and Tanner were soaked and the crowd was wrung out. Yet there was more to come, and the crowd rallied desperately, willing itself back to life to accept the task at hand: to show respect and admiration for Tanner and Kriek. This had long since ceased to be a tennis match. It was spectacular sport being played by two men who had raised themselves and their game to a new—if temporary—level of excellence. Kriek was seeded twelfth: good but not great. At thirty-one, Tanner was a few years beyond his peak. And the winner would be playing Ivan Lendl. For Kriek and Tanner, this was their stage and now was their moment. A deliciously perfect moment, and I wanted it to last forever.

If only it had. Kriek and Tanner traded games to 2–2 and then

Kriek broke and went up 4–2. Tanner countered with three straight to go up one, Kriek tied it, Tanner went up one again, and then Kriek tied it again at 6–6 to give us our fourth tiebreaker of the evening.

But there was something wrong. Reaching for a short drop in the eleventh game, Roscoe had pulled up short on his return. When he walked to the baseline, a slight limp altered his stride. In the tiebreaker, Kriek broke serve five times, a wholly unexpected, almost tragic turn of events after all the pure and perfect, undiluted sport that had preceded it. At 6–2 Kriek, Tanner back-pedaled for a high lob. He hit the return but his backward momentum left him spread-eagled on the court. He lay there for a long moment, then stood slowly, applause rising with him. A ball girl wiped away the sweat that clung to the court, and then Tanner prepared to serve. But he couldn't. He'd been robbed of his ultimate weapon when he needed it most. Standing flat-footed he swiped at a ball, his racket a flyswatter. Long. He pulled a second ball from his pocket and snapped his wrist with the same ineffectual motion. Net.

Game-set-match Kriek.

Later, sleep was impossible. The match refused to go away, and I played it over and over. The next morning, still exhausted, I stayed home and watched Bill Scanlon upset John McEnroe on CBS. The match would have real bearing on the tournament. To listen to Brent Musberger I'd missed the contest of the year, but I knew I hadn't.

The Open wasn't on my original schedule. Although after the Tanner-Kriek match, it was difficult to remember why. I think I wanted to go to the National Air Races in Reno on September 18. But economics ruled against it: I could find no events en route to make the trip cost-effective. And the effects of cost were becoming more affective. Two weeks at the Open meant two subway tokens a day. After that, I could head to Rhode Island for the America's Cup, another event not on my original schedule. But with *Australia II*'s winged keel raising a ruckus, the Cup had become a must-see event.

But first, I had to survive the two-week U.S. Open tennis marathon. How do the players do it? By the time the Open was over I was exhausted, and all I did was sit and watch and try to get people to talk to me. Not that that was an easy task. The tennis crowd was very different from any crowd I'd yet encountered. They arrived at the National Tennis Center in self-contained units of four to six people and remained autonomous. They sat in their little box seats, watched their tennis, and then went home. Finding conversations was difficult. Interplay between these units was occasional at best and usually precipitated by the unusual (Kriek-Tanner, for instance, or the night the number seven subway broke down after a session). Tennis spectators didn't come to the center to become part of what was happening. What was happening was down there on the court and they were here to watch it.

Aesthetically, there isn't much to recommend the center. Twenty-five outdoor courts packed in one right next to the other, with a couple of trees and macadam walkways in between. A few banquet tents and the inevitable village of tennis suppliers neatly lined up in their cute little booths. The clubhouse and nine indoor courts were sheathed inside aluminum siding. The main stadium was a collection of concrete slabs and brown girders specifically designed, it seemed, to create drafty corridors. It was also incongruously named Louis Armstrong Stadium. Nothing about the center suggested this was Satchmo's kind of place.

There was, however, an egalitarianism that was unabashedly commercial and 100 percent American. This was Lee Iococca's kind of place ("If you find a better tennis center, play there!"). There were, of course, selected areas off limits to the general populace, but there remained ample opportunity for everyone to hang out in semiclose proximity to all the stars here to lend their glamor to the event. Especially in the first few days, when there was just too much tennis on too many courts.

The only thing the Open wasn't was whatever the late night CBS report said it was. This was the first event where I could follow the television coverage while attending the event itself, and I enjoyed coming home each night to find out what my day had been like. Seeing one match at the center meant not seeing all the other matches taking place at the same time. So I missed much of what happened but saw all that I chose to watch. Not a bad tradeoff. To me, the Open was a two-week endurance contest that unfolded slowly, its rhythms tuned to the plunk of racket on ball and ball on court and all of it backed by polite applause. The Open of the late-night CBS report was a series of disjointed highlights backed by *Rocky*-esque music and packed to the max with drama.

I'd come home, turn to Channel 2, and find myself saying, "I didn't know that." And I'd start to wonder if maybe they were talking about a different tournament.

I met Kathy Morgan on the first day. A temporary security guard, her job had been to patrol the walkway to the left of the press box on top of the stadium. The walkway was deserted.

Two days later I ran into her in the downstairs interview room. She greeted me effusively. I lamented the fact that she didn't have Tuesday's plum assignment. She shrugged and stuck her hands in the pockets of her official blue uniform, probably to keep her baggy pants from falling down. "This isn't bad at all," she said. "It's air-conditioned, and I get to listen to all the interviews. You just missed Jimmy Connors; Martina, too. Yesterday I didn't do anything. I sat in one of the box seats and worked on my tan." That explained the pinkish sunburn beneath her freckles.

Kathy told me she'd graduated from Springfield College in Massachusetts in June with a Master's degree in athletic administration. And now here she was working the U.S. Open, holding down the interview room. If I came back next year, she said, she might be in charge of hot dogs.

"I took this job for the contacts," she said. "Like yesterday I was sitting in the office and I talked to one of the heads of security. He suggested I talk to a friend of his. I also talked to some guy who works for a racket company, and, hopefully, I'm going to meet a few more people who can help me out."

"What do you think of this tournament?" I asked.

"I'm really impressed. I like the idea of seeing all the stars. And I guess I thought this would be pretty much the way things are: big, fast-paced, very celebrity-fied. I like it. And then sometimes I think, 'Wow, why didn't I play more tennis when I was a little kid?' "

Kathy had played basketball in college. A degree in athletic administration was a way to stay in sports. "I was told it was an upcoming field for women and there might be real possibilities."

"Well?" Well what? Here she was, wearing an oversized monkey suit and guarding empty walkways.

"I thought the degree would be a foot in the door, but it hasn't turned out that way. The degree looks good but it doesn't mean much. Universities are looking to fill one spot and they're going to take the one person who's best qualified."

"How tough is it being a woman?"

"It's tough being a woman and being involved in sports."

"As a player or administrator?"

"In both, I think. Hopefully, when I'm more involved with a sport or a particular organization, I'll have more insights into that. But I think it's still a little too new to a lot of people for women being involved in sports. I mean, in college we were kind of looked at a little weird."

"So, you haven't come a long way, baby?"

"Well, Title IX has done a whole lot for women's athletics, although it's in jeopardy now. But there is definitely a stereotype."

John Lloyd, Brian Gottfried, and Andrea Jaeger walked into the room. Lloyd sat down at the interview table. His eyes were impossibly blue, his smile lighting the entire room. Gottfried and Jaeger sat off to the side. In the corner sat Chris Evert Lloyd, appropriately demure beneath a white visor. There were only a handful of reporters in the room. Most were British.

Kathy craned her neck to get a better look at Jaeger. "See that woman sitting next to Andrea? The lady in the pink? I wouldn't mind a job like her's. I think she's some sort of athlete's escort. And the lady in white"—she pointed to the woman sitting next to John Lloyd—"I've had my eye on her, too."

Lloyd was interviewed, and then Gottfried and Jaeger, and finally Jose Higueras, who had lost to Lloyd. Then it was me and Kathy in the back of the room again, and the woman in white transcribing the interview tapes. She glanced back at us occasionally, obviously trying to figure out why a guy with a yellow "Press A" badge was interviewing a security guard.

"I'm in my incognito suit," Kathy said, talking to the lady in white but loud enough for only me to hear. "You don't know it yet, but I'm gonna win this tournament."

"What would be the ideal situation for your getting a job?"

"The trick would be to meet someone here with a lot of pull who could recommend me to a small college that needs an assistant athletic director and I'd go walking through the door."

"And reality?"

"Reality is I'm not going to get a job unless I make a few decisions. Maybe volunteer to help out with a program somewhere, do some coaching, just to get the experience I need. If I do a good job, you never know, something might open up."

"I would think the traditional method would be . . ."

"To start in a high school, teach and coach?"

"Right."

"I'm not certified to teach and I don't particularly want to."

"So where's that leave you?"

"Workin' two weeks a year as a guard at the U.S. Open!"

"How ambitious are you?"

"I think that's what it all comes down to. If I'm going to make a career of it, I'd like to go as far as I can. I mean, why be a busboy if you can own the restaurant?"

"Would you be interested in the division two and three colleges?"

"Right now I would. I certainly don't have the luxury of saying no. In fact," she leaned down close to my recorder, "Division ten, if you're out there, I'd be more than happy to join your staff." She leaned back. "A small school would be ideal. I could see myself being in a big-time school and getting kind of lost."

We talked about recruiting violations, graduation ratios, the big bucks, the general all-around morass of college athletics today.

"Why do you want to get mucked up in all of that?"

"I just want to give it my best shot. I really like being around sports. I think sports are really valuable to have through life and you can learn a lot through them.

"I have nothing against a school making money. What I would like to try to do is keep athletes on the same level with the rest of the student body. Once an athlete becomes a money maker, all of a sudden he's in a class by himself. He no longer has to take care of himself. He has no sense of being a student and a lot of values are lost. I'd just want to keep control of the situation; I'd love to have that opportunity."

"Okay, well thanks a lot," I said, clicking off my recorder.

"That'll be a thousand dollars," Kathy said, not missing a beat. "I'm unemployed on September 12!"

I left the interview room and oozed myself back into the muggy air. I had no place to go, and in this awful heat—even at 5 P.M.—I wasn't interested in getting there very fast anyway. I walked around the grounds, through the International Food Village, past the three field courts near the main stadium, and over to "The Grove," a small, semigrassy area with a couple of trees. From there I could see the bleachers that flanked court sixteen. The court was hidden behind green windscreens, but the bleachers were packed. I investigated.

Bruce Manson was playing Tomas Smid. Manson led 6–3, 3–6, and 5–4 in the third set. That did little to explain the crowd, which was literally pouring from the bleachers. I checked the 1983 *Volvo Grand Prix Media Guide*:

> Bruce Manson
> Birthdate: March 20, 1956
> Residence: Ft. Worth, Texas
> Ranking: 1982 75 / 1981 42 / 1980 T79
> 1982 Record:
>
> - Semifinalist at Columbus (d. Denton)
> - Semifinalist at WCT/Mexico City (d. Clerc)
>
> Career Highlights:
>
> - U.S. Open quarterfinalist, 1981
> - Defeated Borg at Palm Springs, 1979
> - All American at University of Southern California
> - Two time NCAA doubles champion, 1975/77.
>
> Bruce Manson is one of those players his colleagues just dread facing . . . a mover and shaker off the court as well, taking a keen interest in the affairs of the game and of the Association of Tennis Professionals.
>
> Tomas Smid
> Birthdate: May 20, 1956
> Residence: Prague, Czechoslovakia
> Ranking: 1982 23 / 1981 31 / 1980 T24

1982 Record:

- Won title at WCT/Mexico City
- Won title at WCT/Cap d'Agde
- Runner-up at WCT/Munich
- Runner-up at Geneva (d. Gerulaitis)
- Member of Czechoslovakian Davis Cup team

Career Highlights:

- Won title at Bologna, Stuttgart, 1980
- Italian Open semifinalist, 1980; d. Orantes
- Won doubles title at Hilversum, 1982 (w/Khodes)

. . . add the 1982 earnings of Lendl (more than $1.9 million) and Smid (more than $500,000) and you can see why these guys are going to have to start riding to and from tournaments in armored cars.

Really. But that still didn't explain all these people hanging from the bleachers watching them play. I checked the schedule. John McEnroe was to play a doubles match after this.

Oh.

Manson and Smid took their time resolving their struggle, much to the chagrin of the crowd. They were here to see McEnroe blow his top, "not this other shit," as one person put it, and they cheered for whoever was leading. When Smid beat Manson in the fourth set to put the match into a fifth, the groans were audible. They were here to see McEnroe lose his cool. Only when Manson took control in the fifth set to win 6–4 did the crowd finally respond to the players on the court. Still, after the match the referee stopped the crowd in midcheer when he called for attention. Rumors had been circulating that the McEnroe match had been moved to another court.

"Ladies and gentlemen, ladies and gentlemen." Manson's victory was already ancient history. "There will be one final match on this court." Dramatic pause (this guy knew his audience). "It is a doubles match."

The place went nuts like it never did for Manson. I decided

right then I wanted to interview him. I could watch McEnroe any time. McEnroe walked onto the court as Manson walked off, and the posture of the crowd shifted. A couple of people said, "Nice match," to Manson, but most everyone was on his feet calling to McEnroe. They'd waited a long time to see if he'd lose his cool, and it was clear they didn't wish to be disappointed.

Arranging an interview with Bruce wasn't difficult. He said no problem, but asked that I set up the interview through proper channels. I didn't know there were any.

Channels imposed a certain format to our conversation. I hadn't happened on him at a practice court. It was my job to ask questions and his job to answer. Despite this artificial structure we talked for almost an hour. Articulate and well-spoken, he instilled form and substance to some of the thoughts and ideas I'd been gathering during seven months on the road.

"I've been ranked as high as 39 in singles and 16 or 17 in doubles," he said early on. "This year I think I'm down to 239. But I got to the quarterfinals two years ago, and I think that was part of the reason yesterday's crowd was as big as it was." He stopped and smiled, a boyish grin that complemented his reddish hair and next-door looks. "That and the promise of McEnroe."

"How good would you like to be?"

"I'd like to be number one—for a little while. Look at a guy like Borg or McEnroe. They've lost their private lives. On the other hand, you want to have people notice you." He shrugged. "I would like to be able to attain my potential; go as far as I can go. It would be nice to be one of the top players, but if it doesn't come about, it doesn't come about."

"Was there a point when you had larger aspirations?"

"Absolutely. When you first start out you want to be ranked in the top 100, then the top 50, then the top 20. I sort of stalled at 39."

"What was that like?"

"It was the first time in my life when I didn't excel. I'd never been in a slump, and then all of a sudden, I was having trouble winning. That was tough to deal with. I started to think: Can I win anymore? Can I win the close ones? Can I beat the top players? A real feeling of uncertainty. Anyone who's achieved always has the fear of waking up and not being able to do what they can do. And that fear can be a driving force to make them continue doing it."

"Was there a point early in your life when you realized, 'Hey, I could be pretty good'?"

"Yeah, there was. The guys I'd grown up with through the juniors and in college were turning pro and they were doing well. I said, 'If they can do that . . .' "

"What was it like knowing you could be that good?"

"Startling. When you have an overall plan and you reach your goals you're glad you achieved it, but you're not really surprised because that's what you'd been working for anyway. For me, the goals just all of a sudden appeared."

"Is the tour lonely?"

"Definitely. I don't think there are any real close friendships on the circuit. It's the nature of the competition. With all the money involved, it's more a business. There's not that comaraderie that existed in the Laver-Rosewall era. And the circuit is so widespread, and everyone is living in different areas."

I asked if he had a favorite city: Stockholm and Tokyo. The tour didn't sound so bad.

"To get to those few moments of appreciating Stockholm and Tokyo you have to put in long hours on the court; getting cramps, being sick, being so exhausted you can't get out of bed to practice, but you do. And that's the majority of the time."

"Can the average sports fan appreciate what you just said?"

"Arthur Ashe said, 'Success is a journey, not a destination.' You have to go through it all, the good and the bad and all the stuff in between, to really be able to appreciate it."

"But the fan only sees . . ."

"The final outcome. The fan is seeing the *now.* They're just seeing him on center court making a million dollars."

"How important are the Connorses and McEnroes to the game?"

"They're very important, but I don't think you should classify them by name. If John McEnroe and Jimmy Connors weren't the top players, somebody else would be. Their roles will be filled."

"But with all the attention they get, isn't it almost impossible for a top player not to think he's bigger than the game?"

"Absolutely. Every professional athlete has to have an ego to be good and to succeed. He has to believe in himself, because when he walks out there nobody is going to be telling him he's any good. Because of that ego, when you do achieve and win and get ranked, it goes to your head and you get a feeling of grandeur. The game wouldn't be as healthy or as profitable if the top players weren't around, but I do think there's a tremendous amount of resentment among the rank-and-file players that maybe the top guys have become a little too selfish.

"But I don't think that's necessarily the individual top players' fault. It's the times and the agents and the forces in the game. And the public expects that kind of attitude from the top players now, and that expectation pushes them in that direction."

"But what does the professional athlete owe the public?"

"I think all we owe the paying public is that from the moment we step on the court we try our hardest, give them their money's worth, and retain a certain respectability on court. But because we are public figures, people expect more than that. People are selfish, and that extends to the jealousy that they can't have what we have—or what they *think* we have—and because of that they put more stringent controls on us as a way of bringing us down from the pedestals.

"People have to have something in their lives to look forward to. I think everybody's got to have dreams, and they can't have those dreams broken."

"You're an entertainer."

"When I first started playing tennis I was more athlete than entertainer. Probably 90-10. Now I'd say it's probably the reverse. The game has changed, and maybe too I've grown up and matured and I understand where tennis is and where it's coming from. Tennis is entertainment."

"Does that bother you?"

"No, it's just the facts. I perform for other people and they come out to watch me. And I think the game would be better off if that attitude were taken at the marketing end. It all boils down to people paying money to watch us perform. That's the key."

I checked my notes for more questions. "Why do so many athletes hang on for so long?"

"It can be several different things. One can be they just love the game. And winning is a drug, it really is. Once you've experienced winning, you keep trying to get it back. And people don't like change. If you've been playing tennis since you were ten years old, and now all of a sudden you're thirty-five and you've got to put on a business suit and work nine to five, that can be a real shock."

"What's going to happen to you?"

"I'm going to find—or at least I think I'm going to find—the next part of my life exciting. There are still things I'd like to do."

I asked if he'd ever played Wimbledon, then realized that was a stupid question. "Of course you've played Wimbledon. What's it like?"

"It's like this. It's just another tournament. It might mean a bit more because more people are watching, but you still have to play the same guys under the same conditions. The public puts too much credence in what the media writes. Everyone has told everyone else that these are *the* events, and because everyone says that, then they have become the big events."

"But not to you."

"If I could peak for certain events, I'd like to peak for the majors. But beating McEnroe at Wimbledon or beating McEnroe at Columbus, Ohio, is still a win over McEnroe and it still means a hell of a lot."

"On the circuit a win is a win?"

"Right."

"I'm surprised to hear that."

"If I beat McEnroe here, it would be considered more important. But that's just the media talking. To the players its a huge win anyplace."

I had no more questions, so I thanked him and we parted. But there was one more question I should have asked: "Whom do you play next?" Saturday he lost to Jimmy Connors, 6–0, 6–4, 6–0.

The hot dogs at the Tennis Center were the best of the year. An all-beef frank on a caraway seed roll with sauerkraut and bacon bits topped by Grey Poupon ("made with white wine") mustard. Ask for a dog and for a buck-fifty that's what you got.

Thursday afternoon of the second week, I asked for two and walked to the International Village to eat them. The village was a good place to find conversation. Seven or eight food booths beneath yellow-and-white-striped awnings created a manufactured gaity conducive to tête-à-têtes. Chairs were at a premium, which forced people to sit with me.

I talked to a woman from Connecticut here with her daughter from San Diego. The daughter wasn't impressed and had found the Ivan Lendl–Mats Wilander match boring. "Next time I come here I want to be entertained," she said.

When they left, their seats were taken by two women my age. They were eating tacos, holding tickets from one of their husband's companies, and wearing big circle sunglasses and jeans. "You know what really cracks me up?" one of them said to me, looking around at the tennis crowd. "All the people who come here wearing their little white tennis outfits. What do they think is going to happen? Someone's going to get hurt and they'll be asked to take over?"

They were PE teachers from Long Island. One taught at Stony Brook College, the other in a Port Washington high school. Port Washington liked Bjorn Borg and Jimmy Connors, which Stony Brook couldn't understand because she liked McEnroe, which Port Washington couldn't understand because how can you like McEnroe if you don't like Connors? Whatever. They were both amazed how old and tired McEnroe looked.

"It must be tough to be number one," one of them said. (I could never remember who was who.) "Not to get there, but to stay there. Actually, I don't know why anyone would want it."

"But you know, you've got to hand it to Martina. She doesn't really have a family, you know, coming over here from Czechoslovakia. All she's got is tennis."

"I hope Martina never wins the Open," the other one said. "She doesn't deserve it. What's she done for tennis besides win? She's a machine. She's too . . . too . . ."

"Masculine?" I offered.

"Exactly." They looked at me like I'd unlocked the secrets of the ages. Or at least said it out loud. "I just don't like the way she plays."

Neither did anyone else. Martina was nobody's favorite, and I sensed an undercurrent of dread whenever the prospect of a win by Team Navratilova was discussed. Martina had never won the Open, and as far as most people were concerned, it would be just fine if she never did. Martina wasn't a real woman.

But sexual preference aside, the real worry was the possible effect a Martina win might have on the women's game. A couple of girls who should have been guys would benefit, but what would happen to the little girls in pigtails and frilly underwear? That was *real* women's tennis, and it had to be preserved. That Martina had raised the level of the game—re-created it, really—was neither appreciated nor particularly welcomed. Martina's regimen of diet, weights, and training would turn a little girl into, well, another Martina. It couldn't be worth the price.

Martina seemed confused and deeply hurt by her reception. Martina wore her game, her heart, and her American citizenship up and down her well-muscled arm. She had redefined the game hoping the tennis crowd would clasp her firmly to its bosom and place her on its highest pedestal. But this belief served almost as tragic flaw. She'd assumed that on-court excellence translated into off-court admiration. The realization that it didn't obviously pained her deeply. Whenever I saw her—on the court, in the press room, practicing, or walking across the grounds—I always expected her to turn to the crowd and cry, "Why won't you just *like* me?"

There was only one way they might: She had to lose, gracefully. And even that was not without its risk. She'd played that game in 1981, losing to Tracy Austin, and a reprise might not work. More to the point, there were too many people at the center waiting to claim Martina's defeat as sweet salvation for the women's game. Martina's best hope of acceptance was long-term commitment to the course she'd already set. To thine own game be true and refuse to go away. If she's lucky, hating Martina Navratilova will eventually become too much like work. Till then, she had to keep winning, cry only when alone, and wait.

The finals, finally.

There was only a modicum of suspense regarding the Navratilova–Evert Lloyd final on Saturday afternoon. Could Chris extend Martina past an hour? She did, by three minutes. The rest of the excitement involved speculation about the inside of Martina's head. Was her powerful game held together with the hidden wires and two-way mirrors of a fragile psyche, ready to desert her at the slightest hint of strain? The accepted answer was yes, but when Martina won, the debate continued anyway. She'd won an Open. Big deal. Her real test would be defending her title next year.

The victory did little to quell the spirits lurking within Martina, either. Holding up a silver trophy couldn't put down the anxiety. No, she said in the postmatch interview, it wasn't unfair that the new girls had to play against her; if they wanted what she had they could work just as hard. She was glad the title had stayed home in America; if they'd played the national anthem she would have cried for sure. And she really hoped her style of play influenced future players. After the interview, reporters, USTA officials, and assorted hangers-on surrounded her, but as she moved toward the door she stopped to talk to Frank Deford of *Sports Illustrated.* All schoolgirl shy like she was waiting for a dance, she asked him if this win meant she'd finally get her picture on the cover.

The men's final was played the next day, Sunday, September 11. The temperature was 99 degrees, so I sat high atop the stadium, just beneath the flag, which was flying at half mast in remembrance of the victims of Korean Air Lines flight 007. Up here there was a good breeze. Behind me and across the subway tracks was Shea Stadium, where the Jets were playing the Seattle Seahawks.

The Connors-Lendl confrontation created a problem, at least for me. Connors was the most charismatic, appealing personality I'd seen all year. In the press interviews he'd been, by turns, witty and courteous, funny and gracious, thoughtful and occasionally introspective. A complete charmer. On court, he was totally consumed, all animal and wildly entertaining. And more than any athlete I encountered fully aware of the moment thrust upon him and capable of riding it for all it was worth. Ivan Lendl, meanwhile, was easily the most intriguing personality, and probably the year's most impressive athlete. I wanted them both to win.

I first saw Lendl in an early round against Shlomo Glickstein. Awesome (Ivan, not Shlomo). Like Rod Carew at the All-Star Game, a standout even while surrounded by his peers. An erect, muscular six feet two inches and 190 pounds, with powerful legs and broad shoulders, he covered the court effortlessly, ruling his domain with an imperial air; dark and brooding, mysterious, and totally impervious. He played mainly from the baseline, and surely there can be no more feared shot in the game than Ivan Lendl moving to his right to unleash a crosscourt, forehand winner.

But it was his off-court demeanor that intrigued me. I'd heard all the stories about "Ivan the Terrible," and indeed his court persona did lend credence to that image. On the court he lurked inside a smoldering hostility enhanced by deep-set eyes. But off court he seemed to be trying hard, almost desperately, to be a nice guy. Not what I'd expected.

For the two days leading to the finals I asked reporters their opinions of Ivan Lendl. To a person, they insisted I was seeing a "new" man. Some, in fact, had never seen him like this before. Lendl, they said, is a young man who grew up in a country where you're conditioned not to talk to people, and then, all of a sudden, he was here in the United States and everyone wanted to talk to him. Reporters remembered when his postmatch interviews consisted of "I scored six both times and he didn't." He was, they said, obviously making a conscious effort to be more accessible, more trusting. In fact, in Cincinnati earlier this year he'd called a press conference and told reporters that because they'd been fair with him during the tournament he was going to be more open and talkative.

The reporters agreed it was probably a calculated move, but it had nothing to do with money. Lendl had a $2 million contract from Adidas. He didn't need the money. But he did need to be understood. One reporter told me a story of Lendl's learning Polish as a birthday present to his mentor, Wojtek Fibak, so Fibak would have someone to speak with in his native tongue. I couldn't confirm if the story were true, but it went a long way to explain the Lendl who wanted to be understood.

In the press conferences, Lendl worked just as hard in English—too hard, perhaps—to banter back and forth with the media. Sometimes it worked and sometimes it didn't. His English was letter-perfect, but the nuance of language was absent. His attempts at humor were often clunky, like he was hitting us over the head with his tennis racket. But he never stopped trying to be understood.

So I cheered for Lendl to beat Jimmy Connors, quite possibly the only person in the stadium who did. But this was Jimmy's Open. It was also his court, his championship, his moment, and, finally, his victory. Connors won two of the first three sets and then wiped Lendl all over the Decoturf II surface to wrap it up in the fourth. The guy behind me, listening to the Jets game on his Walkman, kept us apprised of the goings-on at Shea—the Jets lost—and, as Connors pummeled Lendl through the final set, took to yelling, "Ivan the Terrible, Ivan the Terrible," every chance he got.

* * *

Sunday, September 17

I turned off Interstate 95 onto Route 138, a two-lane blacktop in Rhode Island. "I'm going to make my year on the road." The thought slapped me across the face. Six months ago I'd been in Alaska for the North American Sled Dog Championships. Since then I'd been chasing summer around the United States. Spring and summer had become one long season, the days melting one into the next. But now a hint of autumn touched the leaves. I was eight months into my trip! Four more months! I could make it on the weight of my own momentum. The sky was pale blue behind thin clouds. On both sides were thick forests. Newport and the America's Cup lay at the end of the road, but I was in no hurry.

Locust Rock Farm. Brigg's Country Cupboard. A tiny, ancient cemetery. Newman's Egg Farm. John and Cindy's Vegetables ("Our own fresh cauliflower" on a chalkboard sign). The Cookoo Nest. Glass Blowers Gift Shop. A road sign pointing left to Usquepaug. Haines River Baptist Church. Peter Potts Pottery.

Past South Kingston the road deteriorated. The wide shoulders disappeared. So did the forests, replaced by cornfields. For sale: Dog Houses. Log Splitter Rentals.

Kingston: Huge maples lined the road; houses, small and well kept, sat behind the trees. Joggers ran past in the opposite direction. To the left was the University of Rhode Island; nine tennis courts followed by an entrance of polished cement; in the distance many red brick buildings. A gas station on the right still displayed Pegasus, the flying horse.

Sunnyledge Farms beyond Kingston. Farther along, a small white house by a dark pond covered with lily pads. Goldenrod stretched forever to my right. Down a long hill to Narragansett Bay, the road etched between walls of rock. The bridge to Conanicut Island a thin strand of highway stretched from the mainland.

Jamestown on Conanicut. The island large enough to forget I was on an island. Two dollars to cross the Newport Bridge; a man-made hill, from the top of the bridge I could see Newport and the harbor. There were enough boats to walk across the water hopping from boat to boat.

I arrived in Newport at the same time *Australia II* was arriving back in port, fresh from its convincing victory over *Liberty* in the day's race. The Americans still held a 2–1 lead, but the warning salvo had been sounded. *Australia II* was everything everyone had feared it might be: lightning in light winds.

I left Jabba at the Chamber of Commerce parking lot and walked down America's Cup Avenue, Newport's commercial district. An Early New England Seafaring Town playing at the real thing but looking like a freshly salted Disneyland. A certain style but zero depth. Buildings that should have been home to sailmakers and shot-and-a-beer bars were instead inhabited by designer dress shops, cookie outlets, and hand-dipped ice cream parlors, their weather-beaten storefronts renovated to within inches of their lives. I couldn't take any of it seriously, although Newport obviously did.

Worse, I despaired immediately of ever meeting a real live Newporter. The place was overrun with people wearing shoes, but no socks, and sweaters tied around their shoulders. They poured from bars, jammed shops, and sat at small tables at small cafés. Everyone working just as hard at belonging to the scene as Newport did at creating it.

There was, however, much to recommend the place, although I didn't find it until Monday, an off day.

Thames Street connected with America's Cup Avenue at Memorial Boulevard, and extended the commercial district another six or seven blocks. But at the corner of Wellington and Thames, Newport stopped pretending to be an Old New England Town and became an old New England town. The famous eighty-room mansions of Newport's 400 were farther up the hill, but down here was a grid of streets overcrowded with wonderfully quaint Cape Cod-style houses with dormers and steeply peaked roofs and little additions poking out the walls. Tiny front lawns were protected from the street by hedgerows and picket fences. Many houses were a rich, deep blue with white trim. Some could have used a coat of paint, but after the excruciating perfectness of America's Cup Avenue and Thames Street, a house in need of a paint job never looked so good.

My second discovery was the waterfront, which I found when looking for *Liberty*. It is difficult to create a waterfront, especially one given to the serious business of the America's Cup challenge. There just isn't time to consider aesthetics. The docks were functional, utilitarian, *unself-conscious,* teaming with life and alive with a real vitality the renovated sections of Newport could never duplicate. They even smelled better: oil, seawater, and dead fish, a combination that shouldn't smell good but always does.

The waterfront ran parallel to and behind Thames Street, the backlot of the movie set where the real action was unfolding. It was impossible to get anywhere near *Australia II.* The white boat was sequestered behind a well guarded eight-foot, chain-link fence, its mystery keel wrapped in a shroud even when it was in the water. *Liberty* was a little more accessible. It was docked at the end of the Williams & Manchester Shipyard, and although the dock was off limits, I could see the boat hanging in its sling, with *Freedom,* the 1980 defender, sitting in the water next to it.

Most people had the same reaction upon seeing *Liberty* for the first time: ugly. I agreed; I expected more from a twelve-meter boat. Something sleeker, flashier, sexier. Or maybe a twelve-meter boat should never be viewed when it's out of the water. Hanging in its sling it looked like a bloated fish left in the sun. I also didn't like the color, and neither did anyone else. Blood red, perhaps, or maybe even rust. Who wants a rusty boat?

By comparison, *Freedom* looked fantastic. A rich blue with a thin red and white stripe, it was at home in the water and ready to race even as it sat just bobbing on the waves. From our vantage point seventy-five yards away from the two boats, the crowd decided we'd all rather have *Freedom* defend us than *Liberty.*

The America's Cup was not a spectator sport. Boat charters joining the spectator fleet started at seventy bucks and private boat owners were charging at least thirty-five. Tuesday morning, I tried to talk my way onto a boat or two, but was rebuffed immediately. I gave up and decided to watch the race on closed-circuit TV down at the Chamber of Commerce.

But the America's Cup wasn't much of a television sport, either. By the time I arrived, the race had already started and *Liberty* was in the lead. Coverage consisted of a shot of *Liberty* followed by a shot of *Australia II.* Rarely were both boats on screen together. Lag time was filled by an Australian announcer and his American cohort on WADK Newport. Their observations were diverting and entertaining, but as a television production it couldn't have been duller.

Yet the excitement was obvious; the tension visceral. Never mind that television couldn't bring the race to us, or that we couldn't get to the race. This had been no ordinary Cup competition—the winged keel had seen to that—and the only way to experience its impact was to be here, now, in Newport, Rhode Island, while the twelve-meters were out there battling head to head. The rules of twelve-meter racing had been inexorably rewritten. No matter the final outcome, history had been altered. To be here was to understand that intuitively.

I spent the race talking to Alex Patison, an electrical engineer from Sydney, Australia. He was in the middle of an around-the-world trip and had rearranged his plans after hearing that *Australia II* was in the finals. He figured there were about five thousand Aussies here in Newport and that most, like him, were not racing fans as much as they were Australians who happened to be in the neighborhood.

What impressed him most about America, he said, was the size of the cars. "Yank Tanks," he called them. His biggest disappointment was going to the comedy clubs in New York. He'd really been looking forward to that, but once he got there, he realized he didn't understand why anyone was laughing.

When *Liberty* rounded the fourth and final mark, Alex timed *Australia II*'s arrival. His forty-eight-second clocking matched the official time.

"It doesn't look good now," he said.

"Ca-mon mite!" I said. Alex had just given me a lesson in the Australian drawl. "You chap, can't give up there, now. What'd'yu say?" Alex laughed. I dropped the Australian drawl and with mock seriousness intoned: "Remember, it ain't over till it's over." Alex looked at me, his face a blank slate. I looked at him and laughed. "Well," I said, "if you were an American you'd think that was pretty funny."

Liberty won by forty-three seconds, finishing the race at 3:39 P.M., in three hours, twenty minutes, and seventeen seconds. I went back to the Williams & Manchester Shipyard to wait for *Liberty*. So did most of Newport, and by the time the boat was in port the dock was overrun. Things looked no less hectic out in the harbor. The sun was falling toward the horizon, turning the water into a silhouetted forest of masts and guy wires. An occasional canon sounded a welcome, usually followed by choruses of "U.S.A.! U.S.A.! U.S.A.!"

Liberty's crew, minus skipper Dennis Conner, who'd been spirited directly to press headquarters, were heralded as conquering heroes when they walked into the crowd. Dressed in blue bermuda shorts, white shirts, and red blazers, their faces were flushed and beaming with a thrill of victory difficult to contain. Their first two wins had been as much the fault of *Australia II's* equipment as anything they'd done as sailors, and after being soundly thrashed by the winged keel on Sunday, today's triumph was vindication. They'd beaten a boat they had no business beating. Their boat was clearly inferior to the Australian boat, and yet today, by combining luck, pluck, skill, and superior tactics, they'd looked the monster in the face and come away laughing. They had flat-out outsailed *Australia II.* A triumph of the human spirit over technology, and victory doesn't come sweeter than that. Now they commanded a 3–1 lead. There was just no way they could lose three in a row. That would be impossible. A summer's turmoil was one race away from being laid to rest forever.

Watching the celebrations I was suddenly aware how long was the shadow cast by the winged keel. It was not just some thing sticking from the bottom of a boat. The winged keel was a living, breathing presence looming over Newport. It was a topic in all conversations, the subject of most newspaper articles, and the object of intense speculation.

As to questions of its legality, there were as many opinions as there were people to propose them: It was the ultimate twelve-meter; it wasn't a twelve-meter at all. Consensus was impossible, and any discussion tended to the volatile.

There was, however, agreement on one element of the controversy: the role of the New York Yacht Club. Simply put, the NYYC consisted of the most arrogant sons-a-bitches you'd ever want to meet. They'd had their opportunity earlier in the year to determine whether the winged keel conformed to the formula required of twelve-meter boats. Given that the twelve-meter equation was as convoluted a series of numbers as you'd ever hope to add, consensus seemed to indicate that no one would have argued had the keel been ruled illegal right off the bat. But in point of fact the keel had been judged a twelve-meter boat. So what happened? In the qualifying races *Australia II* sailed the halyards off everybody. That got the boys of the NYYC a bit hot under their very proper collars, so they decided the keel required a second look-see.

Here's where consensus reached its zenith—and made tonight's celebration so sweet. Reruling on the keel was dirty pool. Worse, it was poor sportsmanship. No one denied that in past years there hadn't been chicanery regarding the rules. But in the America's Cup, grown men spend years of their lives and tons of other people's money trying to win a silver ewer that resembles a very ugly and *extremely* tacky vinegar cruet. In point of fact, if there was one competition in the world that should epitomize the very purity of what sports can be, the America's Cup should be it. Calling for another ruling was dealing off the bottom of the deck. The place to beat the Aussies was on the high seas. Boat against boat and sailor against sailor in the theater of ultimate competition. If the New York Yacht Club couldn't keep the Cup fair and square, they didn't deserve to have it at all.

Thursday, I ate breakfast at Gary's Handy Lunch, as I'd been doing every morning. The Handy Lunch was on Thames Street, in the heart of the revitalized section, but despite the renovated exterior, the inside remained what it had been since Gary bought the place thirteen years ago: a good place to get a great breakfast. Scrambled eggs, hash browns, toast, orange juice, and coffee for $2.07.

As usual, the place was crowded. I sat at the orange Formica counter. In front of me was a small hole in the wall through which supplies could be purchased at the store next door. Behind me the tables were covered with mustard-and-white-checked tablecloths. The walls, of course, were covered with the requisite scenes of sailing ships. On the end wall, however, was the famous World War II photo of the sailor kissing the girl in Times Square. Next to it was a portrait of a World War II sailor, and next to that a second picture of an elderly couple in Times Square striking the same kissing pose, minus the elasticity. I asked Joe, Gary's son, if the man in the middle photo was the real kissing sailor.

"That's him," Joe said. "He owns the fishing dock right down from here." I remembered *Life* magazine conducting a search for the kissing sailor a few years back.

"Yeah, well, *Life* never admitted he was the man in the photo.

If they had, they'd'a owed him for all the times they used the photo."

Johnny sat down next to me. An old man with a three-day stubble, tan pants, tan shirt, and tan Go to Hell hat with the brim turned up. He said he was seventy-six. When he talked his voice sounded far away, like he was talking through three pieces of cotton stuck in his throat.

"See the Oyster House right down there?" he said. "All fancy now. I was born there. Just a shack then. See that power plant over there?" He pointed in the general direction of the docks. "Well, it don't work no more, you know? I mean, they bring the power in from someplace else now. But I can remember being a kid and going down there—they used to use coal—and after they raked out all the old coal we used to fill our buckets and take the coal home. That's how we used to heat our homes. I still tell my kids that."

Joe placed a cup of coffee in front of Johnny. "Now come on, Johnny, don't be makin' up stories."

"Get outta here," he said. Joe laughed.

"I worked in the gov'ment," Johnny continued. "I was making torpedoes for the navy during World War II. Just about got myself killed workin' on a pile driver puttin' in those big fifty-, sixty-footers. I had a bunch of 'em up one day when the strap broke and goddamn if they didn't all come down right across the top of my head." He took off his hat, rubbed his head, and laughed. "I was laid up for five months. Left a healthy crease in my head, let me tell you. But I went back to work again, doin' this, doin' that, till I had enough time in for my pension. Got a disability, too."

"Has the town changed much?" I asked. I was quite sure I knew the answer.

"Jesus Christ, goddamn right," Johnny said. He pointed to the waterfront. "You used to be able to go down there anywhere and walk the whole way up. Now they got those condominiums and all that down there.

"Different kind of people here now, too. They all got au-to-mo-biles. And the navy pulled outta here, what, ten years ago?" He nudged the man sitting next to him. "Jim here, he remembers."

"Some of it, some of it," Jim said. "I remember one time walking down from where Memorial runs into Thames Street." He pronounced the "th" of Thames, the local pronunciation. "I counted twenty-seven bars from there just down to Wellington Street." The same walk I'd taken Monday. Twenty-seven bars or 127 designer outlet shops in a seven-block area. Are they the only choices we get?

"Yeah," Johnny said, "it's a different kind of town."

I'll bet. I asked how many people the navy brought to the town.

"Don't know," Johnny said. "But I used to work the docks a long time ago. And I can remember one time countin' forty-four ships in here one time. All of them navy."

"You guys did a lot of countin' in the old days, didn't you?" I said. Johnny liked that one. He stood up, laughing, and shuffled toward the door.

The race had started by the time I left the Handy Lunch. For the first time the streets were deserted. Everyone was someplace watching or listening to the race. Enjoying the solitude, I took my time walking to the Chamber of Commerce. The race wouldn't be over quickly. When I got there, the TV announcer was saying, "Everything that could have gone wrong for the Americans has gone wrong." I checked the time board. By the first mark the Australians had a two-minute, twenty-nine-second lead. Yesterday *Australia II* had beaten a *Liberty* crippled by mast problems. Now the boat from Down Under was in position to pull even at three races apiece.

The impossible was beginning to happen.

1 P.M., Friday I walk to the Williams & Manchester Shipyards. *Liberty* is gone. She's been taken somewhere to get her ballast shifted. *Freedom* swings gently in the sling.

Dennis Conner walks down the dock to the chain-link gate and leaves the compound. He's wearing blue shorts and a white shirt with "Freedom 83" on the left breast. Three reporters have been standing outside the gate. Conner stops, although it's obvious he'd rather not. He answers questions politely, the sentences short and clipped, the portrait of a nervous man.

"Given the perfect race for both boats," a reporter asks, "can *Liberty* still beat *Australia*?" Dennis says nothing. Instead, he bites his sandwich.

"I'm not going to answer that," he says after a while. But then going off the record, he says there isn't a twelve-meter boat in the world that can beat *Australia II*.

For a moment the reporters stand in silence, stunned. Then, "I wish that were on the record."

"Well it's not." End of interview. In 1980 Dennis successfully defended the Cup in *Freedom.* But that doesn't matter now.

5:30 Dennis Conner, inside the *Liberty* compound, holds a meeting with the crew. On a bulletin board is a sign: "Supper tonight (Friday) 6:30 P.M. Attitude adjustment at 6 P.M."

Also:

All men dream but not equally

T. E. Lawrence

Kick Ass, *Liberty!*

The meeting takes an informal, off-the-cuff air. Hale-well-fare-thee-well. The crew is robust and sunburned and mostly mustachioed, with sun-bleached, windblown hair.

6:15 I stop to talk to the security guard inside the *Liberty* compound. "Well," I say, "what'd'ya think?" He's about my age, and is wearing a red "Freedom 83" shirt. His cap also says "Freedom 83."

"It's excitin', isn't it?" he says. "All goes down to tomorrow. I always said it was going to go to seven races. I just had that feeling, you know?"

"Why's that?"

"Can't tell you that, man. Confidential."

I tell him my name and where I'm from. For the moment, that's all.

"Fairbanks? Alaska? No shit! You want to know why?" He walks over to the gate. He's wearing sunglasses even though the sun is setting quickly. "Because there is a boat named *Freedom* sitting up in the sling right now and they never gave it a chance to defend its title. That boat's a champion and here they are usin' *Liberty.*"

"Can *Liberty* win?"

"I hope so, man, I hope so. But I doubt it. That Australian boat ain't no fuckin' boat." He laughs at what he's just said. "The motherfucker's got wings, man. You hear what I'm sayin'? Wings!"

"Don't get me wrong, now, I love my country. I fought for it and everything. I was in Nam in '68. I want *Liberty* to win tomorrow, but I just don't think it can. That thing . . . ," he points in the direction of the *Australia II* compound, "is not a twelve-meter boat. A twelve-meter boat is a thing of beauty; it doesn't have any fuckin' wings stickin' out of it. You ever see a twelve-meter boat up close?"

"No, I haven't."

His voice grows enthusiastic and more friendly. "Want to see *Freedom?* The *champion* twelve-meter?"

I'd love to. I step onto hallowed ground, but then stop. I make a clean breast of things. Who I am and what I'm doing. He likes the idea and says don't worry about it.

We walk out to the tip of the dock, a narrow wooden walkway above the water. A stiff breeze sings through the wires. Toward the end of the dock is the *Bermbee;* beyond it, *Freedom.* It is hanging in the sling, silhouetted against an orange sky. It looks just like *Liberty* did hanging there, a big bloated fish—until I am standing next to it, my image reflecting in its deep blue hull.

"Is this a fuckin' boat or is this a fuckin' boat?" he asks.

Yes. I walk to the bow and look down the hull. The lines are fast, clean, precise. Nothing sharp or angled, nothing severe. From bow to stern the lines flow one into the other, creating the very real impression that there is no other configuration the boat could possibly have. The water reflects against it. The hull shimmers with movement and speed.

"This boat's a champion," he says. "Ever touch a twelve-meter? Go ahead. Just run your hand along the side." I do, leaving a faint trail in the dust.

"It's been out of the water all day," he says. Then, mournfully, "They never gave this boat a chance to show what it could do."

I follow the lines down the hull to the keel. At the very bottom is a vague outline, like something wedge-shaped had been attached at right angles and later removed.

"That's where they experimented with wings, isn't it?" I say.

"Yeah, can you believe it?" His voice chokes with indignation. "This boat's the champion and here they are fuckin' around with it."

"Kind of a desecration, huh?"

"That's it, that's it!" he says. "That's exactly what they did! They desecrated a fuckin' champion."

9:45 On the way to the van I stop at Buddy's, one of two remaining tattoo parlors in Newport. There used to be at least seven, so I'm told. In a tiny, glass-enclosed booth some guy is getting "ANDY" tattooed on his upper right bicep.

Buddy (I assume) invites me to look around. The parlor is one bare room with pictures of tattoos painted on flesh-colored paper covering the walls. Lot's of naked women, chains, ropes, eagles, and lions. The cheapest is $40. The most expensive, a huge, snarling panther, is $90. Buddy says business is good. A lot of people come with their own design, and many are women. It's a living.

11:10 Yesterday I talked to Alex Patison. He'd gotten out on the sound to see a race by waiting standby on one of the Coast Guard observation boats. He said it was easy and only $4. "The view is spectacular," he said. "I queued up at 3 A.M." I decide to try it tonight. There is history to be made on the sound tomorrow, and I want to see it.

I drive to the naval station. A guard tells me to wait up the hill. "People'll probably start getting in line about 4 A.M."

I park and ask a couple of Australians in a motor home to pound on the van when they go down. "Sure thing, mite."

11:25 Loud pounding. " 'Ey, mite. We're going down now. But if the queue starts forming up we'll come and get you."

"Thanks," I say, and go back to sleep.

2:30 A.M., Saturday More pounding. "Excuse me, mite," A female Aussie. "The queue's forming up." I try to go back to sleep but can't. I dress quickly, fighting the chill, donning long underwear and a thick turtleneck sweater. By the time I arrive at the gate I am number fifty in line, or queue, or whatever. Everyone is hunkered inside parkas or sleeping bags, hiding from the wind. Everyone but some guy in cutoffs and T-shirt.

"That guy gets my man of the year award," someone says. "Or maybe nut of the year."

"Hey, we all get that." No one argues. This *is* nuts. But no one leaves. A seventh race in the America's Cup, and we can be there.

5:15 The guard begins letting people onto the base, twenty-five at a time so there is no stampede. Most everyone heads to the *Vigilance.* With three others I run to the *Chase,* at the end of the base. When I get there I find I'm number forty in line. We begin waiting again.

6:05 The line snakes around a huge pile of barrels; its tail is almost touching the beginning. I start eating a box of Saltine crackers. I'll get seasick if I don't have something in my stomach.

7:00 The enemy—the pass holders—begin to arrive. The sun arrives, too, bringing warmth.

7:50 A man nods toward an elderly couple, probably in their seventies, standing just off to the side of the front of the line. "What are we going to do about them?" he asks me. "They just got here. I've been here since midnight. If they get on before me. . . ." He walks to the front of the line, near the couple, and then in a loud voice asks another man the same question he'd just asked me. The old couple gets the hint and drifts away.

8:30 The enemy is present and accounted for. The *Chase* is laden with passengers. The ensign counts off the first fifteen in the standby line and allows them to board. We move forward eagerly. A few minutes later another fifteen. I will be in the next wave. But there is no next wave. "I've let on 170 more people than I'm permitted," the ensign says. "I'm very sorry." So are we.

No one leaves until a crane removes the gangplank. The man next to me, a New York cabbie, begins to laugh. "In this game," he says, "there are winners and there are losers. We be the loooooooosers." I laugh, too.

8:45 One final hope. The 250 people who didn't get on the *Chase* walk over to the *Vigilance* and join the 250 people who didn't get on there. The situation is hopeless here, too. I begin to understand the emotions present on the *Titantic.*

9:00 The gangplank is removed from the *Vigilance.* That signals the end. Bedraggled and tired, clutching a half-eaten box of Saltines, I shuffle off the base surrounded by 499 equally dismal-looking souls. "Now I know what it feels like to be a refugee," someone says.

10:30 The Handy Lunch is packed. I am hurried through my pancakes, and then I walk back to the Chamber of Commerce fully intent on watching the race. But I've been up for twenty-four hours and I'm exhausted, and suddenly the race of the century doesn't seem so important anymore. I crawl into the back of Jabba and fall asleep.

12:15 P.M. The chop-chop-chop of a helicopter bounces around inside the van. What is a helicopter doing over here? Unless—the race has been canceled. I call to some people and they confirm it. There was no wind.

The rest of the day I walk zombielike through the streets of Newport. Traffic has come to a virtual stop on Thames. The side-walks are so crowded it is easier to walk in the streets. The whole world, it appears, is here for the weekend. By 8 P.M. I simply must escape. I retreat over the bridge, across Conanicut Island to a friend's place in Narragansett on the other side of the bay. I arrive in time to eat supper, shower, and fall asleep by ten o'clock. I wake up sixteen hours later to discover the Americans have called another lay day. On television Franco Harris becomes the second leading rusher in the NFL.

Monday morning. Another late breakfast at the Handy Lunch. Today it wasn't crowded and neither was Newport. Everyone had left. Joe, standing by the grill, said he was happy to see the tourists leave.

"But you must have done good business," I said. Joe's smile grew larger. He was in his late twenties, I figured, although his round face and short reddish hair gave him a boyish appearance. The kind of guy you couldn't help but like.

"We went through a case and a half of eggs on Saturday," he said. "But a place like this, if you don't have the local trade you won't survive the winter."

By the time the race started, it was just me and Joe. I paid my bill and was about to leave when Joe pulled a beat-up Gold Star TV from beneath the counter. "People don't know it," he said, "but I can get the race here." He put the set on the counter and turned it on.

"I really want to watch this thing," Joe said, growing excited. "These guys are friends. They rented some of our apartments this winter. Sometimes I think I want them to win it more than they do. I've got all kinds of bets out on this thing, and I don't even like to gamble. I popped my mouth off to an Australian reporter."

Liberty established a quick lead, or as quick a lead as can be established in yacht racing. By the second mark, the Americans owned a forty-five-second lead. Joe, too nervous to watch and too scared not to, busied himself at the grill.

A man walked in and ordered a hot dog, then walked over to the TV, his steps long and deliberate. "I'm gonna shut this thing off," he said.

"You do and I'll break your arm!" Joe said. The man cackled, then turned to me. "If *Liberty* wins this thing, you're gonna have to tie Joe down; he'll go crazy."

The announcer said *Liberty* had opened its lead to fifty-four seconds. On the screen we could see *Australia II* send a man up the mast. "Boy," Joe said, "I don't know how they do it; I'd be scared to death. What happens if he falls off? Do they have to go back and pick him up?"

Two mailmen checked in. One carrier had hustled through his route so he could see the race. The other was taking his time, watching the race as he walked from place to place. The TV returned from a commercial. The race was into its third leg.

"Looks like *Australia*'s closed it up a bit, doesn't it?" Joe said. We listened to the announcer. *Australia* had made up fifteen seconds. Joe shook his head.

"Right after they sent that monkey up the mast." He walked closer to the TV. "Looks like *Liberty* doesn't have its spinnaker all the way up. If they don't watch it, *Liberty's* gonna get dirty air."

I'd heard that before. "Dirty air." That and "cover." I'd never learned what either term meant, exactly, but it was obvious they were important. In match racing, near as I could tell, tactics could be worth almost as much as the speed of the boat. The idea was to cover the opponent and block his wind, which resulted in dirty air. Or something like that. Joe got a pencil and a paper napkin and tried to explain it to me.

"Listen to him," the man said, pointing to Joe and looking at me. "The guy's never been on a boat in his life." Joe, still drawing on the napkin, started laughing and finally had to stop with the sketches. The announcer then explained dirty air and cover. I didn't understand what he was saying, either, but it was obviously a different explanation from Joe's. He crumpled the napkins and threw them away.

"So what do I know?"

Gary, Joe's father, walked in, breathless. "I just heard on the radio that *Liberty* is really gaining." On the television, we were seeing 1974 highlights.

"Get that off," Joe yelled at the set. "Where's the radio? We got to find out what's goin' on out there!" The coverage returned to today's race. *Liberty* was at the fourth mark holding a fifty-seven-second lead. Gary clapped and rubbed his hands together.

"I better go get my congratulations sign."

But Joe wasn't celebrating. "This is *Australia*'s leg," he said, more to himself than to anyone else.

Gary returned with a canvas congratulations sign rolled up beneath his arm. "I've done this for every Cup. Although for this year what I did was cut the year off the last Cup's banner.

Joe cocked his ear to the TV. "*Australia*'s catching up dramatically."

"What?"

"They just said it. *Australia*'s only a couple boat lengths behind."

"You can't believe what they say. Turn on the radio."

A radio was found and tuned to the race. *Liberty* was no longer a couple boat lengths ahead. *Liberty* was losing. "That's it, that's it," Joe said, grabbing a broom to sweep the floor. "Once the Australians get the lead they can't be beat. No way."

Australia II was the first boat to pass the fifth marker. We waited for *Liberty* to pass the marker for twenty-one agonizing seconds.

Gary: "I'm gettin' out of town.

Joe: "I guess we're gonna find out if God's an American or an Australian."

Joe walked over to the TV set. The picture was a close-up of the *Liberty*. "My God, can you imagine the tension out there?" No I couldn't. But I was suddenly aware of the tension in the pit of my stomach. I'd been watching this as intently as any contest I'd seen all year. I never thought I'd say that about a boat race.

Gary left his shop, leaving "Congratulations: Dennis and Crew" rolled up on a table. Joe walked to the end of the counter, as far from the TV as he could get. He pulled a Danish from a canister and sat down. "We lost it," he said. "The Cup's gone. Fifty-seven seconds. Fif-ty sev-ven seconds! You know, I had a feeling."

One by one, people stopped in to give Joe the business. Joe was the kind of guy you love to razz because you like him so much and you know he can take it.

"Hey Joe, can I borrow some money?"

"Hey Joe, bon voyage!"

A woman walked in. "Hey, Joey baby." She turned around and flipped the back of her jacket into the air, feigning a moon. Joe sat at the counter, smiling and accepting his fate.

"You wait," he said, turning to me. "We'll go down there and win the Cup back right off. Then they'll have it here the next time and I'll be able to bust their humps. I'd love it."

For one of the first times all day, both *Liberty* and *Australia II* were on screen together. *Australia II* at the top, mirroring every action of *Liberty* at the bottom. It looked like *Liberty* was going to sail head first into the spectator fleet in hopes of crashing *Australia II* into a boat. A voice with a distinct Australian drawl called to Joe.

" 'Ey there mite! You goin' to be open tomorrow?" Then he laughed. Joe waved.

"Get outta here." The man continued down the street. "That's the Australian journalist I was telling you about, the guy I made the bets with.

Joe stood up and ran to the door. "Hey," he shouted, a wide smile breaking across his face. "You think they could use a breakfast shop down in Perth?"

Newport was pandemonium by the time the conqueror and the conquered returned to the waterfront. Helicopters beat the air. Cannons boomed a continuous barrage. Christie's Landing, the unofficial Australian gathering place, was awash in Swan Lager, a beer owned, not coincidentally, by Alan Bond, the head of the *Australia II* syndicate. The Mr. T. Band hammered out "Waltzing Matilda" over and over. The party poured into Thames Street and eventually centered itself in front of the Armory, an imposing stone building with twin turrets that had been used as the press headquarters. More and more lager was quaffed, and finally a couple of Aussies climbed the Armory walls to plant the Union Jack atop a turret. The Bastille had been stormed.

I ran into Alex in an alleyway as I walked down to the slip where *Australia II* was berthed. He was surely the only Australian in the world not at this moment drinking beer. Alex shrugged. "I never acquired the taste."

"Hey look," he said, "there goes the millionaire." Alan Bond scooted past on a yellow moped. Except for Alex, I don't think anyone recognized him. He stopped at the corner on Thames Street, waited for a break in the mob, and then the man who'd spent $16 million to pry a four-pound four-ounce silver cup from a table in New York City disappeared into the night.

A few minutes later John Bertrand, the skipper of *Australia II*, walked up the alley, still wearing the green and yellow slicker he'd had on during the race. He cut a wildly romantic profile, straight and erect, his hair tossed by the wind, his eyes sparkling, his Fu Manchu mustache lending the proper air of intensity. Alex stuck out his hand, "Thanks, mite," he said. Bertrand nodded and continued walking.

I exchanged addresses with Alex and then walked down to *Australia II*. The keel had been unveiled, and like everyone else in Newport, I simply had to see it.

The scene was an archeological dig gone mad. *Australia II* was suspended above the water. Floodlights bathed the white hull. All around it and from underneath it, too, people were reaching out to touch it, feel it, check to see if it was real.

My first view was from directly behind. It looked like the tail section of an airplane stuck upside down on the bottom of a boat. From the side it grew larger. A bulbous snout protruded forward, and from this grew the wings. Wide at the front, they tapered to a razor sharpness at the rear. I guessed their span at six or seven feet. The underneath side was slightly concave. One fanciful element was a white outline of a traditional keel painted over the wings.

I knew nothing about sailing, but was still acutely aware that *Australia II* was unique and awesome. I flipped to the back of my notebook and sketched the keel.

Tuesday morning. I had to get back to the road. But I couldn't leave without one more stop at the Williams & Manchester Shipyards.

The sky was clear, the sun bright, the wind blowing in off the water. I sat on a barrel off to the side of the dock. To my right was the large hangar where *Liberty*'s million-dollar sails were stored. To the left, at the end of the dock, *Liberty* hung in its sling. It still looked like a bloated fish, but I knew better now.

"Hello." I looked up. Halsey Herreshoff, *Liberty*'s navigator, was walking toward me. I was hoping I would see him before I left.

I'd met Halsey a week ago—a lifetime ago, it seemed like now—after *Liberty* had outsailed *Australia II* to take a 3–1 lead in the series. I'd listened to a press conference he'd given down by the dock. Articulate and well spoken, he used words precisely to express exactly what he meant. A naval architect, he'd grown up in Rhode Island and had been sailing "probably since before I was born." Now a youthful forty-seven, he had served on the last six Cup defenses, starting with *Columbia* in 1958. Before that, his grandfather had designed six of the defenders, and built and sailed on eight.

Listening to Halsey during the interview I immediately realized I was in the presence of someone special. He was a member of the New York Yacht Club and, in truth, had been one of the first to blow the whistle on the winged keel—even now he insisted it wasn't a twelve-meter boat. But he firmly believed the argument was best settled out on the Sound. He seemed possessed of a rare insight into the nature of his sport and its relative importance to the rest of the world.

"Well," I said, searching for the kindest and most positive tone I could find, "the sun came up today, didn't it?"

"Yes it did, yes it did," he said softly.

"How'd you sleep?"

"Not too well. I woke up several times." He sat on the barrel next to me. "It's hard to believe that this has happened."

"I've always heard it's the losses that show the measure of the man."

"That's probably true. I think I've always been practical about these things. I believe in working hard and doing everything while the contest is on, but afterward you should have an even perspective."

"I was about to ask how you were measuring up."

Halsey laughed. "Not too well. Right now I can hardly believe it."

"Have you considered that you'll probably be regarded as one of the most famous losers in sports history?"

"Well, it hurts, but it's true. And the fact that some of us have won it quite a few times before will be forgotten. But we knew that going in. I said the same thing to Dennis just last week.

"As far as what we did, I feel we did things pretty much right. We can't say we were perfect because there's always the chance to improve. But what we did was good. It was a hard effort. We worked right down to the final second of the last race. We tried to be excellent. It really is a tremendous pleasure to be involved in something that is excellent."

"But you lost."

"I wouldn't change a thing about my being here and taking part in this. You hate to lose, but if I knew it was going to come out like this and I had to do it all over again, I'd still do it."

"And that's enough of a goal?"

"Yes, I think it is. Some people might say, 'Why do it?' Why put all this money into this when there are people starving and we need medical research and we need to make society better."

"You're creating a good argument for not doing this."

"I know, I know, and I agree with the argument. We do need all those things. But to say we will only do the necessities of society takes away from what society is. We should do some of these more frivolous things, particularly if they are associated with what I call excellence. The pursuit of excellence, doing something hard and doing it well, I think that's enough of a goal.

"Racing like this is a magnificent experience. It's awfully hard for me to put into words the picture I have of sailing a twelve-meter boat. To be on the boat, to see how we work, the close coordination of the crew to make things happen, it's marvelous. Any lapse can make you lose the race, any clever idea might make you win it. And all the different elements, the navigation, the handling of the crew, everything—it all goes on simultaneously in real time. It's fascinating. It was put very well by Baron Bic, the challenger from France. I used to sail with him back in '78 and '79, and one time he said to me, 'When I'm steering this boat I'm the bird in the sky and the fish in the sea.' And you really do have that feeling. You do become one with the boat."

"Will you try for the Cup again?"

"Well, it's too early to tell, but I'd certainly go. Gladly. But you know, I really don't think it will ever be the same again. The fact that it had never been won by anyone else gave it a certain grandeur. And I really don't see how that can be recaptured." He folded his arms and surveyed his surroundings. At the end of the dock *Liberty* rested silently in its sling.

"I just don't think it will ever be the same again," Halsey said after a while. "The Cup's been an important part of my life, and yesterday I really lost something."

I walked back to the van, more reluctant to leave now than I'd been before I'd talked to Halsey. I didn't want to leave behind what clearly was the event of the year. There was much about this sport that didn't recommend it—the New York Yacht Club was a pain; and America's Cup racing could be practiced by one-tenth of 1 percent of the population. But like Halsey had said on Tuesday night in response to a question about the keel: "Once we get out on the water we leave all that behind. Out there it's just a boat race."

And I'd been there to see it. History. A seventh race in the America's Cup finals. The Cup itself on its way to Australia. One hundred thirty-two years of sports legend shattered. Newspapers and television were reaching to great lengths to find comparable accomplishments, but nothing else was close. No event could touch it. For a moment I allowed myself to think I was rather expert on this year in sports. *Sports Illustrated* would have no choice but to declare a boat its Sportsman of the Year.

More important, I'd met Halsey. I would meet no one like him again, of that I was certain. He epitomized the very best that sport can be.

My mind returned to last night after the race was over and *Liberty* was back in port. Choppers were beating the air and everywhere there were cannons being fired and foghorns sounding. In the midst of all this frenzy there was Halsey, reporters all around him, microphones tucked beneath his chin. He was smiling, but his brown eyes betrayed his sadness within.

"I really think this was the essence of sports," he said. "If we'd won I'd cherish this moment, but I cherish it anyway." It was, he said, a great contest. A tremendous story. End of an era. It was a magnificent effort.

Driving up 138 to I-95 I considered ending my year right now. Here. This moment. Because it couldn't get better than this.

CHAPTER 9

* * *

September 28, 1983
Thursday

Dear John–

I have been to the Mountaintop.

Red Sox 3, Yankees 1 at Fenway Park.

I included a side trip to Fenway Park while waiting out a lay day at the America's Cup last week. But it was no mere trip to a ball game. It was a pilgrimage. Because Fenway is no mere ballpark. Fenway is a shrine, and I went to worship.

Fenway is made of brick! I don't know why that should have surprised me, but it did. I've been conditioned to expect steel and concrete. Fenway is a deep red brick and low to the ground and if you don't know it's there you won't know it's there. Only the light towers give it away. When I finally realized I was outside the stadium, and before I could stop myself, I said out loud, "Perfect."

I walked around the stadium twice, savoring each step and every moment of anticipation. I talked to a lot of people, and like a kid with a new bike told them this was my first trip to Fenway. They understood my excitement, and each had a word of advice as to where to sit. But I bought a cheap seat in the bleachers (overpriced at three bucks), and walked through the gates. I got a hot dog (awful), and walked up the steps in dead center field, my eyes locked on the steps in front of me. The plan was to get to the top of the landing and have the Holy Grail unfold before me, its natural green grass funneling into home plate. But that didn't happen. From dead center you get a wonderful view of the right-field foul pole. From my seat in left center I looked directly at the rolled-up tarpaulin up the line from the first-base dugout. By the end of the game the arm rest had gouged a hole in my back. But such are the charms of Fenway that you feel fortunate to have suffered the pain.

Fenway looks like it was designed by a guy who never saw a baseball game in his life, and maybe didn't even know how the game was played. Like back in 1912 they took some guy to a field in Boston, told him they wanted to watch baseball here, explained what baseball was and how it worked, and said have at it. When he was finished, he showed them Fenway Park and said, Is this what you meant? The answer is, of course, no, but don't ever change it.

Fenway is perfect because it's such an imperfect place to play baseball. The Green Monster in left field, the right-field line only 296 feet long, all those nooks and crannies in deep center. Everyone says what a great place Fenway is, but have you noticed the park's never been used as a model for a new stadium?

Maybe that's the point: A game at Fenway is baseball like no place else in the world. You know where you are when you're sitting in Fenway Park. Sense of place is particularized. More important, sense of time diffuses. It could be 1918 and Babe Ruth is walking to the mound; or 1941 and Ted Williams is hitting .406; or 1975 and Carlton Fisk is willing the ball fair as it soars over the Green Monster to beat the Cincinnati Reds in the sixth game of the World Series. New stadiums offer no such continuance and provide the fan with no particular place to be. They could be sitting anywhere (Cincinnati, Pittsburgh, Philadelphia, . . .); worse, they're rooted in the present, watching the ball bounce precisely over a green carpet.

Still, some things remain immutable: The worst baseball game I ever saw was still pretty terrific. Didn't Roger Angell say in baseball you never run out of time, only opportunity? What a concept! I can't understand why people leave a ball game early. Because something always happens at a baseball game. Tonight Reid Nichols, the Sox right-fielder, nailed Dave Winfield at home. (Is there a better moment in sport than a play at the plate?) At every game I've been to this year something has happened. In April, the same Dave Winfield reached over the left-field wall to take a home run away from the Minnesota Twins. In July, Rusty Staub of the Mets hit a three-run pinch-hit homer to beat the Reds.

Something always happens, and it doesn't have to be the mighty and spectacular play. The game of baseball describes a precise geometry upon the ground on which it's played, a series of lines and angles unique to each situation, described for a moment and then vanished forever. The pitcher throws the ball, describing the first line. The batter swings to send the ball on a second line. An infielder moves to the ball, creating *his* own line. The throw to first produces yet another line, as does the runner heading to the base. One line precipitates another, they appear simultaneously, are described precisely, and meet together in the first baseman's glove. And that's just one play. Add base runners and the confrontation becomes more complex, the variations endless, each situation producing a pattern never seen before and maybe never seen again. Given this geometry, the home run becomes almost static while the bunt becomes an intricate equation of angles and converging lines.

Something always happens.

It also always happens in the summertime. If summer didn't exist, it would have to be invented so we could play baseball in it. Baseball is the only sport in synch with the season in which it's played. Basketball was invented to escape the winter. Hockey needs the cold, but did anyone watch it before it moved indoors? Football used to be linked to a snap in the air, raccoon coats and falling leaves, but the USFL seems to be proving that football can be played in the spring even if it shouldn't be.

That leaves baseball and summer. Baseball is exciting and dull at the same time. No mean trick, but necessary if you want to enjoy a game played in 95-degree heat. Something happens, then nothing happens, which allows us time to relax and think about what just happened and what might happen next. The game also has an unbounded capacity to delight. I remember in St. Louis in August watching the Cardinals against the Astros, and sitting next to an old black man who'd been coming to games for so long he'd forgotten when he started. He had a new set of teeth that looked great, but he wasn't used to them yet and they made him drool when he tried to talk. When Andy Van Slyke hit the game winner for the Cardinals in the bottom of the tenth, this old man started dancing and talking and drooling all over the right-field bleachers. I couldn't understand a word he said, but I knew exactly what he was saying. His eyes were as happy as a nine-year-old kid's . . . .

Steve

* * *

A moment of truth: Waiting at a friend's place in Rockville, Maryland, to see which teams made the World Series. Baltimore Orioles or Chicago White Sox, Philadelphia Phillies or Los Angeles Dodgers. The wrong combination of winning teams, available press passes, and money to get there, and I could miss the Series completely.

But not to worry. Baltimore won and so did Philadelphia. Having grown up in York, Pennsylvania, not far from either city, it was like a hometown series. The best of all possible worlds. Or just about. I had credentials for the Phillies but not for the Orioles.

But I drove to Baltimore's Memorial Stadium anyway, through a misty drizzle for the opener Tuesday night, October 11. When I arrived at four o'clock there were plenty of tickets to scalp but the price was steep. All I could do was wait, and hope the price came down.

At five o'clock I positioned myself on the sidewalk of the stadium's main entrance, under a covered walkway, in hopes of spotting a reporter I'd met before who might have an extra ticket. In front of me, standing by the edge of the sidewalk, was a man wearing a black suit with a thin gray stripe, light gray shirt, a red-and-blue-striped tie, and black loafers. Pinned to his lapel was a large white button that read: "Lose weight now! Ask me how."

So I asked.

"Are you serious?" he said, looking right at me, "or just curious?"

"Well, the button said." He clicked into his routine: natural system . . . ten to twenty-nine pounds a month . . . dietary supplement . . . two meals a day . . . not medication . . . important nutrients . . . better than you ever felt in your life. Soon I was laughing and so was he. But he plunged ahead, finishing with you-ask-for-it-you-get-it fervor.

His name was Ken Pittman. He was from Dallas, but lived outside Washington now. He didn't have a ticket either. He looked around, his eyes dancing mischievously. "What I gotta do is find myself some fat people and make a couple quick sales to raise the cash." And then he laughed. Here was a guy who could be fun to spend some time with.

We walked across the main drag to a huge yellow-and-white-striped circus tent. A large "ABC Sports" banner sat over the main entrance. A rent-a-cop stopped us at the entrance. Only people with red and white tickets were allowed inside.

"What is this?" said another man who, like Ken and me, was also on the outside looking in. "So this is where our city taxes go? To feed all the big shots?" Inside was a replica of the sailing ship U.S.S. *Constellation.* It was eighty feet long at least, and sailing directly at a fifty-foot lighthouse. The ship was surrounded by tables covered with silver chafing dishes. There were many people inside, too, sipping drinks and having a grand old time being red and white ticket holders.

"ABC is footing the bill on this one," the guard said. "And all I know is nobody without a red and white ticket is allowed in." Ken and I backed off.

The sidewalk was coming to life with people and vendors and scalpers. A flock of fans plastered from head to foot with Oriole stickers walked by. I could feel the energy levels churning. I'd found the center of the universe. Again.

"You ever been to Dallas?" Ken asked. "You wouldn't believe a Dallas Cowboys football game."

"Why not?"

"Because it's nothing like this at all. It's incredible. Dallas Cowboy fans don't cheer the Cowboys for the next play they're going to run. They're not standing up yelling and screaming, you know, exhorting their team to do it. They don't have to do that, because they know the Cowboys will do it whether they cheer for them or not.

"Football at Dallas Stadium is like nowhere else. The stadium is clean. Everything is perfect. The fans are well dressed. It's a giant social gathering—not a party, a social gathering. It's not like here. This is great. Everybody here in jeans and T-shirts, drinking beer and having a good time. These people are here because they firmly believe the Orioles are going to win because they are cheering for them to win."

A black Cadillac with a man and woman in the front seat pulled to a stop in front of us. The woman lowered the window and the man pointed in our direction. Ken turned to see where he was pointing, then turned back to the man. The man pointed again, adamantly, right at Ken.

"Can you tell me where I'm supposed to park this thing?" he said. The people at ABC said they'd reserve a space. We're the band."

The band?

Ken talked to the guard at the tent, who refused to leave his post. Ken walked back to the Cadillac. The man and woman were unloading their equipment. We helped move it into the tent, and then, back outside, Ken pointed to a small badge on the woman's sweater. It was the size of a Boy Scout merit badge with "ABC Sports" embroidered above the Olympic rings.

"That gets me in and out of the tent," the woman explained. She gave one to Ken and one to me.

Ken removed his "Lose weight now!" button and stuck the ABC Sports merit badge on his lapel. If the band leader thought Ken worked for ABC Sports before, there would be no doubt now. With a square jaw, striking good looks, and vibrant eyes that he could lock right on you, Ken fit the part of the TV personality perfectly. He was also wearing that suit. He looked like television. The kind of guy you're sure you've seen before but can't remember where.

"Hey! Hey! Hey!" A thin black man shouted in my ear. "GET your NEWspaper here! The *BALTimore EVening Sun!* All the WORLD Series INformation you'll need! the LINEups, the STORIES. A special SOUViner keepsake. FOUR-color photos, PLUS a limited-edition FULL-color poster for your home." He opened his arms to reveal the poster tied across his chest. "Hey! Hey! Hey . . ." Ken cut him off.

"What do you do for a living?"

Startled, at first the man couldn't remember.

"I'm, huh, a teacher. Well, sort of. Right now I'm a substitute English teacher."

"How would you like to be a millionaire?"

"A millionaire? Well, uh, sure, yeah, of course, why?"

"My name's Ken Pittman and I work for a nutrition company and I think you have potential . . ." I backed away, laughing. They exchanged phone numbers.

"You recruited him?" I asked when Ken turned back to me.

"Sure. Did you see the way he was selling newspapers? He gets ahold of our product and he'll be bouncing to the sky." Ken stopped and laughed. At himself, at the scene, at everything.

"This is great! This is unbelievable. I've got to come to this corner more often." He smiled broadly, eyes twinkling, and rubbed his hands together. "What's next?"

I pointed to the circus tent. "It's time to eat!"

The guard at the door wasn't impressed with our merit badges, however, and we were forced to suffer the indignity of using the servants' entrance. The tent was crowded, so I found a table while Ken scoped out the food.

"Can you believe this?" Ken placed three dishes on the linen-covered table. Two plates were mounded with fettuccine Alfredo, crab cakes, chicken wings, pickled broccoli, and roast beef. Another was stacked with clams on the half shell. "Maybe I better steal the silverware so I can prove this really happened."

"Can I get you fellows anything?" That from a tall, blond waitress in black tux and hotpants and legs that went all the way up. We ordered a couple of beers, finished our plates, loaded up again, and then went to the dessert tables. All four of them.

By the time we finished, the tent was almost empty. We turned to watch the pregame show on one of the monitors that were spaced throughout the tent. All things considered, this wasn't too shabby a place to watch the game. "Can I get you guys another drink?" It was the short brunette who'd been exchanging glances with Ken. Ken ordered two beers and asked her name. Her name was Lynn. She asked what we did for ABC.

"I do interviews for a local affiliate," Ken said, not missing a beat. Lynn looked at me.

"I'm a writer," I said. And suddenly a fifth wheel. I went looking for the Porta-potties. When I returned Ken and Lynn were still talking. By now, I figured, Ken was either president of ABC or he had sold her a lifetime supply of nutritional weight loss protein. Although she certainly didn't need it. Lynn returned to work. Ken turned to me.

"You're not going to believe what just happened," he said. I was afraid to ask. "After you left, Lynn said, 'I just want you to know that I think you're the best-looking man here.' "

"Getouttahere!"

"No, no. It's true." I howled at that and so did Ken. "I mean," he said, "I mean, it's true that's what she said. Why should I bullshit you now?" He had a point there. And the more I thought about it the more I had to figure Lynn was right. There was just something about the way Ken carried himself. I decided it was the way he wore his suit.

"You know," I said, "I'll bet you were born wearing a suit."

"Well all I know," Ken said, his eyes following Lynn across the room, "is I don't think I'm ever going to take it off!"

On the monitor John Denver was singing the national anthem. "You know what we should do?" Ken said. "We should go over to the stadium and see how far these little merit badges will get us. I'd had the correct amount of ABC's beer to consider that a good idea. And Ken was wearing that suit. He had that executive aura and he looked like television. I was wearing brown cords and a white sweater, but I had a notebook and Sony recorder. Ken was the boss, I was the gopher. Like I said, we'd both had enough beer to think it was a good idea.

The turnstiles were inside the stadium, which meant we were able to walk through the first doors and into a hallway to appraise the situation. To our right was the press entrance. Sitting in front of it was an orange-coated usher. We walked over. "If you guys don't have press passes you're not getting in," he said.

We walked back outside, along the half-moon sidewalk in front of the stadium, and into another entrance at the other end of the same corridor. Turnstiles were in front of us, but to the left, next to a bronze plaque of Brooks Robinson, was an unguarded door. We walked through it, into a long dark hallway. On our right was a door to the Oriole clubhouse. "Hey," Ken said, "these would be great seats!"

But we kept walking down the hallway, into a small, private foyer. At the door at the opposite end sat an old man in an usher's uniform. "Can I help you fellows?" he asked. Ken said yes but walked through the door. The old man didn't say a word. Must have been Ken's suit.

We were in another corridor now, this one shorter and darker. Ticket office on the left, Oriole executive offices on the right. At the end was another door. The roar from the stadium vibrated through the ceiling, the noise beckoning and urging us forward. We walked to gate W-3. A turnstile was on our left. People were streaming through it and up a ramp to our right. We were inside the stadium.

We watched the first two innings standing in the entrance ramps along the right-field line until the ushers chased us out. If they asked for tickets we pretended we were lost and peppered them with questions about the game. Wejustcamedowntogetsome-beer. Overthere. Uphere. Isthissection43? 38? Weheardthe screamingandjustranuptoseewhatitwasallabout. Our answers were fast and furious and usually contradictory, but as long as we talked like we were on speed the ushers couldn't say a word.

We worked our way down to the first-base dugout, where we raced past a couple of ushers asking for tickets. We sat in the empty seats that fanned out behind a column, putting the pole between the pitcher's mound and home plate. The only thing we couldn't see was a millisecond of the pitch. The excitement and nervousness of getting here—we'd seen four people taken away in handcuffs—had sobered us up a bit, and now we were equal parts stunned that we'd actually done it and worried that no one would believe us.

"Tell me I'm really here!" Ken said. "I feel like calling somebody and saying, 'Do you hear that noise? Tell me that's noise from the World Series!' " In the third inning the ushers stopped ushering and they too found seats behind the columns. Ken and I toasted our luck by buying a couple of beers, the only thing we paid for all night.

Oh yeah, the Phillies won, 4–2. It wasn't until later that we learned that President Reagan was at the game, and that security had been extra tight.

The next night I did it again, but without Ken—and his suit—to protect me. For insurance I scalped a ticket at $5 under face, put it in my pocket and retraced last night's route. The old guard stopped me. I pointed to my merit badge. He waved me through. I ran outside, sold the ticket, walked back into the stadium, found the same section, and sat down to watch the game.

I was next to an old guy named Lou. He'd grown up in New York and was a Yankee fan until George Steinbrenner took over. The first World Series game he'd ever seen was in 1936, or maybe '37, he couldn't remember for sure. But Lou Gehrig was his hero and Joe DiMaggio was the greatest player the game had ever seen, period.

"I've been watching baseball all my life," he said. "But it's only been in the last ten years or so I've really started to analyze the game and figure out why I like it so much." And then he stopped.

"Well?" I said. Here it was: On the two hundred fifty-eighth day of the trip, at the second game of the World Series, no less, I was finally going to get The Answer.

Lou looked at me, laughed, and threw his hands in the air helplessly.

"Can I quote you on that?"

John Lowenstein of the Orioles stepped to the plate. "Now there's a player," Lou said. "That one shows why the Orioles are the class of baseball, just like the Yankees used to be before, you know, *him*. Everybody else had given up on Lowenstein, said he can't hit left-handed pitching and he can't play every day. And he can't. But the Orioles use him when they should and he produces."

Lowenstein jumped on the first pitch, and the ball rocketed toward left center, clearing the fence between the 405- and 387-foot markers. The crowd roared, and tucked underneath the upper deck as we were, the noise resounded and refused to go away. Rich Dauer then hit a single, and so did Todd Cruz. We were on our feet when Rich Dempsey, the Baltimore catcher, smacked a double and two runs were scored. Bedlam. Lou turned to me, his face aglow, and screamed at me as loud as he could: "Now that's why I like baseball!" He swept his hand across the field in front of him. "You tell me how to explain all this!"

In the sixth inning, I moved across the aisle and sat with another Lou who'd been at last night's game, too. He was my age, a black man with a sharp profile and close-cropped hair and beard.

"Where's your friend?" Lou asked. You know, that guy . . ."

"In the suit?"

"Yeah."

"He couldn't make it tonight." Lou looked at me hard for a moment.

"You guys really with ABC?"

I started laughing. Without that guy in the suit my cover was blown. I explained who I was and how we'd gotten in last night. I started to tell him about tonight, but he cut me off when I said I'd scalped a ticket for insurance.

"Don't do that. Do what I do. Wait till the game starts. That's when the ushers over in right field bring out the extra tickets and sell them for $5. I don't know how it works, or who's getting the money, but that's how I'll be seeing every game."

Dan Ford stepped in the batter's box for the Orioles. Willie Hernandez was on the mound in relief. "Hey listen," Lou said, "there's no way I'm going to pay $25 a game. I come to thirty, forty games a year. I'm a Baltimore Orioles *fan,* and then all of a sudden they're asking me to pay twenty-five bucks for a seat that costs $3? No way I'm going to pay that, you hear what I'm talkin' about?" He held out his palm. I slapped five.

Hernandez wound up and let go. High and hard. Ford spun and ducked, but the ball caught him in the back of the head and he fell to the ground. Hernandez, eschewing the standard practice of turning his back and rubbing up a baseball, walked down to the batter's box and leaned over Ford. Classiest act of the year. Ford was all right, somehow, and as he trotted down to first, he turned to Hernandez and nodded, ever so slightly.

I asked Lou if the Orioles got good support from Baltimore's black community. He looked at me for another long moment.

"Is this for the book?" he said. Why not? "Well, what it is, is that black people don't go down to the Inner Harbor. It's too expensive. Besides, all they want down there are the folks with the real money. So this is where we go. This is good entertainment, and it's cheap. But you know, for me, my real entertainment is going to watch my boy play." He motioned to his son sitting next to him. He was about eight years old, and at the moment following the flight of a beach ball being batted around the lower deck. "That's my real entertainment, watching him play baseball. He's a pitcher and a catcher."

A guy in a cowboy hat and beard climbed on top of the Oriole dugout and spelled out O-R-I-O-L-E-S with his body. His version of the letters barely resembled the real thing, and he moved in almost melancholy fashion, but the fans ate it up and once again the noise came thundering at us under the upper deck.

"This isn't anything like the real season," Lou said after "ORIOLES" had been spelled. "That's when we get the regular folk in here. The *real* Oriole fans. They can get this place rockin'. I mean rockin'! All we got in here now are all these people who want to be able to say they was at a World Series, you hear what I'm saying? They just want to be here so they can be rubbing elbows with all the other people who are here trying to rub elbows."

A fight broke out down and to our right, but a ring of people formed quickly and we couldn't see what was going on. Lou sighed. "Happens all the time. They get to drinkin' and then they want to mix it just to show how bad they be." He turned to a small scoreboard tucked underneath the upper deck. It was the bottom of the eighth and the Orioles were up 4–1.

"I'll think I'll be takin' my boy home now. I got to get him to bed so I can get him up for school tomorrow. He stood up and put his hand on his son's shoulder. "You be here for the sixth game?" he asked, pointing to my merit badge.

"Sure."

"And getting in the same way, too, I'll bet. So will we. So I'll see you then. We can look on these seats as our private reserved section, you know what I'm sayin'?" We slapped five again. Then he was down the aisle, steering his son wide of the guys showin' off how bad they be.

After the two games in Baltimore, the Philadelphia games were hard-pressed to measure up, and they didn't. They weren't events, they were spectacles. Something for 64,000 people to look at. After the intimacy and energy of the Baltimore games, it was impossible to work up any excitement over baseball played in a mammoth bowl. Lou's observation that the people in Baltimore weren't the real fans was hard to believe, but in Veterans Stadium it was pretty near the fact.

Friday night Steve Carlton lost to Jim Palmer. Palmer relieved in the middle innings and picked up the win. I sat in the upper reaches of the right center-field bleachers and tried to keep warm. (World Series night games are a sin against the natural order. The Series was meant to be played on golden afternoons with long, warm shadows. A pleasant reminder of the summer past and the season completed.) The next afternoon the weather complied but the game was a bust. The Phillies managed only one serious rally, and until it occurred it was like the stands were empty. The game generated zero emotion, and for just a moment I even wondered if maybe it would be better watched on television, where feelings can at least be manufactured.

That night I drove back to Rockville, Maryland. Tomorrow was the National Jousting Tournament on the Mall in Washington, D.C., and I had committed myself to an article on the joust for *American Way* magazine. I was not up for missing the fifth game of the World Series, but I needed the money. Besides, there would be a sixth game. I'd already called Ken Pittman's office and left the message: "See you at game six!" The Orioles were up three games to one, but surely the Phillies could not be swept three straight in Veterans Stadium and lose the series at home.

Sunday I went to the joust. And found the perfect day. The eighty-yard long jousting track paralleled the reflecting pool, and behind it rose the Washington Monument, its edges sharpened by the sun and a brilliantly clear sky. There was that just-right snap in the crisp autumn air. On the opposite side of the track, pick up trucks and horse trailers formed a wagon train paused for the midday meal. Coffee boiled on Coleman stoves, baked beans bubbled. Everyone offered me something to eat. The rich, moist smell of hay and horses and, inevitably, manure, floated across the grounds.

If I had to be somewhere besides the fifth game of the World Series, this was certainly the place.

As for the joust, that was won by Mike Virts, the "Knight of St. Marks," and a truck driver from Petersville, Maryland. He did not, however, unseat a series of challengers to win the crown. This version of modern jousting involves tiny harness rings the size of life savers, cue-stick-sized lances with thin metal points, and more than a little horsemanship. Because the object is to slip the tip of the lance through three harness rings suspended six feet, nine inches off the ground and thirty yards apart while riding a horse. Virts, riding his palamino, Princess, all but floated down the track and picked off two of the three rings.

Later, I got lost trying to leave the District. The van had no radio, and by the time I got to my friend's place in Rockville, the Series was over. Dick Schaap was on TV telling me that the Orioles had won the game 5-0 and the Series 4–1. There'd be no more games for me to see for free. The next day, driving back to New York City, I stopped in Baltimore for the victory parade. Three hundred thousand Baltimoreans, each one fully convinced that there was no place else in the world to live, lined the parade route and screamed and yelled for a group of men who had won a baseball game but who would skip town if the money was right. The emotional outpouring shouldn't have made sense, but it did to those who were there. Back in the van on the road to New York City again, I wished for a moment that I could say I lived in Baltimore, too.

* * *

According to *New York Sports* magazine, 17,165 runners were entered in the New York City Marathon. But I was concerned with only one: Katie McDonald.

> *In early 1981 I was working and running full time when I threw my back out. Something started hurting and I didn't stop running. I thought I was building my muscles but I wasn't. They were deteriorating, until one day I just cried out in pain. After April of that year I didn't run at all. I took months off. I had this general pain that started in my back and went all over my body. Doctors would ask me where it hurt and I could never point to one spot, because everything hurt.*
>
> *This March things started getting better. I'd run and I wouldn't hurt as much. I was able to put in more miles. Then in April the qualifying time for the Women's Olympic Marathon Trials was set: two hours, fifty-one minutes, and six-*

teen seconds, the one-hundredth fastest time by an American woman in the previous twelve months. The time is a little soft, but I can't say it's unfair. This is the first time the marathon for women has been in the Olympics. To me that fact seems much more unfair.

So I decided that might be a good goal: To run the New York City Marathon again and qualify for the first women's Olympic Marathon Trials next May in Olympia, Washington. I entered a few ten-kilometer races and it turned out I was in better shape than I thought I was. This summer I kept running, hitting about eighty miles a week. Then I set a specific twelve-week training program. My weekly mileage had been less than I hoped it would be, but I don't think I should have too much trouble doing the qualifying time. What I'd like to do is 2:45; what I think I can do is 2:48.

What I have to do is 2:51:16. My best time is 2:50:32, but that was three years ago. If anything is holding me back now, it's my mental conviction that I can run that fast again. For the first twenty miles a marathon is a physical race; the last six miles are mental. It's a matter of pushing yourself tremendously. I've run eight marathons, but none in the last three years. So I don't feel particularly confident.

I know there will be a good number of women in the race who will have the same goal I do: to run just under the qualifying standard. So for the first time in a marathon, I expect to be running around a lot of other women for the whole distance. But when you're running marathons you can't listen to anybody else. You've got to listen to yourself, you've got to run your own pace.

I'd like to run the first half of the race at 6:15-mile averages, run thirty-eight- or thirty-nine-minute 10Ks throughout the race, and hit the half in about 1:22 or 1:23. That will give me five or six extra minutes for the second half, which is a fairly reasonable margin. It leaves me a lot of time to fall apart in the second half. If it appears that morning that I'm running 6:25s or 6:30s in the first half, then I'll know that I have to absolutely maintain that pace through the second half of the race. But I should know fairly early on if I'm on pace. If I'm not going to make it I'll probably walk off the course and save my effort till next month and the Phillie

Marathon. If it comes down to the end and I do a 2:52 instead of a 2:51, well, I'll just have to get in a full training week next week to get prepared for Phillie. I'll just keep trying. If I don't make it I'll be disappointed, but that will be temporary. If I do make it I don't think I'll go to Olympia for the trial. I'm thirty-three years old and I'm tired of all this training. I just want to know that I made it.

Katie looked like a runner. Short and thin, almost guant. Her body all angles and points, without an ounce of extra fat. By all rights she should have been blown off the Verrazano-Narrows bridge at the start of the race. Her chin was sharp and her eyes disappeared behind little slits when she laughed. And she loved to laugh.

I'd met Katie at a party at my cousin's place in Manhattan back in June. An enthusiastic woman of boundless, infectious energy, she talked in superlatives all the time. My year on the road, for instance, was the greatest idea in the world. There's little you want to say after something like that, and even less that you can.

As a borderline national-class runner, Katie observed the running scene from a unique perspective. She was part of the big-time, but at the same time she was apart from it. Her position provided a special insight, and it was obvious as we talked that she'd taken the time to think about the running game. At one point she turned the conversation back to my trip and asked me what kind of people I tried to interview. My answer was people like Katie McDonald.

I asked if I could follow her in the New York City Marathon and her attempt to qualify for the Olympic Trials. Reduce the country's largest street theater to a single drama. My plan was to see her once in each borough, not including Staten Island, which most New Yorkers don't include anyway. The idea wasn't original—I'd read about it in *The Runner* magazine—but it sounded fun, although probably impossible. Start deep in Brooklyn for the first sighting. Then take the F train to the GG; get off at the Fifty-ninth Street Bridge for a look in Queens. The RR to Fifty-ninth Street in Manhattan to catch the Lexington Avenue Express to 138th Street in the Bronx and the Grand Concourse, then down to Central Park and the finish line and the final Manhattan look.

Katie thought the idea was the greatest.

Race day I'll get up at 6:30 and have some coffee. I'll take a lot of time getting dressed, putting Vaseline on, and combing my hair. Should I pull it in a braid or shouldn't I becomes this huge question every year and I can never decide what to do. Then I'll walk over to Sixteenth Street to catch the club van going over to Staten Island. There will probably be about twenty-five people waiting. We're a fun group, the Warren Street Social and Athletic Club. It's sort of a renegade running club. Anyway, we'll leave about 8:30 and get out there and expend a lot of energy trying to stay warm and trying to secure a fairly private area to go to the bathroom in. And then we'll get the nod to get on the course and we'll find our way to the front. Before the race I get very quiet. I generally get pretty annoyed with people who get real talkative.

My favorite part of the course? I guess like everybody else it's coming off the Queensboro Bridge, from Queens into Manhattan at Fifty-ninth Street. The bridge itself offers some splendid views. Then you circle around and go underneath the bridge itself, and there's a little uphill on First Avenue, but you see about a million people right out in front of you. That's fun. Harlem is fascinating. The townhouses are beautiful and the people are so supportive, and at that point you're feeling so rotten. The part of the race I dread is at ten miles in the Greenpoint section of Brooklyn. The streets are full of potholes, it's industrial, there aren't many people, and it's lonely.

I do my best in the first ten kilometers because it's so exciting going up Fourth Avenue in Brooklyn. And the second ten kilometers, too, because by then I'll be warmed up and I'll have a feel for how the race is going to come out. The finish is always a surprise because you can't see it until the final couple hundred yards.

I met Marian, Katie's sister, on the RR going to Eighty-sixth Street and Fourth Avenue way down in Brooklyn. A Sunday *New York Times* was scattered on the floor. (Headline: "43 Marines are reported killed in Beirut as bomb levels base.") We arrived at 10:31 A.M., fourteen minutes before the start of the race, and positioned ourselves on the left side of the avenue next to the subway entrance. The racers would be coming at us from the right. The Plaka, a Greek restaurant, sat on one corner; the Golden Dragon, a Chinese place, was on the other. A car alarm shrieked. People milled about restlessly.

"The race has begun," Marian said. I don't know how she knew it. She clicked on her digital stopwatch. When the time clock car drove past Marian checked her watch. She was 12 seconds off.

We didn't recognize the lead runners. They tend to look alike when down to singlets and shorts and grim race faces. They were past us in a flash, the power they generated heard as well as seen.

Katie appeared at 17:40 by Marian's watch. She was easy to spot. We were at about the three-mile mark, but the throng of runners had already spread themselves over the distance. Katie was also in the lanes closest to us, the southbound side of Fourth Avenue reserved at this point for women runners. She was wearing a gray Warren Street singlet and black shorts. Her hair was unbraided, but wrapped around her head. She looked fine and was out of sight quickly.

Marian and I were on the RR heading north by 11:09. "As long as I'm moving I won't be nervous," Marian said. I'd been thinking the same thing. We were relying on the New York City transit system for a split-second performance. A fool's errand.

At least we weren't alone. At every stop the train grew more crowded with people wearing bicycle caps or holding water bottles or frantically scanning subway maps. Plus one very young couple with a newborn baby. They were reading an article in *Mademoiselle* entitled "Don't Take a Chance on Love."

At Ninth Street and Fourth Avenue we all bolted for the F train, save for the young couple and one group of marathon followers still looking at a map. "We better tell them to get out," Marian said. If they didn't, they'd miss any chance of seeing the race in Queens. Marian turned, they all ran from the train, and screamed down the platform. We gave chase and caught them at the F train platform.

They were actually three different groups that had banded together. Five spoke Spanish and one was wearing an orange sweat suit with "COLOMBIA" written across the back. Standing on the platform they pulled out the map again. A guy in a bicycle hat, an American, who had raced from the train with the Colombians, looked at the map, too. Bicycle Hat shook his head. "No, no, no." Then, extra loud and extra slow: "FOL-LOW US! FOL-LOW US!" The GG pulled into the station. The Colombians put away the map and followed.

"Do you know who that guy is?" Bicycle Hat said to me, motioning to the guy in the orange sweat suit. "That's Colombia's number one marathon man. He got here last night but they wouldn't let him run. He's run a 2:12. The other guys are with a Colombian radio network. You should see them, it's great. They're phoning in results as they go along."

"They're calling Colombia from a pay phone?" I said.

Bicycle Hat laughed. He was having a great time all the way around. "Yeah, can you believe it? They're calling collect. They're supposed to be reporting the race, but look at 'em. What do they know? They're just like us. They're making this up as they go along. They asked me to give a report." He laughed again. "At the next stop I'm going to talk to Colombia."

The Americans with the Colombians were actually two groups, one from Philadelphia and one from Jersey. Some had done this before, some hadn't. One wanted to be home watching the race on TV, but the others hooted down his insouciance.

We stopped at Van Alst, two stops from the Queensboro Bridge. And waited. Bicycle Hat and his group debated going straight to the Bronx. But that would mean missing the race at mile twenty-four, and they all agreed that was the best place to watch the race. We waited some more.

"What's going on here?" Bicycle Hat said, his voice filled with righteous indignation. Then, his tone shifting to mock seriousness, "Don't they know they have the new Howard Cosell of Colombia right here in this very car?" The doors snapped shut and the train lurched out of the station. We positioned ourselves in front of the door, Bicycle Hat in the lead.

"Okay," he said, as the train pulled into the Queensboro stop, "get ready to sprint."

Back in 1980 I made kind of a splash by winning $15,000 in the Atlantic City Marathon. I was the first woman to accept money over the table for a track and field event. After that there was a big hubbub about my participation in races. I was a "tainted" runner and I would "contaminate" the *other runners. The AAU actually told me that. In fact, I wasn't allowed to run in certain races. It wasn't that I was one of the best runners in the world—I'm a pretty good metropolitan runner and maybe the East Coast—it was more what I represented: professionalism. But to me, the whole idea of amateur racing in track and field was ludicrous. I felt a lot of pressure to run because I thought it was important to keep the issue alive.*

Before the Atlantic City race there were tremendous questions. And I didn't decide to run until the day before. But I knew the race would be a once-in-a-lifetime thing. So that Saturday I said, "Okay, I'll do it. This is it, this is the only chance I'll ever have." My winning was luck and circumstances. My time was slow—over three hours—and that was embarrassing. Actually, I thought some of the good runners would show up at the last minute and run.

Shortly after that race I received a notice from the Athletics Congress telling me I'd been suspended. That produced a long hearing process. Locally a lot of people took notice. I'd go to races and the top dogs would be there and they'd say, "Oh, so you're Katie McDonald?" And there'd be this certain sneer about the way they said it. Intellectually I knew what I was doing was right, but I was very vulnerable. I'd be running in Central Park and people would go by me and say "We can't run with you, we'll be contaminated." They meant it as a joke, but I could only laugh for the first week. I had friends say to me, "I think what you've done is a pretty great thing, but I just have to tell you I don't think money should enter the sport. I think it's too pure."

Here's how silly the whole thing got. Women athletes were listening to their coaches, who were saying, "Don't run with her, it's too dangerous." But at that time the marathon for women wasn't even in the Olympics. What did they have to lose? Absolutely nothing. After Atlantic City I ran the New York City Marathon and the Rose Bowl Marathon. By then people were saying, "Wait a minute. She hasn't dropped dead because she's won some money." Finally, some of the women started listening to themselves, and after a couple of races that started showing up.

But recently I met a woman who won $250 in a race and

she wouldn't accept it. She didn't believe money should be involved in sports, but she couldn't articulate her reasons. It makes me think there is just a general feeling that life used to be better before money. Her "reasons" were more feelings than any real reason.

I do think the money in sports has really gotten obscene. I mean, there's just so much involved. But I don't know where the line should be drawn and I don't know if it can be. I see some track athletes living comfortably now; Bill Rodgers is a wealthy man and I don't think that's bad. You know, the Olympics were originally started just for the rich. The money makes a lot more things available to a lot more people. Yes, there are dangers in it, but I'd have to say I think there's more good come out of money being involved in American sports than bad.

Grete Waitz ran past as we got to the Queensboro Bridge. Marian and I ran down a street to escape the crush of spectators, then began searching for Katie in the stream of runners slogging past us in the rain. We were beginning to think maybe Katie had dropped out when we finally spotted her.

We yelled. She waved and held up three fingers. If we wanted to make it to the Bronx that was all the time we could spare. We sprinted for the Queensboro station. I stopped suddenly. Marian ran into me. "Why did Katie hold up three fingers?" I asked. Marian had been wondering the same thing.

"What do you suppose it meant?" she said.

"I have no idea."

Marian started running. I followed. She stopped and I ran into her. "Maybe it meant three hours." She looked at me, worried.

"You think she was trying to tell us she wasn't going to make it?"

Marian brushed the thought aside. "It can't mean that," she said, full of conviction. "Can it?"

"No it can't." I said, full of conviction. "Can it?" We turned and ran.

The station was jammed. There was a Manhattan train at the platform, but no signs saying which train it was. At least none I understood. All we had was BMT and IRT, and I'd never learned what they meant or where they went. The train pulled out. A number seven. We could have taken it to Grand Central Station and made the switch there. The train disappeared, and so did our best chance of getting to the Bronx on time.

An RR finally pulled into the station. We jumped on and took it to Fifty-ninth and Lex. Then it was up and down and all around the innards of the city, looking for the Lexington Express. That I recognized the station didn't help at all. This was where I always got lost looking for the train to Yankee Stadium. At forty-six minutes after noon we found the correct platform. We leaned against some pillars to catch our breath and plot strategy. We had to be at 138th Street in seven minutes. There was just no way.

"What we need is for the train to come right now," Marian said, peering into the tunnel, trying to will a train into existence.

"Wait a minute," I said. "Katie gave us a time for when she was getting into the Bronx, right?"

Marian checked her map. "Right. She figured to be at the Willis Avenue Bridge at 12:53."

"But that's going in. How long are they in the Bronx?"

"About a mile," Marian said. Her eyes brightened. "You figure she's running 6:15s; that gives us an extra eight minutes here." Our spirits, about as low as a rat's belly between the rails of a New York subway track, soared.

"We've got plenty of time," I said.

Marian laughed. "Yeah, We can wait here for a while before we have to make another decision."

A few minutes later we made that decision: We'd take the train if it came by 12:50. Even that would be cutting it close. We'd have ten minutes to get to the Grand Concourse. I asked an elderly man how long it took the express to get to the Bronx.

"Ten minutes," he said. I breathed easy. It would be a piece of cake, cut closely. "But that's if everything is running right. Sometimes nothing is running right. Sometimes the four and five are both upstairs. Sometimes just the six is down here. Should always check before you come down. Did you check? Now once up there, where you wanno go? One thirty eight? How 'bout 138th and Third? That depends on which train . . ."

The express roared into the station. It was 12:50 straight up. We hopped aboard.

I really don't think world-class athletes are "normal" people. They can be very neurotic and are compelled by a few things in their lives that really dominate their whole existence. They are very, very focused on single issues, to the point that they're unaware—or unable to make themselves aware—of normal issues.

They're not stupid; it's just that they're so into what they're doing. They are absolute experts on what they do, they really are. They're very thoughtful and able to think critically about any aspect of their sport, but take them outside their sport and they just aren't interested in anything. To compete at that level they have to channel themselves that way.

I'm probably not as competitive in my running as other people are. Certainly not as much as men. Men who run the same pace as I do are more competitive than I am. They're out to get the guy in front of them even if it means giving their life in the last half mile to do it. I'm not going to do that. I do think I'm more competitive than a four-hour marathoner, but I'm not as competitive as a Grete. And I never will be.

This is an area that is difficult for woman athletes. Up until recently this whole area of competitiveness among the women has been such an undercover taboo. Not among the top women, but I think the rest of us are just now grappling with this issue. We are afraid to be aggressive. I've slowed up in races to wait for a friend to catch up with me. Even though there are women who are posting some pretty good times, there was still all this friendly little business before the race: "You look so nice today," and all that. The men say, "I'm going to kick your ass," and then hang onto each other during the race. Until recently no one would even think of hanging onto Grete in a race. I think women becoming aggressive and being able to acknowledge their competitiveness is a good thing, to be more forthright and challenging, to be able to say, "Maybe she will cream me, but I'm going to try to stay with her."

I suspect what happens is some women say, "If that's what it takes to get to the top, then I'm not going to do it." Not among the top women, but for three quarters of the women who will be running the marathon, I really hear a tremendous amount of discouragement: "I don't want my legs to become too muscular," or "How can you bear to look that skinny?"

But recently I have noticed changes. I think there is a difference between women athletes my age and twenty-year-old women athletes who have developed through high school and college. I know at least a dozen college-age-athletes and they're tough. A certain element of competitiveness is a learned process—my first race was when I was twenty-five years old. That's why men are different from women my age right now. But in another fifteen years the thirty-year-old woman athlete will be as competitive as the thirty-year-old man.

The subway exit for the Grand Concourse was less than seventy-five yards from the course and the twenty-one-mile mark in the race.

"This is the place to watch," Marian said. Yes it was. The rain was heavy now and the streets were deserted but for a small, loyal band of spectators huddled beneath an overpass. Forty strong at most, what they lacked in numbers they substituted with enthusiasm as the runners ran between them in single file. I had the distinct impression every member of this group had run the race last year and understood that if a runner ever needed encouragement, now was the time and here was the place.

We left reluctantly. We had missed Katie by three minutes, we figured, and with our own race lost we were in no particular rush to leave. Manhattan would be pushing and shoving and millions of people, most of whom didn't know elbows from sweat socks about running. Meanwhile, up here was this small and loyal band.

Their cheers filtered down to us as we stood on the subway platform. We waited almost ten minutes for a train, and never once did their enthusiasm wane. The more they cheered the glummer we got. We'd lost Katie and now we couldn't even watch the race because we had to wait for a train. When finally a subway came it was marked "express," but it wasn't.

I've been running for thirteen years now. My father died of a heart attack in 1969 when I was a senior in high school.

Right then I made a vow that I would never die of a heart attack. I promised myself I would always physically work at not having a heart attack. This was back when that doctor in Boston was first talking about aerobics and how everyone should exercise.

My father was sixty-two and I was seventeen when he died. He was a cigar salesman all his life—to this day I love the smell of cigars—and he worked hard. He went away to the International Tobacco Convention in Chicago and he died there, without family or friends or anything. I guess it was pretty awful. I mean, the coroner had to call my mother and tell her. She was devastated. Five kids, with two in college. So the number one motivation for my running is to get and stay very, very healthy. Not dying [laughs]. When I was hurt and wasn't running what I missed most was not having control over my own health. That was really frightening. Being fit is extremely important to me. It's a quality I look for in my friends—I don't know too many smokers.

When I was nineteen and a sophomore at Indiana University in Bloomington, a friend and I decided we weren't getting enough exercise. There wasn't much in the way of women's sports then, so we used to meet at a track. We met every night at eleven o'clock because it was dark and nobody could see us. We'd have been extraordinarily embarrassed if anybody had seen us. That's how I started running.

Just before his death my mother and father started taking walks after dinner, just the two of them. That always seemed like such a pleasant activity to me and it's one of the things I really like about running. It allows me to spend time with myself. And I think about my father a lot when I run now. I put off grieving his death for a long time. Only later did I realize, "Geez, I never took time out for that." So yeah, I think of him quite a bit when I run. I offer things up. Like when I was running my first marathon and I was really struggling over those last six miles I said, "Okay, Dad, pull me through."

Riding down Lexington Avenue I asked Katie's father to pull her through again. My father had died of a heart attack when I was a senior in high school, too. He was fifty and I was sixteen. He died at home, right after watching the *Immortal Man* on television. I was the only one home and I was taking his pulse when it stopped. Three years ago, at age twenty-eight and done playing basketball and volleyball, I'd suddenly realized I needed to physicially work at not having a heart attack. I started running, and the month before leaving Alaska I'd completed the Equinox Marathon in Fairbanks.

Heart attacks. Hitting the wall. Getting in shape. Running scared. I understood everything Katie had said.

Marian wondered aloud if Katie had made it. We took turns telling each other she had. "You know," Marian said, "I used to think that anybody who could say they were in the Olympics or even the trials had to be some kind of major athlete or something. But now, with Katie trying for it, it's just that . . ." She stopped, searching for the correct word.

"You're finding out she's just your sister?" I said.

Marian looked at me. A woman of delicate, almost fragile beauty, she had clear white skin and brown eyes that could look right through you. "That's it," she said, the realization more revelation than disappointment. "You know, if Katie makes it today she'll always be able to say she made the Olympic Trials. That's something no one will ever be able to take away from her."

The race was exactly two hours and forty-eight minutes old when we walked up Central Park South, fighting crowds and umbrellas. We looked for Katie, but didn't want to see her. We were a mile from the finish and if we saw her now she'd never make the trials. At Central Park West we turned right. There was no getting into the park, so our best bet was to hang out here and hope we ran into someone we knew or maybe even Katie herself. Near Seventy-second Street we saw a station wagon with a Warren Street banner draped across it.

"Wait a minute," Marian said. "There's Elaine." Marian walked over to Elaine, who was pulling on a pair of sweats, and asked how she did.

"I finished in 2:48 something," Elaine said. She'd made the trials, but at the moment was too tired to be ecstatic. "I was right behind Katie."

"Katie made it?"

"Yep. Katie made it."

I think so many people run marathons because this tends to be an age of proving oneself, of distinguishing oneself. Our society has gotten pretty nameless, and I think people use something like a marathon to give them some personal accomplishment. That's very important. It's also gotten rather fashionable and trendy. That's how I see the masses running marathons.

But I'm not sure how much that has to do with why I run marathons. I started running before most people got into running. I watched the running boom grow up around me. That put me in a good place because I was a little ahead of where other people were and I think it encouraged me. It was also very satisfying knowing that I'd gotten the idea before everyone else.

I run marathons because compared to other people doing the same thing, I'm pretty good. I would run whether there was competition or not—it's healty and it's helping me develop a strong cardiovascular system—but the fact that I receive a sort of universal approval for what I accomplish is a lot of reward for me.

I think we place more significance on these kinds of things than they really deserve. In the face of death and destruction and wars, it's not the least bit important to know how fast we can run a marathon. And there's nothing really special about the marathon, or running twenty-six miles or harkening back to the boys of ancient Greece. But in the face of dreams and the athletic pursuit, it really is important. We have to know how good we can be.

Katie appeared a few minutes later, wrapped in an aluminum foil space blanket and looking like an undernourished baked potato with a bad case of the shakes. She'd finished in 2:48:16. Her chin stuck out from a makeshift hood she'd formed in the foil and her lips were blue. Her legs were all goose bumps, and she didn't warm up until she was inside two sweatsuits and inside Martin's Deli near Lincoln Center.

She didn't sit down so much as melt into the seat. A waiter brought a pitcher of beer. Katie downed a couple of quick glasses. Sometimes, running is just an excuse to drink beer earlier in the day than you should.

Katie returned to earth slowly. I sat and listened as she talked nonstop, reliving every step of the race. I interrupted only long enough to find out that her three-finger wave near the Queensboro Bridge meant that she was on her third borough. "Didn't you get the message?" she said.

"Sure we did, Katie, sure we did," I said, and then I shut up. I envied her the emotions that swirled within her. The having done, the goal accomplished. I even envied the physical sensation the marathon can produce, that feeling of being turned inside out and having nothing, virtually nothing, left inside you. Suddenly, she stopped talking, and sank deeper into the seat. "I am now tired," she said, as if to officially verify the moment.

"I could have done better," she said, her voice no longer urgent and excited. The race was behind her now and she could look at it. "I didn't push myself at all. I knew I was going to make it the whole time. That was great. At the finish it all came crashing down around me. All at once, you know? I crossed the finish line, and all of a sudden I said to myself, 'It's all over,' I didn't want it to end."

I asked if she would run the trials now that she had really made it. Katie didn't answer right away. She started once, stopped, started again. "I don't know . . . well, maybe . . . yeah, I think so." Then she smiled, her face still flushed with victory.

"Yeah," she said, "I'm gonna do it."

CHAPTER 10

* * *

Introduction

Jabba is gone. Stolen. Last seen on DeGraw Street Tuesday night, October 18, across from the apartment. The next morning the cops said it was probably in five hundred pieces in five hundred places. My reaction was no reaction. No outrage, no despair. Since moving to New York City, I suppose I've always expected that someday something would happen. I never liked that van anyway.

But what of the trip? The immediate impulse was to bag it completely. Two weeks ago in Philadelphia the van had been broken into and all my clothes taken. (Somewhere in the City of Brotherly Love walks a thief with hands hidden beneath the sleeves of a forty-two extra-long sports coat.) Calling it quits once the van was stolen seemed the better part of intelligent.

But a year by any name would still be twelve months long. Buy another van? Never. The only "solution" was thirty days on a Trailways bus ("Go Big Red"). I must remember the advice a *Boston Globe* sports columnist imparted in Newport: "Everything that happens adds to the charm of the trip." Easy for him to say.

I picked the best thirty days to be on the road between now and the first of the year: November 11 to December 12. Next weekend I'll be in Denver for a Nuggetts–Houston Rockets NBA game and a Bronco–Seattle Seahawks NFL game. The day after Thanksgiving it's Caesars Palace in Las Vegas for the Larry Holmes–Marvis Frazier fight. Two days later I'll see the Chicago Bulls against the Lakers at the Forum in Los Angeles, then get to Oklahoma City the first weekend in December for the National Finals Rodeo.

I'll finish my year in Florida during the first three weeks of 1984. Miami for the Orange Bowl and Tampa for the Super Bowl.

Some events had to be scrapped. (Marvin Haglar versus Roberto Durran being the most prominent). Also out is the National Surfing Championships in Hawaii between the Orange and Super bowls. Too bad. I'm the Alaska chairman of the National Surfing Association. (I've got the letter to prove it. When I first wrote requesting info they wrote asking if I knew anyone interested in the position. I said I didn't, so they named me to the post.)

Because I'll be tied to Trailways, I've prearranged some of this thirty-day excursion. I can no longer pour my wallet into Jabba's gas tank and just go for it. I'll interview Reggie McKenzie of the Seahawks in Denver; and Tommy Bonk, the *Los Angeles Times*'s Laker beat writer in L.A. With that as framework, I'll wing it as best I can.

But first, this weekend in Chicago. Bulls–Boston Celtics tomorrow night, Bears–Philadelphia Eagles Sunday afternoon, Blackhawks–Edmonton Oilers Sunday evening. Three sports in one city in twenty-four hours. I've been wanting to do that all year. That the city is Chicago is perfect. No other city can usurp Chicago as my favorite stop on the road. I've got friends and a place to stay, and I've enjoyed every stopover. I want to get back to Chicago one more time before my year is over.

Day Two I watched the Celtics-Bulls game at a court-side press seat. Down here I could see the players' eyes, and I was suddenly aware of a brand-new dimension of the game. I noticed it first in Robert Parish, the Celtic center. He grabbed a rebound, faked right, dribbled once to his left, and lofted a short jumper. I'd glanced at his face when he feinted right and for the briefest of moments the scene was frozen, like a snapshot, his eyes two darts to the right inside their sockets. Here was a part of the game I had never seen before, and it was difficult now to look at anything else. I spent the rest of the game taking snapshots with my eyes, shooting quick glances at the players to record for just a moment a moment of their game. Disgust. Pain. Elation. Frustration. Deviltry. Mischief. Parish, with his hawkish profile and deep-set eyes, remained the most intriguing player to follow. He seemed to be operating from inside an impermeable shell, quiet and self-contained, totally impervious and supremely aloof. For minutes on end I followed him up and down the court snapping off little pictures of how he played his game.

Afterward (Celtics won, of course), I waited at gate 3½ with about fifty fans waiting for the players. One man kept telling his group he could get them introduced to Quinn Buckner of the Celtics.

As the players emerged it was readily apparent that neither side, fans nor players, was terribly enamored of the other. The players wary and distrustful, the fans antagonistic and more than a little jealous.

The guy who said he could get introductions to Quinn Buckner got them. Buckner shook hands dutifully, saying the name of each one as he did. The guy who got the intros beamed.

Two women in tight jeans approached a player. One of the two asked why he hadn't called her. The player looked at the ground. "I've been busy," he said.

"You've got my number?"

"Yeah." Silence.

"Give me a call. Anytime. Please." More silence. Then a quick touch of a gloved hand to the player's face. "You look good." She walked into the parking lot alone.

Kevin McHale walked over to a woman who looked to be his mother. Other players walked through the crowd, trying to ignore everyone until they found the people who mattered to them. Players with no one waiting walked quickly to the Celtic bus or their own cars. Robert Parish attracted much attention; he accepted it with the same game face I'd studied inside. Larry Bird walked out behind him, however, and he immediately became the focus. People asked for autographs with one breath, then taunted Bird with questions about his preseason fight with Marc Ivaronni with the next. Parish was left alone, and as he talked to his friends his game face disappeared. It was like he was a completely different person.

Day Three Sunday afternoon the Bears beat the Eagles in the first game played at Soldier Field since George Halas's death. The game was a sellout, and I waited for the crowds to thin before walking back to Irene's car.

Along the way I met Barry, a black college student taking a year off from the University of Illinois Chicago-Circle and working as an usher at Soldier Field and Comiskey Park.

"Tell me something," I said. "When you put on your uniform, do you get an urge to lead the band.?" Barry laughed. He was soft-spoken and gentle, and it seemed important to him that I know his being an usher wasn't his career.

"It was either take this job or work at a little grocery store right in my neighborhood," he said. "But if I'd done that I'd just be bouncing off the same people all the time. You know, people just like me. But this job . . ."

"You get to bounce off sixty thousand people every Sunday?"

"Yeah, I guess so. Something like that anyway. But like I said, this isn't my life's work. Not by a long shot. But I love these stadiums. What other city has all its teams playing in their own stadiums? Bulls and Hawks play together, but the Sox and the Cubs and the Bears all got their own place to play. It's great. And all the stadiums have long traditions and the seats aren't miles away. It's not like a Veterans Stadium in Philly."

"What's it like bouncing off sixty thousand people?" I said.

"Oh man, I seen it all," he said. The boy become a man. "Everything. Heart attacks, you name it. At this point nothing can shock me. One time at Comiskey during a rain delay they almost had a riot. I don't even think about what happens anymore. The first time something happened I took too much time thinking about what was happening and I was shocked. Now I just react. But you know, you gotta figure: You get thirty thousand people at a ball game and the law of averages says somebody isn't going to make it through the afternoon." I told him I'd keep that in mind next time I was at a ball game.

I drove Albert, Irene's rusted yellow Volkswagen, to Chicago Stadium, picked up my credential, and went to the press room on the mezzanine level to eat. I loaded up my plate and sat in my seat, the old and venerable Chicago Stadium spreading out before me.

My Chicago weekend was proceeding better than planned. Chicago teams were 1-1 going into tonight's game. More important, now that I'd been to Soldier's Field, I'd batted the cycle and been in all four Chicago parks. I'd missed seeing the White Sox, but I'd seen the All-Star Game at Comiskey.

Soldier Field had surprised me. Pillars and archways gave it the look of a Roman coliseum, but the field was astroturf. The press room was ultramodern, too, and so were the locker rooms. But Lake Michigan had been a cold, gray slate, and snow flurries had swirled around the stadium. The feelings were right. George Halas isn't really gone. Barry was right when he said Chicagoans were fortunate to have four great places to to watch their teams play ball.

Chicago Stadium was equally impressive, an ancient-looking place that dripped with character. Even the cheap seats were great. The highest seats shared space with dusty girders, a few championship banners, and some pigeons. This was the kind of place where people were part of the game being played. I'd just seen two games in twenty-four hours, but sitting in a stadium like this—in a city like Chicago—I couldn't wait for the next game to begin. But there was still two hours to go. I looked for someone to talk to. Directly below me was a woman in a pink sweater, alone in the arena, sitting next to the ice and eating a sandwich.

"How you doin'?" I said as I walked down the ramp. Then, to start the conversation, "Who are the Hawks playing tonight?" She looked at me like I'd just crawled out from underneath a rock.

"Edmonton," she said, glancing at me and then my credential and then back to me.

"Oh," Edmonton! Wayne Gretzky! Power offense! The team that had eliminated the Blackhawks in last year's play-offs! Who didn't know *that*? I felt like I'd just crawled out from underneath a rock. To salvage my credibility, I quickly explained who I was and why I was so stupid.

Her name was Sue Cohn. She was a producer for SportsVision, the Chicago cable system that carried the city's teams. Her hair was curly and raven black, which contrasted sharply with her very white skin. She was short, twenty-three, and looked sixteen.

"I really wanted to work for a network," she said, "but because

I'm young I need all the experience I can get. In Philly I was doing three minutes for the five, the six, and the eleven o-clock news. Here I'm doing three hours live. I never thought I'd be doing that as quickly as I am."

"How much are you hampered by being (a) a woman, (b) young, and (c) little?"

Sue finished her sandwich and wrapped the wax paper into a little ball. "I don't care what anybody says about women having a chance to compete and all that stuff. If I was a blond I'd really be in trouble. People just don't believe a woman's place should be in sports."

"How 'bout the locker room?"

"Women are allowed in the locker room," she said, "but I don't like to go in. I'm not afraid of seeing the guys; it's just I know if I was a guy I wouldn't want women traipsing in with a microphone. It's a matter of mutual respect. I'll tell an athlete I'd like to talk to him and then I wait outside. That attitude has always worked for me. It takes time, but it's usually worth it."

Sue started her career doing color for Cornell hockey, but she no longer worked in front of the camera. There was, she said, no market for the lady sports broadcaster.

"I've also never seen a woman who was any good at it, either," she said. "And anyway, all they want is Miss America behind a desk. Whenever I tell someone what I do, they immediately say, 'Oh, like Phyllis George?' " Sue shrugged. "Like I said, there just isn't the market for the woman sports announcer. Men are just not going to watch a woman tell them about sports. Sports is the last bastion of the male's domain."

"So why do you want to be involved in it?"

"Well, I'm no bra burner, you know what I mean? I do this because I like sports and love television. I'm fascinated by the technical aspects of directing a game, of producing a feature. So I'm combining the things I know the most about: sports and television. To me there's no greater thrill than producing a good segment or directing something that comes out right."

Sue planned to stay in Chicago for a couple more years. She liked it well enough, but she grew up on the East Coast and wanted to get back. To the biggest market, the toughest competition. She loved the competition. "I've had people come up to me and say, 'I think the work you're doing is great, but I can do it better.' I remember the first time I pulled up the wrong graphic I was physically removed from the truck. That's the thing about television, it's so competitive. Not everybody can make it. That's why they have places like Peoria and Kansas City."

I told her about a place called Alaska, and how being up there and far away I felt trapped by television.

"And," Sue said, "you started to wonder if what television was bringing you really was the truth, right?"

"So you tell me, Ms. Producer, is TV bringing me what really happens?"

"That depends."

"Thanks."

Sue laughed. "I know that sounds awfully generic, but it really is true. But I'll be specific. The higher up you go, the less objectivity there is."

"The higher up what you go?"

"The higher the network. SportsVision, for instance, is regional. If a skater goes to the penalty box and he's swearing, we'll let it go on the air. We're cable, what the hell. What it all boils down to is we're dealing with a product: entertainment."

I told her about last night, the scene outside the gate. "That just reinforced what I've been seeing all year: a wide, wide gulf between the players on the courts and the people in the stands. I don't think fans understand what an athlete's life is about," I said.

"And I don't think they care, either," Sue said. "They paid their eighteen bucks for their seat, five for parking, and two for a beer. They've invested themselves in a win. The fans here tonight will be looking for a happy ending. That's it."

I watched the first period outside gate 3½, inside the SportsVision production truck, a cramped compartment with carpet on the walls and coaxial cables snaking all over the floor. A narrow passageway connected five small cubicles. The biggest area barely had room for three chairs in front of a wall covered by twenty-four monitors. The only light was the glow of the television screens. From the moment I entered, the outside world ceased to exist. It was like I'd crawled inside a hole a million miles beneath the surface of the earth.

There were eight people in the truck. Three in production, one each in audio, transmission, and video, and two in videotape in the rear. Inside the stadium were four people behind cameras. All twelve were hooked together via their headphones, and they turned on the overhead speaker so I could listen in. As game time approached the tensions increased, but so did the barbs and insults, and their collective sense of humor served as an irreverent buffer between them and the pressure of being ready to go when the red light blinked.

The director was Brian. He sat in the middle chair between Mark and Sue. Sue's job was communication with the studio. Brian called the shots he wanted played, and near as I could tell Mark was in charge of getting these shots onto the right monitor. The large monitor on the right showed the picture that was being beamed to "the entire free world," as they like to call it. Four of the smaller monitors showed what was being seen by each of the four cameras inside the stadium.

I spent the period second-guessing Brian's shot selection. My eyes scanned the screens looking for the best image: in tight, wide angle, behind the net, isolation. I forgot there was a real game being played. The figures running back and forth across the monitors were just pieces of an electronic puzzle that needed to be fit together in rapid succession. The combinations were endless. The period flew by. When it was over I didn't know the score, but my eyes burned and a dull headache pressed across my forehead.

Back inside the stadium for the second period, there was no way not to know the score. The Hawks were down just one to nothing against the strongest offense in the league!

The second period was one long, ecstatic ride. Denis Savard scored at 1:04 for Chicago; ten minutes later Bill Gardner put the Hawks up 2–1. At 12:51 Jari Kurri tied it for Edmonton on an assist by Gretzky, but with three and a half minutes left Rick Paterson gave all of Chicago (or so it seemed from inside the stadium) a 3–2 lead to take into the locker room.

In the final period, neither team scored for almost seven minutes. Then Steve Larmer scored for Chicago at 13:10, and 17,534 people erupted, everyone of them begging and beseeching the Hawks to give them their happy ending. With two minutes remaining Edmonton scored to make it 4-3, and with fifty seconds left, the Oilers pulled their goalie to gain a man advantage. Thirty seconds later Gretzky stole the puck at mid-ice, and with nothing between himself and the net but Tony Esposito, skated for the goal.

But the night belonged to Tony. He had latched onto one of

those rarified performances an athlete can't predict but can only grab hold of when they happen. He stopped The Great One, the Hawks scored an open-net goal with eight seconds remaining, and all of Chicago lived happily ever after.

Day eleven Denver has a new saint. Number eight, quarterback Gary Kubiak. Forget Steve DeBerg; he missed the game with a separated shoulder. Scratch John Elway; he woke up vomiting at three o'clock Sunday morning. That placed the game in the hands of one Gary Kubiak, six feet tall and 192 pounds, a rookie eighth-round draft choice from Texas A&M, who makes in a year the kind of money Elway makes when he puts on his helmet. Prior to yesterday's game Kubiak had been on the field once, as holder for an extra point that failed. Sunday he passed for one touchdown, ran for another, and led the Broncos to a 38–27 victory in the kind of game that keeps little boys dreaming. Denver is beyond euphoric. One game does not a season make, but for the moment, at least, Denver is prepared to ride Gary Kubiak to the Super Bowl.

My press pass got me into the game but not into the press box. I had to find my own seat. No mean trick in a stadium that's been sold out ninety-seven times in a row. I finally found one in section 440 of the upper deck (Mile and a Half Stadium, I was told). But I was on the fifty-yard line and the view was superb. The game unfolded like a schematic diagram. When Kubiak hit Steve Watson with a seventy-eight-yard touchdown pass, I knew it would work before Kubiak was two steps into his drop. So did everyone else in the upper reaches, and I watched and listened as this understanding swept through the lower decks until the entire stadium erupted.

No one was more enthusiastic than the woman behind me. She was about forty and blond, and she just loved her Broncos. When I told her what I was doing for the year she responded with: "You won't find anything like this anyplace else in the country." I didn't tell her people had been telling me that everywhere I'd been. Instead, I asked her to explain Broncomania.

"The only way to get to a Bronco game is if you know someone who got tickets as part of their divorce settlement. That's why I'm here today. The lady I'm with has been coming to games for thirteen years. People will give up their house if that's the only way they can keep their Broncos. And I'm only exaggerating a little bit.

"But you know what it is? This is a city of Easterners. Everybody here is from someplace else. Following the Broncos is a good way to follow your old hometown team. I'm from Cleveland. I started going to Browns games with my father when I was sixteen. I love it when the Browns come here. I can't lose. I stand through the whole game. Everybody's got to have roots, right?"

I asked about a particular Bronco player and his rumored connection to cocaine. "I don't want to talk about it," she said. "I'm just sick about it.

"The coaches are being real tight-lipped. We're not getting any pertinent information. He was my hero." She laughed. "He has the best fanny in the NFL. But really, I'm heartbroken. He was a real figure in the community. He was great with kids. Everyone looked up to him. I guess you can't take that away from him, but after this . . . ," her voice trailed away. She was a social worker and she worked with teenage boys.

"That's why I get so angry when something like this happens. Great role model, huh? The kids don't come right out and say, 'Well look at him, he does it,' but I know they're thinking it. I just know they are."

My interview with Reggie McKenzie went very well, although credit belongs to Reggie. Early in the second half he'd taken a shot to the head and had to be helped from the field, but in the locker room afterward he insisted he'd only been dinged. "You stick your head in there, you got to expect to get it hit," he said.

The locker room was small and crowded. Clumps of grass were ground into the carpet. Tape everywhere, huge chunks of it discarded on the floor, still in the shape of the ankles and hips and elbows and knees they had recently encased. Players and reporters and camera crews jockeyed for space to twist out of uniforms or get quotes explaining the whipping the Broncos had just administered.

Reggie and I were the last to leave. I enjoyed his company, and sensed that he enjoyed mine. Large and muscular, he had an ugly dark scar in the middle of his forehead and a thin white-line scar across his nose. His beard was thick and rough. When he laughed his face disappeared behind his mouth. He shed his uniform piece by piece but didn't grow smaller as each layer hit the floor. He had appeared rather menacing encased inside his battle dress, but once freed from it, he was warm and sincere, even gentle.

"How'd you come to pick Reggie?"

"You were my second choice," I said. He looked at me with feigned indignation and then laughed. I'd wanted Kellen Winslow but had gotten no where with Charger public relations. Reggie was a twelve-year pro and had blocked for O.J. Simpson at Buffalo. "You were the next person to come to mind." I said.

"Fair enough. Ask away." I did. He had much to say, and seemed to appreciate the opportunity to say it.

On education: I graduated in four years from Michigan. That degree was very important to me. My part of the deal was that I play football; their part of the deal was that I get an education. I tell the young kids coming up to be like Reggie. To be like an O.J. or a Curt Warner. I tell the kids that if they're good enough physically, to go for it. But develop the mind along with it. Don't lose out on your end of the deal.

Mental preparation: During the season everything else is secondary. As the coaches say, "You got to fine-focus in." You've got to be totally committed. You've got to be mentally tough. You've got to go out there every Sunday and do it. You got to be out there doing the job. If you're not doing your job they'll just get somebody else.

The fans: They don't understand. They don't see July, they don't see August. They don't see the bumps and bruises. They don't see Monday morning. They don't want to see it, really. They just want to see the finished product. It all goes back to the days of the Roman gladiators. You win or you lose; thumbs up or thumbs down.

Money: I enjoy what I do. I enjoy the camaraderie. But let me tell you something, I understand the game on this level. I learned from an old pro when I first came in. He said, "You want to do the best you can and you want to win; that's built into all of us as competitors. But the most important thing is that you get paid. As long as you get paid, you're okay." People—especially the money people—try to tell you it isn't about the money. But they just want you to lose sight of what it's all about. And it's about the money.

O. J. Simpson: My most memorable moment is the year we took the division and his 2003 yards. He was one of the best, maybe the best ever. Nobody else had ever done it; nobody else had ever dared to think it. It was all confidence. Something that was created over an extended period of time. The confidence that we could do, *you know?*

Violence: This is a violent game played by violent men. There's no other way to put it. In this game you got to get to the point where you kind of enjoy the hitting because you're going to have to do it anyway. But it's the people in the stands who get off on it. What's the worst thing that could happen out on the field? Somebody could get killed. But the fans will love it until somebody gets killed.

Injury: It's gonna happen. It's as much a part of the game as puntin' the football. I was operated on once, but I played 142 consecutive games before I got my knee. You're all but guaranteed to get a knee playing football.

Pressure and responsibilities: The average NFL life span is $4\frac{1}{4}$ *years. At that point—if a guy lasts that long—he begins to realize he has responsibilities. You've got to understand, a guy comin' out of college is twenty-one years old. He doesn't know what his responsibilities are. Some of them handle it; some of them don't. The ones that don't you read about.*

Reggie left to shower. When he came out, a towel wrapped around his waist and another draped over his head, he waved a finger at me. He'd been talking about being a black athlete and the extra layer of responsibility that entailed.

"When you're black, being an athlete is your way out," he said. "Now the Man, he don't want to let you out. He don't care what you got in your head, he just wants to squash you. Why does somebody like Doug Williams have to sign with the USFL Oklahoma Outlaws? He's a top-notch quarterback. They just don't want to pay him what they're paying the white guys. How many black reporters you see in here right now, understand?"

I bounced an observation off him: "The success of black athletes has worked against blacks being successful in other areas." Reggie looked at me, measuring both me and the statement. People have conceded athletics to blacks, but use that attitude to keep blacks out of everything else.

"A lot of people stereotype," Reggie said. "It comes from the years and years and years gone by. A lot of people think a young black man coming into college can't get his degree. I've had people say, 'You know, I didn't know you could talk.' " His face broke into a wide laugh of disbelief.

I asked about retirement. It wasn't a subject he liked to think about, he said, although he'd been thinking about it since he was traded before this season.

"I was with Buffalo for eleven years," he said. "For the first ten years I didn't miss a game, but when it came time to negotiate my contract they just turned the shoulder on me. That's what I've been saying here. What's the most important thing? The money. Because there ain't no loyalty." He shrugged. He understood the game at this level. "There was no sense getting mad. I mean, what's another black man getting mad?" Reggie laughed.

"You should be happy with what you got?"

"Right. Exactly. That's the attitude most of the time." He laughed again.

He dressed in a gray suit and light gray shirt and put a heavy gold chain around his neck. He tried to put his suit coat on, but couldn't twist his left shoulder to get his arm into the sleeve. I reached to help. He pulled away.

"I'm all right," he said, still struggling.

"Sure you are." He looked at me and chuckled. At me, at himself. How many times had he used that line? So many times that saying it now was automatic. Like it was me who'd decide if he played next week and collected his check.

"Yeah, right," he said, still laughing. "I'm okay, Coach, put me in." Still, he put his coat on by himself, and then we walked out.

Day Fifteen, Las Vegas, From the Passport to Caesars Realm:

> I, CAESAR, greet you as your host to my Royal Wonderland, created solely for the enjoyment of my citizen guests.
>
> My Palace of Pleasures, built with the wondrous elements of historic fact, romantic legend and myths of the gods is a haven of boundless delights. Within these lavish confines you will be treated to unparalleled entertainment, teased with exquisite food and drink and challenged by games of chance. To rejuvenate the spirit, two vast pools and fields of combat await, with Roman baths and solaria to

relax and comfort you. . . . For you, O Noble Guest, shall the gates of my Palace swing wide. . . .

Alone in Las Vegas was no way to spend Thanksgiving. Finding conversation was impossible. Everyone was pursuing the grim-looking business of having fun. Even winning produced no joy. People stood by their slot machines as silver dollars cascaded into their buckets like they were walking their dog and it was pooping all over the sidewalk and they were trying not to notice. When the money stopped falling they slid the silver they'd just won back into the slots.

As for the Larry Holmes–Marvis Frazier fight, the whole thing stunk. All two minutes fifty-nine seconds of it. It wasn't a championship match. It was an attempt by two men to exorcise their demons. Neither succeeded.

At the last minute the bout was moved inside to the 5,000-seat Olympic Forum. The weather was cold and nasty, the promoters said. They'd also sold only 1,000 tickets. The Forum was behind the Garden of the Gods and the Palace Pools and sat in the shadow of the Olympic Stadium, an erector set of rusty pipes and unpainted wood. The Forum itself was an aluminum airplane hangar with blown insulation hanging from the rafters.

In the featured preliminary Boom Boom Mancini beat his opponent in one minute fifty-eight seconds. The fear was that Larry Holmes would do the same to Marvis Frazier. An unwarranted concern, because Larry needed another 61 seconds to beat the absolute bejeezus out of Marvis. The crowd filed out quietly. We'd been had, but this was Vegas. In Vegas, you know what you're getting before you get here, and once here, you get it.

At the postfight press conference Larry Holmes was the first to take a shot at expelling the spirits that lurked within. He was visibly relieved that Marvis had escaped with less than three minutes of punishment, but furious that as heavyweight champion of the world he'd been forced to fight Marvis in the first place. He was the champ. He had paid his dues, waited his turn. He'd defended his title sixteen times and was undefeated in forty-four professional fights. Now here was some twenty-two-year-old named Frazier with ten professional fights standing in the ring with him. How could anyone think for a minute that Marvis could have taken his title? But when it was suggested that Larry looked insulted in the ring, Holmes's entire demeanor changed. Insult had nothing to do with it. Give him the money and he'd fight anybody.

Holmes was an open book that invited dime-store analysis. He laid his guts all over the table, daring people to figure him out, then berating them when they wandered too close to the mark. There was little about him that elicited sympathy. He wanted, demanded, *craved* respect, but then made sure he'd never get it. He was vindictive and biting, unpredictable and caustic. But mostly he was angry, at everything and everyone, including, it seemed, himself. One phrase struck me: "This is a hard, dirty-ass, rotten game, gentleman." A native-born son in the Land of Opportunity, and the best shot he could get was beating people up.

Then it was Joe Frazier's turn, all chin and all pride, standing next to son Marvis. He was the only person in the room—with the possible exception of Marvis—who hadn't been terrified at the prospects of sending a twenty-two-year-old against the heavyweight champion of the world. What inner demons could still be dancing with Joe's ego to have made him do a thing like that?

Even more terrifying was the son's acceptance of his father's will. Marvis stood behind the microphones, an NBC cap cocked at a crazy angle, a self-conscious smile on his boyish face. All he needed was a fishing pole and he'd have been Huck Finn. Someone asked what he planned next. "That's up to Pop," Marvis said, and a shudder ran through the room.

After the interviews I listened as Larry Merchant of the *New York Daily News*, Dave Anderson of the *New York Times*, and Colin Hart of the *London Sun* commiserated with Eddie Futch, Larry's trainer. Eddie had trained Joe Frazier for all his title bouts and had watched Marvis grow up. He considered Marvis a grandson. He had not wanted him to fight Larry, and had said so before the fight. The kid was young, the kid was inexperienced. The kid was still a kid. That's what hurt the most.

"Marvis is a fine, fine, kid," Eddie said, with obvious affection. He looked tired and more than a little sad. His soft brown face held expressive eyes that disappeared behind their wrinkles when he laughed or scrinched his face to make a point. "I went to see him win his Junior Olympic wrestling title."

"Was there ever a time when you said, 'He can be a fighter'?" Dave Anderson wanted to know.

"I never really thought about it too much. He was going about his own ways. Swimming, football, wrestling. I thought that would be his own niche, you know? Just a real good athlete." Colin Hart suggested that Marvis would be better off working toward an Olympic gold medal as an amateur boxer. Eddie agreed wholeheartedly.

"Marvis was a very good amateur boxer," Eddie said. He stated again that he was sad to see Marvis being trained by his father. Marvis was tall and strong and had that great athletic ability. He could have been a fine boxer. Joe wanted to make him a puncher.

"Joe is making the mistake most great boxers make when they turn trainer. They try to cut everybody in their own mold."

"And now Joe is trying to make Marvis another Joe," Anderson said.

Eddie nodded, full of regret. "Nobody could tell Joe that this wasn't the way Marvis should fight."

The four continued to talk. It was agreed that Joe had once been a great champion and was a superb father now. No question about it. Joe as professional trainer was another story altogether. A story these reporters didn't want to write. Putting Marvis in the ring against Larry had been a huge mistake.

"So much has been lost that didn't need to be lost," Eddie said. "He wasn't ready; he shouldn't have been there."

Larry Merchant wondered if Marvis might quit.

"Joe won't let him," Eddie said.

A television monitor was turned on. With a fight this quick everyone needed to see it again. Marvis, wearing a pair of green shorts that hung to his knees and looked ridiculous, threw one punch at the opening bell. That was it. Midway through the fight he dropped his hands and stood flat-footed, trying to slip punches.

A reporter joined us when the final flurry began, "I want to count the punches," he said. I watched Eddie and listened to the reporter call the hits one after the other in rapid succession. Eddie didn't move. He just sat and looked at the monitor, his face scrinched, his eyes hidden, his arms folded across his chest. The reporter stopped at thirteen.

Day Seventeen At the end of the third period the Lakers were down by five. The Chicago Bulls had taken away the running game by walking the ball up court, and L.A. was out of its rhythm. The Forum was deathly quiet.

But then the Laker girls pranced to center court, shimmering in purple and gold. Their break-dance routine pumped new blood through the sagging crowd. Suddenly they were up. On edge. Aggressive. The noise climaxed when the Lakers returned to the court. "You kind of get the feeling," said the guy next to me, "that the person who yells the loudest thinks he's gonna get laid!" The Lakers delivered immediately. The five-point deficit quickly became a five-point lead, and the Lakers held on to win 103–100.

I'd met Tommy Bonk once before but didn't know it. At the U.S. Open Tennis Championships in September he'd been a columnist for the *Houston Post,* where he worked for eleven years. I'd talked to him briefly. Now he was the *Los Angeles Times*'s Laker beat writer. The change had happened overnight but he was happy with the switch.

"People have asked me how I could have given up a column to become a beat man again," he said, "but I'd rather be covering this beat in Los Angeles than be a columnist in Houston. Things are going real well for me now. I'm covering a team that could win the NBA title; I'm living in Los Angeles and working in the market I want to be working in. This is the best of both possible worlds."

Tommy was the writer who had coined the University of Houston's "Phi Slamma Jamma" slogan that had run amok at the NCAAs in Albuquerque. It had been the inescapable hype of the tournament, and I remembered an irrational desire to strangle the writer who'd dreamed it up. "Tell me about it," Tommy said. "I spent more time at the championships doing interviews than I did writing stories. It was supposed to be a throwaway line." I accepted his remorse and allowed him to live.

We met in the Laker press room, then walked out to the Forum and sat near the court. The game was an hour away. The Laker girls, in sweats and leg warmers, were on the floor rehearsing later enticements.

Tommy was well over six feet tall, with brown curly hair and sharp, handsome features. He was stylishly attired in lavender shirt, charcoal-purple slacks, and a pastel knit tie. The entire package bespoke a cool, totally competent professionalism. I asked if he felt it necessary to answer the critics who degraded sports reporting as hack writing.

"I've always considered myself a reporter and a writer who just happens to be covering sports," he said. "People who turn up their noses at sports are probably out of it anyway. Sports cuts across all kinds of lines. It's a social common denominator and I think that kind of reporting is important.

"A sports reporter has to know about labor law, the cost of bail bonds (not for himself); he has to be versed in the sport. He has to be a social commentator within the framework of the game and do it in an entertaining way.

"That's quite a bit of pressure if you stop to realize you only have forty minutes to write a thousand-word story that two million people are going to read."

"Ever get writer's block?"

Tommy shook his head. "You do what you have to do. And the Lakers make my job easy because they're so wonderful to work with. They're very quotable. And of course they win all the time, which helps their demeanor. They also realize they are competing for the entertainment dollar in a large market. The Lakers are very public relations–conscious.

"Do the Lakers school their players?"

Tommy didn't think so. "I think the players just intuitively know it or they don't last here. It's a very important part of the makeup of the club."

"What do you think the players think of you?"

"Hopefully they feel the same way about me that I feel about them. We're both trying to do a job and we're both working at the same time. I really don't care if they like me, as long as they respect me. And I have to earn their respect, just as they have to earn mine. I think athletes can take tough stories as long as you're fair about it. If you praise an athlete you have the right—and the duty—to criticize when they screw up. Athletes know what the truth is. They know when they've screwed up. They're not dumb."

"Why have I found so much cynicism in the press boxes I've been in this year?"

"That goes with the whole newspaper business. You have to realize, a lot of people tell you things because that is the way they wish to appear. It isn't the way the reality is. You have to have a sixth sense to understand when someone is feeding you a line. There's so much untruth that we have to deal with that it develops a certain cynicism."

"Do players have a duty to talk to the press?"

"Yeah, I think they do. They don't have an obligation to talk to a particular reporter, but they do have an obligation to the fan who spends money to come see them play. I think it's pretty short-sighted to turn your back on the people who are making these huge contracts possible."

"Is it easy for the press to misrepresent a personality simply because that person is easy to talk to?"

"No question about it. There are reporters who have their favorites and they go to them for quotes and will make them appear what they are not. That's a real problem, dealing with the intimacy we have with the players. I mean, we see them every day for seven months. There are people that you're going to get along with. And there is a definite danger in that."

The Lakers walked onto the court to shoot around. The game was twenty minutes away. The Forum was almost empty. "How much of a cheerleader are you expected to be for the Lakers?"

"In some other markets and at some other levels I think there is the idea that reporters should be part of the team. You'll hear reporters refer to the team as 'we.' That's not expected here and I would never do it. There has to be a certain adversarial relationship between myself and the players. I work for the *Times*; we pay our own way. The most important thing in reporting is credibility. My stories are written from a Laker point of view, and rightfully so, but the moment you drop the typewriter and pick up the pom-pom you're through. No one will ever believe you again." A pep band behind us jumped into an enthusiastic rendition of "Rocky." The interview was over.

During the game Tommy kept track of all shots, fouls, the time of every basket, and a commentary of notes explaining specific plays. He also wrote the "A" matter, a running story to be sent immediately after the game to meet first-edition deadlines. When time warranted, he kept an eye on the stands and told me to do the same. They were all here tonight, he said, referring to the regular retinue of good looking Forum women. I was free to look where I pleased. Tommy was right. Best-looking fans of the year.

After the game, Tommy hustled to the press room and filed his first story. Then it was down a long corridor to the Lakers' locker room. "This entire postgame locker room stuff is demeaning," Tommy said, jogging along. "To the players and to me."

"How do you put up with it?" I asked.

Tommy shrugged. "It's the nature of the beast. I've learned to block it all out and get what I need."

The locker room door was closed; a handful of reporters waited outside. The door opened and Pat Riley, the Laker coach, walked into the hallway. Reporters surrounded him, but Tommy ignored the coach and went right inside. He talked to Jamaal Wilkes first and was able to ask a couple of questions before the Laker forward was enveloped by TV cameras. Tommy moved to James Worthy, then tried Magic Johnson, but he was buried beneath a pile of cameras and microphones. He tried to listen from the periphery, gave up, and walked outside. Riley, by himself now, was leaning against the wall, his hands in his pockets.

"Hey, Bonk, how ya doin'?" the coach said, his voice friendly. "What can I do for you?" The two exchanged friendly insults and on the next beat Tommy asked a question. Riley's answer was as Tommy had said it would be: thoughtful, articulate, and complete.

"I'm lucky," Tommy had told me. "I'm working in the best media market with the best coach in the NBA from a reporter's point of view. Pat knows how to talk, and being in L.A., he understands his responsibilities to the media. This is a hype town and he knows it. And television loves him. He talks in thirty-second segments. It's uncanny."

"They controlled the tempo," Riley said, answering Tommy's question. "They sustained a hell of a defensive effort against us. Last time that was done to us was San Diego. They picked up Magic full court and bump, bump, bump, bump. We had a hard time. We got the least number of fast breaks that we've had all year. I don't know the number but Bill sort of threw it out at me. But they controlled the tempo and they banged the boards. If you want to stop the running game, those are the things you're going to have to do. On the offensive boards, they took that away from us, too. But we ground it out, Tom. I think it's important that when you're a running team you're not going to have eighty-two great running games. You're going to have probably sixty. The other twenty-two are probably going to be grind-out games. You just got to win those games, and we did. I thought we played as well as we could play under the conditions."

When the interview was over Riley playfully flipped Tommy's tie. "You look like a rock star," the coach said. "Oh, and I liked the story you did on Scott. I liked that one line, 'Scott is destined for more minutes . . . .' What was the rest of it? Is that like stream-of-consciousness writing?"

"I don't know, Pat, the wine was kicking; I don't know."

"Well it was a good story. The kid needed it."

Tommy thanked Pat warmly and went back inside. He found Magic for a one-on-one interview. On the way out he talked briefly to Scott; then it was through the door and down the corridor in high gear. He was wired tight. "The only thing I didn't want was an overtime," he said. "You know, I don't really care who wins or loses; I've got to write a story no matter what happens. The only thing I want is for the game to end in two hours."

He checked his watch as we neared the press room. "Okay, now the jammin' starts."

LAKERS WALK OVER BULLS . . . SORT OF

by Thomas Bonk, *Times* Staff Writer

Contrary to what others may believe, Pat Riley said the Lakers are simply not going to have 82 running games.

"You'll have, say, 60," Riley guessed. "The other 22, you just have to grind out. And this was one of them."

The Chicago Bulls accomplished what few other teams have been able to do this season against the Lakers—keep them from fast-breaking. But Sunday night at the Forum, it didn't make much difference. The Lakers won in a walk, not a run, 103–100.

"It wasn't exactly picturesque, but we're glad to have it," said Jamaal Wilkes.

And so it went for forty minutes and one thousand words for two million people to read tomorrow morning. When he finished punching the story into his computer, he called the *Times* office, put the phone in a special holder on top of the computer, pressed a button, and left. He returned a few minutes later and picked up the receiver. "All right?" Short pause. "All right." He hung up the phone.

We walked from the Forum together. Tommy was still wired. "The problem with this job is that there is always another story to write," he said. "And your only as good as your last fuckin' keystroke."

Days Nineteen to Twenty-one. Escape from L.A. Thirty days on a Trailways bus is a jail sentence, but seventy-two hours in southern California without transportation is cruel and unusual punishment. I was locked in a prison with freeways for fences, an alien being in a land where pedestrians obey the Don't Walk sign. I left Tuesday night and have been traveling east to the rodeo ever since. I have lost track of time, space, and reasons to live. It is Tuesday, Wednesday, maybe Thursday.

Reality has been reduced to the inside of a Trailways bus. Rational thought is difficult. I keep thinking that this ordeal has been orchestrated by Jabba to force me to say that I miss the van. If so, I'll concede. In Jabba, I always had a place to sleep. In Jabba, wherever I went, there I was. On a Big Red bus, wherever I go, I'm still here. On a Big Red bus.

Oklahoma City, 6 A.M. Frozen puddles and a dusting of snow on the street. I take a room at the Peacock Brothers Hotel near the bus depot. For $12 I get a windowless room that smells of Lysol, has fake paneling on the walls and real mold in the corners. I turn on the TV, searching for static. It will drown out the ringing of the pinball machine in the lobby. I throw my sleeping bag on the bed—no way am I getting in it—and sleep for ten hours.

Days Twenty-three to Twenty-five The National Finals Rodeo was a ten-day marathon that stretched to December 11. To remain within my bus pass I stayed only three days, but that was enough, in a manner of speaking, because the same thing happened every night. The top fifteen cowboys in each of the six events competed in their specialties, amassing money night by night. The man with the most money at the end of the ten "Go-Rounds" (plus money won leading to the finals) was the champion. In that sense I could watch just three sessions and still see it all.

The first event was bareback riding, followed by steer wrestling, team roping, saddle bronc riding, calf roping, and bull riding. There was also one event for women, the barrel race, sandwiched between calf roping and bull riding. But it was a token gesture, more seventh inning stretch than real event. A rider would execute a cloverleaf pattern around three barrels and then be gone. The best horsewomen took about seventeen seconds to complete the course. The riders and the horses looked the same, as if they'd sneaked into the arena and were trying to steal a moment's glory before being run out.

Also the same from night to night was the opening ceremony, a twenty-minute celebration of God, America, and the Cowboy Way of Life. The first night I had trouble taking it seriously, and dismissed it as saccharine and sentimental. The second night I was surprised when the entire ceremony was rolled out again. The third night I viewed it much less critically, principally because it was delivered with as much gusto and honesty as it had been the first two nights.

There were, of course, plenty of Stetsons and Wrangler jeans walking around the Myriad Convention Center. And cowboy boots and spurs and belt buckles the size of serving platters. (Rodeos don't give trophies, they give belt buckles.) I was the only person out of uniform. But that didn't matter, and in fact probably made it easier for me to talk to people. I was made to feel more than welcome. Everyone was genuinely friendly, not so much unsophisticated as unpretentious. People seemed anxious to talk to me, to make sure I was having a good time, to listen to my thoughts about the rodeo. Their earnestness was grounded in their belief that rodeo was the greatest sport on God's good earth, but it seemed generated by a fear that the rest of the world thought them a bunch of bowlegged yahoos. That I was an outsider who'd taken the time to come to their event pleased and flattered them, and no one, it seemed, was about to let pass an opportunity to say something good about the rodeo.

The first weekend of the finals was also the Beauty and the Beast Contest. Beauty was the Miss Rodeo America finals, a sort of Miss America on horseback. Beast was the World Championship Bullfight finals.

American bullfighting has evolved from the sport of bull-riding, and bears scant resemblance to its more illustrious Spanish counterpart. For one thing, bullfighters double as clowns. Their real job, however, it quite serious. A Brahma-crossed bull weighs about a ton and will attack its rider once he's been thrown. It's the bullfighter's job to distract the bull in that one second after the rider is thrown and before he hits the ground. The idea is to make the bull attack the bullfighter, who is in a much better position to protect himself than the rider. The fighter provides that distraction by running up to the bull, tapping it on the forehead, and then beating a hasty retreat, taking the bull with him.

In 1979 Wrangler turned this job into a contest. A series of bullfights were held throughout the country, with the top six money-winning fighters coming to the national finals to face the bulls in two days of fighting. Skipper Voss won that first contest, and he was back again this year defending his 1982 title.

The "Wrangler Trail," as the national bullfight was called, was divided into two categories: freestyle fighting and protection. The protection phase was straightforward. A bull rider would take his ride and the fighter would be scored on how well he protected the rider.

In the freestyle phase a bull was released into the ring and a fighter would take a turn dodging and chasing and "fighting" it. The idea was to come as close as possible to being gored, trampled, or killed without being gored, trampled, or killed. With the exception of Skipper Voss, the fighters were little and quick and wonderfully agile. A second ninety-second freestyle phase employed hornless bulls. This allowed the fighters to get even closer, and the results were as expected.

I was, of course, asked what I thought about this bullfighting stuff. This time the friendly inquiry came from a man dressed all in black and sporting a gold tooth.

Well, I told him, I rather liked the protection phase. It was a competition designed to hone the skills needed to protect the bull riders. That made a great deal of sense. But I didn't like the free-style phase. (I'd learned that when people asked my opinion they generally appreciated a direct response.) On one level it was absolutely riveting: man against beast, a fundamental struggle. And what these guys could do was insanely entertaining, even if I was uncomfortable admitting that there was something enjoyable about watching people almost get killed. But my initial impression had been even more basic. This wasn't freestyle fighting; this was freestyle tormenting. The idea seemed to be to antagonize the bull into chasing a man around the ring so the people in the stands could have some fun squealing and groaning. I looked at the man with the gold tooth and shrugged my shoulders. He'd asked me.

He didn't look surprised by what I'd said, nor was he particularly offended. He just told me a story, an observation I could take or leave. A couple of years ago he'd gone to his first hockey game. He went with a friend and had done everything he could to get into the game. Had a couple of beers, yelled at the players, the whole bit. But he still hadn't liked it. To him hockey was just . . . . He stopped, searching for a phrase. I found it for him: a bunch of grown men beating each other with sticks.

"That's it," he said. "That's it exactly. I figure you're what, twenty-eight?"

"Thirty-one."

"Well, there you go. That's about how old I was when I went to see that hockey game. You got to be brought up with rodeo. You got to understand from the time you're little. Rodeo's got to be in your blood. It's got to be part of what you are."

I told the man in black I'd remember that.

On Sunday Miss Wyoming, Sandy Kay Meyer, won the Miss Rodeo America title and Bob Smets won the Wrangler Trail Bullfighting Championship. Skipper Voss, the four-time, defending national champion bullfighter, finished last. In the protection phase he'd handled his bulls and protected his riders expertly, but in the freestyle phase, when he was required to move and junk and outrun the bull, he spent most of his time trying to limp on two bad knees. At one point he was able to confuse the bull so completely with fakes and feints that the bull fell over, but later the bull caught Skipper on the left hip and flipped him like a rag doll. The other bullfighters in the competition, banded together by their special brotherhood, ran into the ring to distract the bull and give Skipper a moment to regroup. He did so quickly and was back on his feet hobbling after the bull in a matter of seconds.

I arranged to talk to him Monday morning at the downtown Sheraton, but standing in the lobby I tried to figure out how I'd recognize him. In the ring he wore a yellow fright wig underneath a beat-up purple hat with pink band, a flowered shirt, and threadbare cutoff jeans. His nose was painted red, and his eyes and mouth were exaggerated by white clown makeup.

But for all that disguise he was easy to spot at the Sheraton. He was the cowboy trying to limp on two bad knees.

Skipper Voss was thirty-eight years old. He started in the rodeo as a bull rider, but when he realized he was spending $500 to win $100, he wisely gave it up. Ten years ago he turned to fighting bulls. The money was nothing spectacular, but it was a way to stay with the rodeo. He was also damn good. In 1973, his first year with the Professional Rodeo Cowboys Association, he worked 130 performances, and was a bullfighter much sought by rodeos all over North America. In 1974 and again in 1978 he was chosen to work the national finals as one of the bullfighters used to protect the cowboys during the bull riding competition, a singular honor. He retired at the end of the '78 season, but the next year Wrangler began its bullfighting series and Skipper was back.

But now he was up against it. He was nine years older than Leon Coffee, the second oldest bullfighter in the competition. The rest were in their early twenties. Skipper was running out of youth. (He'd long since run out of knees; Tuesday he'd be under the knife for his seventh operation.)

We sat in the coffee shop, Skipper lowering himself into his chair and then using his hands to straighten out his legs. He reminded me of Walt Garrison, the former Dallas Cowboys football star and now a rodeo cowboy. Square jaw, deep-set eyes, prominent nose, a creased and lined face that made him look older than he was. He spoke in a slow and comfortable drawl, his voice tired and weary, just like the rest of him.

"This is the first last place that I ever won," he said. "I don't particularly like it. I kind of feel like I'll be back next year, but if I can't beat 'em I don't want to stay. But if I can go to a rodeo and make 'em say, 'We've got to beat Skipper,' well, then I'll keep going."

"Why?" I said.

Skipper laughed, a knowing and telling chuckle. "Boy, that's a good'n. It's kind of a funny thing, but in the rodeo you feel like you belong. It's kind of a fraternity party. You know everybody. You can go from one rodeo to the next and you won't know who's going to be there and then you get there and there's guys you haven't seen all year long. It's that kind of thing. And maybe there's a guy you saw just last week, too, but it's like you're seeing him brand new."

"But," I said, "you don't have any legs left."

Skipper shook his head. "When I'm out there fighting bulls I never notice it. It's like those guys trying to ride bulls with a broken arm or a broken ankle." I started to ask why again, but Skipper cut me off with that laugh of his.

"The Code of the West?" he said.

"Well, yeah," I said. "I want to say this with respect for what you guys do, but it just seems like cowboys work when they're really hurt. You've got the limits pushed way, way beyond the line. You know what I mean?"

"I know what you mean and I don't know the answer. You're going to get hurt in the rodeo. It's just a question of when and how bad. From losing your life to being paralyzed to broken backs and arms and legs. But, see, a rodeo clown don't get paid if he don't work. Same for everybody. You just have to get to the point where you just go on with the pain. It's gotten to the point where I just warm up and bear down. There isn't enough money in the world to do what we do."

There was a whole lot less than that. Total prize money here at the finals was $800,000, but that was being spread among 116 competitors. The best cowboy usually won the most money, but the difference between championship payoff and consolation prize was no big deal. It didn't pay to be good. Coca-Cola, Dodge Trucks, Coors, R. J. Reynolds, and Wrangler were the finals' heavyweight sponsors, so there had to be money in rodeo, but the cowboys were being paid in pride, love, and admiration. Estimable, but the bottom line was the cowboys were putting it on the line in a dangerous sport while someone else was making their money. The Cowboy Way of Life was being used against them.

"Sometimes you have to wonder why we do it," Skipper said. "Some of the things we've done, well, it's just been stupid to get out there and work as hurt as some of us have been. But what can you do if you don't? To me that's one of the worst things about the rodeo. You rodeo all your life, and if you're not a really big winner where you could put something aside to invest, you're going to have to go to work. Now, work to a cowboy isn't a dirty word. I mean, these boys have worked ranches, they've worked cattle. They ain't bothered by work. It's that eight-to-five drudgery of getting up in the morning after livin' a free life. You know, nobody tells a cowboy what rodeo to enter, when to get up, where to go. Nothin'. They're their own boss and have been the whole way through. They've been able to rely on their own abilities to make their money. Then all of a sudden they've got to work for somebody else. That's a hard transition."

An elderly woman stopped at our table and asked Skipper about his leg. It wasn't too bad, he asid. Last week's bad leg was this week's good leg. The woman liked that and told Skipper how much she enjoyed watching him fight the bulls.

When the woman left I asked, "Is that what keeps you in the rodeo, the worry that once you're out people won't be asking you how you are?"

"In a way it is," he answered. "It seems that in rodeo once you're gone you're forgotten. In this business the turnover is so great. Every couple of years there's all these new faces. There's a lot of guys here that I don't know at all. It's not that people will ignore me or anything like that; it's just that they won't know who I am. If I quit, in a couple of years I could go to a rodeo and nobody'd know who I was. Only way they'd know is if they saw my belt buckle or my name was announced as being in the audience. Then people'd say, 'So you're Skipper Voss. I've been hearing about you since I was this high.' Skipper shrugged and leaned back, carefully, so as not to disturb his knees.

"I don't know," he said, "funny business, isn't it?"

Days Twenty-five to Thirty Mechanical failure in Kansas; five hours in a garage, waiting. Toothache in Nebraska; dentist prescribes medicine, cautions it will knock me out. I grab the pills eagerly. My next game is still twenty-eight hours away in Allentown, Pennsylvania.

A blizzard east of Chicago. The bus driver is from Washington, D.C., pressed into duty on the Chicago–New York line. Crossing Indiana the driver volunteers information that she has never driven in snow. I take another pain pill.

Philadelphia fourteen hours late and I've missed the day's last connection to Allentown. I grab a bus to Reading. Plan: sleep in Reading bus station and thumb to Allentown in morning. Arrive Reading at 11:30 P.M. Bus station locked. When did I lose control of this trip? I have little choice but to thumb to Allentown tonight. It is midnight. It is raining. Of course.

A sign on Route 422 says Allentown is thirty-five miles away. I stick out my thumb and scrunch my neck against my coat collar to keep out the rain. At 12:22 A.M. Harvey Smithburger picks me up. He is a poor man's Truman Capote and gets me to the other side of Temple, where he drops me off underneath a sign that says Allentown is twenty-nine miles away. It is raining harder.

This is not my idea of good time. It becomes less so when I take further stock. I am six feet eight inches tall, I've got a beard, and I need a haircut. I'm wearing an army surplus parka, and I've got a large duffel bag sitting next to me. It is ten minutes to one. I would not pick me up.

"Where you going?" The voice startles me. It is coming from the blue Horizon that has pulled over going in the opposite direction of where I want to be.

"Allentown." The girl in the car thinks about that for a moment, says okay, and spins the car around. I throw my stuff in the back and get in.

"I just hope you don't have a gun," the girl says. It's a little late to hope that, I think, but don't say it. Instead, to allay her fears—and ensure my ride—I tell her everything about myself as fast as I can, keeping it as complex as possible so she'll know I'm not making it up.

"I'm Sally," she says when I run down. "This is my dad's car. I'm just out cruisin'."

"Isn't your dad going to be wondering where you are?"

"He's asleep. Hell, he's been asleep since nine-thirty."

"How old are you?" I say, casually conversational.

"Twenty-four," she says. I don't believe her.

She tells me she lives in Freemont and that she works in a

cracker factory. "Well, I sort of work there. I haven't worked in a while, but I'm hoping to be going back soon."

"You live in Freemont all your life?"

"Yeah. Where else am I going to live?"

We drive in silence for a while, the truck in front spraying water and smearing the windshield.

"You mind if I get personal?" Sally says.

I think about that for a moment, then say no, go ahead.

"How old are you?" I tell her. "Married?" Yes. "Any kids?" No. She lapses back to silence.

"Why do you ask?"

Sally doesn't answer right away. Then, "I just wonder what it's like to have kids." I begin thinking of a question to ask about her parents, but she cuts me off. "You have a license?"

"Yeah, why?"

"You want to drive?" No I don't. But I also don't want to lose my ride to Allentown. She pulls over and we change places. The car has snap and a lot of pep.

This is stupid. The realization bangs me across the forehead. Read, *real* stupid. I pose no threat to Sally; Sally poses no threat to me. But what if something happens? An accident? A cop pulls me over? I'm driving Sally's father's car down Route 422 away from Freemont toward Allentown, Pennsylvania.

But pragmatic gallantry clouds my thinking. Sally is better off with me than anyone else. Besides, it's raining even harder. I will drive to the Allentown bus station and hope it's open.

"Boy," Sally says, "you must think I'm a real jerk, just driving around and then agreeing to take you to Allentown." Well yes, but why tell her that? Sally turns away and stares out the window.

Allentown doesn't look very familiar. It's been twelve years since I've been here. "Tell you what," I say, "I'm just going to drive around a little bit and look for the bus station. If I can't find it I'll get out and look for it on my own." Sally's head snaps back to me.

"Jeez," she says, voice quavering. "Why do you have to do that? What'd I do to you? You don't have to get out."

"I just think that would be the best thing."

We reach the square and I know where I am. Right on Seventh, left on Walnut. Down one block, a left on Sixth, and there's the station.

"I don't know where I'm at," Sally says. "I won't know how to get back to 422." I drive across Hamilton and turn left on Linden; 422 should be straight ahead about ten blocks. I reach into the back seat to get my stuff.

"You know," Sally says, "you don't have to get out right now. We can drive around some more if you want."

"I know," I say, "but I think I'd better. Thanks a lot. I didn't know what I was going to do when I was stuck back there and it was really starting to rain."

"Yeah, sure," she says.

The interior light clicks on when I open the door. For the first time I see Sally. Frizzy brown hair, a couple of pimples. She is not twenty-four. But her eyes are rimmed with red. I think for a minute of closing the door. We could drive around, go to an all-night diner. But no; there's too much about this situation that's no good. I pull my stuff onto the curb and close the door behind me, then lean down and thank Sally again.

"Can I give you a little advice?" I say. "I wouldn't make a habit of picking up strange men at one o'clock in the morning."

"Just thanks for being nice to me," Sally says, "that's all."

The bus station is locked and now it's 4 A.M. I park myself in an all-night diner on Linden and treat myself to pancakes and eggs. That leaves $5.50 to get to New York City tomorrow.

I leave at seven. Allentown College of St. Francis de Sales is about ten miles away, south on 309. The college has been my goal since I left Oklahoma City 108 hours ago. The Allentown Centaurs are playing the Muhlenberg College Mules in a basketball game in seven hours. Nine years ago I graduated from Allentown. I played on the basketball team. My senior year we were 8 and 12. I haven't seen a game in eight years and haven't been back to the school in six. This game is self-indulgence, a reward for having endured my thirty-day bus pass. I've earned it.

I get a ride to Center Valley, the real home of Allentown College. Walking toward the school, it strikes me that this is how I've always arrived at Allentown College: duffel bag over my shoulder and $5 in my pocket. Only now it is nine years later.

One impressive homecoming.

Day Thirty-one Allentown lost to Muhlenberg 56–50 and their record dropped to 5 and 5 going into the Christmas break. The next day I hopped my final Trailways for the four hours back to New York City. Along the way I calculated my expenses for the past thirty days. Everything—room, board, transportation, and tickets—came to just over $600, about what I would have spent for gas had I done the trip in Jabba.

Back in New York City there was more good news: The insurance paid $2,300 for the van, $600 more than I'd paid for it 12 months ago.

On December 30, down at my mother's place in Matlacha, Florida, waiting for the Orange Bowl in Miami and the SuperBowl in Tampa, I watched Florida beat Iowa in the Gator Bowl on television. I wanted to see Rickie Tibbs, an Iowa football player whom I'd met on Trailways between Denver and Las Vegas. He'd been on his way to California for the Thanksgiving break before returning to Iowa to prepare for the Gator Bowl. He'd said he was a wide receiver. "I don't want to brag or nothing," he told me, "but I got the greatest pair of hands you'll ever see."

We had talked through all the breaks and during lunch. An unplanned, lucky moment of the year: finding a football player from California who played for Iowa while I was traveling across Colorado, Utah, and Nevada.

But in Florida, at the Gator Bowl, there was no Rickie Tibbs. The next day I listened to my tape of the conversations. His NFL chances as a step-too-slow black wide receiver, the rumors that Hayden Fry, the Iowa coach, might go to the Houston team in the USFL, recruiting, the joys of the game, big-time football, the little perks. No way this guy wasn't on the team. I called the sports information director at Iowa and told him my story. He started laughing. "Nobody on our team by that name," he said.

"Is this the team that lost to Illinois 33–0?" Rickie couldn't believe that the Hawkeyes could have been beaten that bad.

"Right."

"He said he caught eleven passes against Northwestern and scored a touchdown. Can you check your records?"

"I don't have to. Nobody caught eleven passes for us all season. But tell you what, if this guy's as good as he says he is, tell him to give us a call."

"Thank you," I said, and hung up. Seventeen days late, but the Big Red Month was finally over.

CHAPTER 11

* * *

One more Big Red bus. This one in Miami, right outside the Orange Bowl. This one a *real* big red bus, a schoolbus painted red, with "Big Red Bus" written in white letters across the front. I had to investigate.

Inside, red carpeting covered the floor, the walls, and the ceiling. And in case anything suddenly turned another color, there was an open can of red paint sitting on a table. There were also a dozen guys inside, each one changing into his red football jersey and shouting and yelling and drinking beer and adding his own signature to the redolence of hamburgers, onions, and sweat.

They were, they told me, the red-shirted walk-ons of the University of Nebraska's football team. I didn't believe them. There wasn't a single body that approached the standard dimensions of a division I football player. But that's what they were. They'd made the trip from Lincoln, the costs picked up by an alumni group back in Nebraska. Such excursions weren't exactly legal, but, they said, just between you and me, it's one of the perks of big-time football.

Ten of them left. The Cornhuskers would be warming up by now, and they wanted to get to their seats in the first rows of the stands right behind the bench. That left two in the bus. One was a 205-pound lineman, the other a 170-pound wide receiver. They told me their weights defiantly, as if to ensure that I wouldn't come back with the obvious rejoinder ("Linemen at Nebraska weigh more than 200 pounds!"). I held my tongue.

The lineman said he was playing behind four other guys, the wide receiver behind six. But the lineman figured he was better than two of the guys in front of him, and the wide receiver said he had a shot at passing three of the guys in front of him. I started to ask how many players Nebraska recruited each year, but didn't.

"I had a scholarship to the University of Nebraska at Omaha," the lineman said, "but all I've ever wanted to be was a Cornhusker." The wide receiver shook his head firmly.

"That's it," he said. "We both come from the same town in Nebraska. Twenty-two hundred people. When we go back home, people worship us. You see, it don't matter if you're first string, third string, or a red shirt. Everybody wants to be a Cornhusker."

"I'll bet you," the lineman said, "that between the two of us we've taken back at least thirty footballs autographed by the team. Everybody in town wants one."

I asked if they figured ever to be starters. Neither did. In fact, they said, they'd be lucky if they ever got in a game.

"But you see," the lineman said, "I got a chance to get a national championship ring. I've got my Big Eight ring back home. Haven't even taken it out of the box yet." He held up an index finger. "Numero uno. How many people can say that?" The wide receiver shook his head again.

"We know guys who played football for Nebraska ten, twelve years ago," he said. "People still come up to them and want to look at their rings."

I'd taken a Greyhound to the Orange Bowl, although I hadn't wanted to go. Four months ago I'd watched Nebraska humiliate Penn State 44–6 in the Kickoff Classic at the Meadowlands. Since then the Cornhuskers had racked up scores of 56–20, 84–13, 42–10, 63–7, 14–10, 34–13, 69–19, 51–25, 72–29, 67–13, and 28–21. They'd been threatened only twice and scared but once. They were The Greatest Team That Ever Played The Game, and everybody knew it. Miami didn't stand a chance. They were 10–1, but they'd won with mundane scores like 29–17, 17–7, and 20–3. Plus a 12–7 win over East Carolina and a 17–16 last-second victory over Florida State. There was no way the Hurricanes could beat Nebraska, and if they didn't watch out they could be blown into the Atlantic Ocean.

This game was a moral obligation: A year of American sports required a New Year's bowl game.

I stayed with a friend and got my ticket from him. He'd been to a New Year's Eve party and five people offered him tickets. He didn't want to go, but I took a ticket on the forty-yard line of the north stands to watch the Fiftieth Orange Bowl "Celebration." (There was no mention on the ticket about a football game.) The stadium was fifty years old, too, and looked it. Gray steel and concrete, the steep walkways sticky with five decades of beer. The seats were painted orange, of course, but they were faded and chipped and looked rusty. The field was a lush, rich green, although on closer inspection I realized that was the TV paint.

I'd planned to find my seat and then walk around the stadium looking for conversations, but once I wedged myself into my seat there was no getting out. The aisles were narrow and the walkways were worse. I was locked in for the duration between an Irish priest and an elderly woman who'd been to the twenty-fifth Orange Bowl. The priest was absolutely bonkers about American football. Back in Ireland he'd followed Irish football, rugby, and soccer, but once he'd come over here he'd taken to the American game with a passion. He had season tickets for the Dolphins and was still praying for their departed souls; yesterday they'd been eliminated from the play-offs by the Seattle Seahawks.

The woman on my right was upset, too, but for a different reason. She'd forgotten her book. She hated football and was here for the halftime show. She couldn't remember who played in the game twenty-five years ago (Oklahoma 21, Syracuse 6), but she did tell me all about the 1959 halftime festivities. There'd been lots of floats with oyster shells and pearls. A short, chubby woman with white hair, she wore rectangle glasses and looked like George Washington. Her husband was three seats away, sitting with his football-watching buddy. The buddy was with his wife, too, but in self-defense she'd learned the game. So my Mrs. Washington was really here by herself. The only plays she liked were the ones that didn't stop the clock.

I cheered for Miami. Cheering for Nebraska would have been like rooting for the atom bomb. Besides, Miami's colors weren't red, and I'd come to hate the color red. North Carolina State and Houston at the NCAAs, the Phillies in the Series, even *Liberty* at the America's Cup had all been red. Now here was Nebraska, which wasn't just red, but "Big Red," like a Trailways bus. Miami's colors were aquamarine and orange.

There was, thankfully, little red to be found in the Orange Bowl. This was more a Miami home game than a bowl game to decide the national championship. When the Cornhuskers took the field the hooting and hollering rained down. That gave way to a steady chorus of boos, and then was replaced by "Go home, hillbillies," and other intelligent comments. But then the catcalls suddenly stopped. Seventy thousand Miami fans had just gotten their first real look at the mighty midwestern juggernaut that masqueraded as a college football team. An audible gasp filled the stadium: "These guys are big!" followed immediately by, "and quick, too!" When the Hurricanes stormed the field the roar was deafening, but the enthusiasm was held aloft on the strength of its own desperation. If Miami fans were going to cheer, they had to do it now, before the game began and the atom bomb was dropped. I settled into my seat, fully prepared for the rout, content, at least, that my year on the road had included a New Year's bowl.

Nebraska received the kickoff. On the first play from scrimmage Mike Rozier of Nebraska ran through the Hurricane defense like it was a late-afternoon drizzle. Two plays later Nebraska was lined up for a field goal. But the kick was blocked, and there was quarterback Bernie Kozar, the nineteen-year-old freshman, trotting onto the field for Miami. Fifty-seven yards, six plays, and three minutes later, it was Kozar to Dennison for a two-yard touchdown. Nebraska tried again but had to punt, and after running twice and throwing six times, the Hurricanes got a forty-five-yard field goal. Nebraska tried again, but was intercepted. This time it took Miami all of four plays and forty-eight seconds to throw a twenty-two-yard touchdown pass from Kozar to Dennison. Suddenly it was 17–0 Miami and there was still 1:08 left in the first quarter.

The Orange Bowl ripped itself limb from limb in paroxysms of absolute delight. Jammed in cheek to jowl as we were, we'd spent the first fourteen minutes of the game rising en masse every time Kozar dropped back to pass, all the while telling each other none of this was supposed to be happening and yet all of it was. In the second quarter Nebraska scored twice, which brought the Orange Bowl back to earth. The Cornhuskers' two drives used twenty-two plays and $9\frac{1}{2}$ minutes and plowed up 138 yards. As the first half ticked away, no one seemed anxious for the second half to begin. But it sure'd been fun while it lasted.

I remember little of the halftime show. It was a celebration of the last forty-nine halftime shows, which is saying something. I scribbled "psychedelic ant farm" in my notebook, but at some point I lapsed into sensory overload, a condition caused, no doubt, by the Spanish dancers, Rockettes, square dancers, a salute to Broadway, the Statue of Liberty, at least one thousand American flags, fireworks, rockets, and 40,000 light bulbs. According to my Mrs. Washington, however, the best touch came when the lights were turned out and we were asked to "crack" the six-inch phosphorescent light pens we'd been given when we entered. The ant farm became a giant jar of lightning bugs.

Ninety-six seconds into the second half, Nebraska kicked a field goal to tie the game at 17. That did more than just even the score. The first half was history; now was reality. Kozar had had his fun, and for that matter so had we. How many times could we expect him to reach into his bag of tricks and pull out *one more* desperately needed play?

The answer was simple: as many times as we wanted him too. Miami scored twice in the third quarter to go ahead 31–17.

The final period belonged to Nebraska. Their first drive chewed up five minutes and took thirteen plays, including a fourth-down conversion. Their second drive was a little different. It included things like the forward pass and took less than a minute to bring the Orange Bowl to its knees. With forty-eight seconds remaining, Turner Gill, the Nebraska quarterback, ran to his right, waited until the penultimate moment, and then pitched the ball to Jeff Smith, who ran twenty-four yards to score six points. That brought Nebraska to within 1 at 31–30, and guaranteed that my "moral obligation" of a New Year's bowl had instead become the finest contest of the year.

During the timeout that preceded what would surely be Nebraska's two-point conversion, I stood with the rest of the Orange Bowl, gleefully chastened. To think I really considered not coming to this game! Twenty-four hours ago I'd arrived in Miami full of myself and wonderfully self-confident. I had, after all, been on the road for almost a year, and I had, after all, seen it all. Surely there was nothing left that could surprise or delight me. Except I'd forgotten one thing. I'd forgotten about the game.

The game! Turner Gill dropped back and rolled to his right, then lofted a short pass to a man in red. Ken Calhoun, the Miami defender, in the air and parallel to the ground, strained to reach the ball and at the last possible moment, a moment he will never forget and never again equal, tipped the ball away from Nebraska to make Miami the national champion.

* * *

Life between Bowls

I lost $14 betting the greyhounds at Hollywood Park. No combination worked. Not my anniversary (7-8), my birthday (1-7), Noreen's birthday (1-8), my mother's birthday (2-4), my sister's age (3-4), or Noreen's grade point average (3-8-5). A less than knowledgeable system, but what did I know from greyhounds? The closest I came to a winner was the eighth race. I didn't bet Basic Dream because the program said "erly spd. gv way," and "no threat," and "no factor" in his last two races. Basic Dream wiped himself all over the track going into the first turn. He started rolling on the inside lane and wound up against the outer rail. I claimed a moral victory.

Never a fan of gambling, my first trip to a track did little to sway my opinion. (The object of gambling isn't to win; it's to lose without seeming to care.) The romance of the wager is best left to the fanciful pens of Damon Runyon and Pete Axthelm. The reality is decidedly unglamorous and tinged with a seeping, pervasive despair. Hollywood Park was tacky and garish and bereft of imagination, a fifties-style fantasy reduced to gloomy absoluteness. Tile floors and harsh lights, rows of betting windows stretching forever down long corridors. A functional workplace designed to separate people from their money. That the majority of people looked like they couldn't afford the severance only enhanced the pallor.

The next day Jesse Jackson negotiated the release of navy flier Robert O. Goodman, Jr., in Syria. I went to World Jai Alai Miami and saw the future.

Lesson of the year: The distance between players and fans is wide and getting worse. Lip service is paid to the bond between athletes and fans, but that's to ensure that the turnstiles spin and—more important—the television is watched. Jai alai is the future because it admits that there need be no bond between players and fans for the money to be made.

The jai alai matches weren't athletic contests; they were performances. The fronton, 176 feet long, 40 feet high, and 50 feet wide, was a stage. A screen separated the players from the spectators (for safety, obviously, but the effect was no less clear). Interplay between athletes and bettors was minimal and probably discouraged. A game consisted of 8 two-man teams playing each other in round-robin fashion. When a game was completed and a combination of numbers produced, the players retired to a guarded training room while the spectators raced to collect winnings or place new bets. Twenty minutes later the players reappeared for another game. Playing order and team combinations were arranged by oddsmakers, and a player in a red jersey for one game might wear black and play against his former teammate—now wearing blue—in the next game. I was invited backstage to talk to a some of the American players, and before I could ask the question they offered that yes, they felt like the greyhounds I'd seen the night before.

Back on Florida's west coast I searched for more "events," and found the international bait casting champion, or some such title holder. He was talking to a local fishing club. After his presentation he traded tales with a couple of the guys, and after that I approached him.

One more time I pulled out my spiel: who I was, what I was doing, and could I interview him?

"How much?" he asked.

"How much what?" I said.

"How much money do I get for the interview?"

"You don't get any."

"How do I know you're not trying to steal my secrets?"

I looked at him, dumbfounded. I'd traveled the country, talked to all kinds of people. No one had ever asked for money—no one had ever even brought it up.

"I can't give myself away."

"You're a fisherman," I said. A *fisherman.* I wanted to ask what it's like to catch the big one, get your feet wet in a new stream, feel a strike while the sun sets over your shoulder.

"If I don't get paid I don't do the interview. I gotta protect myself."

* * *

Los Angeles Raiders' press tent. Tuesday, January 18, 9:45 A.M. Super Bowl week.

A large blue and yellow circus tent behind the Airport Hilton. Inside there was room for about one hundred tables in its main areas. A row of serving tables sat directly in front of the entrance. Eggs Benedict, sausage, quiche, pastries, and pancakes simmered in serving dishes. One nook housed a wet bar. Another cranny had been arranged with 300 chairs lined up in rows in front of a table with a podium in the middle. In front of the podium were thirty microphones.

At the moment, the second half of the tent was empty save for the forty-eight tables that filled that area. Each table was ringed by ten chairs, and on each table was a numbered index card. The numbers ranged from six to ninety-three. This was where the Raiders would sit, one player per table, during the press conference. The front half was filled with the press corps eating eggs and drinking Bloody Marys. No one seemed particularly anxious for the press conference to begin.

When it did, there was no immediate rush to get interviews. The players trooped in single file, found their tables, and sat down. As members of the press finished eating, they moved unhurried to the players' area. Only slowly did the aisles between the tables fill with reporters, camera operators, and broadcasters, until they finally flowed together to form a gelatinous mortar circulating around the tables.

Reporters moved from Raider to Raider gathering bits of conversation, or camped at one table recording every word a player said. Jim Plunkett was always surrounded by forty people. So was Lyle Alzado. Ted Hendricks was worth thirty sets of ears, Lester Hayes twenty. Todd Christensen arrived late, asked an imaginary waiter for a "table for ten," then distributed copies of "Pressure," his latest attempt at iambic pentameter. Raiders' coach Tom Flores stood behind a podium and answered the questions of seventy-five reporters. Special-teams players sat by themselves, their tables on the outer fringe, reading the paper or surveying the scene. A couple of them played cards, but they had to deal from table to table because all players were required to remain at their numbered spots.

Irv Cross filmed a segment for the CBS Super Bowl show. Dick Schaap of ABC surveyed the scene from the other side of the tent. Eukie Washington, a Fort Meyers sports announcer, was filmed while a Raider taught him to play cribbage. Everywhere was noise. Forty-eight football players answering the same questions makes for a lot of noise.

There was, however, no frenzy. Or at least none of that feverish excitement I'd experienced at other events. Orderliness had replaced the deadline-pressure atmosphere; the reports didn't need to rush. They were going to get their stories. Because this was Super Bowl week, and the rules had been changed. The media was in charge.

I spent only one day in Tampa during Super Bowl week. But I missed little. Tampa was the smallest city ever to host the Super Bowl, and the game was the city's bid for big-league status. The entire west coast of Florida was trying to ride the coattails, and the resulting hype was inescapable. (The *St. Petersburg Times,* for instance, published a 100-page insert extolling the virtues of its city.) Last year the Super Bowl had been swallowed by the Rose Bowl and southern California. The worry this year was we'd drown before the game began.

But the hype, as I'd seen at the Raiders' press conference, was what this game was all about. History has proved that we can't rely on the game, but we can rely on the hype. And it was obvious as I walked around the circus tent that the press knew it and so did the players. The hype justifies the hype. The more you have the more you need; it holds itself up. Super Bowl week is but one week out of fifty-two, but for those seven glorious days, the press is more important than the game they cover.

It was difficult, however, to decide who was exploiting whom. The players and the press were in this media game together, but they often worked at cross purposes. The Raiders were portrayed as a bunch of semi-illiterate animals who enjoyed beating up their mothers—a catchy image easily digested and long remembered. It was in the Raiders' own best interest to foster this image, but they were quickly trapped within it. A newscast early in the week showed the Raiders checking into their hotel, with an off-screen interviewer commenting to Lyle Alzado that the team was arriving more peacably than expected. "We kind of thought you'd beat up a couple bellboys on the way in," the voice said. Alzado started to disagree, but then he stopped, reconsidered, and jumped back into character. "Yeah," he said, "we left a couple of 'em bloodied up in the corner." Image and reality mesh, and the beat goes on.

From the circus tent behind the Hilton I took a media bus back to NFL central at the downtown Hyatt Regency. The press room was an entire banquet area, with three long rows of tables in the middle surrounded by cordoned-off work areas for the *New York Times,* the *Washington Post,* AP and UPI, and the rest of the heavyweights.

The information room provided information:

- "Redskins worked for two hours in the rain."
- "[Redskin coach Joe] Gibbs also said he was 'very much pleased with the security around our practices.' The field is heavily secured, including new draping around the cyclone fence of the field."
- "During practice, a plane flew over several times, towing a banner which read, 'L. Alzado wears pantyhose! Wash. D. C. Ad Club.' "
- "Two thousand Super Bowl programs will be delivered Friday to United States Marines stationed in Beirut, Lebanon."
- "Gibbs said . . . that all the talk preceding the game itself will have little influence on the outcome."

Between the information and press rooms was the Tampa Bay Chamber of Commerce booth. Included in the display were two members of the Tampa Bay Buccaneer cheerleaders. Their orange and white outfits didn't conform to their bodies so much as create a standard that their figures had to meet. The women were exhibited in three-hour shifts. Besides sharing the obvious characteristics, they displayed decided confusion over what to do with their hands.

I walked into the hospitality room and sat down at a table littered with the sports pages of the major dailies of the United States. I read the stories and columns about the upcoming game, cruising through the hype until I got to an article about Jimmy the Greek's French poodle, Napoleon. This was hyperspace. I flipped the paper back onto the table, found a comfortable chair, and fell asleep. That's where I was when Gerald Williams found me.

Gerald Williams was a radio and television tennis commentator for the BBC. An elderly man in a red-and-white checked shirt and blue sports jacket and white pants, I'd first noticed him at the Raiders' circus tent, standing off to the side, bemused and bewildered. I thought he might be a good person to comment on this wholly American scene, and I arranged to talk to him back at the Hyatt. But before I could solicit his opinion (after he'd woken me), we started talking about English football and it's predilection to violence.

"It's my opinon that soccer is in a steep decline in Britain," he said, his voice all English and totally BBC. "And that's an opinion from one whose first love was soccer and whose first job was a soccer writer. The ordinary person's idea of fun isn't to listen to baying terraces of idiot youths screaming obscenities at each other and trying to knock the hell out of each other, and then walking home through streets where everybody is trying to knock the hell out of each other. That just isn't fun."

"Are they taking the game too seriously?"

"The game has nothing to do with it. I don't believe there is anything wrong with the game. It's just that they've chosen soccer as the place to have their fights. I'm sure that if soccer was stopped they'd fight somewhere else. Soccer is, basically, the game that has come out of the lower classes, although one is always reluctant to use those sorts of terms."

"Is a lot of it fueled by alcohol?"

"Of course. But I still don't think that's the reason. It's the yobs."

"Yobs?"

"You don't have yobs?"

"I don't know. What's a yob?"

"A cretin. An idiot." I assured Mr. Williams that we had our share of yobs here in the United States. What we didn't have, though, were the intense, violent outbursts endemic to British soccer.

"I have a theory about that," he said. "Fans can't afford to get from Los Angeles to New York. In Britain it's quite simple to get from Manchester to London to watch Manchester United. We get these massive crowds of touring supporters. Another thing is your stadiums are much newer than ours. Many of ours are old and decrepit. That just breeds depression. All in all, the reputation of British soccer is seriously impaired."

I turned the conversation to American football. More specifically, the Super Bowl.

"Oh, I think this is terrific fun," he said. "I'm thrilled to see the whole town involved, and it all seems so innocent. For all its hyperbole, for all its in many ways juvenile enthusiasm, I think there is really something very wholesome about this.

"This is quite different from anything we have in Britain. We have our major events, certainly, but there is never any doubt that the match is the be-all and end-all. Over here it seems that the game, the Super Bowl, is the least important thing going on. I get the feeling the most important thing is the journalists. In England the journalist is sometimes regarded almost as an impediment to the proceedings. I spend quite a bit of time over here, and quite frankly I've been spoiled. It seems that the English reporter often spends his time freezing in a car park to try to talk to a player."

"Why in Britain," I said, "is the game the thing, as opposed to over here where everything else is the thing?"

"I'm not quite sure, actually. It seems to me that it's part of the British personality that we are highly suspicious of having a good time." He laughed at that, a dry, English chuckle.

"What's the American approach?"

"In the main it always seems to me to be more family fun. More wholesome. I don't know if it actually is, though. I detect a greater undercurrent of violence over here than in our country. But usually over here I get the feeling that families go to sports events. It's all good, clean fun."

I asked him what he would want to import to England from the American sports scene. Again, it was the willingness of a city like

Tampa to pitch into making the game a success. That just didn't happen in England. I reversed the question: What would he want to export from England to America. "A slightly more objective view of things," he said dryly.

"What would you like to keep from crossing the Atlantic back to England?" I asked. He thought for a moment, reminded me that he was generalizing to make a point, and pitched in.

"I find the American obsession with style a little sickening. I think you often have an unhealthy enthusiasm for the adulation of people who are, quote, 'successful.' You're a country that absolutely idolizes television and I personally don't like that. You put people up on pedestals simply because they are on television." With that he stopped. I sensed there was more he could have said, but in the interest of hands-across-the-water it would be best to refrain.

"When you go back home, what will you tell people about the Super Bowl?"

"I'll say it was like nothing we have and that it was enormous fun and that it was fabulous seeing an entire city being invaded by everybody and everyone enjoying themselves without any social unrest. To me that is the great thing about this. It's marvelous. Absolutely marvelous."

But the Super Bowl wasn't marvelous. That enormous surge of energy that had carried me to the stadium disappeared immediately when I walked inside. Being *at* the Super Bowl obviously wasn't as important as getting *to* the Super Bowl. For players and fans alike. And who can blame them? Midway through the third period Marcus Allen ran seventy-two yards for a touchdown, ensuring that a relatively dull game was indeed spectacularly awful. The Raiders won 38–9, the best (or worst) margin of victory in Super Bowl history. Once again, America's greatest unofficial holiday produced an official case of the national blahs.

I watched the final ten seconds standing by myself in an auxiliary press box high atop the stadium, the two thousand reporters having left their seats for the locker rooms and interview areas with seven minutes remaining. I stood on the bleacher seat with my hands in my pockets and counted down the final ten seconds out loud. Afterward, I watched on the giant scoreboard televison as President Reagan called the winning locker room and suggested that maybe Marcus Allen and the rest of the Raiders should be put in the missile silos instead of the MX missiles. Not wanting that to be my final image of the trip, I wandered downstairs. Inside the Raiders' locker room, jammed and exploding with players and press and cameras and steam, I listened to Al Davis hold court, while all around me people were shouting the standard platitudes ("This is the greatest team EVER!"). Then I walked over to the Redskins' locker room, where Joe Theismann stood, deserted by his teammates, facing the reporters alone. He was standing next to his locker, stripped to the waist, arms folded across his chest, still talking. Live by the tongue, die by the tongue.

Between the locker rooms was a large cement-block corridor. Arranged around the open space were a series of platforms, each one occupied by a Star of the Game, who was placed—quite literally—on a pedestal. Bands of reporters surrounded each player, each group a circular wave about to crash down on its victim. Security guards scurried from pedestal to pedestal collecting autographs. The shouts and screams of people outside the stadium filtered into the corridor, the excited buzz adding fuel to the hysteria that already surrounded me.

My year on the road was over. The realization didn't surprise me, but I was suddenly aware that the trip wasn't going to come to any grand denouement. It was just going to stop. Not exactly how I'd planned it. I had always expected that at this Final Moment someone would tell me something witty, wise, and wonderful that would wrap my year into one all-encompassing quote. I could see now that that wasn't going to happen. I was going to walk outside the stadium and that would be it.

But before I left I toyed with the idea of talking to Jim Plunkett, who was standing on the pedestal right in front of me. His rags-to-riches story had been three times lived and many times told; surely his life's experience could provide me with an appropriate closing sentence. But getting that quote now would be impossible. He was surrounded by at least thirty reporters, and this was not the appropriate moment to break through their ranks and shout: "Tell me, Jim, what does all this MEAN?"

So I slipped my notebook into my pocket and walked outside, through the crush of people crowded around the players' entrance, and out into the parking lot. I was about to turn around for a final look at the stadium when a man walked over and asked if he could have my press pass. I didn't give it to him, but I should have. My year was over; my trip was done. I'd taken my best shot at painting a portrait of American Sports, and that picture, however incomplete, was finished. Now there was a brand new year of events poised on the horizon, each event awaiting its turn to be the center of the universe. I should have given that guy my press pass. It was time for someone else to take the journey.